MW01517687

Inclusive Physical Activities

A volume in
International Advances in Education: Global Initiatives for Equity and Social Justice
Elinor L. Brown and Rhonda G. Craven, *Series Editors*

Inclusive Physical Activities

International Perspectives

edited by

Alexandre J. S. Morin
Concordia University

Christophe Maïano
Université du Québec en Outaouais

Danielle Tracey
Western Sydney University

Rhonda G. Craven
Australian Catholic University

≡**IAP**

INFORMATION AGE PUBLISHING, INC.
Charlotte, NC • www.infoagepub.com

Library of Congress Cataloging-in-Publication Data

A CIP record for this book is available from the Library of Congress
http://www.loc.gov

ISBN: 978-1-68123-852-4 (Paperback)
       978-1-68123-853-1 (Hardcover)
       978-1-68123-854-8 (ebook)

Printed in the United States of America

CONTENTS

PART I

STRATEGIES TO MAXIMIZE PARTICIPATION OF CHILDREN AND ADOLESCENTS WITH SPECIAL NEEDS IN PHYSICAL ACTIVITY AS A GLOBAL PRIORITY

PART II

STRATEGIES TO MAXIMIZE THE SOCIAL INCLUSION OF CHILDREN AND ADOLESCENTS WITH SPECIAL NEEDS IN GENERAL PHYSICAL ACTIVITIES

PART III

EFFECTIVE PHYSICAL EDUCATION STRATEGIES TO ENHANCE BIOPSYCHOSOCIAL OUTCOMES FOR CHILDREN AND ADOLESCENTS WITH SPECIAL NEEDS

PART IV

ADVANCING THE PRACTICE OF EDUCATORS AND COACHES TO CULTIVATE THE SOCIAL INCLUSION AND PARTICIPATION IN PHYSICAL ACTIVITY OF CHILDREN AND ADOLESCENTS WITH SPECIAL NEEDS

PART V

CHALLENGING THE MEANING AND IMPLEMENTATION OF INCLUSIVE PRACTICES IN PHYSICAL EDUCATION GLOBALLY

FOREWORD

Today our society struggles with many challenges. One of these challenges is peoples' attitudes toward individuals with special needs. It is a remarkable observation that on the one hand, people adapt very rapidly to new and quickly changing technologies; but on the other hand, changes in peoples' attitudes take up so much time and energy. Inclusion or the act of accepting people with special needs as an equal part of our society is one of the strategies aiming to accelerate this process. In a society that is increasingly moving toward the right political spectrum, all initiatives for equality and social justice are in need of a strong support. In order to increase awareness and recognition, attention should be drawn to all of these initiatives.

In the last decade, undeniably some progress has been made, but before the idea of inclusion is accepted by our entire society, worldwide and without exceptions, there is still a long way to go.

Today everybody is convinced that physical activity, besides the somatic effects, also has important psychosocial effects (i.e., improving feelings of well-being and quality of life), and that physical activity is crucial in daily life. At the same time, our society is confronted with new health issues due to a lack of exercise, such as increasing sedentary behavior and mental illnesses. Even a simple, inexpensive, and accessible intervention like regular physical activity requires too much energy. People prefer taking medications rather than changing their lifestyle and exercise behavior. Changing lifestyle and behavior demand a lot of intrinsic motivation.

The editors and the authors of this volume present the readers with a plethora of social inclusion possibilities by means of using physical activity

Inclusive Physical Activities, pages ix–x
Copyright © 2017 by Information Age Publishing
All rights of reproduction in any form reserved.

in children and adolescent populations. In their development, children and adolescents with and without special needs deserve a fascinating and challenging life. "Inclusion" and "physical activity" are two concepts that respond to the demands in this field and that are relatively easy to achieve. New individual tailored strategies must be developed continuously. Unfortunately, the experience teaches us that in practice this is far more difficult.

All contributors to this volume have recognized the need to assimilate the rapidly growing research into an up-to-date synthesis concerning strategies to maximize participation in physical activity in an international perspective and from different points of view (society, educators/coaches, etc.). To achieve this goal, the authors provide the readers with a lot of cornerstones and highlight the importance of inclusion by using physical activity to increase social integration. That makes this volume both practical and insightful. This is not just a book; this book is in sharp contrast to other books because it contains a message of hope for a better future for children and adolescents with special needs.

This book includes 14 chapters and provides essential information from different continents that will be useful to those involved in research and practice involving children and adolescents with special needs. The main objective of this book is to provide examples of effective theory, research, policy, and practice that were developed with the objective of improving the quality of life of children and adolescents with special needs through physical activities.

This information carries a rich potential to reinforce practical treatments. At the same time, it is an important contribution for a better understanding of the inclusive physical activity concept, not only for physical educators but also for policymakers. For a layman, this book might be an eye opener. At the end of this book, the reader will undeniably be convinced about the benefits of participation in physical activity and sport. It is a wonderful experience, not only for children and adolescents with and without special needs, but also for their entire life contexts. Now it is time to bring all these new ideas into practice!

—**Michel Probst**
Catholic University of Leuven

INCLUSIVE PHYSICAL ACTIVITIES

International Perspectives

International Advances in Education: Global Initiatives for Equity and Social Justice is an international research monograph series of scholarly works that focuses primarily on empowering children, adolescents, and young adults from diverse educational, socio-cultural, linguistic, religious, racial, ethnic and socio-economic settings to become non-exploited/non-exploitive contributing members of the global community.

The series, edited by Professors Elinor L. Brown and Rhonda Craven, draws on the international community of distinguished scholars to serve as guest editors for each volume, and prominent investigators, academics, and community organizers to contribute to the evidence base for developing sound educational policies, practices, and innovative programs to optimize the potential of all students. Each themed volume includes multi-disciplinary theory, research, and practice that provides an enriched understanding of the drivers of human potential via education to assist readers in exploring, adapting, and replicating innovative strategies that enable *all* students to realize their full potential.

Inclusive Physical Activities, pages xi–xii
Copyright © 2017 by Information Age Publishing

Current volumes in print include:

Religion and Spirituality, Ethnicity and Race: Creating Educational Opportunities Around the Globe
Refugee and Immigrant Students: Achieving Equity in Education
Communication and Language: Surmounting the Barriers to Cross-Cultural Understanding
Indigenous Peoples: Education and Equity
Migrants and Refugees: Equitable Education for Displaced Populations
Poverty, Class, and Schooling: Global Perspectives on Economic Justice and Educational Equity
Inclusive Education for Students With Intellectual Disabilities
Comparative International Perspectives on Education and Social Change in Developing Countries and Indigenous Peoples in Developed Countries
E-Learning and Social Media: Education and Citizenship for the Digital 21st Century
Inclusive Physical Activities: International Perspectives

Volumes in press include:

Global Perspectives on Gender and Sexuality in Education: Raising Awareness Fostering Equity, Advancing Justice

Volume 12 presents an outstanding array of research-based evidence on the physical activity needs of children with intellectual limitations and the importance of implementing inclusive physical education activities. The editors of volume 12 have compiled an outstanding array of research-based evidence on the physical activity needs of children with intellectual limitations and on how inclusive physical education can positively influence the physical, social, and mental health of special needs children. Authors of the 14 chapters demonstrate the importance of providing physical activity for all children and provide many strategies and tools for implementing programs and activities that are both inclusive and challenging for all students.

—**Elinor L. Brown**
University of Kentucky

Rhonda G. Craven
Australian Catholic University

VOLUME INTRODUCTION

Increasing numbers of children and adolescents internationally are being diagnosed with secondary health problems (e.g., overweight-obesity, diabetes, asthma, anxiety, etc.) due in part, or at least related to, a lack of physical activity. Children and adolescents with various forms of special needs (for example, children and adolescents with physical or intellectual disabilities, children and adolescents from disadvantaged social backgrounds, and children and adolescents with chronic illnesses) seem to be particularly at risk for secondary health problems, which in the end limit their social participation and inclusion, as well as their ability to achieve their full potential and to lead happy and fulfilling lives. For these children and adolescents, involvement in regular physical activities (including fitness activities and sports) may have far-reaching benefits. For instance, organized physical activities are known to represent an effective vehicle for interventions for children and adolescents with special needs who do not seem to benefit as much as others from more traditional, verbal-oriented approaches. Organized physical activities (in or out of school) further provide these children and adolescents with opportunities to interact in a positive manner with prosocial peers and adults who may serve as positive role models for them. There is currently a paucity of research about physical activities that effectively include children and adolescents with a range of special needs or research that identifies evidence-based strategies that seed success in

Inclusive Physical Activities, pages xiii–xx
Copyright © 2017 by Information Age Publishing

maximizing the involvement in, and the positive biopsychosocial outcomes associated with, the practice of physical activity. This dearth of research is impeding progress in addressing the biopsychosocial disadvantage that these children and adolescents encounter, the development of new solutions for enabling full potential, and ensuring that children and adolescents with special needs not only succeed, but also flourish in life.

This volume includes examples of theory, research, policy, and practice that will advance our understanding of how best to encourage these children and adolescents to participate regularly in physical activity, how to maximize the biopsychosocial benefits of involvement in physical activities, and how to ensure that these physical activities are inclusive for children and adolescents with special needs. The focus will be placed on research-derived physical activity practices that seed success for children and adolescents with special needs; and new directions in theory, research, and practice that have implications for enhancing physical activity practices with at-risk children and adolescents.

The themes covered in this volume include:

1. Strategies to maximize participation of children and adolescents with special needs in physical activity as a global priority.
2. Strategies to maximise the social inclusion of children and adolescents with special needs in general physical activities.
3. Effective physical education strategies to enhance biopsychosocial outcomes for children and adolescents with special needs.
4. Advancing the practice of educators and coaches to cultivate the social inclusion and participation in physical activity of children and adolescents with special needs.
5. Challenging the meaning and implementation of inclusive practices in physical education globally.

STRATEGIES TO MAXIMIZE PARTICIPATION OF CHILDREN AND ADOLESCENTS WITH SPECIAL NEEDS IN PHYSICAL ACTIVITY AS A GLOBAL PRIORITY

This section focuses on practices that are likely to increase the participation of children and adolescents with special needs in physical activities so they can access the well-documented benefits of this participation. More specifically, the chapters in this section identify barriers and enablers to participation in community-based sports and leisure programs; provide a detailed case study of the impact of transitional services; and highlight the need to promote physical activities for children and adolescents who live with chronic illnesses.

Yolanda Fernandez, Jenny Ziviani, and Monica Cuskelly's chapter highlights that despite the well-demonstrated benefits of participation in community-based sports and leisure programs, many children with special needs do not participate in these programs, but rather participate in solitary and informal home-based physical activities. In response to this problem, the chapter encourages stakeholders to investigate ways to best support participation in physical activity both in and outside of school. The chapter examines recent research to identify the barriers to participation for children with special needs as well as strategies that enhance enjoyment and engagement in active leisure and sporting programs. The chapter concludes that supporting more positive and inclusive leisure experiences in the community may provide the key to strengthening children's engagement in regular physical activity.

Anna Cadzow, Motohide Miyahara, and Ruth Cutfield's chapter provides an illustrative longitudinal case study to demonstrate how a young boy with a developmental coordination disorder experienced two transitive intervention services from home to school and community as a long-term process that resulted in his participation in extracurricular physical activities. The chapter employs the transactional model of personal and environmental factors to explain the intervention focus and provides extensive contextualized descriptions of how the student experiences the transitive services of the Family Focused Intervention and the Movement Development Clinic over 3 years. The case study culminates with an interview with the boy and his mother where barriers and enablers for participation in extracurricular physical activities after exiting the transitive services are clearly identified. As a result of the case study, the chapter concludes with recommended strategies to facilitate participation in physical activities for youth with special needs.

Fiona Moola and Elizabeth Huynh assert that despite the increase in the number of children living with chronic illnesses, little is known about the physical activity needs of these children. This chapter presents a body of research that has been conducted over one decade to distill the lessons learned in this important area of need. First, the historical context and psychological and sociological aspects of living with chronic illness are described. Importantly, the stereotype that these children are "too fragile" for physical activity is challenged and the benefits of such participation championed. Next, the barriers to physical activity—from personal to systemic—are critiqued. The chapter concludes by signaling the dire need to recognize and nurture the physical activity needs of children who live with chronic illnesses and dismantle the systemic barriers that these children face in their efforts to be physically active, so that they too are free to play.

STRATEGIES TO MAXIMIZE THE SOCIAL INCLUSION OF CHILDREN AND ADOLESCENTS WITH SPECIAL NEEDS IN GENERAL PHYSICAL ACTIVITIES

One of the most pressing criteria used to determine whether inclusive education has been achieved is the extent to which children and adolescents with special needs are socially included. This section investigates this issue within the context of general physical activities. The chapters provide explicit recommendations about how best to enhance the quality of social interactions between children and adolescents with special needs and their peers, and the attitude of peers toward children and adolescents with special needs. Strategies to achieve these outcomes include focusing on disability-ability awareness, the training of educators, curriculum design, and ensuring the voices of the children and adolescents with special needs are considered when identifying the barriers and enablers.

Bethany Hersman and Samuel Hodge recognize the benefits for both children and adolescents with special needs, and those without, when children and adolescents with special needs are included within various physical activity settings. The social aspect of inclusion can be considered one of the greatest benefits of including children and adolescents with and without special needs together. The research, however, informs that the social interactions are often unidirectional where youth with special needs typically initiate the interaction rather than the interaction being reciprocal. The chapter presents a critique of the research investigating the nature of these social interactions and, importantly, provides strategies to promote social inclusion and social interaction between children and adolescents with and without special needs in physical education and activity settings. The chapter advances the social inclusion of children and adolescents with special needs by providing recommendations for best practices.

Tânia Bastos, Joana Teixeira, Mariana Cunha, and Rui Corredeira's chapter recognizes that frequently children with special needs report negative experiences during social interactions with their peers, which leads to social exclusion from physical education activities. The attitude of children without special needs is positioned as one of the most important factors to achieving a successfully inclusive physical education setting. The chapter presents a detailed analysis of the impact of a Paralympic educational program on the attitudes of peers toward disability. Based on this analysis, educators are urged to implement disability-ability awareness activities and design Paralympic educational programs that focus on peers' social interactions. Recommendations provided in the chapter seek to promote social inclusion, respect for individual difference, knowledge about disability sport, and foster positive interactions between children with special needs and their peers.

Martin Block, Michelle Grenier, and Yeshayahu "Shayke" Hutzler's chapter questions what can be done to help children and adolescents with special needs have a more positive experience in general physical education, where they are socially and academically included and not just physically present in the class. The chapter seeks to address this key question by illustrating three key practices that can promote social acceptance and social inclusion of children and adolescents with special needs in general physical education. The first strategy focuses on preparing peers without special needs to communicate, understand, accept, and appreciate classmates with special needs; implementing international disability awareness programs; and the adoption of peer tutoring. Second, the chapter recommends that educators and training bodies embrace new ways of preparing physical education teachers and supporting current physical education educators. Finally, the chapter presents several models, such as Universal Design and STEP, to modify physical education and sport activities, and strategies such as cooperative learning so that children and adolescents with special needs can be included in physical education.

Janine Coates advocates that children's perceptions of physical education lessons are at the core of understanding inclusion, yet research infrequently asks children about their experiences and too often relies on the perceptions of other stakeholders. This chapter explores some of the emerging literature in this field and then presents findings from a study that aimed to understand inclusion in physical education from the perspective of a heterogeneous group of children with a range of special needs. The key findings of the study form the basis of the chapter's recommendations, which seek to advance knowledge and practice to assist educators to develop inclusive physical education environments that nurture relationships between children with special needs, their teachers, and their peers.

EFFECTIVE PHYSICAL EDUCATION STRATEGIES TO ENHANCE BIOPSYCHOSOCIAL OUTCOMES FOR CHILDREN AND ADOLESCENTS WITH SPECIAL NEEDS

The biopsychosocial benefits of effective physical education curriculum and pedagogy are well recognized among researchers and educators. This section seeks to showcase and critique a number of strategies for use with children and adolescents with special needs with a particular emphasis on youth living in poverty. Strategies include introducing play fighting to the curriculum to reduce aggressive behavior; enacting outdoor and adventure education to enhance social skills; and starting a school-based health initiative to promote health opportunities for children and adolescents.

Erica Gobbi and Attilio Carraro describe the emerging problem of aggressive behavior among youth from disadvantaged backgrounds in Italy. The school, and in particular the physical education class, is positioned as a location to deliver strategies to address this issue, and more specifically through the delivery of play fighting. The chapter presents a series of studies that demonstrate in the short-term, play fighting appears to significantly reduce aggressive behavior (especially the physical dimension of aggression) and enhance the quality of school life and interpersonal relationships. This chapter advances knowledge and practice not only by demonstrating the impact of play fighting, but also by presenting a best practice approach to designing and delivering a play fighting intervention within physical education classes.

Daniel Tindall, Jack Neylon, Melissa Parker, and Deborah Tannehill introduce educators to outdoor and adventure experiences as a potential strategy to enhance the social skills of adolescents with special needs. Outdoor adventure education has been demonstrated to enhance motor functioning for adolescents with special needs; however, less is known about its impact on social and psychological outcomes for adolescents with special needs. This chapter advances knowledge about this emerging field within inclusive physical education. More specifically, the chapter defines the adventure education model and identifies how its implementation as part of a learning experience can help foster social skill development for adolescents with special needs. Viewed primarily from an Irish context, this chapter emphasizes the development of evidence-based, practice-focused, effective teaching to promote physical activity for adolescents with special needs. It contributes to educator's knowledge of constructivist pedagogies and provides specific examples to enhance application.

Alex Garn, Jeffrey Martin, Brigid Byrd, and Nate McCaughtry's chapter draws attention to the health inequities faced by children and adolescents living in poverty and proposes that school-based programming could be one solution to reducing such obstacles. In this chapter, the Detroit Healthy Youth Initiative is showcased as a proactive collaboration between Detroit Public Schools and Wayne State University to mitigate some of these obstacles. This initiative uses school programs as a hub for health promotion across primary, middle, and high schools and delivers programming before, during, and after school. The chapter presents the origins and overview of the Detroit Healthy Youth Initiative and highlights research findings, with an emphasis on social determinants of physical activity, associated with the initiative. Finally, evidence-based recommendations are discussed to support educators in developing school-based programs that promote health opportunities and equity for children and adolescents living in poverty.

ADVANCING THE PRACTICE OF EDUCATORS AND COACHES TO CULTIVATE THE SOCIAL INCLUSION AND PARTICIPATION IN PHYSICAL ACTIVITY OF CHILDREN AND ADOLESCENTS WITH SPECIAL NEEDS

Educators and coaches play a vital role in developing physical activities that foster social inclusion and participation for children and adolescents with special needs. This section describes and critiques an internet-based initiative to train facilitators to enhance participation, and also provides an assessment of the role and training of various educators in the United Kingdom and their capacity to promote social inclusion and participation.

Kwok Ng, Matthew Rogers, and Ken Black's chapter recognizes the imperative to ensure that coaches and educators are appropriately trained to effectively plan and deliver adapted physical activities and sports to maximize social inclusion and participation for children and adolescents with special needs. The internet provides an opportunity to improve access to such training for coaches and educators. This study investigates the utility of an Internet-based initiative entitled Volley*SLIDE* as a means to train coaches and educators about best practice in the sport of sitting volleyball. The chapter contributes toward our understanding of not only how to train coaches and educators to effectively deliver an adapted sport, but also investigates the underlying principles of social media as a tool for learning.

Philip Vickerman and Anthony Maher begin by highlighting the health and social benefits gained from participating in physical education and the international commitment to promoting equal access for children with special needs. Despite these convictions, this chapter clearly identifies some of the existing barriers that limit the inclusion of children with special needs in physical education. The role of the teacher and other related professionals is cast as a critical factor influencing this inclusion, with particular emphasis on their training, collaboration, and responsibilities. Current policies and practices occurring in the United Kingdom are critiqued to enhance our understanding of these contributing factors. Finally, the chapter advocates for the Eight P Inclusive Framework as a strategy for realizing the full inclusion of children with special needs in physical education.

CHALLENGING THE MEANING AND IMPLEMENTATION OF INCLUSIVE PRACTICES IN PHYSICAL EDUCATION GLOBALLY

Inclusive education is a complex concept that requires much more than simply having children and adolescents with special needs placed in the same educational environments as their peers. This section challenges educators to consider and reflect on not only the discourse that underpins their professional practice, but also to advance their understanding of the differing inclusive policies and practices that occur across diverse parts of the world.

Donna Goodwin's chapter challenges educators to consider and reflect on their professional practice, and the construction and discourse of disability that underpin their practice. A social justice lens is brought to our understanding of the meaning of disability and a critical examination of the social model of disability is presented. The chapter encourages educators to acknowledge and value alternative embodiments to those typically reflected through cultural norms. Throughout the chapter, issues of social justice are used as a pedagogical tool for shifting discussions of disability as an individual problem to be treated and eradicated, to a progressive understanding of disability as a way of being in the world.

Justin Haegele, Bethany Hersman, Samuel Hodge, Jihyun Lee, Amaury Samalot-Rivera, Mayumi Saito, Takahiro Sato, and Anselmo de Athayde Costa e Silva's chapter highlights the expanding international support for the concept of inclusion. Despite such consistent support, the meaning and implementation of inclusive practices in physical education vary in different countries. This chapter explores current inclusive physical education practices across a number of countries including Brazil, Japan, South Korea, and the United States including Puerto Rico. A critique of the various philosophies and practices is presented. The chapter contributes to our understanding of cross-cultural inclusive practices in physical education that will advance the knowledge of both educators and researchers working in these contexts. Finally, the chapter identifies strategies that are effective in promoting the physical activity of children and adolescents with special needs.

ACKNOWLEDGMENTS

The editorial efforts leading to the development of this collective work was realized in the context of, and made possible by, a grant from the Australian Research Council (DP140101559) awarded to Alexandre J. S. Morin, Rhonda G. Craven, Danielle Tracey, and Christophe Maïano, and grants from the the Social Sciences and Humanities Research Council of Canada (430-2012-0091, 435-2014-0909) awarded to Christophe Maïano, Alexandre J. S. Morin, and Danielle Tracey. The editorial team would also like to thank Hua Flora Zhong and Zhu Chen who greatly assisted throughout the production of this book.

Alexandre J. S. Morin
Christophe Maïano
Danielle Tracey
Rhonda G. Craven

PART I

STRATEGIES TO MAXIMIZE PARTICIPATION
OF CHILDREN AND ADOLESCENTS WITH SPECIAL
NEEDS IN PHYSICAL ACTIVITY AS A GLOBAL PRIORITY

CHAPTER 1

PARTICIPATION IN COMMUNITY LEISURE PROGRAMS

A Vehicle for Enhancing Physical Activity in Children with Developmental Difficulties

Yolanda Fernandez and Jenny Ziviani
The University of Queensland

Monica Cuskelly
University of Tasmania

CASE VIGNETTE, OLLY: A MOTHER'S DILEMMA

It's a story I've heard many times before in my occupational therapy clinic room. Whether it be about joining the local football or cricket club, doing dance classes or... "Gymnastics. Yeah, I wanna do gymnastics just like all the other kids," proclaims 7-year-old Olly, an energetic cheerful boy who enjoys playing on his portable electronic device, running around, and building with blocks. Olly also has some attention, learning, and motor coordination difficulties. These developmental difficulties are having an impact not only on his performance at school, but also on his ability to participate in community leisure and sports activities. Janine lowers her head in dismay as she places her hand on her son's shoulder.

"Love, you know we've tried that before. Remember what happened?... It was a bit tricky for you." "Awwh, but Mu-um!" And with that, Olly dashes off across the room to explore a set of blocks that have caught his eye, almost tripping over his backpack on the way. Janine turns to me, lowering her voice, "You know, we had a go and went along to a few kids' classes at the local gymnastics club. For the first couple of sessions, Olly was alright. He was having fun. But then, as they got more into it, they added more and more steps, and trickier stuff... and things got faster. Olly just couldn't keep up with it all. Half the time he wasn't even keeping up with the instructions the coaches were calling out. It was *so* obvious. I started to feel really frustrated with the whole thing, too. It was hard for me to watch. And the coaches, they just didn't seem to get it. They would let Olly 'sit out' for some of the tricky stuff, while the other kids did it. He'd just sit out to the side with his head hanging, fiddling with the cord on his pants. He wouldn't say anything about it to the coaches or to me, but I could tell he was feeling a bit... you know, a bit down and embarrassed. What's that gonna do for his self-esteem?"

Sensing that Janine has more that she needs to share with me, I nod and pause. She continues, her voice quivering. "He keeps asking me about joining this or that club activity or sport... and I really want to be able to say yes, I really do... because I know he needs to be doing something physical for his body, and it would be great if he could make some new friends outside of school, too. Not to mention, it would also help him get some more skills and confidence so that he can join in more with the kids at school when they're running around playing soccer or footy and stuff but... (sighing) I just don't know what to do. I don't want to put him through that again ... I don't think I can risk it." Olly bounces back over to his mum and leaps into her lap nearly bowling her over with a huge bear hug. Janine smiles as she hugs him back and quickly wipes away a tear. It is clear that she is feeling torn: On the one hand, she really wants to support her son's development and participation opportunities, and on the other, she is burdened by her worries for him and past negative experiences.

Participation in community-based leisure programs outside of home and school environments provides children with an opportunity to become involved in a regular organized form of physical activity. It also offers an important means of connecting with peers, developing physical and social skills, and enhancing self-confidence (Hood & Carruthers, 2013; Mota, Barros, Ribeiro, & Santos, 2013), which are key contributors to health, well-being and resilience. Children with developmental difficulties, however, do not participate in physically active leisure programs to the same extent as their peers (Arim, Findlay, & Kohen, 2012; Potvin, Snider, Prelock, Kehayia, & Wood-Dauphinee, 2013; Shikako-Thomas et al., 2013). A sedentary lifestyle and inactivity places these children at higher risk of obesity, decreased self-esteem, and social isolation (Murphy & Carbone, 2008). Exploring ways to support their participation in physically active leisure programs within the comunity setting could prove a valuable vehicle for enhancing their health and well-being. In this chapter, an overview of recent research and key theoretical frameworks within the field of child development and leisure participation will be presented. These will provide the basis for exploring the dimensions of leisure participation and informing practice with respect to how to effectively support children who are developmentally vulnerable and "at risk" of avoiding or disengaging from community leisure programs.

LEISURE: A KEY OCCUPATION OF CHILDHOOD

Some may view leisure as an optional part of life; however, leisure should be considered a key occupation and an important part of a balanced and healthy lifestyle. For school-aged children, leisure provides time away from the demands of home, school, and other commitments where they can rest, recharge, and enjoy preferred activities (Majnemer, 2010). These activities may encompass a range of informal and organized games, sports, relaxation and/or hobbies (WHO, 2007). Experiencing a sense of "freedom" from other life demands, choice, and enjoyment are key defining elements of leisure (Majnemer, 2010). Other important aspects can include intrinsic motivation (being moved from within to participate), perceived competence, and a sense of satisfaction (Hurd & Anderson, 2011). These subjective elements are critical to determining whether an experience is perceived as leisure or not by an individual.

Benefits of Leisure Participation

Although the contribution of leisure participation to health and developmental outcomes continues to be under appreciated, there is now a growing body of evidence that points to the significance of leisure and the positive contribution it can make to children's health and well-being. Participation in physically active leisure contributes to health and fitness (Janssen & Leblanc, 2010), mental well-being (Biddle & Asare, 2011; Kremer et al., 2014) and children's happiness and positive self-concept (Holder, Coleman, & Sehn, 2009). Leisure pursuits can also offer children opportunities to develop and master skills, enhancing their sense of competence

(Majnemer, 2009), provide dedicated downtime for enjoyment and relaxation (Poulsen & Ziviani, 2010), and emotional release (Jessup, Cornell, & Bundy, 2010; Majnemer, 2010). Furthermore, for school-age children participation in organized activities outside school hours has been associated with higher social and academic self-concept, general self-worth (Blomfield & Barber, 2009), and more positive peer and identity experiences (Blomfield Neira & Barber, 2012). These physical and psychosocial benefits are known to be key contributors to children's overall health, well-being, and resilience (Jessup et al., 2010; Rutter, 2013). For children with developmental difficulties, however, leisure participation can be compromised.

CHILDREN WITH DEVELOPMENTAL DIFFICULTIES AND DISABILITIES

A variety of terms are used in the literature to describe developmental conditions and childhood disabilities. The most recognized of these are developmental disability and neurodevelopmental disorder. Majnemer (2012) described developmental disabilities as encompassing delays or deficits in one or more developmental domains (e.g., motor, cognitive, behavioral, speech, language) that "have an impact on that person's ability to perform age-appropriate everyday activities and functions" (p.10). Developmental disabilities are a diverse group of conditions and disorders that begin in childhood and can influence children's trajectories into adulthood. Although a clear cause for the disability is often not known, it is considered attributable to an underlying intellectual and/or physical impairment (Mason & Smith, 2005). The *Diagnostic and Statistical Manual of Mental Disorders* (DSM -5; American Psychiatric Association, 2013) classifies developmental disabilities within the category of neurodevelopmental disorders, which includes conditions such intellectual disability, communication disorders, autism spectrum disorder, and cerebral palsy. About 5% of children have a detectable biological medical condition, intellectual or physical disability that can be diagnosed early in life (Australian Government, 2016; Curtin, Madden, Staines, & Perry, 2013).

There is a considerable proportion of school-age children who do not have a diagnosed medical condition or disability, but who do experience developmental difficulties that impact their ability to participate in everyday activities, such as schoolwork and learning, playing games and sports, interacting with their peers, and being able to care for themselves. International data indicates that in addition to the approximately 5% of children with recognized conditions based on medical diagnosis, about another 22% of children are identified at school entry as being "of concern," with vulnerability identified across one or more domains of development (Curtin et al.,

2013; Australian Government, 2016). Although these children are identified as having additional health and developmental needs, because they do not have a medical diagnosis they will not meet the special needs classification for support (Australian Government, 2016). Data trends suggest an increasing presentation of children with a range of learning, attentional, behavioral and social emotional difficulties that impact their ability to engage in age-appropriate activities and opportunities (Halfon, Houtrow, Larson, & Newacheck, 2012).

To date, most leisure studies have focused either on typically developing children or children with specific developmental disabilities, such as cerebral palsy. There has been a paucity of research on children who may experience developmental difficulties and vulnerabilities (Majnemer, 2010), such as those highlighted in the aforementioned data. It is this group of children our research focused upon. For the purposes of this chapter, this group of children will be referred to as children with developmental difficulties; that is, children who experience difficulties and vulnerabilities in one or more areas of their development that impact their ability to participate in everyday life activities—children just like Olly. Although Olly has no diagnosed medical or health condition, nor a recognized developmental disability, his mother has brought him to occupational therapy because he is struggling to participate in many daily activities and childhood occupations that he needs to do, wants to do and is expected to do. Olly is described by his parents and teachers as being quite clumsy and uncoordinated, struggling with learning and staying on task, as well as playing with his peers. This has an impact not only on Olly, but also causes worry and concern for his parents.

So why have we chosen to focus on this group of children? Firstly, we believe these children are a vulnerable group who are at risk of being overlooked, precisely because they do not have a recognized disability. Second, these children represent a large proportion of school-aged children identified with developmental needs; and finally, research investigating their participation needs is almost nonexistent. Research in this area is not only relevant, it is greatly needed to address this gap. As a starting point, we have drawn on the existing literature on children with developmental disabilities to inform our research.

Leisure Participation of Children With Developmental Disabilities

Children with developmental disabilities do not participate in community leisure programs to the same extent as their peers. Instead, they are more likely to participate in solitary, sedentary, and informal home-based activities rather than active physical pursuits or organized leisure programs in the community (Jarus, Lourie-Gelberg, Engel-Yeger, & Bart, 2011; Potvin et al., 2013; Shikako-Thomas et al., 2013). This is concerning, as participation in a variety of activity opportunities, across different domains and settings, has been found to result in positive academic and social outcomes (Bohnert, Fredricks, & Randall, 2010), and enhanced quality of life (Dahan-Oliel, Shikako-Thomas, & Majnemer, 2012). Children who participate predominantly in solitary and sedentary activities are missing out on the physical and social benefits that more physically active leisure within the community context can provide (Murphy & Carbone, 2008).

Barriers and Bridges That Influence Children's Leisure Participation

A number of environmental and psychosocial factors have been found to influence children's leisure participation, over and above the influence accounted for by person-specific variables such as age, gender, physical skill, or type or level of disability (Badia, Orgaz, Verdugo, Ullan, & Martinez, 2011; King, Law, Petrenchik, & Hurley, 2013). These factors include opportunities, time, cost, access to programs (Arim et al., 2012; Barnett, Dawes, & Wilmut, 2013; Shimmell, Gorter, Jackson, Wright, & Galuppi, 2013), and for those with physical impairments, the impact of pain and fatigue (Barnett et al., 2013; Shimmell et al., 2013). Factors within the social environment such as the level of support, understanding, and attitudes of others—such as peers, teachers, and coaches—can also support participation or act as a barrier (Barnett et al., 2013; Dahan-Oliel et al., 2012; Shimmell et al., 2013).

In terms of factors that can support more positive participation experiences, a number of key themes have emerged from the research literature with children and adolescents with developmental disabilities. For example, being able to engage in activites of their choosing within a social context (Dahan-Oliel et al., 2012; Majnemer et al., 2008; Shikako-Thomas et al., 2013) was found to be important and contributed to quality of life and happiness (Dahan-Oliel et al., 2012). Having independence and choice, having fun, doing and being with others, and feeling successful are the key aspects of activity participation (Heah, Case, McGuire, & Law, 2007), and physically active leisure (Shimmell et al., 2013) which children and adolescents find most meaningful.

Parental beliefs may also influence children's participation. Pitchford, Siebert, Hamm, and Yun (2016) found that the physical activity level of youth with developmental disabilities was significantly associated with parental beliefs regarding the importance and benefits of physical activity.

Findings suggest that youth with disabilities whose parents held more positive beliefs, participated in more physical activity.

An interesting finding that has also emerged has been identified as *perceived barriers*, or aspects that appear daunting to an individual, which may or may not hold true. Perceived barriers may relate to perceptions individuals hold of their own skills and abilities, as well as their perceptions of activity demands and the environment, both physical and social. For example, feeling their skills, abilities, and fitness were not "good enough" have been cited as preventing children and adolescents from participation opportunities (Arim et al., 2012; Badia et al., 2011; King et al., 2003). Feeling worried about being teased or embarrassed has also been identified as a perceived barrier to participation (Badia et al., 2011; Shimmell et al., 2013).

Perceived barriers may develop as a result of a range of other complex variables such as coaching approach, attitudes of others, and the actual activity itself. The level of skill proficiency, competition, and performance grading that is often associated with many physical activity programs such as sports, dance, and gymnastics may discourage the participation of children and adolescents who have conditions such as developmental coordination disorder (Barnett et al., 2013; Poulsen, Ziviani, & Cuskelly, 2006). Past negative experiences have also been identified as not only impacting self-efficacy, but also a willingness to try new activities (Barnett et al., 2013).

This research highlights the complexity of interrelated personal, activity, and environmental factors that may influence children's leisure participation. Collectively, these data also illustrate the importance of taking a more holistic and deeper view of leisure participation in future research.

Theoretical Frameworks and Models of Health, Well-Being and Participation

To inform our research, we chose to draw on key theoretical frameworks with a holistic perspective of health and well-being, and a focus on participation outcomes. During the last 30 years, there has been a dramatic shift in the way health is viewed, with growing recognition of the need for a broader lens and more positive perspective. This has led to traditional medical and deficit-based approaches being replaced with understandings of health and function derived from an ecological-behavioral perspective, sometimes referred to generically as biopsychosocial or person-environment fit models (Halfon, Larson, Lu, Tullis, & Russ, 2014; Soresi, Nota, & Wehmeyer, 2011). This means our perspective has shifted from focusing on individuals and their "problems," to more attention now being given to interactions between individuals and the environments in which they live and participate (Soresi et al., 2011). Bronfenbrenner was one of the early theorists to describe this broader perspective in relation to human social development. He conceived the ecological systems theory (Bronfenbrenner, 1977) to explain the interdependence of social environmental systems of the home, family, school, and work along with the influence of the broader cultural and socioeconomic context on child development.

Two theoretical frameworks that align with this more holistic view of health and well-being, while also providing an overarching guide to practice and research, are the International Classification of Functioning, Disability and Health for Children and Youth (ICF-CY; WHO, 2007) and the Person-Environment-Occupation model (PEO; Law et al., 1996). The ICF-CY was developed by the WHO and was derived from the original universal classification system, the International Classification of Functioning, Disability and Health (ICF; WHO, 2001). It reflects a biopsychosocial framework and emphasises the dynamic interrelationships of biological components, tasks and activities, people's involvement in life situations (participation), and personal and environmental factors. Refer to Figure 1.1.

Similarly, the PEO model was developed by occupational therapists to guide professional assessment and practice: it highlights that practitioners need to attend to person-specific factors (P), environmental considerations (E), and occupation (O) or tasks/activities in order to optimize performance and participation outcomes, thereby enhancing health and well-being. Refer to Figure 1.2.

The use of arrows in the ICF model and overlapping circles in the PEO highlights that no one area stands in isolation and that all aspects can influence one another. For example, person-specific factors may include a

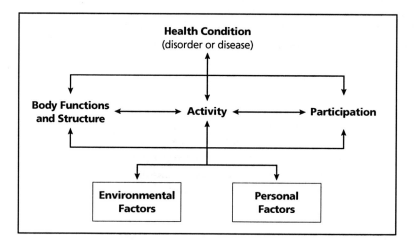

Figure 1.1 International classification of functioning, disability and health (adapted from WHO, 2001).

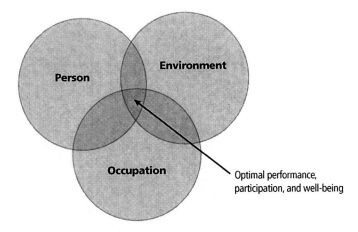

Figure 1.2   Person–environment–occupation model (adapted from Law et al., 1986).

child's age, skills and abilities, interests, values, culture, self-esteem, and confidence. Many of these factors can be influenced by what the child needs to do and is expected to do (occupations and activities), but also by the environment and context in which he or she participates. The environment includes both the physical and social environment (such as attitudes of others). Given our focus on leisure participation within a community context, frameworks such as these are particularly pertinent and helpful when we begin to explore the leisure participation of children with developmental difficulties. But is this sufficient?

Participation and Engagement From a Self-Determination Theory Perspective

Some authors have proposed that we need to re-examine our conceptualization of participation from a deeper perspective. In their conceptual models of participation, Bohnert et al. (2010) and King, Rigby, and Batorowisc (2013) described two distinct concepts that underscore involvement in life activities: participation and engagement. They described participation in terms of "the doing" and "taking part," while engagement was described as a behavioral, emotional, and cognitive concept that reflects the deeper "experience" of participation for the individual: doing, being, and feeling. This important distinction between participation and engagement allows for a better understanding of the different elements of involvement and the possible contributing factors. These authors also emphasized that participation and engagement are very much interconnected. Engagement is the mediating variable that leads to more positive outcomes in activity participation and a state of "flow" (Csikszentmihalyi, 2009), providing opportunities for children to "develop new competencies and strengthen their sense of mastery" (King, Rigby, et al., 2013, p. 1579). King, Rigby, and colleagues (2013) have proposed that when optimal engagement is achieved, it is more likely that children will continue to be involved in activities.

Self-Determination Theory. Another important theoretical perspective that can guide our understanding of children's engagement in life activities, and in particular what drives and motivates sustained involvement, is self-determination theory. Self-determination theory is a theory of human motivation, development, and wellness (Deci & Ryan, 1985). Individuals may behave in particular ways as a result of their response to external factors; such as reward systems, evaluations, or the opinions of others. Equally, people can be motivated from within themselves by their interests, values, and inner yearnings. This latter is referred to as intrinsic motivation and describes the innate motivation from within the individual that drives and sustains passions, creativity, and ongoing efforts, without necessarily being externally rewarded or supported (Deci & Ryan, 1985, 2000). The interplay between extrinsic influences acting on individuals, and intrinsic motives and psychological needs inherent in human nature is the territory of self-determination theory.

Deci and Ryan proposed that humans have three basic psychological needs.

- Autonomy: The need to experience a sense of volition, integration, and psychological freedom; to have life's activities concordant with one's sense of self; taking personal ownership; and having choices.
- Relatedness: The need to experience a sense of connectedness and belonging, to feel connected to others, to care for others, and to be cared for.
- Competence: The need to experience a sense of effectance, to feel effective in one's environment, and to experience opportunities to develop one's capabilities.

According to self-determination theory, these psychological needs can be described as essential human *nutriments* that influence our thinking, feeling, and behaving (Deci & Ryan, 2000). They are an innate part of human nature, essential for optimal development and psychological health (Deci & Vansteenkiste, 2004). Furthermore, engagement and psychological well-being is optimized when all three psychological needs are met.

The issue for children with developmental disabilities (and indeed, we would propose, for children with any developmental difficulties) is that their leisure activity choices may be limited. Misconceptions and concerns about the skill proficiency, safety, and susceptibility of children with disabilities to injury—particularly in regards to physical activity and sports—may result in well-meaning parents and service providers limiting students' participation options or believing they should make choices for them (Badia et al., 2011; Murphy & Carbone, 2008; Shields & Synnot, 2016). Since one of the core elements of leisure is freedom–freedom to choose and freedom from daily demands–we would propose that children with developmental disabilities and those with developmental difficulties are at risk of not having the same opportunities and, therefore, not experiencing the same benefits that physically active leisure can provide for typically developing children.

ENHANCING PHYSICAL ACTIVITY THROUGH COMMUNITY-BASED LEISURE PROGRAMS

The focus of health interventions has often been on individuals and how to improve their physical activity and fitness. Health interventions are now emerging that endorse a more community-based approach. A small number of recent studies have creatively used leisure programs to maximize physical activity participation and address specific health and therapeutic goals. Madsen, Thompson, Adkins, and Crawford (2013) used an after-school soccer program to address youth obesity and enhance health. Those youth most at risk of weight-related comorbidities benefited the most in terms of health and fitness indicators, including an increase in physical activity. Gilmore, Ziviani, Sakzewski, Shields, and Boyd (2010) and Sakzewski et al. (2011) experimented with the use of a circus-themed day camp to motivate and engage children with unilateral cerebral palsy in pursuing therapeutic goals and physical activity with positive results. These preliminary results appear promising and warrant further investigation.

AIM AND CONTEXT

As identified, most leisure studies to date have focused on typically developing children or children with specific developmental disabilities. Although this is understandable, there remains a significant gap in the research: examining the leisure participation of children who have developmental difficulties and vulnerabilities, but for whom there is no clear medical diagnosis (international data indicates approximately 22% of school-age children). This is a considerable proportion of children who are potentially at risk of having their participation needs overlooked or misunderstood. This provided the impetus for our research.

Our study aimed to explore the community leisure experiences of children with developmental difficulties examining: (a) the psychosocial elements of leisure, including what they enjoy and value most; (b) whether they experience any barriers and enablers to participation; and (c) how this compares to research on children with developmental disability. We also sought to explore whether a scaffolded community participation opportunity (providing targeted support and skill development) could act as a bridge toward broader participation in the community and further engagement in physical activity. We specifically aimed to examine any changes with respect to children's self-efficacy, motivation, confidence, and leisure aspirations. Our broader aim was that this research would inform future endeavors to promote and enhance the engagement of children in physically active leisure.

For the purposes of this study, children with developmental difficulties included children who experience difficulties in one or more areas of their development (cognitive, attention, motor, language, social-emotional) that impacted their ability to participate in activities of everyday life.

METHODS

A partnership between a community leisure organization that runs circus programs for children and youth in Brisbane (pseudonym—Circus Club) and an occupational therapy practice (pseudonym—Children's Therapy) led to the introduction of a circus program for children with additional support needs. This existing partnership provided the opportunity for our study. A Brisbane City Council Community Development Grant provided funding that enabled a group of children attending occupational therapy services to participate in a supported leisure program at Circus Club free of charge.

Participants

Twenty children with developmental difficulties were recruited from two occupational therapy services in Brisbane, Australia, using the following inclusion criteria: (a) attending mainstream school; (b) aged 5 to 10 years; and (c) referred to occupational therapy due to concerns regarding participation in daily occupations such self-care, school work, play, and leisure. Children were excluded if they had been identified as having a significant intellectual, communication or physical impairment (e.g., cerebral palsy); had attended a circus program previously; and/or did not have sufficient English to participate in interviews. See Table 1.1 for descriptions of participants.

Leisure Program Details

The community-based leisure program was collaboratively designed by staff at Circus Club and Children's Therapy. It was designed to provide a noncompetitive, supportive environment focused on skill development and

TABLE 1.1	Characteristics of Participants	
Characteristic	**Category**	**No.**
Children interviewed ($N = 20$)		
Age (years:months)	5:0–6:11	9
	7:0–10:11	11
Gender	Male	13
	Female	7
Presenting difficulties	Complex (motor, learning, attention, communication, and/or social-emotional difficulties; impacting on participation in life activities)	14
	Predominantly motor (impacting on participation in life activities)	6
Medical diagnosis	Not known/specified[a]	18
	Autism Spectrum Disorder	1
	Genetic disorder	1
Parents interviewed[b]	Mothers	17
	Fathers (interviewed in addition to the mother)	4
Level of interviewee education	High school	1
	Trade or apprenticeship	4
	Tertiary	16

[a] Two participants had a provisional diagnosis of Pervasive Developmental Disorder (PDD-NOS).
[b] Three pairs of siblings with developmental difficulties were recruited—twin girls, twin boys, and a set of brothers. Thus, 17 families participated in the study.

confidence-building through physical activities such static trapeze, group acrobatics, lyra (aerial hoop), tissu (aerial acrobatics in double silk straps), trampolining, floor-based exercises, and strength activities.

Study Design

A mixed-methods design was employed with both quantitative and qualitative methods (Cresswell & Plano Clark, 2007) to enable a deeper understanding of the leisure participation experience from the perspectives of both children and parents. As this was an exploratory study focusing on understanding the leisure participation experiences and perceptions of a group of children for whom little data exist, a comparison group was not used (Table 1.1).

Tools and Measures Employed

Parents completed a demographic questionnaire prior to their child commencing the leisure program. Each child and parent/s also participated in in-depth, semi-structured interviews following the completion of the program. The following standardized tools were used to collect data pre and post participation in the leisure program:

- Perceived Efficacy and Goal Setting System (PEGS; Missiuna, Pollock, & Law, 2004). The PEGS can be used to elicit children's perspectives about how well they feel they can perform everyday tasks including self-care, leisure, and learning activities. Picture cards depicting drawings of children doing these everyday tasks are used to support children's reflection and understanding of these concepts. The parent version of the PEGS is used to gain parents' perspectives on their child's performance in everyday activities. The PEGS is one of only a few tools for this age-group (Missiuna, Pollock, Law, Walter, & Cavey, 2006) that focuses on children's abilities and perceived performance in daily life tasks (including leisure). The PEGS is client-centered and is sensitive to the issues that are important to children and their parents (Galvin, Randall, Hewish, Rice, & MacKay, 2010). Good construct and content validity is reported, and test-retest reliability ranges from 0.95 to 0.99 (Missiuna, et al., 2004; Missiuna et al., 2006).
- Children's Leisure Assessment (CLASS; Rosenblum, 2010). The CLASS was used to capture children's reflections on their participation in leisure activities: the types of activities, with whom they participated, and their level of enjoyment. The CLASS also includes a section that asks children to reflect on activities they would like to do in the future (leisure aspirations). Parents are able to support their child's responses. The CLASS was selected for this study because it can be administered in a semi-structured interview format, which allows both for flexibility and for rich data to be gathered (Rosenblum, Sachs, & Schreuer, 2010).
- Dimensions of Mastery Questionnaire (DMQ-17; Morgan, Busch-Rossnagel, Barrett, & Wang, 2009). The DMQ-17 gathers parent perceptions of children's mastery-related behaviors. It assesses aspects such as the child's mastery pleasure, persistence with activities, general competence, and any negative reactions to failure. The DMQ-17 is one of the only tools available for this age group that measures these aspects across children's occupations, and has shown robust properties in terms of reliability and validity for children with motor performance difficulties (Miller, Ziviani, & Boyd, 2014).
- Paediatric Volitional Questionnaire (PVQ; Basu, Kafkes, Schatz, Kiraly, & Kielhofner, 2008). The PVQ is one of the only observational assessment tools available to examine children's volition (their motivation for occupation) by observing their behaviors during activi-

ties and daily tasks. Ratings are systematically recorded for aspects such as mastery pleasure, initiation of tasks, attempting to solve problems, practicing skills, investing energy and attention, seeking challenges, showing curiosity and pride, and trying new things. By capturing these data during children's participation in activities, the PVQ provides insight about what drives a child, and how the environment may affect motivation and engagement in activities. It has been shown to be a valid tool (Andersen, Kielhofner, & Lai, 2005).

- Social Emotional Assets and Resilience Scales (SEARS; Merrell, 2011). The SEARS allows parents to report on their child's strengths, competence and abilities. At the time of this study, the SEARS was a relatively new tool. It was selected due to its strengths-based perspective (which contrasts to the negative orientation so often found in other questionnaires) and because it is based on strong research focused on resilience. The SEARS has robust psychometric properties with factor validity ranging from 0.87–0.95, high internal consistency (0.96), strong interrater reliability (0.72), and consistent sensitivity to group differences based on gender and disability status (Merrell, Felver-Gant, & Tom, 2010).

Procedures

In the month prior to commencing the leisure program, children completed the PEGS and CLASS. Parents also completed a demographic questionnaire, DMQ-17, SEARS, and parent-version of the PEGS.

Children then participated in the circus program, which consisted of 10, one-hour group sessions held each Saturday afternoon. Children were divided into two groups for classes. There was one group for younger children aged 5–6 years ($n = 9$; all boys), and another for children aged 7–10 years ($n = 11$; mix of boys and girls). Two circus trainers facilitated each group, one who had extensive experience working with children with additional support needs. An occupational therapy aide from Children's Therapy also supported the younger children's class. These classes took place alongside other circus classes taking place within the center. Circus Club trainers and managers, along with the Children's Therapy practice manager met with the research team prior to and during the program to discuss students' support needs, progress and engagement.

While observing children participating in the program, the first author completed the revised edition of the PVQ. Data were recorded for each child across three observations in the 10-week period. Photos were taken and video footage recorded of each child.

Within one month following the completion of the program, each child, together with his/her parent/s, attended a follow-up session. Using the photos and video footage to stimulate discussion, an in-depth semi-structured interview was undertaken separately with the child and his/her parent/s. Children had the option of having their parent present if they wished. The interview focused on the experience of the circus program, how this compared to other leisure experiences, what children enjoyed and valued most, barriers and challenges, and any aspirations for future leisure participation. Measures completed prior to commencing the program were also repeated.

Data Analysis

Baseline and follow-up data were screened and analyzed descriptively in the first instance. Tests of normality were undertaken prior to statistical analyses. In addition, the internal consistencies of the measures for our present sample were investigated using Cronbach's alpha. To explore if any changes had occurred that may have been associated with this leisure participation experience, differences in performance on measures of children's perceived efficacy, mastery related behaviors, and social-emotional competencies and skills were calculated using appropriate parametric tests. Frequencies for participation in physically active leisure and leisure aspirations at baseline and follow-up were also analyzed.

Interviews were audiorecorded and transcribed verbatim. Data from interviews were analyzed thematically. Three researchers, none of whom had an affiliation with the circus or occupational therapy organization, read the transcripts independently, and used selective highlighting to identify statements that conveyed children's and parents' views. Common categories and themes were then coded from these statements following the process outlined by Graneheim and Lundman (2004).

RESULTS

The measures used all showed acceptable to excellent levels of internal consistency (reliability) for our sample. The DMQ scales had good to excellent alpha coefficients ranging from .74 to .91. The PEGS child report had fair reliability for the self-care scale (.68), and good reliability for the productivity (.82) and leisure (.80) scales. Parent PEGS had an acceptable level of reliability for the self-care scale (.74), and good reliability for productivity (.81) and leisure (.84). The SEARS had excellent internal consistency for all scales (.90 or above). The PVQ also showed excellent internal consistency (.93). The CLASS was not assessed for internal consistency as this tool was used as a more descriptive and qualitative tool.

Paired-samples t-tests were conducted to compare children's perceived efficacy, mastery related behaviors, and social-emotional competencies and skills pre- and post-participation in the leisure program. As indicated in Table 1.2, there was a significant difference in children's efficacy scores from baseline to post participation, both on child and parent reports.

There was a significant difference in scores for children's gross motor persistence and cognitive persistence on the DMQ-17. Although there were improvements in other mastery-related behaviors, such as children's social persistence and mastery pleasure, these were not statistically significant. There was a significant difference in overall social-emotional competencies and skills scores at post participation in comparison to baseline values.

A paired-samples t-test was also used to compare observations of children's participation and level of engagement (based on a 4-point rating scale) from the initial sessions to the observations taken in the final sessions. A significant difference was found ($p < 0.01$). There was a steady improvement in the scores for children's level of engagement across the three observations during the 10-week period that the program was running (mean scores of 2.47, 2.72, and 3.04, respectively).

The three most preferred and enjoyed leisure activities in which children participated across the week remained the same at baseline and post participation. These were (a) watching television and videos, (b) playing games on portable electronic devices, and (c) indoor and outdoor unstructured play (creative, pretend, unstructured play). At baseline, 17 out of

TABLE 1.2 Perceived Efficacy, Mastery-Related Behaviors and Social Emotional Competence

	N	Pre-test Mean	Post-test Mean	p value
Perceived efficacy	19			
Children's perceived efficacy		64.2	73.9	<.001
Parent report child efficacy		53.8	64.4	<.001
Mastery-related behaviors (parent report)	20			
Cognitive persistence		2.7	3.1	.002
Gross motor persistence		3.01	3.49	.009
Social persistence–child		3.67	3.79	.234
Mastery pleasure		4.11	4.15	.748
Social emotional competencies and skills	17			
Self-regulation and responsibility		40.47	42.52	.120
Social competence		39.29	42.88	.011
Empathy		42.76	45.76	.017
Overall T-score		39.58	42.47	.017

the 20 children (85%) had aspirations to participate in leisure activities in which they were not currently involved. Of their leisure activity choices, 53% were physically active community-based activities. Post participation, the same 17 children continued to aspire to participate in additional activities, with 59% of these activity aspirations being for physically active community-based pursuits. The most popular physical activities that children aspired to participate in were dance classes, gymnastics, and martial arts. Enrollment data indicated that at least six children from the study had re-enrolled in Circus Club's regular suite of beginner circus classes. Three of these children also enrolled in a performance stream, which required a commitment to additional training sessions.

Four main themes emerged from the interview data in relation to what children and their parents perceived as being the most positive and valued aspects of a physically active leisure experience in the community. Enjoyment and having fun, as well as the opportunity for social connections and making friends, were valued aspects of leisure. The third subtheme was a sense of competence. Parents described the importance of the "just right" approach and "just right" expectations (not too easy, not too hard). Parents felt that when children were able to accomplish activities that they thought difficult and challenging, this resulted in a sense of achievement, and provided a boost to their confidence and sense of competence. The final subtheme was about the value and benefits of physical activity itself, including associated psychosocial benefits such as increased confidence and sense of achievement.

Parents also discussed barriers and constraints they believed were affecting their child's ability to access and participate in appropriate leisure programs in the community. Four main subthemes emerged: (a) reduced skill proficiency compared to peers, (b) past negative experiences, (c) limited activity/ program options available in the community, and (d) cost, time, and demands of family life. Parents indicated that these factors were often interrelated and that it was a combination of factors that had an impact. Data also emerged that these factors had resulted in parent worries and concerns for their child, which had led them to being hesitant about accessing participation opportunities. Some parents reported that they had reduced their child's choices and leisure options, even for activities in which the child had expressed an interest. The data from this qualitative component of the study are described in more detail in Fernandez, Ziviani, Cuskelly, Colquhoun and Jones' paper (under review).

DISCUSSION

In this chapter, we have described theoretical frameworks that support our understanding of children's participation, health, and well-being. A review of the research literature and our own exploratory study examining the leisure participation experiences of a small group of children with developmental difficulties has also been presented. Together this information provides us with a holistic understanding of children's participation in life activities, and more importantly can inform us regarding the strategies and actions that could be undertaken to maximize the participation of children at risk of inactivity and social exclusion due to developmental difficulties or vulnerabilities.

Positive changes were seen on a number of measures after children participated in the supported physical activity leisure program used in our study. Children's perceived efficacy improved, and parent's perception of children's efficacy (in a range of self-care, productivity, and leisure activities) also improved. Children's mastery-related behaviors also increased both as observed in the program and on parental reports. An improvement in social emotional competencies was also reported by parents. These findings suggest that children had a higher drive to participate and were feeling more confident in their abilities, as were their parents.

Prior to commencing the program, most children in our study had aspirations for taking up new physical activities and programs in the community; however, it seemed that parental concerns were getting in the way of children taking up opportunities. Our interviews with parents indicated that many of them had limited their child's choices in the past due to their concerns that their child may not keep up with peers and be embarrassed. This parental concern appears to have been a significant barrier to participation. Children's aspirations for physical activity remained high following their participation in the program, with a slight increase indicated. Most interesting is the high number of children who re-enrolled in circus and in other sports and community leisure clubs. These data add weight to our hypothesis that a supported participatory experience in a physically active leisure program could act as a bridge to further participation in physical activities in the community.

Similar to children with specific developmental disabilities, our study found that children with developmental difficulties also experience compromised participation opportunities in the community. Children and their parents expressed similar views and experiences regarding barriers and facilitators of participation as those reported in leisure research studies with other vulnerable populations. Perceived barriers, negative past experiences, along with coaching styles and attitudes were viewed as being particularly limiting. Enjoyment and having fun, as well as the opportunity for socializing with others were valued aspects and facilitators of physical activity and participation, reflecting other studies (Heah et al., 2007; Jaarsma, Dijkstra, de Blécourt, & Geertzen, 2015; Shimmell et al., 2013).

Although our participant sample was small, our findings contribute to a growing body of research that highlights that there are key person, activity and environmental (both social and physical) factors that could be addressed to support improved participation opportunities for school-aged children (Shimmell et al., 2013). The ICF-CY and the PEO model offer frameworks that can guide practitioners in supporting children and their families in addressing these factors. These findings also highlight the importance of the deeper elements of participation, those that promote engagement and enjoyment of participation, as well as include the elements of human needs identified by Self-Determination Theory. So pulling all of this information together with our collective experience, what actions do we believe are needed?

RECOMMENDATIONS AND IMPLICATIONS

It is critical that we consider how we can support children with developmental difficulties to not only become more physically active but stay active across the longer term. Supporting children to participate in physically active leisure programs in the community could be a pivotal way of keeping them engaged in a regular form of physical activity, especially if these activities are meaningful and enjoyable. Informed by the growing body of research literature, we believe there are four key overarching strategies, with several actions stemming from these, which could be applied to enhance enjoyment and engagement in leisure programs, while also addressing some of the key barriers that have been found to inhibit and thwart participation and enjoyment. These strategies are outlined below and are also synthesized in a visual representation in Figure 1.3:

1. Information sharing
   – Information for parents about the important benefits of physical activity, as well as information about physically active leisure programs available in the community, including sports programs.
2. Education and training
   – Further education/training of leisure providers, coaches and trainers regarding:
      ▷ Child development and developmental vulnerabilities, and
      ▷ Inclusive practice and coaching techniques to support children's autonomy, relatedness, and competence.
   – Further education/training of health and education professionals (such as occupational therapists, physiotherapists, school health nurses, physical education teachers) regarding:

▷ Benefits of children's participation in physically active leisure programs in the community;

▷ Importance of promoting physically active leisure participation within a community context as part of a holistic approach to children's optimal development, health and well-being.

3. Service delivery and programming

– Children and parents supported to find physical activities that are meaningful to them and a good "fit." Consultation with an occupational therapist could support parents and children in this process.

– Targeted skill development programs to support children to engage more successfully in specific sports and physically active leisure programs of interest, while also building their confidence. Consultation with an occupational therapist, physiotherapist, and leisure coach could support this process.

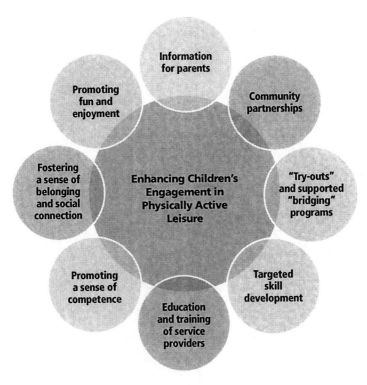

Figure 1.3 Key ingredients to enhance children's engagement in physically active leisure programs in the community.

- "Bridging" programs that can act as stepping stones to participation in more community leisure programs–enabling children and their parents the opportunity to try-out and experience activities in a supportive atmosphere focused on building confidence, developing skills and competencies, and addressing any concerns and worries. These should be available as part of the regular suite of options and classes provided by community leisure and sports organizations.
4. Community partnerships
   - Collaboration and partnerships between health services, schools, and community leisure/sports providers

CONCLUSIONS AND FUTURE DIRECTIONS

The benefits of physical activity to children's health and well-being are well documented. For school-aged children with developmental difficulties, participation in physical activity can be compromised. Supporting participation in physically active leisure programs within the community context that foster success, fun, and the opportunity to socialize with others could provide the vehicle for enhancing children's engagement in physical activity, while also supporting their social inclusion and well-being.

SUPPORTING OLLY'S PARTICIPATION

At our next occupational therapy session, Janine and I discuss her goal for Olly to be able to participate in a community-based physical activity or sport. I explain that we could work together on a plan to help Janine support Olly's participation in an activity that is positive for him and that he can enjoy. Prior to today's session, I have spent some time looking into programs that are available in the local area that could be a good fit for Olly and his family, including a noncompetitive gymnastics program that promotes having smaller group classes, as well as a "bridging" class for new students and those needing a little extra support. I gather some more information from Janine about what activities and strategies they've already tried and what's most important to her. We do some solution-finding together and discuss some ideas. I also show Olly some pictures of children playing different sports and physical activities, and explore with him a little more about what interests him. . . .

ACKNOWLEDGMENTS

The authors thank the children and families who participated in this study for sharing their stories and experiences. The program support provided by Flipside Circus and OCC Therapy is also gratefully acknowledged.

REFERENCES

American Psychiatric Association. (2013). *Diagnostic manual of mental disorders* (5th ed.; DSM-5). Arlington, VA: American Psychiatric Association.

Andersen, S., Kielhofner, G., & Lai, J.-S. (2005). An examination of the measurement properties of the pediatric volitional questionnaire. *Physical & Occupational Therapy in Pediatrics, 25*(1/2), 39–57. doi:10.1300/J006v25n01_04

Arim, R. G., Findlay, L. C., & Kohen, D. E. (2012). Participation in physical activity for children with neurodevelopmental disorders. *International Journal of Pediatrics.* doi:10.1155/2012/460384

Australian Government. (2016). *Australian early development census (AEDC) national report 2015: A snapshot of early childhood development in Australia.* Retrieved from www.aedc.gov.au

Badia, M., Orgaz, B. M., Verdugo, M. A., Ullan, A. M., & Martinez, M. M. (2011). Personal factors and perceived barriers to participation in leisure activities for young and adults with developmental disabilities. *Research in Developmental Disabilities, 32*(6), 2055–2063. doi:10.1016/j.ridd.2011.08.007

Barnett, A. L., Dawes, H., & Wilmut, K. (2013). Constraints and facilitators to participation in physical activity in teenagers with developmental co-ordination disorder: An exploratory interview study. *Child: Care, Health and Development, 39*(3), 393–403. doi:10.1111/j.1365-2214.2012.01376.x

Basu, S., Kafkes, A., Schatz, R., Kiraly, A., & Kielhofner, G. (2008). *Pediatric volitional questionnaire (Version 2.1).* Chicago, IL: MOHO.

Biddle, S. J. H., & Asare, M. (2011). Physical activity and mental health in children and adolescents: A review of reviews. *British Journal of Sports Medicine, 45*(11), 886–895. doi:10.1136/bjsports-2011-090185

Blomfield, C. J., & Barber, B. L. (2009). Brief report: Performing on the stage, the field, or both? Australian adolescent extracurricular activity participation and self-concept. *Journal of Adolescence, 32*(3), 733–739. doi:10.1016/j.adolescence.2009.01.003

Blomfield Neira, C. J., & Barber, B. L. (2012). Exploring the positive peer and identity experiences occurring in Australian adolescents' leisure activities. *The Australian Educational and Developmental Psychologist, 29*(1), 44–51. doi:10.1017/edp.2012.8

Bohnert, A., Fredricks, J., & Randall, E. (2010). Capturing unique dimensions of youth organized activity involvement: Theoretical and methodological considerations. *Review of Educational Research, 80*(4), 576–610. doi:10.3102/0034654310364533

Bronfenbrenner, U. (1977). Toward an experimental ecology of human development. *American Psychologist, 32*, 513–531.

Cresswell, J. W., & Plano Clark, V. L. (2007). *Designing and conducting mixed methods research.* Thousand Oaks, CA: SAGE.

Csikszentmihalyi, M. (2009). *Flow: The psychology of optimal experience.* New York, NY: Harper Collins.

Curtin, M., Madden, J., Staines, A., & Perry, I. J. (2013). Determinants of vulnerability in early childhood development in Ireland: A cross-sectional study. *BMJ Open, 3*(5), 1–9. doi:10.1136/bmjopen-2012-002387

Dahan-Oliel, N., Shikako-Thomas, K., & Majnemer, A. (2012). Quality of life and leisure participation in children with neurodevelopmental disabilities: A thematic analysis of the literature. *Quality of Life Research, 21*(3), 427–439. doi:10.1007/s11136-011-0063-9

Deci, E. L., & Ryan, R. M. (1985). *Intrinsic motivation and self-determination in human behavior.* New York, NY: Plenum.

Deci, E. L., & Ryan, R. M. (2000). The "what" and "why" of goal pursuits: Human needs and the self-determination of behavior. *Psychological Inquiry, 11*(4), 227–268. doi:10.2307/1449618

Deci, E. L., & Vansteenkiste, M. (2004). Self-determination theory and basic need satisfaction: Understanding human development in positive psychology. *Ricerche di Psicologia, 27*(1), 23–40.

Fernandez, Y., Ziviani, J., Cuskelly, M., Colquhoun, R., & Jones, F. (under review). *Leisure participation, health and well-being: Experiences of children with developmental difficulties and their families.*

Galvin, J., Randall, M., Hewish, S., Rice, J., & MacKay, M. T. (2010). Family-centered outcome measurement following pediatric stroke. *Australian Occupational Therapy Journal, 57*(3), 152–158. doi:10.1111/j.1440-1630.2010.00853.x

Gilmore, R., Ziviani, J., Sakzewski, L., Shields, N., & Boyd, R. (2010). A balancing act: Children's experience of modified constraint-induced movement therapy. *Developmental Neurorehabilitation, 13*(2), 88–94. doi:10.3109/17518420903386161

Graneheim, U. H., & Lundman, B. (2004). Qualitative content analysis in nursing research: concepts, procedures and measures to achieve trustworthiness. *Nurse Education Today, 24*(2), 105–112. doi:10.1016/j.nedt.2003.10.001

Halfon, N., Houtrow, A., Larson, K., & Newacheck, P. W. (2012). The changing landscape of disability in childhood. *The Future of Children, 22*(1), 13–42. doi:10.2307/41475645

Halfon, N., Larson, K., Lu, M., Tullis, E., & Russ, S. (2014). Lifecourse health development: Past, present and future. *Maternal and Child Health Journal, 18*(2), 344–365. doi:10.1007/s10995-013-1346-2

Heah, T., Case, T., McGuire, B., & Law, M. (2007). Successful participation: The lived experience among children with disabilities. *Canadian Journal of Occupational Therapy, 74*(1), 38–47. doi:10.2182/cjot.06.10

Holder, M. D., Coleman, B., & Sehn, Z. L. (2009). The contribution of active and passive leisure to children's well-being. *Journal of Health Psychology, 14*(3), 378–386. doi:10.1177/1359105308101676

Hood, C. D., & Carruthers, C. P. (2013). Facilitating change through leisure: The leisure and well-being model of therapeutic recreation practice. In T. Freire

(Ed.), *Positive leisure science: From subjective experience to social contexts* (pp. 121–140). New York, NY: Springer.

Hurd, A., & Anderson, D. (2011). *The park and recreation professional's handbook.* Champaign, IL: Human Kinetics.

Jaarsma, E. A., Dijkstra, P. U., de Blécourt, A. C. E., & Geertzen, J. H. B. (2015). Barriers and facilitators of sports in children with physical disabilities: A mixed-method study. *Disability and Rehabilitation, 37*(18), 1617–1625. doi:10.3109/0 9638288.2014.972587

Janssen, I., & Leblanc, A. G. (2010). Systematic review of the health benefits of physical activity and fitness in school-aged children and youth. *International Journal of Behavioral Nutrition and Physical Activity, 40*(7), 1–16. doi:10.1186/1479-5868-7-40

Jarus, T., Lourie-Gelberg, Y., Engel-Yeger, B., & Bart, O. (2011). Participation patterns of school-aged children with and without DCD. *Research in Developmental Disabilities, 32*(4), 1323–1331. doi:10.1016/j.ridd.2011.01.033

Jessup, G. M., Cornell, E., & Bundy, A. C. (2010). The treasure in leisure activities: Fostering resilience in young people who are blind. *Journal of Visual Impairment & Blindness, 104*(7), 419–430.

King, G., Law, M., King, S., Rosenbaum, P., Kertoy, M. K., & Young, N. L. (2003). A conceptual model of the factors affecting the recreation and leisure participation of children with disabilities. *Physical & Occupational Therapy in Pediatrics, 23*(1), 63–90.

King, G., Law, M., Petrenchik, T., & Hurley, P. (2013). Psychosocial determinants of out of school activity participation for children with and without physical disabilities. *Physical & Occupational Therapy in Pediatrics, 33*(4), 384–404. doi:10.3109/01942638.2013.791915

King, G., Rigby, P., & Batorowicz, B. (2013). Conceptualizing participation in context for children and youth with disabilities: An activity setting perspective. *Disability and Rehabilitation, 35*(18), 1578–1585. doi:10.3109/09638288.2012.748836

Kremer, P., Elshaug, C., Leslie, E., Toumbourou, J. W., Patton, G. C., & Williams, J. (2014). Physical activity, leisure-time screen use and depression among children and young adolescents. *Journal of Science and Medicine in Sport, 17*(2), 183–187. doi:10.1016/j.jsams.2013.03.012

Law, M., Cooper, B., Strong, S., Stewart, D., Rigby, P., & Letts, L. (1996). The person-environment-occupation model: A transactive approach to occupational performance. *Canadian Journal of Occupational Therapy, 63*(1), 9–23.

Madsen, K., Thompson, H., Adkins, A., & Crawford, Y. (2013). School-community partnerships: A cluster-randomized trial of an after-school soccer program. *JAMA Pediatrics, 167*(4), 321–326. doi:10.1001/jamapediatrics.2013.1071

Majnemer, A. (2009). Promoting participation in leisure activities: Expanding role for pediatric therapists. *Physical & Occupational Therapy in Pediatrics, 29*(1), 1–5. doi:10.1080/01942630802625163

Majnemer, A. (2010). Balancing the boat: Enabling an ocean of possibilities. *Canadian Journal of Occupational Therapy, 77*(4), 198–208. doi:10.2182/cjot.2010.77.4.2

Majnemer, A. (2012). The purpose and framework for this text. In A. Majnemer (Ed.), *Measures for children with developmental disabilities: An ICF-CY approach* (pp. 10–15). London, England: Mac Keith Press.

Majnemer, A., Shevell, M., Law, M., Birnbaum, R., Chilingaryan, G., Rosenbaum, P., & Poulin, C. (2008). Participation and enjoyment of leisure activities in school–aged children with cerebral palsy. *Developmental Medicine & Child Neurology, 50*(10), 751–758. doi:10.1111/j.1469–8749.2008.03068.x

Mason, A., & Smith, M. (2005). Developmental disabilities. In N. J. Salkind (Ed.), *Encyclopedia of human development* (pp. 360–363). Thousand Oaks, CA: SAGE.

Merrell, K. J. (2011). *Social emotional assets and resilience scales (SEARS).* Lutz, FL: PAR.

Merrell, K. W., Felver-Gant, J. C., & Tom, K. M. (2010). Development and validation of a parent report measure for assessing social-emotional competencies of children and adolescents. *Journal of Child and Family Studies, 20*(4), 529–540. doi:10.1007/s10826-010-9425-0

Miller, L., Ziviani, J., & Boyd, R. N. (2014). A systematic review of clinimetric properties of measurements of motivation for children aged 5–16 years with a physical disability or motor delay. *Physical & Occupational Therapy in Pediatrics, 34*(1), 90–111. doi:10.1111/dmcn.12356

Missiuna, C. A., Pollock, N. A., & Law, M. (2004). *Perceived efficacy and goal setting system (PEGS).* San Antonio, TX: Psychcorp.

Missiuna, C. A., Pollock, N., Law, M., Walter, S., & Cavey, N. (2006). Examination of the perceived efficacy and goal setting system (PEGS) with children with disabilities, their parents, and teachers. *The American Journal of Occupational Therapy, 60*(2), 204–214. doi:10.5014/ajot.60.2.204

Morgan, G. A., Busch-Rossnagel, N. A., Barrett, K. C., & Wang, J. (2009). *The dimensions of mastery questionnaire (DMQ): A manual about its development, psychometrics, and use.* Fort Collins, CO: Colorado State University.

Mota, J., Barros, M., Ribeiro, J. C., & Santos, M. P. (2013). Leisure time, physical activity, and health. In T. Freire (Ed.), *Positive leisure science: From subjective experience to social contexts* (pp. 159–174). New York, NY: Springer.

Murphy, N. A., & Carbone, P. S. (2008). Promoting the participation of children with disabilities in sports, recreation, and physical activities. *Pediatrics, 121*(5), 1057–1061. doi:10.1542/peds.2008-0566

Pitchford, E. A., Siebert, E., Hamm, J., & Yun, J. (2016). Parental perceptions of physical activity benefits for youth with developmental disabilities. *American Journal on Intellectual and Developmental Disabilities, 121*(1), 25–32. doi:10.1352/1944-7558-121.1.25

Potvin, M. C., Snider, L., Prelock, P., Kehayia, E., & Wood-Dauphinee, S. (2013). Recreational participation of children with high functioning autism. *Journal of Autism and Developmental Disorders, 43*(2), 445–457. doi:10.1007/s10803-012-1589-6

Poulsen, A., & Ziviani, J. (2010). Enablement of children's leisure participation. In S. Rodger (Ed.), *Occupation-centered practice with children: A practical guide for occupational therapists* (pp. 248–273). Oxford, England: Wiley-Blackwell.

Poulsen, A., Ziviani, J., & Cuskelly, M. (2006). General self-concept and life satisfaction for boys with differing levels of physical coordination: The role of goal orientations and leisure participation. *Human Movement Science, 25*(6), 839–860. doi:10.1016/j.humov.2006.05.003

Rosenblum, S. (2010). *Children's leisure assessment (CLASS).* Haifa, Israel: University of Haifa, Occupational Therapy Department.

Rosenblum, S., Sachs, D., & Schreuer, N. (2010). Reliability and validity of the children's leisure assessment scale. *American Journal of Occupational Therapy, 64*(4), 633–641. doi:10.5014/ajot.2010.08173

Rutter, M. (2013). Annual research review: Resilience—clinical implications. *Journal of Child Psychology and Psychiatry, 54*(4), 474–487. doi:10.1111/j.1469-7610.2012.02615.x

Sakzewski, L., Ziviani, J., Abbott, D. F., Macdonell, R. A., Jackson, G. D., & Boyd, R. N. (2011). Participation outcomes in a randomized trial of 2 models of upper-limb rehabilitation for children with congenital hemiplegia. *Archives of Physical Medicine and Rehabilitation, 92*(4), 531–539. doi:10.1016/j.apmr.2010.11.022

Shields, N., & Synnot, A. (2016). Perceived barriers and facilitators to participation in physical activity for children with disability: A qualitative study. *BMC Pediatrics, 16*(9), 1–10. doi:10.1186/s12887-016-0544-7

Shikako-Thomas, K., Shevell, M., Lach, L., Law, M., Schmitz, N., Poulin, C., . . . group, Q. (2013). Picture me playing—A portrait of participation and enjoyment of leisure activities in adolescents with cerebral palsy. *Reearch in Developmental Disabilities, 34*(3), 1001–1010. doi:10.1016/j.ridd.2012.11.026

Shimmell, L. J., Gorter, J. W., Jackson, D., Wright, M., & Galuppi, B. (2013). "It's the participation that motivates him": Physical activity experiences of youth with cerebral palsy and their parents. *Physical & Occupational Therapy in Pediatrics, 33*(4), 405–420. doi:10.3109/01942638.2013.791916

Soresi, S., Nota, L., & Wehmeyer, M. L. (2011). Community involvement in promoting inclusion, participation and self-determination. *International Journal of Inclusive Education, 15*(1), 15–28. doi:10.1080/13603116.2010.496189

World Health Organization. (2001). *International classification of functioning, disability and health: ICF.* Geneva, Switzerland: World Health Organization.

World Health Organization. (2007). *International classification of functioning, disability and health, children and youth version: ICF-CY.* Geneva, Switzerland: World Health Organization.

CHAPTER 2

A LONGITUDINAL CASE STUDY APPROACH TO DESCRIBING A BOY WITH DEVELOPMENT COORDINATION DISORDER EXPERIENCING TRANSITIVE INTERVENTION SERVICES TOWARD INCLUSIVE SCHOOL- AND COMMUNITY-BASED PHYSICAL ACTIVITIES

Anna Cadzow, Motohide Miyahara, and Ruth Cutfield
University of Otago

When a child has a recognized disability, parents and educators usually endeavor to include the child in the educational system and the community as much as possible. What about a child with a "hidden disability" whose

Inclusive Physical Activities, pages 31–52
Copyright © 2017 by Information Age Publishing
All rights of reproduction in any form reserved.

difficulties are overlooked and unnoticed? The child may be regarded as slow, lazy, clowning, or unmotivated. The parents and educators may pressure the child to try harder and to do more. After all, the child looks "normal," and most of the time behaves "normally," For this reason, the child's alleged lack of effort and intention tend to be blamed for any deviations in academic, behavioral, social, and physical performance. If parents and educators have such a mindset toward the child's difficulties at school, they may make few adjustments to meet the child's unique needs and to include him or her into school and community. This kind of story is rather common, and we are going to tell you how such a story can change its course when appropriate transition support is provided. Our story culminates in an interview to identify barriers and enablers to participation in extracurricular physical activities. We hope that our story will generate reflections, insights, and solutions.

The authors of this chapter have a long history of supporting children who are medically diagnosed with learning disorder, attention deficit hyperactivity disorder, autism spectrum disorder, developmental coordination disorder (DCD) and other developmental disorders. Some of these conditions may be considered "hidden disabilities." In the case of children with DCD, difficulties with motor coordination are not easily recognized in the absence of observable physical, cognitive, and psychosocial differences from those of typically developing children until the children with DCD try to perform particular age-appropriate tasks, such as eating, dressing, tying shoelaces, writing, throwing and catching a ball, or riding a bicycle. Then they may avoid these motor tasks and physical activities, or perform them extremely poorly when compared with typically developing children of a similar age.

Working directly with children with DCD, in particular, by supporting Family Focused Intervention (FFI; Miyahara, Butson, Cutfield, & Clarkson, 2009) and when teaching at a university-based teaching lab, the Movement Development Clinic (Miyahara, Yamaguchi, & Green, 2008), we conducted case study research (Yin, 2014). Case study research differs uniquely from typical quantitative and qualitative research in three ways. First, case study research involves a single case or a small number of cases, in contrast to other quantitative and qualitative studies that sample dozens of participants (Reid, 2000). As such, case study research allows for a detailed and thorough investigation of each case. Second, due to the small number of cases, findings from case study research may not be generalizable to other cases or contexts because of a lack of external validity. Third, as Yin (1984) maintained, case study research employs theoretical replication that generalizes from case study to theory, rather than statistical generalization from sample to population. Although results from a sample or a population in one part of the world may not be applicable to those from other parts of the world, a good theory should be an invariably descriptive and explanatory tool in any part of the world (Deutsch, 1997). Our single case study can be justified because it meets the conditions of the single-case design proposed by Yin (2014): (a) a critical test of existing theory, and (b) a common case where the case serves a revelatory or longitudinal purpose.

We drew on the transactional model of personal and environmental factors (Adelman & Taylor, 1993) to guide the focus of transitory support interventions. Our single case study first presents extensive contextualized descriptions of how a boy with DCD experiences two types of transitive support interventions, namely FFI and the Movement Development Clinic, to transform him from being a sedentary boy at home to being a physically active boy playing sports at school and in the community. After describing the transformation and the boy's transition from a sedentary lifestyle at home, our case study draws conclusions about how the boy with DCD, and his mother, perceived barriers and enablers to the boy's participation in physical activities at school and in the community, with reference to the model of 11 factors affecting the participation of children with disabilities (King, Law, King, Rosenbaum, Kertoy, & Young, 2003).

Our case account, based on the two theoretical models, will help the reader to apply the theory to solve similar relevant problems regarding inclusive physical activity.

This longitudinal case study was partially presented at the 9th International Conference on Developmental Coordination Disorder in Lausanne, Switzerland, in 2011 (Miyahara, Cutfield, Clarkson, & Butson, 2011) and at two national conferences in New Zealand afterwards. Some audience members at the conferences asked for more details of this case, and we are glad to provide full details in this chapter.

DCD AND EMERGING INCLUSIVE PRACTICES

If we trace the history of how people with disabilities have been placed and treated in social systems, we soon realize that the current model of inclusion is a relatively new ideal to strive for. Inclusion in the context of physical activity can be defined as opportunity and choice in that "all individuals have the chance to benefit from inclusive and accommodating programming regardless of age or ability level" (Kasser & Lytle, 2013, p. 11). Only within the last 40 years has there been a shift from segregated education in separate schools and classes to inclusive education in mainstream schools and classrooms (Mitchell, 2010). In the case of children with mild disabilities such as developmental coordination disorder (DCD), the problems are so subtle that parents, teachers, and physical activity leaders can easily overlook the youngster's hidden difficulties. In a sense, young people with DCD are often in inclusive environments in education, sports, and recreation systems. However, it is the exception rather than the rule that their movement difficulties are systematically recognized and adequately catered for, so they can succeed in self-care at home, learning at school, and in playing sports and participating in physical activities at school and in the community (Miyahara et al., 2008). In fact, only the relatively affluent developed countries tend to pay attention to children with DCD, formerly called clumsy children (Cratty, 1994).

The term developmental coordination disorder was first coined by the American Psychiatric Association (1987) to describe a marked impairment in the development of motor coordination. The first international meeting regarding DCD was held by leading researchers and clinicians in 1995, when DCD started to gain international attention. Although the number of studies conducted on the identification, assessment, diagnosis, and management of children with DCD has been increasing exponentially, only a limited number of studies have investigated participation in physical activity. None has detailed longitudinal transitory intervention support processes, and none has captured the perspectives of children and parents regarding environmental barriers and enablers (Magalhães, Cardoso, & Missiuna, 2011).

Contesting and Complementing the Dominant Research Methods

The literature around increasing participation in physical activity is frequently one-sided: targeted specifically for coaches or for parents (Kleinert, Miracle, & Sheppard-Jones, 2007; Murphey & Carbone, 2008). Factors affecting participation have been written mainly from a parent's perspective (Brittain, 2004; King et al., 2003; Law, Petrenchik, King, & Hurley, 2007).

It was not until 2010 that researchers started listening to children's voices (Hilderley & Rhind, 2012) and finding out whether factors identified as barriers were the most important obstacles for children themselves.

Much of the previous literature is generalized to large populations such as those of the United States or the United Kingdom (King et al., 2003; King et al., 2006; Law, Petrenchik, King, & Hurley, 2007; Murphey & Carbone, 2008). In contrast to case studies, group studies seek universal principles and laws that can be generalized to populations, but overlook the more detailed explanations that can be gained from personal experiences (Reid, 2000). Law et al. (2007) developed a bank of potential barriers to participation that was considered to apply to all children with disabilities. This was beneficial in the way it could be related to everyone, but no details of individual participants or disabilities were given. Law et al.'s (2007) broad view lacked the context and comprehensive accounts of a case-study approach.

Methodology is contested in the literature, with previous studies concerning participation for children with disabilities tending to follow a questionnaire- or interview-based framework. Questionnaire-based studies have targeted large samples involving hundreds of participants (e.g., King et al., 2006; Law et al., 2006; Law et al., 2007). Law et al. (2006) aimed to comprehensively describe the participation of children with disabilities, but found their questionnaire failed to uncover reasons for participation and instead provided only a list of all activities completed by children in the study. An interview-based study conducted by Brittain (2004) was beneficial because it provided more data and descriptions from the participants, explaining why their participation was limited. Therefore an interview method is desirable to answer the "why" questions about participation in extracurricular physical activities (Yin, 2014).

To start filling the gap in the current literature about inclusive physical activities for individuals with DCD and other similar hidden disabilities, we employed a longitudinal case study of a child with DCD whose details are elaborated in the method section of this chapter. The child received two transitory intervention services as part of the authors' research projects, namely, FFI for children with DCD (Miyahara et al., 2009) and the Movement Development Clinic (Miyahara et al., 2008). The focus of each transition service was identified by the transactional model of personal and environmental factors (Adelman & Taylor, 1993) and the child's perspectives on the environmental factors, as well as personal and family factors, were examined with regard to the model of 11 factors affecting the participation of children with disabilities (King et al., 2003).

Theoretical Framework

Transactional Model of Personal and Environmental Factors

To help students with various forms of disability achieve inclusive physical activity, sport, and physical education, it is important to consider the personal and environmental factors (World Health Organization, 2007) of each individual. At the same time, it is useful to estimate the degree to which each personal and environmental factor contributes to participation. In the context of learning problems and disabilities, Adelman and Taylor (1993) created a transactional model to help decide how much emphasis to place on a continuum of problems from those caused primarily by environmental factors to problems derived mainly from personal factors (Figure 2.1).

Type I problems have mainly environmental causes with a minimum contribution of personal factors. The primary focus of intervention should be environmental adjustments, including of teaching and learning space, time, equipment, staffing, and so on. Type 2 problems occur when both personal

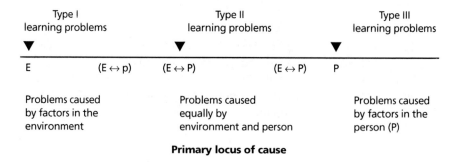

Type I learning problems		Type II learning problems		Type III learning problems
▼		▼		▼
E	(E ↔ p)	(E ↔ P)	(E ↔ P)	P
Problems caused by factors in the environment		Problems caused equally by environment and person		Problems caused by factors in the person (P)

Primary locus of cause

Figure 2.1 A continuum of learning problems reflecting a transactional view of the locus of primary instigating factors (Adelman & Taylor, 1993). *Note:* This figure is included in the document: Center for Mental Health in Schools (2010). *Youth Substance Use Interventions: Where Do They Fit Into a School's Mission?* Los Angeles, CA: Author. The reproduction of the entire document is granted.

and environmental factors contribute significantly. This is where an individualized approach to intervention is paramount. Physical education teachers and facilitators of sports and physical activities need to modify teaching and coaching strategies, rules of games, and so on. Type 3 problems are attributed primarily to personal conditions, such as diagnosed developmental disorders like autism spectrum disorder, limb deficiency, cerebral palsy, or intellectual disability. Although a desirable environment can maximize learning outcomes and enhance the quality of physical activity for these individuals, additional strategies for inclusion must be developed and implemented. Thus, it is helpful to identify the relative contributions made by personal and environmental factors when planning the logistics of intervention.

The relative contributions of personal and environmental factors are not always obvious, however. For instance, a child may have a motor learning problem because of an inadequate social background (Type 1), and the problem may be alleviated by treating a previously overlooked medical condition (i.e., a personal factor). Conversely, a barrier to physical activity for a person with a severe disability (Type 3) can be largely environmental, such as accessibility (i.e., an environmental factor). Regardless of which factor appears to be dominant for a particular problem, the areas where educators and physical activity leaders can intervene and which they can modify are mostly environmental in nature, so it is always worth suspecting the possibility of a Type 1 problem first (Adelman & Taylor, 1993).

There are two points that we need to discuss about the transactional model. First, just because a person has a diagnosed health condition or disability (Type 3), educators and physical activity leaders should not assume the person has "special needs." These people have the same desires, aspirations, and dreams as people without disabilities, and we must respect their independence, rights, and dignity. Second, the existence of Type 1 and 2 problems can be ascertained only after trying out a type-specific environmental intervention and examining the effect of the intervention. Particularly in the case of mild developmental disabilities (such as learning disorder, attention deficit hyperactivity disorder, high functioning autism spectrum disorder, and DCD), the first course of action should be provision of the best possible environment for learning and physical activity. If the case turns out to be Type 3, then necessary adjustments need to follow toward inclusive physical education, sports, and physical activity.

Model of 11 Factors Affecting the Participation of Children With Disabilities

The transactional model proposed by Adelman and Taylor (1993) consists of three types of problems and three corresponding loci of instigating personal and environmental factors as the focus for intervention. A more complex model, which consists of 11 factors affecting the participation of children with disabilities, was proposed by King et al. (2003). The 11 factors are classified into environmental, family, and child (personal) levels as shown in Table 2.1.

To identify specific barriers and enablers to participation in extracurricular physical activities, we examined whether the barriers and enablers identified in our case study could be classified into one or other of the 11 factors. If the 11 factors were not sufficient, we would modify the model,

TABLE 2.1   Eleven factors in the three levels classified in the Model of Factors Affecting the Participation of Children with Disabilities
1. The environmental level
A. Supportive physical and institutional environments.
B. Presence of supportive relationships for the child.
C. Presence of supportive relationships for the parents.
2. Family level
D. Absence of financial and time impact on the family.
E. Supportive family demographic variables.
F. Supportive home environment.
G. Family preference for recreation.
3. Child level
H. Child's self-perceptions of athletic and scholastic competence.
I. Child's physical, cognitive, and communicative function.
J. Child's emotional, behavioral, and social function.
K. Child's activity preferences.

Source: King et al., 2003

because theory building is an important aspect of case study research (Eisenhardt & Graebner, 2007).

Our longitudinal single case study answers the following two research questions:

1. What did a boy with DCD experience and gain long term from two transitive intervention services from home to school and community?
2. How did the boy and his mother perceive barriers and enablers to participation in activities at school and in the community after the interventions?

METHOD

Participant

This case study describes our interactions with Henry (pseudonym), diagnosed with DCD, through three research and clinical projects over 3 years, starting shortly after Henry's seventh birthday and continuing until he was 10 years of age. Henry first took part in FFI for children with DCD (Miyahara et al., 2009) as a 7-year-old. From 8 to 9 years of age, Henry attended the Movement Development Clinic (MDC). After being discharged from the clinic at aged 10, he moved on to extracurricular hockey. At that time Henry and his mother were interviewed concerning their views on barriers and enablers to participation in extracurricular physical activities. Henry and his mother agreed to participate in these projects by signing the informed consent forms approved by the University of Otago Human Ethics Committee.

Diagnosis of Developmental Coordination Disorder (DCD)

When the FFI project was conducted in 2008, DCD was defined by the *Diagnostic and Statistical Manual of Mental Disorders* (4th ed.; American Psychiatric Association, 1994). Table 2.2 gives a list of names and results of assessments used to evaluate the diagnostic criteria for Henry.

Among other tests, we administered the Movement Assessment Battery for Children, Second Edition (Henderson, Sugden, & Barnett, 2007) test repeatedly throughout this longitudinal case study, and thus monitored Henry's motor-development status as a personal factor. When Henry was first assessed, his overall motor development was placed in the 16th percentile, just above the cutoff of the DCD criterion (Figure 2.2).

TABLE 2.2   A List of Assessment Batteries to Examine the Inclusion and Exclusion Criteria of DCD in DSM-IV

DSM-IV Diagnostic Criteria for DCD	Assessment Used	Assessment Results
A. Substantial delay in motor development	Movement Assessment Battery for Children, Second Edition	Manual dexterity: 63rd percentile: Absence of difficulty Ball skills: 16th percentile: Absence of difficulty Balance: 9th percentile: At risk of difficulty Total: 16th percentile: Absence of difficulty
B. Impact of the delay on academic achievement and activities of daily living	Developmental Coordination Disorder Questionnaire '07	36: Indication of, or Suspect for DCD
C. Exclusion of Pervasive Developmental Disorder	Children's Autism Rating Scale	No autism
D. Exclusion of Mental Retardation (Nonverbal)	Colour Progressive Matrices	28/36: No intellectual disability
D. Exclusion of Mental Retardation (Verbal)	British Picture Vocabulary Test	26th percentile: No intellectual disability

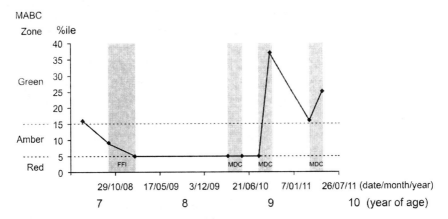

Figure 2.2   Changes in the percentiles of the Movement Assessment Battery for Children, Second Edition, Total Score (Henderson, Sugden, & Barnett, 2007) across the periods of participating in transition support of the Family Focused Intervention (FFI) and the Movement Development Clinic (MDC). The green zone (>15th percentile) is considered as being free from a motor difficulty; the amber zone between the 5th and the 15th percentiles is regarded as at risk of having a movement difficulty; the red zone represents a high likelihood of movement difficulty. The zone (>15th percentile) is considered as being free from a motor difficulty; the amber zone between the 5th and the 15th percentiles is regarded as at risk of having a movement difficulty; the red zone represents a high likelihood of movement difficulty.

Following the assessment, a senior pediatrician took a developmental history and conducted a neurological examination. During the history taking, Henry's mother reported that Henry had had no delayed achievement in motor milestones, including sitting and walking. However, Henry was reported to be clumsy, dropped things often, and was poorly coordinated for sports. With all assessment results, developmental history, and neurological examination considered, the diagnosis of developmental coordination disorder was confirmed by the pediatrician.

Procedure

This section first introduces two transitive support interventions: the FFI for children with DCD, and the Movement Development Clinic. The interventional focus of the FFI was on Henry's environment through practice at home, whereas the focus of the MDC was on improving Henry's personal motor skills. Second, we explain how the interview with Henry and his mother was conducted and analyzed.

Family Focused Intervention for Children With DCD

Through a workbook, weekly telephone support, and a blog the FFI for children with DCD (Miyahara et al., 2009) guided parents to develop a case formulation (Sperry, Gudeman, Blackwell, & Faulkner, 1992) by identifying movement problems, hypothesizing about underlying mechanisms or processes, and deciding on the tasks, equipment, and environment for their children to practice target motor skills. Support and guidance was delivered via telehealth, using information and communication technologies (website and blog) to provide health care when a provider and a recipient were separated by distance.

Henry and his mother were one of 11 children and their families who participated in the FFI pilot study (Miyahara et al., 2009), and the FFI was delivered to Henry's family from July till September 2008. Henry's family found out about the FFI in a local newspaper article. Except for the face-to-face assessment before and after the intervention, the third author (RC) communicated with Henry and his mother by weekly phone calls. Henry's family did not have access to a computer or the Internet, so email communication was not an option. Information was gathered from the phone log and from the logbook completed by Henry's mother.

As its name indicates, the FFI attempted to remediate Type III environmental problems in the transactional model (Adelman & Taylor, 1993).

Movement Development Clinic (MDC)

The MDC is a teaching and research lab in the University of Otago, School of Physical Education. Established in 1950, this on-campus clinic is one of the first and the longest-lasting laboratory of this kind in the world (Miyahara et al., 2008; Haywood, Roberton, & Getchell, 2012). At the time of this case study research, undergraduate students enrolled in courses entitled PHSE305 Lifespan Human Development and PHSE427 Case Study Research taught weekly lessons to children with a wide range of movement difficulties on a one-on-one basis over a seven- or eight-week period each semester. The students were assigned to conduct an intake interview and write an initial assessment report with long-term goals and intervention strategies; compile daily lesson plans with behavioral objectives and teaching strategies; carry out daily teaching evaluation against behavioral objectives and provide evaluation for further needs; and complete the final progress report, including the result of the final assessment, the course of intervention, and future recommendations.

Raw clinic data for Henry consisted of the initial assessment reports, clinic observations, daily teaching evaluations, as well as the final progress reports, the notes from the interviews, fieldnotes following clinic lessons in the third semester, and information gained from Henry's mother during the initial interview in the third semester of his involvement in the MDC. These multiple sources of evidence added to the content validity of the study (Yin, 2014).

Henry attended the clinic in the first and second semesters of 2010, and the first semester of 2011. The first author (AC) directly taught him in the second semester of 2010, and observed another student teaching Henry in the first semester of 2011.

Interview

The interview took place four months after Henry's third semester of intervention at the MDC, when he was 10-years-old. The first author conducted telephone interviews with Henry and his mother. Prior to the interviews the interviewer reminded Henry and his mother that they had the right to refuse to answer any questions to which they did not wish to respond.

Henry and his mother were interviewed separately over the telephone. The interviews were not audiorecorded. Instead, the interviewer took notes throughout the interview. Although specific questions were not predetermined, the discussion with Henry's mother was guided toward Henry's experience with extracurricular sport, benefits Henry gained from his participation, differences from previous extracurricular activities he had been involved in, barriers to participation, and future recommendations for extracurricular involvement. The interview with Henry was also conversation based. The interviewer planned to discuss the sporting activities Henry participated in at school and how he liked them, past and current extracurricular activities and his experience, assistance and guidance provided by any coaches, activities Henry would like to try in the future, and the differences between the MDC and extracurricular activities for Henry.

The interviewer (AC) planned to obtain specific information regarding what Henry and his mother perceived as barriers and enablers to Henry's participation in extracurricular physical activities. The previous discussion guides were preplanned to obtain anticipated information from the interviews and to increase construct validity in later discussions (Yin, 2014). After the interviews with Henry and with his mother, the second author reviewed the notes taken by the interviewer.

Analytical Procedure for Interview Data

Since the purpose of the interviews was to examine pre-existing theoretical constructs in the model of 11 factors affecting the participation of children with disabilities (King et al., 2003) from the perspective of Henry and his mother, a deductive approach (Gale, Heath, Cameron, Rashid, & Redwood, 2013) was used to analyze the interview data. After the first author transcribed the interview, she familiarized herself with the whole interview by reading the transcriptions several times. Subsequently she coded each meaning unit and categorized it to one of the three elements from the theoretical model: (a) environmental factors, (b) family factors, and (c) child factors, and further to one or more of the 11 factors from King et al.'s model (2003). The second author served as methodological auditor (Lincoln & Guba, 1985) to ensure the credibility of the categorization made by the first author.

RESULTS

This section explains how we describe the progress made by Henry throughout the two transitive support interventions, namely, the FFI for children with DCD and the Movement Development Clinic, and the results of the interview to identify enablers and barriers to participation in extracurricular physical activities.

Family Focused Intervention for Children with DCD

The FFI study period commenced over the school holidays while the family were away, so the family did not initiate intervention at that time. In Week 4 the family were ready to start the FFI process. Henry's mother chose to work on goals with both Henry and his older sister so that Henry did not feel singled out.

The goals they agreed to work on were:

1. To tie shoelaces.
2. To improve Henry's swimming ability.
3. To improve his ball skills.

It was often difficult to make contact with the family due to their busy schedule and lack of voicemail or email. In Week 8, Henry's mother discussed their lack of practice and progress. Although an option was given to terminate the FFI and be reassessed at that point, Henry's mother was very keen to continue in the hope that they would make some progress over the next school holidays.

Tying Shoelaces

Henry thought this was a good goal, so he could get shoes with laces, not shoes with Velcro. His mother thought the skill acquisition was practical because "Velcro does not last long on shoes." When it came to practice, his mother found working toward the goal difficult to initiate and Henry found it too hard, protesting: "I can't do it! I won't do it!" Henry's parents were frustrated and believed the activity might be too hard for Henry: "It is too daunting to try, as Henry struggles with complex instructions."

After very little practice, the family made up for lost time during the last week of the study period with almost daily entries in their workbook. This practice was mainly focused on the shoelace goal. The family commenced practice by viewing an instructive shoelace-tying DVD (Miyahara & Van der Vyver, 2008) supplied by the FFI study. Henry tried first with his father's shoes. His mother struggled to demonstrate because she was right-handed and Henry is left-handed. They decided that the best strategy in the end was for Henry's older sister to teach him since he had taken instruction better from her than from his parents. The sister taught Henry the double-bow technique and he succeeded at last. Their mother commented that Henry was "extremely resistant" to this activity at first. She stated that "his resistance to a difficult or new task is a huge problem for us. However, he did manage to tie a shoelace and he was very proud."

Swimming Technique: Freestyle

Henry was attending structured swimming lessons during the study intervention. He thought it was going pretty well, but his mother reported that he could not get his arms, legs and breathing working together. The practice sessions at home were frustrating for his mother because "Henry thinks he is good at this, so he won't keep trying."

During the Week 4 phone call, Henry's mother explained that Henry lost his rhythm when attempting to use his arms and legs at the same time. We discussed breaking down the activity, providing positive performance feedback to Henry and measuring his progress so Henry could perceive improvement. In Week 6, the weekly telephone discussion was concerned with Henry's swimming difficulties again, without any breakthrough. To encourage Henry's mother and make her feel that she was not the only one who was struggling with such a task, RC printed out the swimming information from a discussion page on the FFI website (see Miyahara et al., 2009 for more detail), and sent it by postal mail to the mother. The following week Henry's mother said she found the swimming information helpful and was particularly interested that other families had similar difficulties, but she still did not manage to find time to help Henry to practice. In Week 8, Henry's mother was reluctant to engage in the weekly phone call, probably because she had had no time to practice and felt embarrassed. It was clear that she was still keen to participate in the FFI program, and on discussion we decided that just focusing on one goal at a time for frequent practice sessions of short duration might help. Henry and his mother agreed on shoelace tying because this was the goal that was most important to Henry, so no further swimming practice occurred.

Ball Skills

Henry wanted to improve his ability to hit a ball, so he could play tennis at school with his friends. He also wanted to kick a ball more skillfully for soccer games. His parents were supportive of these goals. Over the course of the FFI program, Henry's family found very little opportunity to practice toward these goals because the weather was not always conducive to going to the park for practice. In Week 9 during the school holidays, Henry finally went to practice kicking with his father. This was documented in the logbook as being unsuccessful because Henry was reluctant to listen to his father's advice. During that week Henry's mother reported very little progress or practice. She felt that she had the skills to help him at that time, but she still found it hard to find the right time. She would like the weekly phone calls to continue even though she did not need more assistance.

Reassessment at the end of FFI program:

- Shoelace tying: achieved.
- Swimming: ongoing.

Henry's mother felt that the best thing they learned from participating in the FFI program was a realization that Henry could achieve new skills if they put in the practice. Some barriers to success for this family appeared to be finding motivation and time to practice at home. When they focused on only the one goal at a time, Henry achieved success in shoelace tying in quite a short time. Another barrier might have been the lack of access to a computer. Henry's mother found that the information from the web discussions, which had been printed and posted out to her, was useful, but she was unable to access this resource directly. Henry was quite often reported as not wanting to take advice or instruction from his parents. But he achieved success when his older sister gave the instructions to him. He also achieved success in the goal that was most important to him.

Movement Development Clinic (MDC)

Henry's first intervention at the MDC in 2010 focused on improving static and dynamic balance, throwing and catching skills, soccer technique, skipping, swinging, and other general motor skills such as jumping. These areas were identified as important to work on by Henry himself and by his mother during interviews before the first semester of weekly lessons began. As indicated in Figure 2.2, Henry's overall coordination stayed at the same level at the 5th percentile. In the following semester Henry returned to the clinic.

On his first day back to the clinic in the second semester, the first author (AC) met Henry and his mother and interviewed them. The mother reported that Henry was "a very outgoing and enthusiastic child who loved to give everything a go." Henry's second semester intervention focused on two long-term goals that were developed alongside the aspirations of Henry and his mother: (a) to improve Henry's balance skills and explore the possible links between balance and the locomotive patterns of walking and running; and (b) to learn fundamental motor skills and patterns that allow the mastery of skills indigenous to tennis and hockey.

The second semester of weekly lessons involved a program to specifically address these two goals. First, AC set up a balance beam at the clinic gym. When he first saw the set-up, Henry seemed to be determined to walk along it. Initially, Henry found it difficult to maintain his balance and he could barely hold a standing position on the beam. However, he faced the challenge and turned it into a competition with his sister at home. This seemed to make his balance practice fun and his improvements were beyond AC's expectation; he was not only able to walk from one end of the balance beam to the other, but he also progressed to balancing on one foot, completing a 360-degree turn, swapping places on the beam with AC, bending down and touching the beam, and throwing and catching a ball with AC. Henry's mother and sister acted as his audience and they were enthusiastically supportive of his achievements. Even during the clinic session Henry's sister could not wait until going home to ask him to teach her the new routine, which seemed to give Henry a great sense of self pride and achievement.

To objectively assess Henry's running forms and stability, kinematic data of his leg movements were compared before and after the intervention in the second semester. The comparison indicated a greater flight between strides, the swinging leg to flex to 90°, and the swinging leg to be traveling forward-back and not on an angle. Thus, Henry was able to maintain stability throughout a stride by the end of the second-semester intervention.

Henry's third semester at the MDC focused on applying the acquired fundamental movement skills in the context of sports and other activities such as bike riding, hockey, tennis, golf, soccer and swinging. Henry brought his own bicycle to the clinic and learned to cycle downhill and around obstacles. He also learned basic sports skills so he could participate in soccer, hockey, and tennis games at school or with friends. Thus, Henry transferred his fundamental movement skills to sports settings. As a result, Henry went on to participate in a hockey team for his age group—one of his ultimate goals!

Longitudinal Changes in the Results of Motor Coordination

Despite the FFI program, Henry's overall coordination, measured by the Movement Assessment Battery for Children (2nd ed.; Henderson et al., 2007) declined from the 16th percentile to the 5th percentile, and stayed at the same level throughout the nonintervention period and the first semester at the MDC. At the end of the second semester at the clinic, his assessment result improved dramatically, to the 37th percentile, and remained in the "free from a motor difficulty" zone (Henderson et al., 2007) throughout the third intervention period at the MDC. Thus, Henry's Type 1 and 2 problems as construed in the transactional model (Adelman & Taylor, 1993) were confirmed by the effects of the two transitive support interventions.

Interview Findings

During the interview Henry stated that he had played soccer for a school team for two seasons 2 years previously, before attending the MDC. Henry specified that he did not like soccer much because he always "got cold and didn't enjoy it." Henry's mother backed up his statement as a reason for withdrawing from soccer saying, "It wasn't the right sport; he got very cold when playing." She also added that his soccer skills were below the level of his teammates and he found it difficult to run and kick the ball at the same time.

During an initial interview before Henry's second semester at the clinic, his mother emphasized that their family did not use the words "developmental coordination disorder." They instead treated movement difficulties as "things that needed more practice." Henry's mother felt that the MDC was a good steppingstone for her son before he tried extracurricular sport again. This idea was expressed in an evaluation form in which she wrote: "He gets tastes of activities, so they are not confronting him for the first time in a more public space, i.e., school. This helps him merge more with the kids at school."

After the success of the three clinic intervention periods, Henry moved on to play hockey for a school team. When asked about his hockey experience, Henry simply stated, "It was really fun. We only won one game!" which highlighted that winning and being in the strongest team were not so valued by Henry as participating and having fun. Henry attributed this attitude to the coach, who was always fair and gave everyone a turn at playing, no matter who was the best player in the team. Henry's mother complimented the coach, saying that the coach was great at adapting to all the children's abilities and at teaching them skills in a simple way, so they could understand.

Henry mentioned that he would love to continue with hockey during the next season; he also wanted to try tennis and volleyball over the summer because he had already tried out these sports' skills at the MDC. All Henry's friends played hockey and tennis. Now he could join in with them and it made "playing sport more fun." His mother also recognized that hockey had enriched Henry's social life and said she would support his involvement in hockey in the next season.

Theoretical Interpretation of Interview Data

We drew on the three-level model of 11 factors affecting the participation of children with disabilities (King et al., 2003) to examine whether the 11 factors covered Henry's perceived barriers and enablers. The following interpretation refers to this model, as presented in Table 2.1.

Both Henry and his mother offered similar reasons for Henry's withdrawal from soccer, being that Henry always got cold. However, when talking to Henry's mother separately, she mentioned Henry's personal factor—that he was behind in his soccer skills compared with his teammates. This was not something that was talked about with Henry because his family chose not to focus on things that Henry could not do. It thus appears that the reasons for Henry's withdrawal from soccer were different for Henry and for his mother. But his mother followed what Henry said in order not to emphasize Henry's lack of skills.

At the environmental level, perceived barriers and enablers were identified from the soccer and hockey examples. Firstly, an important enabler to participation was the greater value placed by the hockey coach on participation than on winning. This can be best categorized in "B" in the model:

"Presence of supportive relationships for the child." Secondly, becoming cold while participating in soccer made Henry's soccer experience less than enjoyable. This barrier relates to the absence of "A" in the model: "Supportive physical and institutional environments."

At the level of the family, all Henry's family members were very supportive of Henry's attempts at playing new sports at the MDC. Henry's mother was eager for him to participate in extracurricular physical activities, so she applied for help from the clinic. During FFI Henry took instruction better from his older sister than his mother and father. During the MDC phase, the older sister served as a competitor for tying shoelaces, and as an encouraging audience for Henry's balance act along with their mother. Once Henry's motor skills had improved, the family encouraged him to play in a hockey team. While these examples of support are at the family level, none of the four factors in the model (D, financial and time impact on the family; E, demographic variables; F, home environment; and G, preference for recreation) suitably explains how Henry's family enabled him to participate in extracurricular activity. Perhaps the family could afford money and time to take Henry to the clinic, and to play soccer and hockey. In addition to such tangible and instrumental support, the family's moral support, as well as the family's preference for sports in addition to recreation, needs to be included in the model.

At the level of the child, it was evident from the interview with Henry that he enjoyed being able to participate in sports with his friends. Henry emphasized that his group of friends all played hockey and tennis, and it was fun that everyone could play the same sports together. This fact relates to J in the model: child's emotional, behavioral, and social function. Henry disliked soccer, which corresponds to K, child's activity preferences. As a possible reason for Henry's withdrawal from soccer, his mother mentioned that Henry's ability fell behind that of his teammates. This barrier can be categorized into H, child's self-perceptions of athletic and scholastic competence.

Overall, barriers to participation in soccer for Henry were mostly environmental. However, some factors at the child level relating to motor ability contributed indirectly. The interview with Henry uncovered mostly enablers to his participation in hockey. These were predominantly family factors concerning support and encouragement. However, child and environmental factors were also evident as enablers. It is therefore difficult to conclude that any one element had the greatest effect on participation. Instead it is observed that environmental, family, and child factors were interlinked for Henry.

As a theoretical framework, we subscribed to the transactional model of personal and environmental factors (Adelman & Taylor, 1993) to indicate the focus of intervention in the FFI and the MDC. During the FFI, the no intervention period, and the first period of the MDC, Henry's motor skills, assessed by the Movement Assessment for Children (2nd ed.; Henderson et al., 2007), showed no sign of improvement. Note that Henry did learn how to tie shoelaces during the FFI. During the second MDC intervention period, Henry's engagement in and his enjoyment of a creative game on the balance beam were paramount in the dramatic improvement in his movement assessment test results, which rose beyond the diagnostic cutoff for DCD, although his improvement tapered off later. During the third semester of the MDC, Henry practiced soccer, hockey, and tennis skills, which enabled him to participate in extracurricular physical activities. Thus, both environmental and personal interventions through FFI and MDC were not very successful until Henry enjoyed the balance beam activity at the MDC and home, and improved on his balance skills.

IMPLICATIONS AND FUTURE DIRECTIONS

Four weeks after Henry last attended the MDC, Henry and his mother were interviewed over the telephone to identify enablers and barriers to his participation in extracurricular physical activities. The interview data were categorized into the three-level model of 11 factors affecting the participation of children with disabilities (King, et al., 2003). At the environmental level, the cold climate was perceived as a barrier to participating in soccer, whereas the hockey coach's emphasis on enjoyment over winning served as an enabler for Henry to participate in hockey. At the family level, Henry's family's moral support did not fall into any factors in King et al.'s model (2003). At the child level, Henry's insufficient soccer skills were considered by his mother as a barrier to his participation in soccer. In contrast, his enjoyment of hockey and his socialization with his teammates acted as enablers to participation. Thus, our data confirmed some parts of the 11-factor model, but additional factors need to be considered in any future study.

In accordance with the suggestion by Magalhães, Cardoso, and Missiuna (2011) concerning directions for future research, we conducted case study research on the participation in physical activity of a child with DCD over a period of three years by describing how the child experienced the transitive support interventions of the FFI and the MDC programs, and by analyzing what worked and what did not in the particular case. By incorporating the child's perspectives regarding his personal and environmental factors, we gained insight into his inner world to find what motivated him and what turned him away. The enablers included family support, the selection of a suitable movement coach and competitor (his sister in Henry's case), improved sports skills, his desire to be included in sports teams with his friends, and his hockey coach's emphasis on enjoyment over winning.

We also identified barriers, such as the cold weather, the child's motor-skill level, and unsuitable movement coaches (his parents, for specific tasks).

This longitudinal case study applied local and specific examples of intervention services, and identified barriers and enablers to participation. Due to the constraint of its being only a single case study, the findings can be generalized to theory, but not to a population of all children with DCD (Yin, 1984, 2014). Because a case study must be complete on its own (Yin, 2014), we do not propose that future quantitative research should confirm our findings. We would rather suggest that other researchers, teachers, and clinicians might want to conduct similar case study research to investigate the promotion of inclusive physical activities in specific contexts by testing and further building theoretical models. It is our hope that our case study research is beneficial to parents, teachers, clinicians, and coaches because it suggests that a range of factors involving the child, the activity environment and the family can be interacting as barriers and enablers to participation. By identifying barriers and finding solutions that transform them into enablers, our goal of truly inclusive physical activities can be achieved.

ACKNOWLEDGMENTS

We thank "Henry" and his family for their participation. We also thank Tessa Pocock for her editorial comments on the earlier version of this manuscript, and Julie White-Robinson for her graphic arts skills.

REFERENCES

Adelman, H., & Taylor, L. (1993). *Learning problems and learning disabilities: Moving forward.* Pacific Grove, CA: Brooks/Cole.

American Psychiatric Association. (1987). *Diagnostic and statistical manual of mental disorders* (Rev. 3rd ed.; DSM–III–R). Washington, DC: Author.

American Psychiatric Association. (1994). *Diagnostic and statistical manual of mental disorders* (4th ed.; DSM-IV). Washington, DC: Author.

Brittain, I. (2004). Perceptions of disability and their impact upon involvement in sport for people with disabilities at all levels. *Journal of Sport and Social Issues, 28(4)*, 429–452.

Cratty, B. J. (1994). *Clumsy child syndrome: Descriptions, evaluation and remediation.* Langhorne, PA: Harwood Academic.

Deutsch, D. (1997). *The fabric of reality.* New York, NY: Penguin Books.

Eisenhardt, K. M., & Graebner, M. E. (2007). Theory building from cases: Opportunities and challenges. *Academy of Management Journal, 50*, 25–32.

Gale, N. K., Heath, G., Cameron, E., Rashid, S., & Redwood, S. (2013). Using the framework method for the analysis of qualitative data in multi-disciplinary health research. *BMC Medical Research Methodology, 13*, 117.

Haywood, K., Roberton, M. A., & Getchell, N. (2012). *Advanced analysis of motor development.* Champaign, IL: Human Kinetics.

Henderson, S. E., Sugden, D. A., & Barnett, A. L. (2007). *Movement assessment battery for children* (2nd ed.; MABC-2). London, England: Harcourt Assessment.

Hilderley, E., & Rhind, D. J. A. (2012). Including children with cerebral palsy in mainstream physical education lessons: A case study of student and teacher experiences. *Graduate Journal of Sport, Exercise & Physical Education Research, 1,* 1–15.

Kasser, S. L., & Lytle, R. K. (2013). *Inclusive physical activity: Promoting health for a lifetime.* Champaign, IL: Human Kinetics.

King, G., Law, M., King, S., Hurley, P., Hanna, S., Kertoy, M., & Rosenbaum, P. (2006). Measuring children's participation in recreation and leisure activities: construct validation of the CAPE and PAC. *Child Care, Health and Development, 3(1),* 28–39.

King, G., Law, M., King, S., Rosenbaum, P., Kertoy, M., & Young, N. (2003). A conceptual model of the factors affecting the recreation and leisure participation of children with disabilities. *Physical and Occupational Therapy in Pediatrics, 23(1),* 63–83.

Kleinert, H., Miracle, S., & Sheppard-Jones, K. (2007). Including students with moderate and severe disabilities in extracurricular and community recreation activities. *Teaching Exceptional Children, 39(6),* 33–38.

Law, M., King, G., King, S., Kertoy, M., Hurley, P., Rosenbaum, P., . . . Hanna, S. (2006). Patterns of participation in recreational and leisure activities among children with complex physical disabilities. *Developmental Medicine and Child Neurology, 48,* 337–342.

Law, M., Petrenchik, T., King, G., & Hurley, P. (2007). Perceived environmental barriers to recreational, community, and school participation for children and youth with physical disabilities. *Archives of Physical Medicine and Rehabilitation, 88,* 1636–1642.

Lincoln, Y. S., & Guba, E. G. (1985). *Naturalistic inquiry.* Beverly Hills, CA: SAGE.

Magalhães, L. C., Cardoso, A. A., & Missiuna, C. (2011). Activities and participation in children with developmental coordination disorder: A systematic review. *Research in Developmental Disabilities, 32,* 1309–1316.

Mitchell, D. (2010). *Education that fits: Review of international trends in the education for students with special educational needs.* Wellington, New Zealand: Ministry of Education's Current Review of Special Education.

Miyahara, M., & Van der Vyver, R. (2008). *Tying shoelaces* [DVD]. Dunedin, New Zealand: University of Otago, School of Physical Education.

Miyahara, M., Butson, R., Cutfield, R., & Clarkson, J. E. (2009). A pilot study of family focused tele-intervention for children with developmental coordination disorder: Development and lessons learned. *Telemedicine and e-Health, 15,* 707–712.

Miyahara, M., Cutfield, R., Clarkson, J., & Butson, R. (2011). *Family-focused tele-intervention for children with DCD: Development and lessons learned.* Paper presented at the 9th International Conference on Developmental Coordination Disorder, Lausanne, Switzerland. Abstract retrieved from http://ic-dcd.org/conference/wp-content/uploads/2014/pdf/DCD-9-Abstract.pdf

Miyahara, M., Yamaguchi, M., & Green, C. (2008). A review of 326 children with developmental and physical disabilities, consecutively taught at the Movement Development Clinic: Prevalence and intervention outcomes of children with DCD. *Journal of Developmental and Physical Disabilities, 20(4),* 353–363.

Murphey, N., & Carbone, P. (2008). Promoting the participation of children with disabilities in sports, recreation, and physical activities. *Pediatrics, 121(5),* 1057–1062.

Reid, G. (2000). Future directions of inquiry in adapted physical activity. *Adapted Physical Activity Quarterly, 52,* 369–381.

Sperry, L., Gudeman, J. E., Blackwell, B., & Faulkner, L. R. (1992). *Psychiatric case formulations.* Washington, DC: American Psychiatric Press.

World Health Organization. (2007). *ICF-CY, international classification of functioning, disability, and health: children & youth version.* Geneva, Switzerland: Author.

Yin, R. K. (1984). *Case study research: Design and methods.* Beverly Hills, CA: SAGE.

Yin, R. K. (2014). *Case study research: Design and methods* (5th ed.). Beverly Hills, CA: SAGE.

CHAPTER 3

FREE TO PLAY

The Role of Physical Activity in the Lives of Children With Chronic Illnesses

Fiona Moola and Elizabeth Huynh
University of Manitoba

TWO STORIES OF PHYSICAL ACTIVITY IN THE LIVES OF CHILDREN WITH CHRONIC ILLNESSES

Layla

Layla is a 15-year-old girl living with severe cystic fibrosis (CF) in Toronto, Ontario, Canada. Her parents emigrated from Afghanistan several years ago. They live in a low-income housing project in an impoverished neighborhood in the city. Layla has six other siblings, one of whom also has CF. Layla complied with the hospital's request to do daily treatment until she was about 12-years-old. After the age of 12, she began to fully comprehend the effects of CF. On a cold winter day in Toronto—when interviewing Layla for a research study—she came to a profound conclusion. She said that since CF is life limiting and the outcome is always negative, there is simply "no point" in doing therapeutic treatments for her illness. She

Inclusive Physical Activities, pages 53–71
Copyright © 2017 by Information Age Publishing
All rights of reproduction in any form reserved.

proceeded to disclose how she often throws medication away or flushes it down the toilet. During an 8-week counseling intervention, Layla became more physically active. She also demonstrated enhanced quality of life and a broadened sense of personal health and well-being. She began to recognize the importance of physical activity as a tool to aid in self-care. Despite the important gains that Layla made during a physical activity counseling intervention, her carriage was always one of great despair, sadness, and despondency.

Gretchen

Gretchen is an intelligent, inquisitive, and ambitious 25-year-old. She lives with her fiancé in a historic Toronto home and works in the television industry in the city. Although Gretchen was always a very active child—a natural athlete of sorts—she experienced frightening and frequent bouts of dizziness during her youth. Since Gretchen's respiration and heart rate dramatically changed at night, she greatly feared falling asleep. At first, Gretchen's strange symptoms of dizziness and fatigue were attributed by doctors to causes such as anxiety or behavioral issues. A physician at a children's hospital correctly diagnosed her with congenital complete heart block at the age of 14. At that time, a pacemaker was inserted into Gretchen's chest to regulate her heart rate. Gretchen's health rapidly improved after her pacemaker surgery. She actively participated in many high school sports—such as field hockey and basketball—and was encouraged to do so by her parents, teachers, and coaches. During university—where Gretchen obtained a journalism degree—she continued to regularly exercise, participating in activities such as running, Ultimate Frisbee, and walking. Gretchen underwent a planned pacemaker surgery at the age of 23 to replace the battery of the device. Gretchen has recently experienced deterioration in her health after doctors diagnosed her with worsening heart function. During this time of deteriorating heart function, Gretchen's cardiologist recommended physical activity restrictions. As such, Gretchen was not advised to engage in any strenuous physical activity. Most recently, Gretchen's heart function has improved with the help of medication. While she has been advised by her physician to walk for 5 kilometers a few times a week, Gretchen has had difficulty doing this since it "does not feel like real exercise." Gretchen's cardiologist has referred her to cardiac rehabilitation in the hospital, where her cardiac activity can be safely monitored during exercise sessions. Gretchen appears to be dealing well with the numerous health-related changes she has recently experienced. Her ultimate career aspiration is to be a nurse.

Lessons Learned From These Two Stories

These two vignettes capture the vast range of health and physical activity experiences of young people living with chronic illnesses. Some youth with chronic illnesses such as Layla display difficulty engaging in health promoting pursuits like physical activity for much of their lives. Others, like Gretchen, defy myths and misconceptions about chronically ill children by maintaining active and healthy lifestyles and a true devotion toward activity. In what is to follow, we outline contemporary research on the role of physical activity in the lives of young people living with chronic illnesses. We also discuss physical, psychological, and social barriers that detract from enjoyment in physical activity. We propose suggestions on how to develop appropriate guidelines for physical activity participation in this population of youth. In so doing, we advocate for enjoyable and inclusive physical activity opportunities.

THE ROLE OF PHYSICAL ACTIVITY IN THE CHRONICALLY ILL CHILD

Given rapid advances in medicine, healthcare providers are better able to manage the complex needs of medically fragile children. Improved medical intervention and management has contributed toward increased survival among these children. As a result, these children are living longer lives with illnesses that were at one time regarded as fatal. While estimates vary, approximately 31% of children are affected with chronic illnesses (Newachek & Taylor, 1992).

In this article, we define a childhood chronic illness as a condition that lasts longer than six months and significantly affects the child's overall functioning and well-being. Chronically ill children typically consume a disproportionate amount of healthcare resources in relation to their healthy peers (Newachek & Taylor, 1992). Cystic fibrosis, acute lymphoblastic leukemia, congenital heart disease, and HIV/AIDS are contemporary examples of chronic childhood illnesses.

Physical Activity in the Chronically Ill Child

The topic of physical activity participation for chronically ill children did not develop until the early 1970s. The absence of research prior to this time period is not entirely known. However, given the long history of oppression and neglect that people with chronic illnesses and disabilities have faced, it is likely that the physical activity needs of this population were not viewed as important. Given the limited life expectancy of many chronically ill children, the physical activity needs of this population were likely not regarded as relevant. Finally, as discussed further in this chapter, chronically ill children were most often restricted and prevented by parents, coaches, teachers, peers, and doctors from engaging in activity due to the misconception that physical activity was dangerous. Cumulatively, these three factors likely shaped the lack of historical research on the physical activity needs of chronically ill children.

In the 1970s, research on physical activity participation among chronically ill children began to emerge. Bar-Or and Rowland's (2004) seminal scholarship was critical to furthering the idea that physical activity participation affords numerous physical benefits to children with chronic illnesses. As the field of adapted physical activity began to burgeon, scholars produced research that testified to the psychological and social benefits of physical activity participation, with a particular focus on children with disabilities (Goodwin, 2001; Goodwin, Thurmeire, & Gustafon, 2004; Goodwin & Staples, 2005). We will briefly review literature that has had a groundbreaking influence on how we conceptualize activity for the chronically ill child.

Meta-Analysis and Systematic Reviews

A number of researchers have conduced meta-analyses and systematic reviews of literature pertaining to physical activity among children with chronic illnesses. Quirk, Blake, Tennyson, Randell, and Glazebrook (2014) conducted a meta-analysis and systematic review to examine the influence of physical activity on children with type 1 diabetes. Although physical activity can delay the onset of cardiovascular disease in children with type 1 diabetes, there is a lack of studies that are guided by well-developed psychological theories to inform such interventions. Further, most studies do not emphasize the importance of sustained, lifelong activity or focus on psychological outcomes. The authors found that physical activity interventions in children with diabetes had a moderate effect size on triglycerides and lipid levels. Thus, physical activity has the potential to improve the lipid profiles of diabetic children (Quirk et al., 2014). Despite knowledge on the importance of physical activity in delaying adverse outcomes among diabetic patients, however, there is an overall lack of information on how to promote activity among children with type 1 diabetes.

Umpierre et al. (2011) also conducted a systematic review and meta-analysis to examine the impact of structured exercise training versus exercise advice only program for children with type 2 diabetes. The authors found that structured aerobic and resistance exercise reduces glycated haemoglobin (HbA1c) levels in children with diabetes. Exercise in excess of 150 minutes per week was associated with a greater reduction in HbA1c levels in comparison to exercise that was less than 150 minutes per week. Exercise advice only appeared to reduce HbA1c levels when it was used in conjunction with dietary counseling. The authors concluded that exercise should be viewed as a tool to aid glycemic control in children with diabetes.

Longmuir et al. (2013) wrote an evidence-based consensus statement to guide physical activity recommendations for children and adults with congenital heart disease. They emphasized that with the exception of those patients with electrical diseases, people with CHD should not be restricted from physical activity. Patients with CHD are at long-term risk of developing obesity, poor psychosocial outcomes, and sedentary behavior. Longmuir et al. (2013) concluded that regular exercise promotion should be a routine component of clinical care.

Randomized Controlled Trials

Researchers have conducted a few recent randomized controlled trials (RCTs) related to physical activity for chronically ill children. For example, Baleman, van Wely, Becher, and Dallmeijer (2015) conducted an RCT with American children that have cerebral palsy (CP). The intervention involved a physical fitness training program focusing on gross motor activities, anaerobic fitness, muscle strength, counseling, and home-based physical therapy. Activity monitor questionnaires were employed. The authors found that children with bilateral spastic cerebral palsy benefited from the enhanced physical fitness necessary to improve physical activity levels. However, no increase in fitness or physical activity was observed in children with unilateral spastic CP. The authors did not find a correlation between physical fitness and self-reported fatigue in children with CP. While they found that there is an important correlation between enhanced physical fitness and increased physical activity levels, the authors suggested that different interventions might be necessary for children with bilateral versus unilateral CP.

Kriska et al. (2013) conducted a large RCT with American children that had recently been diagnosed with type 2 diabetes. The researchers employed accelerometers to objectively measure physical activity. Diabetic children were found to be less physically active than their same aged peers. The authors concluded that future interventionists should focus on reducing sitting time and sedentary behavior among diabetic youth.

Pre- and Post-Test Studies

Pre and post-test research designs are most commonly used when assessing physical activity levels in chronically ill children. Akber, Portale, and

Johansen (2014) developed a pedometer-based intervention to increase physical activity participation among children with chronic kidney disease in the United States. Pedometers, a quality of life assessment tool, as well as the 6-minute walk test were employed. The intervention did not result in increased physical activity for children with kidney disease. However, changes in physical activity were related to changes in physical functioning as well as an observed improvement in the children's physical performance. From this, we can conclude that physical activity is a successful means to improve function and physical performance among children with chronic kidney disease.

Wilson et al. (2014) sought to measure physical activity levels among childhood survivors of cancer in the United States. Questionnaires were employed to measure the correlates and factors associated with activity status in pediatric cancer patients. Declining activity levels among pediatric cancer survivors were associated with not completing high school, female gender, and higher body mass index. Low physical activity levels were also associated with the presence of musculoskeletal conditions. Poorly educated female pediatric cancer survivors with a greater body mass index were also found to be particularly at risk of declining physical activity. Although there were no differences between survivors and their siblings, cancer survivors consistently reported low physical activity levels. Given the onset of chronic illnesses that are associated with cancer survivorship, physical activity has the potential to be successfully employed as an intervention to help manage the ongoing health issues associated with cancer survivorship.

Orsey, Wakefield, and Cloutier (2014) sought to examine physical activity levels and sleep quality among American pediatric cancer survivors. Questionnaires were employed. Although pediatric cancer survivors demonstrated poor sleep quality overall, physical activity was associated with improved sleep. They concluded that physical activity should be targeted as a modifier to enhance sleep quality among pediatric cancer survivors.

Ewalt, Danduran, Strath, Moerchen, and Swartz (2012) employed accelerometers to objectively measure physical activity levels among American children with and without congenital heart disease (CHD). Children with and without CHD failed to meet physical activity recommendations. Although children with severe CHD were less active than healthy peers, children with stable CHD were as active as non-CHD participants. To encourage lifelong physical activity participation among CHD patients, the authors recommended developing early childhood physical activity interventions for this special population.

Kimmelblatt (2012) examined the impact of a summer camp that involved physical activity on children living with type 1 diabetes. The camp involved a wide range of physical activities and the authors employed questionnaire methods. Levels of depression and anxiety decreased for all participants across the course of the intervention. The participants demonstrated higher self-concept as well as an improved attitude toward illness after camp. The authors concluded that camp might be a useful psychosocial intervention to improve health outcomes among children with diabetes.

Wu, Prout, Roberts, Parikshak, and Amylon (2010) also assessed the experience of American children with cancer and their siblings at a summer camp. Questionnaires were employed and parental reports were included. Campers, siblings, and parents all reported positive perceptions and evaluations toward the camp experience. Campers enjoyed engaging in recreation at camp and forging new friendships. Camp also provided them with a sense of respite from the stress and strain associated with everyday life. Parents felt that camp had a positive impact on their child's behaviors. They also benefited from the caregiving respite that camp provided. Camp appears to be a therapeutic intervention for children living with cancer as well as their siblings, and their parents.

Cross-Sectional Studies

Many cross-sectional studies have been conducted in the field of physical activity and childhood chronic illness. Fischetti (2015) conducted a cross-sectional study in the United States to examine the correlates of physical activity among youth living with type 2 diabetes. A questionnaire method was employed to collect data. Fischetti (2015) found that youth with type 2 diabetes who participated in leisure time physical activity intervention perceived diabetes to be a life-threatening disease. Additionally, participation in even mild physical activity allowed youth to feel a sense of control over their illnesses. This finding underscores how physical activity might modify disease beliefs among chronically ill children. This is especially important given low the self-efficacy and a sense of hopelessness that is demonstrated by many chronically ill youth (Moola, Faulkner, Kirsh, & Kilburn, 2008; Moola & Faulkner, 2014).

Rintala et al. (2011) employed a cross-sectional method to assess the physical activity levels of children with long-term illnesses in both Canada and Finland. Surveys were widely distributed to collect data. The authors found that both girls and boys with chronic illnesses were inactive. However, physical inactivity levels appeared to be no different than their healthy peers'. Since this finding is not consistent with many other reports, further investigation is warranted and no solid conclusions can be drawn.

In a landmark cross-sectional study, Schneiderman-Walker et al. (2005) assessed the correlates of physical activity in a large cohort of girls and boys with CF. Questionnaire methods were employed. Inactive girls with CF had a greater rate of lung function decline in comparison to active girls with CF. In contrast, boys with CF demonstrated similar lung function decline regardless of activity status. Overall, boys with CF were much more active than girls. All participants demonstrated increased physical activity in the summer months as compared to other months. Schneiderman-Walker et al.'s (2005) study draws attention to how girls with CF appear to be particularly vulnerable to the negative effects of physical inactivity. Alarmingly, they found that inactive CF girls have a steeper rate of lung function decline, which might hasten mortality. Thus, it is all the more imperative to include physical activity as a part of disease management among adolescent girls with CF.

Bell and Davies (2010) employed a cross-sectional research design to assess the physical activity levels of American children with cerebral palsy in comparison to typically developing children. They used a range of clinical measurements. They found that in compassion to typically developing children, children with CP expend more energy during walking. Further, they found that children with CP have lower physical activity levels and energy requirements in comparison to typically developing children. These results imply that when designing interventions, it is imperative to appropriately assess the energy requirements of children with CP. The authors conclude that physical activity is very helpful in the management of CP.

Using a correlational research design, Gannoti, Veneri, and Roberts (2007) assessed the weight status and physical activity levels of third graders with chronic illnesses in the United States. Children with asthma, sensory impairments, and physical disabilities were more likely to be overweight in comparison to peers. Children with chronic health conditions watched more television than peers, and their parents reported worse physical and mental health. Higher body mass index, Hispanic background, and living in an urban dwelling were associated with physical inactivity. Higher body mass index was also associated with more nonparental care arrangements, fewer siblings, low socioeconomic status, increased television viewing, asthma, and poor parent mental and physical health. The authors concluded that the development of family-centered care for all children with chronic health conditions would be useful. These findings also suggest that interventions to increase physical activity in children with asthma, sensory, and physical disabilities are warranted.

Qualitative Research

Researchers have conducted several qualitative studies in the field of physical activity and childhood chronic illness to explore how chronically ill children feel about engaging in physical activity. Azmeh and Leo (2014) sought to investigate how American children with asthma feel about physical activity. The researchers found that the children tend to manage asthma symptoms by avoiding physical activity rather than using medication. The students experienced asthma symptoms during physical education class. Rather than using medication, they coped with these symptoms by stopping activity and drinking water. Most students did not carry medication on them, due to the misbelief that they were not allowed to. Rather, they thought that the school nurse was responsible for medication. The students also feared taking medication in front of their peers and worried that they would be teased. Rather than trying to prevent asthma symptoms, the students tended to focus on dealing with present symptoms. The authors concluded that children with asthma face major barriers toward medication adherence as well as physical activity participation. Educating families and children affected by asthma about the importance of management with medication as well as physical activity might go a long way toward enhancing the health of children with asthma.

Moola and Faulkner (2014) undertook a qualitative study with Canadian children that have CF. Using the case study methodology, the authors sought to contrast and compare the physical activity stories of two children living with CF. Such cases serve as exemplars for broader physical activity narratives that pertain to chronically ill children. Layla, whose narrative was presented in the introduction of this chapter, displayed a narrative of despair, emphasizing how her illness made her feel helpless and depressed. Prior to a physical activity program, she demonstrated a "don't care" attitude toward physical activity, regarding it as unimportant to her life. After a physical activity intervention, Layla's attitude toward CF and physical activity began to change, as she recognized the importance of self-care. Nevertheless, Layla's prevailing health and illness narrative remained one of despair, hopelessness, and sadness. In sharp contrast, Chase demonstrated a narrative of resilience in the face of CF. He sought to live his best life regardless of his diagnosis. Despite CF, he maintained an active social life, was dedicated toward academic studies, and held important goals for the future. Chase felt even more empowered to engage in a physically active lifestyle after a counseling intervention and spoke of feeling inspired for the future. The authors suggest that chronically ill children draw on many narrative tropes to explain their health and physical activity experiences. The narratives that chronically ill children use to make sense of health and illness appear to exert a profound influence on physical activity (Moola, Faulkner, Kirsh, & Schneiderman, 2011).

Since it is well known that parents exert a great influence on their children's physical activity behaviors, a team of researchers also sought to explore the perceptions of parents toward their child's physical activity (Moola, Faulkner & Kirsh, 2011a, 2011b). The parents in this qualitative study provided care to children with congenital heart disease and cystic fibrosis. Parents discussed numerous benefits and barriers associated with physical activity for their child, such as being bullied by peers in physical activity spaces. Interestingly, parents also felt that physical activity was an important health enhancing tool to employ in their own lives. Indeed, while they were not always able to be active themselves due to time constraints, they recognized physical activity as a health enhancing pursuit that would in turn allow them to be better caregivers to their children. Parent's physical activity narratives toward both their child and themselves were negotiated within a broader context of stress and complexity. The authors concluded that these complex families lived with a sense of constant stress. Physical activity interventions could be developed not only for children with CF and CHD, but for caregivers and parents as a tool to cope with chronic stress and worry.

SUMMARY

After undertaking the review of literature that has been discussed, it is evident that studies pertaining to physical activity and the chronically ill child are a burgeoning and contemporary area of inquiry. Studies are mainly of the cross-sectional and pre and post-test type, which greatly hinders the ability of scholars to comment on whether long-term gains in physical activity are possible. Most studies have been conducted in the United States. This precludes a greater understanding on whether cultural and geographic factors also shape physical activity, such as climate or cultural norms and conventions. Studies have been conducted with variable disease types, although there appears to be a greater focus on youth with type 2 diabetes currently. This is likely the result of the significant increase in the prevalence of type 2 diabetes among the pediatric population in the last two decades. These youth are being diagnosed at earlier ages and living longer lives with diabetes. This raises concern about declining physical activity levels. Most researchers conclude that physical activity should be promoted as a health-enhancing tool for chronically ill youth, but that specific strategies on how to do so are warranted.

Barriers to Physical Activity

In reviewing the literature, it is evident that children with chronic illnesses encounter numerous barriers to physical activity. According to a social-ecological approach, these barriers occur on multiple scales of influence.

Intrapersonal Barriers

Psychologically, children with chronic illnesses demonstrate low perceived confidence toward physical activity (Moola, Faulkner, Kirsh, &

Kilburn, 2008). Weak self-efficacy toward physically active endeavors might lead these youth to avoid being active. As a result, weak self-efficacy may also lead these youth to seek out other activities in which they feel a sense of mastery and control. Interventionists need to specifically target low self-efficacy toward physical activity and work toward creating the mastery experiences that are needed to foster better physical self-efficacy. Since physical self-efficacy is related to physical activity behaviors, this is critical.

Intrapersonally, youth with chronic illnesses perceive physical activity to be "unimportant" to their lives. They ascribe more value to spending time with friends and family or attaining a job in the future (Moola et al., 2008). Indeed, within the context of numerous other stressors—such as doing treatment everyday—not engaging in physical activity is understandable. However, interventionists could work with youth to help them to re-prioritize life goals and ambitions. For example, interventionists might help youth to recognize that "being healthy" through activity is critical to attaining other life goals, such as meaningful careers. Interventions that foster positive peer relationships may prove invaluable to alleviating feelings of loneliness during physical activity. Cognitive behavioral-based physical activity interventions for youth with chronic illnesses might help them to better recognize the importance of physical activity to their lives.

Interpersonal Barriers

For decades, it has been well documented that the parents of chronically ill youth often pose formidable barriers toward physical activity (Moola, Fusco, & Kirsh, 2011a, 2011b). For example, research has found that parental overprotection and avoidance of physical activity strongly shapes the aversion that many chronically ill children display toward physical activity. If parents are not educated about the benefits of physical activity for their child, it is likely that they will view activity as a dangerous and unsafe pursuit. Parents of chronically ill youth often view their child as delicate, fragile, and vulnerable (Moola et al., 2011a). Such perceptions—while understandable—are ultimately damaging as they serve to foster physical activity fear and avoidance (Bar-Mor, Bar-Tal, Krulik, & Zeevi, 2000). Given that physical activity can be safely undertaken by most chronically ill children, efforts could be made to educate parents on the benefits of physical activity for their child. Indeed, parents could be encouraged to view physical activity as a safe and normal pursuit for their child. Interventionists could educate parents on the benefits of physical activity for their child and encourage them to view it as a normal and safe pursuit. Since health providers—such as physicians—powerfully shape parents' attitudes toward their child's health, they could be encouraged to teach and educate parents about the benefits of activity for their child (Moola et al., 2011a, 2011b). Parents are influential role models of their children's health behaviors; indeed, children will mimic and follow the exemplars that parents provide them with (and, as of late) greater importance is being given to the benefits of family-based interventions. For this reason, parents could also be encouraged to engage in activity with their children at home. When the parents of chronically ill youth regard their child as fragile and keep them in a "bubble" for fear of injury, it serves to damage the child's sense of self, overemphasize illness as a marker of identity, and prevents inclusion with same age peers. Parents could be encouraged to normalize their child's life and to promote their integration into society. However, as the two vignettes earlier in this chapter demonstrate, the way in which a child understands his/her illness varies greatly. Thus, parents could be encouraged to identify the best strategies for integration and normalization with their child. Children are often mirrors of their parents; in this regard, positive parental mirroring could be encouraged and promoted.

School

Multiple barriers toward inclusive physical activity exist within the education system. Recent physical education graduates have not completed advanced course work in inclusive physical activity during their university degrees. As such, they might lack the necessary knowledge and skills to appropriately adapt physical activity for students with disabilities or chronic illnesses. It has been reported that a considerable number of physical educators possess negative feelings toward inclusion (Block & Obrunikova, 2007). However, these feelings are likely to stem from the perception of being inadequately trained due to lack of experience and knowledge to successfully include children with disabilities and illnesses. Even when physical education teachers do have such skills, large class sizes and a lack of adapted physical activity equipment might pose challenges toward the development of inclusive physical education programs. Students with disabilities and chronic illnesses consistently report that they feel "left out" and excluded from physical education (Moola et al., 2008). Many report being exposed to both overt and covert teasing and bullying by able-bodied peers in physical education classes (Moola et al., 2008). Systemic changes are needed within the education system to enhance inclusive physical education opportunities for youth with chronic illnesses and disabilities (Poursanidou, Garner, & Watson, 2008). Mandatory training on inclusive physical education design is needed so that teachers have the skills and abilities to appropriately adapt the curriculum. Administrators could allow for flexibility in the curriculum so that physical education teachers can create new and improved curriculum to include chronically ill children within classes. This involves reconceptualizing the traditional ways that teachers view assessment, and a willingness to be flexible and accommodating with assessment items. Fellow peers and students could be educated and encouraged to celebrate difference and diversity as a normal part of the human experience. Recognizing and celebrating diversity in human abilities could be encouraged just like valuing racial and cultural difference. Young people with disabilities spend more time with adults in comparison to able-bodied youth. Peer-to-peer interaction is absolutely critical to optimizing development and social skill acquisition. While a full discussion of integrated versus segregated classrooms is beyond the scope of this chapter, where possible, teachers could seek to integrate and include students with illnesses within their classes. Doing so will ultimately normalize illness as an intrinsic part of the human condition.

Community, Culture, and Society

There are also barriers to physical activity participation in communities and neighborhoods. There is much research to show how factors in the built, purposeful environment strongly shape physical activity behaviors. Parents and youth frequently report that there is a lack of physical activity opportunities specifically for those young people with illnesses in the community (Goodwin & Staples, 2005). In this regard, there are few community-based physical activity programs—such as adapted hockey, swimming, or skating—designed to specifically meet the needs of those with illnesses. This lack of access to such programs in the community means that parents have few options when it comes to physical activity planning. Many parents are not able to register their child for physical activities in the community due to the fact that few opportunities are available. Alternatively, they fear that their child will be injured or hurt during "regular" community-based programs that are not specifically designated for children and youth living with disabilities or illnesses (Moola et al., 2011a).

Variety Village is a physical activity center designed specifically for people with disabilities and chronic illnesses in the east end of Toronto, Ontario, Canada. It serves as an exemplar of what community-based physical activity initiatives for special populations could be comprised of. Variety Village has a long legacy of providing high quality adapted physical activity programs for those with disabilities and illnesses across all seasons. Architecturally, the Variety Village space is entirely inclusive; based on the principles of universal design, everyone—regardless of their degree of limitation—can safely use the space. Facilities like Variety Village are rare. Unlike the city of Toronto, which is relatively affluent, many Canadian cities do not have the funds available to create such spaces. Government funding and funding from the private sector might be necessary to create community-based physical activity opportunities for those with illnesses, as well as integrated classes to allow those with and without illnesses to be active together.

Policymakers contribute to shaping contemporary attitudes toward topics such as the inclusion of people with illnesses. The rights of people with disabilities now feature in the Canadian Charter of Rights and Freedoms (Government of Canada, 2016). Although this piece of legislation has vastly improved the social conditions of those with disabilities, it took several decades of lobbying by the disabled community to have such rights recognized. Although Canada now has a national physical activity policy, no such policy exists for those with disabilities and illnesses. A national physical activity policy for people with disabilities and illnesses might pave the way for important community and school-based initiatives and serve to place the physical activity needs of people with illnesses and disabilities higher on the Canadian national agenda.

IMPLICATIONS

While this chapter has not exhaustively discussed all factors, it is evident that multiple barriers detract from optimal physical activity participation for children with chronic illnesses. These barriers range from the person to society. Deeply held misconceptions about the inability of chronically ill children to participate in physical activity abound in culture and society (Moola et al., 2011b). With a few notable exceptions, most children with chronic illnesses can and should safely participate in physical activity (Moola, McCrindle, & Longmuir, 2009). Pending restrictions from a health provider—such as a physician—chronically ill children should be included in physical activity. Further education and opportunities are needed to change deeply held and incorrect misconceptions.

More research is needed to document the physical, psychological, and social benefits of physical activity for chronically ill children. Given the importance of lifelong physical activity to the attainment of important health outcomes, longitudinal research designs that promote and track physical activity over the course of time are warranted. Further qualitative research is also warranted to understand disease specific barriers to physical activity, as well as to comprehend the various meanings that chronically ill children ascribe toward physical activity.

Theory provides a well-tested road map to develop relevant behavioral interventions. For example, self-efficacy theory, the theory of self-determination, the theory of planned behavior, social cognitive theory, and the transtheoretical model of change have all been successfully employed in the field of physical activity intervention development (McAuley, 1984; Prochaska, DiClemente, & Nocross, 1992). Researchers in the field of childhood chronic illnesses and physical activity could rely on theory to develop meaningful and relevant physical activity interventions. This will increase the chances of developing physical activity programs that make sense to the everyday realities and dilemmas of children living with chronic illnesses.

The government, local municipalities, and the private sector could combine resources to create more sustainable, high quality community-based physical activity centers for people with disabilities. Without such top-down involvement, young people with disabilities are likely to continue to be deprived of such opportunities to be active.

Type 2 diabetes and childhood obesity are two relatively new illnesses of childhood that have emerged over the past two decades, particularly in developed nations. Previously, such disease entities did not exist. Since a significant component of disease causation is attributable to lifestyle factors—such as diet and inactivity (Dietz & Gortmaker, 2001)—this issue has generated much controversy. Many argue that diabetes and obesity should not be considered as childhood illnesses given that they are not congenital. Regardless of the philosophical approach taken, diabetes and obesity constitute the greatest threat to children's health today. Both are regarded as a major public health threat facing 21st century children. In 2013, across the globe, the Childhood Obesity Foundation estimated that 42 million infants and children were overweight or obese. For example, 13% of children and youth suffer from obesity in Canada and 17.5 % of American children are obese (CBC News, 2015). Additionally, it is estimated that 25, 693 Canadian children and youth live with diabetes (Public Health Agency of Canada, 2011), as well as 208,000 American young people (American Diabetes, 2016). These numbers are likely to be underestimates as the prevalence of obesity and diabetes continue to increase. Further, current figures may be hampered by a lack of diagnosis. Physical activity promotion is particularly important for youth living with diabetes and obesity.

Medicalization was a term originally proposed by Zola (1982) and later taken up and adapted by other scholars. Medicalization refers to the infiltration of medicine into our everyday lives. In a society of medicalization, the importance of health and illness to well-being is overemphasized. Medicalization also contributes toward a "society of risk" that is perhaps overly concerned with various health threats. Although health providers could encourage physical activity as a central component of illness management, it is perhaps not advisable to overemphasize activity as a medical entity. Indeed, disability scholars have drawn attention to how physical activity for people with disabilities is often only encouraged through a dominant discourse of "therapeutic rehabilitation." Rather, physical activity should be regarded as a pursuit that is not only fun and safe, but also a normal component of childhood regardless of its "medical benefits."

LIMITATIONS

This chapter focused on the role of physical activity in the lives of children with chronic illnesses more broadly. Opting for breadth rather than depth, we have provided a general outline of the physical, psychological, and social benefits of physical activity for a broad range of chronically ill children. It is noteworthy to mention that this chapter was limited to children with chronic illnesses that are currently well-researched. As such, chronic illnesses that are less common in the academic literature are missing, and their relation to physical activity remains unknown. Thus, specific physical activity guidelines have not been provided in this chapter. Readers who are interested in specific chronic illnesses should seek out advanced scholarship and physical activity guidelines for the particular condition in question. Physical activity consensus statements have been developed for many disease groups. For example, Moola, McCrindle, and Longmuir (2009) have produced a consensus statement on physical activity recommendations for children with congenital heart disease.

CONCLUSION

The two vignettes provided in the introductory components of this chapter testify to the vast range of physical activity experiences that young people with chronic illnesses encounter. Some, like Layla, feel excluded from physical activity and regard it as unimportant to their lives. Others, like Gretchen, dispel deeply held misconceptions about the inherent inability of young people with chronic illnesses through their active engagement in sport. By outlining contemporary research that attests to the benefits of physical activity for chronically ill youth, we hope that we have provided a compelling rationale for the inclusion of these children into physical activity. However, we also hope that we have drawn our readers' attention to the barriers that detract young people with chronic illnesses from engaging in physical activity. Scholars, students, educators, and health providers could advocate for the physical activity needs of young people with chronic illnesses, and act as allies for this cause. By providing physical, social, and psychological benefits, inclusive environments in which physical activity occurs offer countless potential benefits for children and youth living with chronic illnesses. In so doing, we hope that the exclusion young people with chronic illnesses have faced in activity might be a thing of the past. We hope that in the future, young people with chronic illnesses might be "free to play."

REFERENCES

Akber, A., Portale, A. A., & Johansen, K. L. (2014). Use of pedometers to increase physical activity among children and adolescents with chronic kidney disease. *Pediatric Nephrology, 29,* 1395–1402.

American Diabetes Association. (2016). *Statistics about diabetes.* Retrieved from http://www.diabetes.org/diabetes-basics/statistics/

Azmeh, R., & Leo, H.L. (2014). In-school asthma management and physical activity: Children's perspectives. *Pediatrics, 134,* S180.

Balemans, A. C. J., van Wely, L., Becher, J. G., & Dallmeijer, A. J. (2015). Longitudinal relationship among physical fitness, walking-related physical activity, and fatigue in children with cerebral palsy. *Physical Therapy, 95,* 996–1005.

Bar-Mor, G., Bar-Tal, Y., Krulik, T., & Zeevi, B. (2000). Self-efficacy and physical activity in adolescents with trivial, mild, or moderate congenital cardiac malformations. *Cardiology in the Young, 10,* 561–566.

Bar-Or, O., & Rowland, T. (2004). *Pediatric exercise medicine: From physiologic principles to health care application.* Leeds, England: Human Kinetics.

Bell, K. L., & Davies, P. S. W. (2010). Energy expenditure and physical activity of ambulatory children with cerebral palsy and of typically developing children. *American Journal of Clinical Nutrition, 92,* 313–319.

Block, M. E., & Obrusnikova, I. (2007). Inclusion in physical education: A review of the literature from 1995-2005. *Adapted Physical Activity Quarterly, 24,* 103–124.

CBC News. (2015). *Child obesity at highest level in Canada and U.S.* Retrieved from http://www.cbc.ca/news/health/child-obesity-at-highest-level-in-canada-and-u-s-1.3203561

Dietz, W., & Gortmaker, S. (2001). Preventing obesity in children and adolescents. *Annual Review of Public Health, 22,* 337–353.

Ewalt, L. A., Danduran, M. J., Strath, S. J., Moerchen, V., & Swartz, A. M. (2012). Objectively assessed physical activity and sedentary behavior does not differ between children and adolescents with and without a congenital heart defect: A pilot examination. *Cardiology in the Young, 22,* 34–41.

Fischetti, N. (2015). Correlates among perceived risk for type 2 diabetes mellitus, physical activity, and dietary intake in adolescents. *Pediatric Nursing, 41,* 126–131.

Gannotti, M., Veneri, D., & Roberts, D. (2007). Weight status and physical activity in third graders with chronic health conditions. *Pediatric Physical Therapy, 19,* 301–308.

Goodwin, D. (2001). The meaning of help in PE: Perceptions of students with physical disabilities. *Adapted Physical Activity Quarterly, 18,* 289–303.

Goodwin, D., Thurmeier, R., & Gustafson, P. (2004). Reactions to the metaphors of disability: The mediating effects of physical activity. *Adapted Physical Activity Quarterly, 21,* 379–398.

Goodwin, D., & Staples, K. (2005). The meaning of summer camp experience to youths with disabilities. *Adapted Physical Activity Quarterly, 22*, 160–178.

Government of Canada. (2016). *Rights of people with disabilities.* Retrieved from http://www.canada.pch.gc.ca/eng/1448633334025

Kimmelblatt, C. A. (2012). *Diabetes summer camps: Improving the psychosocial functioning of children with type 1 diabetes* (Doctoral dissertation). Retrieved from ProQuest (UMI No. 3547527).

Kriska, A., Delahanty, L., Edelstein, S., Amodei, N., Chadwick, J., Copeland, K., . . . & Syme, A. (2013). Sedentary behavior and physical activity in youth with recent onset of type 2 diabetes. *Pediatrics, 131*, e850–e856.

Longmuir, P. E., Brothers, J. A., de Ferranti, S. D., Hayman, L. L. Van Hare, G. F., Matherne, G. P., . . . Joy, E. A. (2013). Promotion of physical activity of children and adults with congenital heart disease. *Circulation, 127*, 2147–2159.

McAuley, E. (1984). Modeling and self-efficacy: A test of bandura's model. *Journal of Sport Psychology, 7*, 283–295.

Moola, F., & Faulkner, G. E. J. (2014). A tale of two cases: The health, illness, and physical activity stories of two children living with cystic fibrosis. *Clinical Child Psychology and Psychiatry, 19*, 24–42.

Moola, F., Faulkner, G. E. J., Kirsh, J. A., & Kilburn, J. (2008). Physical activity and sport participation in youth with congenital heart disease: Perceptions of children and parents. *Adapted Physical Activity Quarterly, 25*, 49–70.

Moola, F., Faulkner, G. E. J., Kirsh, J. A., & Schneiderman, J. E. (2011). Developing physical activity interventions for youth with cystic fibrosis and congenital heart disease: Learning from their parents. *Psychology of Sport and Exercise, 12*, 599–608.

Moola, F., Fusco, C., & Kirsh, J. A. (2011a). The perceptions of caregivers toward physical activity and health in youth with congenital heart disease. *Qualitative Health Research, 21*, 278–291.

Moola, F., Fusco, C., & Kirsh, J. A. (2011b). "What I wish you knew": Social barriers toward physical activity in youth with congenital heart disease (CHD). *Adapted Physical Activity Quarterly, 28*, 56–77.

Moola, F., McCrindle, B., & Longmuir, P. (2009). Physical activity in youth with surgically corrected congenital heart disease: Devising guidelines so Johnny can participate. *Pediatrics and Child Health, 14*, 167–170.

Newacheck, P., & Taylor, W. (1992). Childhood chronic illness: Prevalence, severity and impact. *American Journal of Public Health, 22*(3), 364 —371.

Orsey, A. D., Wakefield, D. B., & Cloutier, M. M. (2014). Physical activity and sleep among children and adolescents with cancer. *Pediatric Blood & Cancer, 60*, 1908–1913.

Poursanidou, K., Garner, P., & Watson, A. (2008). Hospital-school liaison: Perspectives of health and education professionals supporting children with renal transplants. *Journal of Child Health Care, 12*, 253–267.

Prochaska, J., DiClemente, C., & Nocross, J. (1992). In search of how people change: Application to addictive behaviour. *American Psychologist, 47*, 1102–1114.

Public Health Agency of Canada. (2011). *Diabetes in Canada: Facts and figures from a public health perspective.* Retrieved from http://www.phac-aspc.gc.ca/cd-mc/

publications/diabetes-diabete/facts-figures-faits-chiffres-2011/chap5-eng.
php

Quirk, H., Blake, H., Tennyson, R., Randell, T. L., & Glazebrook, C. (2014). Physical
activity interventions in children and young people with type 1 diabetes mellitus: A systematic review with meta-analysis. *Diabetic Medicine, 31,* 1163–1173.

Rintala, P., Valimaa, R., Tynjala, J., Boyce, W., King, M., Villberg, J., & Kannas, L.
(2011). Physical activity of children with and without long-term illness or disability. *Journal of Physical Activity and Health, 8,* 1066–1073.

Schneiderman-Walker, J., Wilkes, D. L., Strug, L., Lands, L. C., Pollock, S. L. Selva-
durai, H. C., . . . Corey, M. (2005). Sex differences in habitual physical activity
and lung function decline in children with cystic fibrosis. *Journal of Pediatrics,
147,* 321–326.

Umpierre, D., Ribeiro, P. A. B., Kramer, C. K., Leitao, C. B., Zucatti, A. T. N., Aze-
vedo, M. J., . . . Schaan, B. D. (2011). Physical activity advice only or structured
exercise training and association with HbA1c levels in type 2 diabetes. *JAMA,
305,* 1790–1799.

Wilson C. L., Stratton, K., Leisenring, W. L., Oeffinger, K. C., Nathan, P. C., Wasilews-
ki-Masker, K., . . . Ness, K. K. (2014). Decline in physical activity level in the
childhood cancer survivor study cohort. *Cancer Epidemiol Biomarkers Prev, 23,*
1619–1627.

Wu, Y. P., Prout, K., Roberts, M. C., Parikshak, S. & Amylon, M. D. (2010). Assessing
experiences of children who attended a camp for children with cancer and
their siblings: A preliminary study. *Child Youth Care Forum, 40,* 121–133.

Zola, I. (1982). *Missing pieces: A chronicle of living with a disability.* Philadelphia, PA:
Temple University Press.

PART II

STRATEGIES TO MAXIMIZE THE SOCIAL INCLUSION
OF CHILDREN AND ADOLESCENTS WITH SPECIAL
NEEDS IN GENERAL PHYSICAL ACTIVITIES

CHAPTER 4

STRATEGIES TO INCREASE SOCIAL INCLUSION OF STUDENTS WITH DISABILITIES IN PHYSICAL EDUCATION SETTINGS

Bethany L. Hersman
Wright State University

Samuel R. Hodge
The Ohio State University

In the United States as well as in other countries, many students and individuals with disabilities are included in general education settings including school physical education and sports programs (Fitzgerald, 2006; Hodge et al., 2009). Internationally, inclusion has increasingly been seen as a way to support and welcome all individuals and to eliminate social exclusion of people regardless of their race, ethnicity, religion, gender, sexual orientation, or ability level (United Nations Educational, Scientific, and Cultural

Inclusive Physical Activities, pages 75–89
Copyright © 2017 by Information Age Publishing
All rights of reproduction in any form reserved.

Organization, 2005). The term inclusion traditionally has been used to discuss different options for placing individuals with disabilities (e.g., cerebral palsy, visual impairments, autism) into settings with individuals who do not have disabilities as long as the needs of each person can still be met successfully (Block, 2016).

As such, one potential benefit of an inclusive setting is that all individuals who have disabilities can benefit from the positive social interactions they may experience with their peers without disabilities (Block, 2016). For example, being included with peers without disabilities can help students with disabilities learn appropriate behaviors such as taking turns or cooperating with their classmates. However, even though people with and without disabilities often are located in physical education settings together, we do not always observe these positive interactions occurring between the groups (Hersman, 2007). Possibly it could be due to the fact that individuals view people from other "groups" as different, it could be because they do not know how to interact, or are fearful about interacting with one another. In any case, there are many ways that as physical education professionals, we can help to educate individuals and provide positive experiences and role model appropriate and positive interactions between all the people we work with regardless of how they are similar to or different from one another.

Seeing that individuals with and without disabilities are included in physical education settings together, it is important that all individuals have their needs met while providing positive experiences both socially and physically. Mindful of these needs, the first purpose of this paper is to describe inclusion and social inclusion and the benefits for both individuals with and without disabilities in physical education settings. A second purpose of this paper is to discuss strategies that physical education professionals can utilize to maximize the participation and social inclusion of individuals with disabilities within inclusive contexts.

This topic has become increasingly important as many people in the United States have at one time or another been in the same setting as someone with a disability. But in many cases, if they were asked whether they spoke with or interacted in any way with the individual, they (if honest) will tell you no. In fact, research on social inclusion in physical education has highlighted the lack of meaningful social interactions between individuals with disabilities and their peers (Butler & Hodge, 2004; Place & Hodge, 2001). Typically, they experience a form of social isolation where they may be physically included in a setting (Place & Hodge, 2001), but there are no meaningful or appropriate social interactions, so the individuals with disabilities are not truly fully included with their peers. There is a need to not only include individuals with disabilities, but also to provide all individuals with the tools they will need to interact positively with one another in these inclusive physical education settings.

DESCRIPTION OF INCLUSION AND SOCIAL INCLUSION IN THE UNITED STATES

Inclusion in Physical Education

In education, inclusion typically refers to educating individuals with disabilities in one of many least restrictive environment settings. When possible and appropriate, students with disabilities are educated in a social and physical environment with individuals without disabilities where the individuals can thrive and succeed as any other student (Block, 2016). In recent years, estimates indicate that approximately 93% to 96% of children with disabilities receive school physical education in inclusive classes (Block & Obrusnikova, 2007; Hodge, Lieberman, & Murata, 2012; Lieberman & Houston-Wilson, 2009). The Individuals with Disabilities Education Improvement Act (2004) guarantees students with disabilities the opportunity to receive a free and appropriate education in what has been termed the least restrictive environment (LRE). The LRE is the environment where students with disabilities can participate, have their needs met, and be successful. The LRE can range from self-contained special education classes (including physical education) to fully included general education classes. In most cases, as mentioned previously, that setting happens to be inclusive, especially in the physical education setting.

In the research on inclusion in physical education, there have been many postulated benefits for both students with and without disabilities (Block, 2016). For example, an inclusive setting can provide opportunities to learn and practice social skills in more natural environments such as those we see every day in the real world. Secondly, students with disabilities can learn appropriate behaviors by observing their peers without disabilities. The interactions between students with and without disabilities who can act as peer models have been supported in the literature as well (Block, 2016). A final benefit of participation in an inclusive setting is developing relationships with others who are perceived as different (Block, 2016), which can include race, gender, or ability levels among other socially constructed attributes (Hersman, 2007; Hodge et al., 2012).

Social Inclusion in Physical Education

There are many benefits to the inclusion of individuals with disabilities in an inclusive physical education class for all involved. Teachers as well as students with and without disabilities can benefit from a successful inclusive physical education program (Block, 2016). Research has indicated that one of the main benefits of an inclusive physical education class for students with disabilities is that of social acceptance and interaction with peers (Block, 2016; Block & Obrusnikova, 2007). Ideally, social inclusion is demonstrated by students who engage in "positive personal interactions with classmates that contribute to feelings of accepting and liking each other" (Sherrill, 2004, p. 242). Further, Sherrill identified social inclusion in one of two ways. It can be unidirectional, meaning the students with disabilities most often initiate the interactions, so the relationships are one-way rather than two-way, or have equal status. Equal status interaction refers to reciprocal relationships where both students with and without disabilities interact and initiate interactions among one another (Sherrill, 2004). Unfortunately, much of the research that has been initiated on social inclusion has shown that interactions that occur between students with and without disabilities in inclusive settings are limited and unidirectional, which are often initiated by the student without disabilities (Butler & Hodge, 2004; Place & Hodge, 2001). Findings from earlier research on social inclusion indicate a need for an increase in equal status relationships between students with and without disabilities, which would promote social inclusion in physical education and beyond (Butler & Hodge, 2004; Goodwin, 2001; Goodwin & Watkinson, 2000; Place & Hodge, 2001). There is also a need for physical education professionals to step up and encourage interpersonal relationships between all individuals they work with, regardless of any differences between the participants. It is the role of the physical education teacher to help develop and foster positive and meaningful social interactions between individuals with and without disabilities. Interactions can occur occasionally, but it is important that the interactions are meaningful and that they occur voluntarily and not out of obligation.

More than 60 years ago and on the issue of race relations, Allport (1954) articulated contact theory and stated that placing together individuals who are different would not necessarily improve attitudes or dispel stereotypes that may already exist. Tellingly, earlier research on social inclusion indicated that meaningful interactions do not always occur between students with and without disabilities in general physical education (GPE) classes (Butler & Hodge, 2004; Place & Hodge, 2001). These findings lend support to Allport's (1954) postulates that proximity will not necessarily lead to attitude change, instead there is a need for something to happen that will help break down barriers and preconceived notions or fears that individuals may have. Early research on attitude change in inclusive physical education settings has also shown that structured and meaningful contact between students with and without disabilities do in fact improve attitudes more so than when there is unstructured contact (Archie & Sherrill, 1989; Block & Zeman, 1996; Slininger, Sherrill, & Jankowski, 2000; Tripp, French, & Sherrill, 1995). In brief, Allport's (1954) contact theory maintains that there are four conditions that must be present in order for positive and meaningful interactions to occur. These are: (a) equal status contact; (b) sharing of common goals; (c) intergroup cooperation; and (d) an environment that supports contact between the individuals. Although contact theory was originally created as a way to understand and explain interactions between different racial and ethnic groups, this theory has over the years been used by adapted physical education researchers to explain the educational contexts between students with and without disabilities in inclusive physical education (Archie & Sherrill, 1989; Block & Zeman, 1996; Slininger, et al, 2000; Tripp et al., 1995). Contact does not ensure meaningful relationships or increased social inclusion. Therefore it is important that cooperation, common goals, and a supportive environment also exist in order to decrease the social isolation that many students with disabilities experience in inclusive GPE settings.

STRATEGIES TO MAXIMIZE PARTICIPATION AND SOCIAL INCLUSION

The second purpose of this paper is to present as many strategies as possible to help ensure that students with disabilities are included both physically and socially in their physical education classes. Although this list may be extensive, it is by no means exhaustive. As discussed previously, there exists a significant need to employ strategies that help students with disabilities to feel included by their peers. This section will discuss the following general strategies a physical education teacher can utilize to increase participation and social interactions between all participants. The general strategies are: (a) be a role model, (b) teach appropriate interactions, (c) reinforce appropriate interactions and behaviors, (d) work with the paraeducators, (e) implement a peer tutoring program, (f) implement universally designed instruction into the curriculum, (g) organize students strategically, (h) promote disability awareness, and (i) utilize community resources. For discourse on specific strategies for teaching students with various different types of disabilities in inclusive physical education, we direct you to the works by Block (2016), Hodge et al. (2012), Lieberman and Houston-Wilson (2009), Sherrill (2004), and Winnick (2011), just to name a few useful resources.

Be a Role Model

Teachers, parents, coaches, and fitness instructors are role models to the individuals they instruct. Most actions and behaviors are learned through imitating what other people do. As is the case with many children, they oftentimes look up to their teachers or coaches as role models (Block, 2016). So what does this mean? A teacher should always be respectful to and welcoming of any individual regardless of ability, gender, ethnicity, or any other socially constructed attributes. For example, if a physical education teacher is working with an inclusive class arrangement, it is important that all students are actively engaged in the lesson's activities. The students may not all be doing the exact same thing, but everyone is included and participating at their ability levels (this will be discussed in more detail in the Universal Design of Instruction section).

By not segregating students and by giving equivalent attention to all, the teacher is showing the class that everyone is important. If the teacher gives high fives at the end of the class, it is important to do so for every student, even those with motor or orthopedic disabilities. Giving feedback is an important part of being a physical education teacher, so making sure that every individual receives an adequate amount of attention and specific feedback is a good practice to adopt. The teacher should exude a positive attitude and make it clear that each student is an important part of the class. Communication is key! Speak to all students in the class, not just boys or girls, or students with or without disabilities. By making an attempt to interact with everyone, the teacher is setting a positive example and showing everyone that it is okay to speak to the child who is perceived as "different" because he or she speaks with an accent, has a disability, or comes from a different socioeconomic status than other students in the class. This is especially important with students who have speech or language disabilities or even for those who may not speak at all. Interacting with everyone will set a positive example for all to see.

Teach Appropriate Interactions

It is also important that the teacher speak to students with disabilities just as she or he would speak to others in the class, and to let the students with disabilities communicate back in their preferred form of communication. If the student uses sign language, the use of an interpreter would be helpful, but it is also important that the teacher take the time to learn key words and phrases using sign language and then also teach those signs to the rest of the class so that they can learn to communicate with that student. Language can be a barrier to social inclusion, but by taking the appropriate steps to overcome this barrier and by making an active effort to interact with students with disabilities, that teacher is showing every student that it is important to include everyone.

It is common in sport and physical education settings to focus on competition and winning. A teacher should encourage appropriate interactions and positive sport behavior between all individuals involved. In particular, students with autism, learning disabilities, or emotional disabilities tend to exhibit inappropriate behaviors in situations where they become frustrated, overwhelmed, or uncomfortable (Schonert-Reichl, 1993; Vaughn, Elbaum, & Scumm, 1996). In these situations, the physical education teacher needs to teach students with disabilities as well as students without disabilities how to show their emotions in healthy or positive ways, and how to express that they are uncomfortable or upset in the form of acceptable behaviors. It is perfectly okay for a student to take a break from activity when he/she is becoming upset or agitated, in fact, there are teachers who use *thinking benches* where a student can go to get away from a situation rather than staying in that situation and letting negative behaviors escalate. In this specific example, the thinking bench should never be used as a time-out tool, or students will see it as a punishment rather than a place to take a moment to calm down and refocus.

Reinforce Appropriate Interactions and Behaviors

All individuals should be constantly encouraged to interact with one another and when the teacher sees students without disabilities interacting appropriately and particularly with students who have disabilities, those appropriate behaviors should be encouraged and reinforced regularly (Lavay, French, & Henderson, 2016). Reinforcement should only happen after a desired behavior occurs, such as a student without a disability explaining the activity to a student with a disability. As a result, that behavior would be more likely to happen in the future (Cooper, Heron, & Heward, 2007). A teacher should know his or her students and what motivates them. For example, if a teacher were to present a student with the opportunity to go play baseball if he did all his work quietly, that may not be a reinforcer for him if he does not particularly enjoy baseball, so he would not care as much about being quiet since he would rather be rewarded with a game of soccer as opposed to baseball.

In addition, a lot of times teachers simply react to a situation that occurs by calling out students who are misbehaving rather than catching them while they are being good and reinforcing appropriate behavior rather than punishing a negative behavior (Lavay et al., 2016). This requires the teacher to be in tune with what is happening in the environment and to watch for certain antecedents (triggers) that may stimulate or lead to misbehavior or inappropriate behaviors and to be proactive in dissipating situations before they occur (Lavay et al., 2016).

Work With the Paraeducators

If a student with a disability is working on a skill or activity with his/her adapted physical education teacher or paraeducator, the physical education teacher should attempt to include the student with a disability in activities with peers, rather than always allowing that student to participate with an adult (e.g., adapted physical education teacher or paraeducator). By participating with an adult, that student is not benefitting from interactions with other students in the class, and the physical education teacher is unknowingly fostering social isolation, or in some cases physical isolation where the student with a disability is included with the class, but is physically separated from the rest of the class (Place & Hodge, 2001). By allowing students with and without disabilities the opportunity to participate together and to interact freely, the teacher is fostering the social and physical inclusion of all students in the class.

According to Lieberman and Houston-Wilson (2009), paraeducators are present to help facilitate inclusion of students with disabilities. They are there to support students in making activity modifications and to assist the physical education teacher in implementing best practices for the student. However, Lieberman and Houston-Wilson also mention that a paraeducator is there to shadow a student with a disability and his/her peer tutor or partner and help by providing suggestions and feedback through the use of instructional strategies that promote inclusion of the student with a disability. Worth mentioning, however, is the fact that students without disabilities tend not to interact with students who have a paraeducator (Causton-Theoharis & Mamgren, 2005). This is especially evident in situations where the paraeducator is constantly in physical contact with the student with a disability, sits directly next to the student with a disability, allows that student to sit in his/her lap, or speaks for the student with a disability.

The physical education teacher should discuss and define the roles of the paraeducator within the gymnasium and specific inclusion strategies that should be utilized in order to facilitate inclusion as well as social interactions between students with and without disabilities (Lieberman & Houston-Wilson, 2009). Instead of always stepping in as a partner to a student with a disability, the paraeducator can teach other students in the class how to interact with the student who has a disability; it is important to keep in mind that the goal is to help the student with a disability become independent and to interact in natural settings with peers (Causton-Theoharis & Mamgren, 2005).

Implement Peer Tutoring Program

A physical education teacher should also prepare the students without disabilities for the experience they will have in the inclusive physical education context. Peer acceptance is an extremely important component to a successful inclusive arrangement, and peer rejection can result in limited social learning opportunities in physical education for the students with disabilities (Block, 2016). Unfortunately, a lack of experience and knowledge on how to interact with individuals with disabilities can lead to an unfavorable attitude toward inclusion, therefore it is important to train peers without disabilities and prepare them on how best to interact with the students with disabilities (Block, 2016).

There are several different types of peer tutoring programs that can occur in an inclusive physical education context. It is important to mention that training should occur first before partnering students with and without disabilities together in a peer-tutoring context (Lieberman & Houston-Wilson, 2009). The first type of program is called unidirectional, where the peer is teaching the student with a disability the entire time and tends to work well with students who have more severe disabilities (Hodge et al., 2012). A second option that tends to work well with students who have mild disabilities is known as reciprocal peer tutoring where the students with and without disabilities take turns teaching one another, giving a leadership role to both students at different times in the lesson (Hodge et al., 2012). Third is a strategy known as classwide peer tutoring, where the entire class is broken into small groups or dyads and they take turns teaching, modeling, and giving one another feedback. This type of a program also works well with students who have mild disabilities and is a way to utilize peer tutoring without singling out the students with disabilities as everyone is partnered up or in a small group (Hodge et al., 2012).

Hodge and colleagues (2012) provide several guidelines in preparing a peer tutoring program. First, whenever possible, include the student with a disability into the training so the tutor and tutee can provide input into the activities. This will also help the student without a disability learn more about the student with a disability. Second, during the training program, provide different scenarios so the pair can practice the teaching, modeling, and feedback that will need to occur during the lessons. Third, it is a good idea to train multiple peers without disabilities to work with the students with disabilities because this will ensure that there is always someone who is trained and available to help during the year. Fourth, keeping in mind that the tutor is not a trained teacher and in some cases this may be that individual's first experience teaching so the teacher should be available to provide guidance, feedback, and suggestions throughout each activity.

Lieberman and Houston-Wilson (2009) provide an extensive example of how to set up a peer-tutoring program. They suggest first to have an application process so that interested individuals can apply to be a peer tutor rather than requiring or assigning a student to be a peer tutor. If a student wants to be a peer tutor, he/she will have the intrinsic motivation and desire to do so and to do a good job, rather than being asked to do so by the teacher and feeling obligated to say yes.

Second, if the peer tutor training is to occur outside of the school day, the teacher should ask permission from parents or guardians as well as from administrators. Third, the teacher should utilize disability awareness activities (discussed in what follows) to teach peers about the disability and strategies that may work best. Fourth, communication techniques should be discussed that are appropriate to each student' disability. For example, students with autism have a hard time understanding sarcasm, so that should be avoided when interacting with someone who has autism (Winnick, 2011).

Fifth, a physical education teacher should teach peer tutors about using teaching strategies where prompting is utilized, but the least amount of prompting that is required is used rather than a more intensive form of prompting. For example, if a student with a disability is able to listen to a verbal prompt and then do the activity correctly, a peer tutor would not need to provide physical guidance prompts. The use of feedback and teaching cues should also be taught to the peer tutors so they know what to tell their tutee during the activities.

Next, the use of specific teaching scenarios can be presented to the tutors to monitor their level of understanding. This can be followed by checking or testing for their understanding and monitoring their progress as tutors throughout the duration of the program.

Lastly, if the student with a disability has any behavior plans, it is a good idea to tell the tutor, but it is still the responsibility of the teacher to ensure the behavior plan is carried out effectively (Lieberman & Houston-Wilson, 2009).

Implement Universally Designed Instruction Into the Curriculum

Universally designed instruction (UDI) is utilized in education in order to provide built-in access for all students to the activities, equipment, and instruction at a level that is appropriate for each student (Lieberman & Houston-Wilson, 2009). What sets UDI apart from any other teaching strategy is that the functioning of the students, objective of the activity, and modifications are considered ahead of time during the lesson planning phase rather than at the time the activity is happening in class (Lieberman, Lytle, & Clarcq, 2008). This allows the teacher to plan ahead for all the different levels of student functioning (both for students with and those without disabilities) based on the activities that will be taught; and then the teacher can make any minor adjustments as needed during the activities in class. Ensuring that all students have access to the activities at a level that is appropriate for each student is how a physical education teacher can help students experience an increase in motivation and personal success, as well as foster inclusion of students without disabilities (Lieberman & Houston-Wilson, 2009).

Utilizing a UDI approach, a physical education teacher can build social interactions into the curriculum through the use of cooperative learning activities, adventure education, or the sport education curricular model (Hodge et al., 2012). In the case of each of those curricular choices, social interaction can and should be an important component of the activities. For example, in adventure education and cooperative learning, the premise of many of the activities is that participants need to interact with one another in order to successfully complete the activity or initiative presented by the teacher. Hersman (2007) used the adventure education model as an intervention to improve the social inclusion of students with disabilities in an inclusive physical education setting, and found that inclusion and acceptance of students with disabilities are benefits of an effectively facilitated adventure education curriculum. In the sport education model, students are placed in teams where they develop a sense of togetherness as a part of that team for an entire sport season in the class. For more information on adventure education, sport education, and cooperative learning, the reader is referred to Frank (2004), Siedentop, Hastie, and van der Mars (2004), and Dyson and Grineski (2001), respectively.

Organize Students Strategically

Place and Hodge (2001) found that students with disabilities (in this case, three students) tended to group themselves together rather than interacting with their peers without disabilities. Therefore, the physical education teacher needs to be aware of this tendency and to put thoughtful preparation into how students will be grouped. Utilizing classwide peer tutoring as previously mentioned is one way to avoid students with disabilities always grouping themselves together in physical education. A similar grouping can be seen when larger groups of students with disabilities participate in inclusive physical education classes with their adapted physical education teacher or paraeducators. At times, it can appear as though there are two separate physical education classes going on in the gym at the same time. This should be avoided, however, because by not physically and socially including the students with disabilities, the physical education teacher is perpetuating the myth that students with disabilities are not able to participate in inclusive settings.

In addition, allowing the groups to separate from one another, the teacher is not allowing the students to learn from one another, interact with one another, or allowing the opportunity to learn about individual differences. When grouping students in inclusive classes, the teacher should consider the needs of the students. For instance, some students cannot be a part of large groups (e.g., due to overt aggressiveness or violent behavioral problems), while others may thrive in a large group environment. Behavioral considerations are also important as some students may not work well with others. This is why it is important to learn about the students' abilities and their needs so that these students can receive the best possible experience that allows them the opportunity to learn how to interact appropriately with one another.

Promote Disability Awareness

Promoting disability awareness is another way a physical education teacher can create an atmosphere of understanding and accepting of differences for students with disabilities. Through various awareness activities, students without disabilities can gain more knowledge and even experience what it might be like to have a disability, which in turn can help them to be more accepting of others who may be different. Lieberman and Houston-Wilson (2009) offer three different levels of disability awareness: exposure, experience, and ownership. Activities at the first level may include having guest speakers with disabilities present to the class, showing videos of disability sports, and possibly having the students do a research project on a disability through looking at websites or reading articles on athletes with disabilities. Level two activities would allow students without disabilities to experience what it might be like to have a disability and to try to participate in a physical education lesson or a sport while having that disability. For example, a teacher could have students put on blindfolds and try to kick a moving ball that has bells inside so they can experience the level of difficulty a student who is blind would face in physical education. Finally, the ownership level would result in students becoming advocates for individuals with disabilities both in the school setting and within their community.

Another form of disability awareness might take place outside of the school setting, but can promote peer support and acceptance through supporting students with disabilities who may participate in sports within the community. For example, Special Olympics is an international sport organization that supports individuals with intellectual disabilities as well as those individuals on the autism spectrum disorder continuum. One division of Special Olympics is called Unified Sports and allows teams of individuals with disabilities and their peers without disabilities to participate and compete on teams together to promote the growth of understanding and relationships between participants. For more information about the Special Olympics, visit the official Special Olympics website (www.specialolympics.org).

Utilize Community Resources

Community based instruction is a way that a physical education teacher can prepare a student with a disability to transition from physical activity at school to engaging in physical activity within the local community (Hodge et al., 2012). Teaching an individual with a disability to utilize the resources her or his community may have (such as fitness centers, parks, and recreation areas) is one way to ensure that an individual will feel comfortable engaging in different activities outside of school. By doing so, the individual is taught how to act and interact appropriately in these settings, how to use the facilities and equipment safely and responsibly, and how to ask for help if it is needed. This is an important component to transitioning to life outside of the school setting and can aid in promoting the socialization and social skills of individuals with disabilities (Lieberman & Houston-Wilson, 2009).

CONCLUSION

Although the early social inclusion literature has shown that at times, students with disabilities tended not to be socially included (Butler & Hodge, 2004; Place & Hodge, 2001), the extant body of research provide options that physical education teachers can take advantage of that will foster positive interactions and acceptance of students with disabilities in physical education (Hersman, 2007).

The purpose of this paper was twofold: to present a brief description of inclusion and social inclusion in physical education settings, and to present strategies to improve the social inclusion of students with disabilities in physical education settings. It is important to keep in mind that these strategies can be utilized in conjunction with one another in order to promote a fully inclusive environment for students with disabilities. The teacher should get to know the individual with the disability in terms of his or her abilities and strengths as well as needs and ability to communicate with others in order to develop an environment that is inclusive to all. Each and every student with a disability is an individual, and what works for one person may not work for another so it is very important to be flexible and adapt as needed.

REFERENCES

Allport, G. (1954). *The nature of prejudice.* Reading, MA: Addison-Wesley.

Archie, V., & Sherrill, C. (1989). Attitudes toward handicapped peers of mainstreamed and non-mainstreamed children in physical education. *Perceptual and Motor Skills, 69,* 319–322.

Block, M. (2016). *A teacher's guide to including students with disabilities in general physical education* (4th ed.). Baltimore, MD: Paul H. Brookes.

Block, M. E., & Obrusnikova, I. (2007). Inclusion in physical education: A review of literature from 1995–2005. *Adapted Physical Activity Quarterly, 24*, 103–124.

Block, M., & Zeman, R. (1996). Including students with disabilities in regular physical education: Effects on nondisabled children. *Adapted Physical Activity Quarterly, 13*, 38–49.

Butler, R. S., & Hodge, S. R. (2004). Social inclusion of students with disabilities in middle school physical education classes. *Research in Middle School Level Education, 27*(1), n.p. Retrieved from http://nmsa.org/research/rmle/winter _03/27_1_preface.htm

Causton-Theoharis, J., & Mamgren, K. (2005). Building bridges: Strategies to help paraprofessionals promote peer interaction. *Teaching Exceptional Children, 37,* 18–24.

Cooper, J. O., Heron, T. E., & Heward, W. L. (2007). *Applied behavior analysis* (2nd ed.). Upper Saddle River, NJ: Pearson.

Dyson, B., & Grineski, S. (2001). Using cooperative learning structures in physical education. *Journal of Physical Education, Recreation, and Dance, 72*(2), 28–31.

Fitzgerald, H. (2006). Disability and physical education. In D. Kirk, D. Macdonald, & M. O'Sullivan (Eds.), *The handbook of physical education* (pp. 752–766). Thousand Oaks, CA: SAGE.

Frank, L. S. (2004). *Journey toward the caring classroom: Using adventure to create community.* Oklahoma City, OK: Wood 'n' Barnes.

Goodwin, D. (2001). The meaning of help in PE: Perceptions of students with physical disabilities. *Adapted Physical Activity Quarterly, 18*, 289–303.

Goodwin, D., & Watkinson, E. J. (2000). Inclusive physical education from the perspective of students with physical disabilities. *Adapted Physical Activity Quarterly, 17*, 144–160.

Hersman, B. L. (2007). *The effect of adventure education on the social interaction of students with disabilities in general physical education* (Doctoral dissertation). Retrieved from https://etd.ohiolink.edu/!etd.send_file?accession=osu1186493 320&disposition=inline

Hodge, S. R., Ammah, J. O. A., Casebolt, K. M., LaMaster, K., Hersman, B. L., Samalot-Rivera, A., & Sato, T. (2009). A diversity of voices: Physical education teachers' beliefs about inclusion and teaching students with disabilities. *International Journal of Disability, Development and Education, 56*(4), 401–419.

Hodge, S. R., Lieberman, L. J., & Murata, N. M. (2012). *Essentials of teaching adapted physical education: Diversity, culture, and inclusion.* Scottsdale, AZ: Holcomb Hathaway.

Individuals with Disabilities Education Improvement Act (IDEIA) of 2004, PL 108–446.

Lavay, B. W., French, R., & Henderson, H. L. (2016). *Positive behavior management in physical activity settings* (3rd ed.). Champaign, IL: Human Kinetics.

Lieberman, L. J. & Houston-Wilson, C. (2009). *Strategies for inclusion: A handbook for physical educators* (2nd ed.). Champaign, IL: Human Kinetics.

Lieberman, L. J., Lytle, R., & Clarcq, J. (2008). Getting it right from the start: Employing the universal design for learning approach to your curriculum. *Journal of Physical Education, Recreation, and Dance, 79*(2), 32–39.

Place, K., & Hodge, S. (2001). Social inclusion of students with physical disabilities in general physical education: A behavioral analysis. *Adapted Physical Activity Quarterly, 18,* 389–404.

Schonert-Reichl, K. (1993). Empathy and social relationships in adolescents with behavioral disorders. *Behavioral Disorders, 18,* 189–204.

Sherrill, C. (2004). *Adapted physical activity, recreation, and sport: Crossdisciplinary and lifespan* (6th ed.). Boston, MA: McGraw Hill.

Siedentop, D., Hastie, P. A., & van der Mars, H. (2004). *Complete guide to sport education.* Champaign, IL: Human Kinetics.

Slininger, D., Sherrill, C., & Jankowski, C. (2000). Children's attitudes toward peers with severe disabilities: Revisiting contact theory. *Adapted Physical Activity Quarterly, 17,* 176–196.

Tripp, A., French, R., & Sherrill, C. (1995). Contact theory and attitudes of children in physical education programs toward peers with disabilities. *Adapted Physical Activity Quarterly, 12,* 323–332.

United Nations Educational, Scientific and Cultural Organization (UNESCO). (2005). *Guidelines for inclusion: Ensuring access to education for all.* Paris, France: Author.

Vaughn, S., Elbaum, B., & Schumm, J. (1996). The effects of inclusion on the social functioning of students with learning disabilities. *Journal of Learning Disabilities, 29,* 598–608.

Winnick, J. P. (2011). *Adapted physical education and sport* (5th ed.). Champaign, IL: Human Kinetics.

CHAPTER 5

PHYSICAL EDUCATION AND SPORT AS A MEANS TO EMPOWER CHILDREN WITH DISABILITY IN EDUCATIONAL AND COMMUNITY SETTINGS

The Contribution of Paralympic Education Focusing on Peers' Interactions

Tânia Bastos
*University of Porto
and University Institute of Maia*

Joana Teixeira
Futebol Clube do Porto

Mariana Amaral da Cunha
University of Porto

Rui Corredeira
University of Porto

Inclusive Physical Activities, pages 91–108

Policies on inclusive education are spread worldwide. According to UNES-CO (2008), the goal of inclusive education is to provide quality education for all students and communities according to their specific needs, abilities, characteristics, and learning expectations. Moreover, inclusive schools strive to erase all forms of discrimination while respecting diversity. It is generally accepted that inclusion in physical education (PE) refers to the inclusion of children with special educational needs (SEN; e.g., autism, learning disabilities, and cerebral palsy) in regular PE classes where children can have a different learning process (i.e., instruction and support) according to their specific needs (e.g., personnel, equipment, and communicational).

All the authors in this chapter have an academic and professional background in PE and adapted physical activity and advocate the inclusion of students with SEN in regular PE classes. It is our belief that the PE teacher is the leader of the inclusive process in the PE classroom. PE teachers must be active participants in all instructional decisions of students with and without SEN (Lieberman & Houston-Wilson, 2009). However, solely the action of the PE teacher is not enough. The peers without SEN who represent the majority of the students in the class can have a crucial role in the successful inclusion of students with SEN in PE and also in the community setting. Peers without SEN can act as facilitators of inclusion, and therefore have to be educated to become advocates of inclusive practices inside and outside the schools walls. The school setting is an appropriate place to foster positive and favorable attitudes toward children with SEN.

The goal of this chapter is to compile the most relevant body of research about the importance of PE and sport for the empowerment of children with SEN in educational and community settings, with particular foci on the traditional types of disability (i.e., physical, sensory, and intellectual disability). In addition, we provide inclusive strategies for PE teachers focusing on peers' education. Specifically, we examine four broad areas that include the following: inclusion in PE, designs of effective disability-ability awareness programs in PE, methodological issues and suggestions for future research, and practical recommendations for PE teachers.

INCLUSION IN PHYSICAL EDUCATION

Perspectives About Inclusion

Research supports several positive aspects of appropriately implemented inclusion (e.g., Lieberman, James, & Ludwa, 2004; Mauerberg-DeCastro, 2005; Morley, Bailey, Tan, & Cooke, 2005). First, students' social skills can be improved when they are educated in an inclusive environment. Students with and without disabilities have demonstrated favorable attitudes toward peers, coaches, and teachers as a result of inclusion (e.g., collaboration, tolerance and a better understanding of other people). Second, inclusion promotes personal development in both students with and without disabilities (e.g., self-perception, self-esteem, and loyalty). Third, students without disabilities benefit from inclusion because it prepares them to deal with disability in their own lives. In particular, inclusive environments enable students without disabilities to cultivate a sense of acceptance of varying interests, backgrounds, abilities, and learning needs, as well as to develop social skills such as cooperative work, responsibility and maturity.

Although research have explored the benefits of inclusion in PE, a PE class is not always a truly and positive inclusive context with equal learning opportunities and a friendly environment for all students regardless of their abilities. Qi and Ha (2012) mentioned that students with disabilities experience less motor engagement than their peers without disability and social isolation in PE settings. More specifically, Place and Hodge (2001) described social inclusion behaviors (e.g., social talk, praise, physical contact) of students with physical disabilities included in general PE and found that not frequently students with and without SEN engage in social interaction. Moreover, interaction between students with SEN is more intensive than with classmates without SEN. Similar findings were reported by Ellis, Wright, and Cronis (1996) regarding instructional and social interactions of students with intellectual disabilities included in general PE.

Several authors (e.g., Goodwin, 2001; Goodwin & Watkinson, 2000; Hutzler, Fliess, Chacham, & Auweele, 2002) have explored the perspectives of children with physical disabilities regarding their experiences in PE classes and identified a variety of positive as well as negative episodes. Goodwin and Watkinson (2000) interviewed elementary school-aged students with physical disabilities and reported a combination of positive (i.e., good days) and negative (i.e., bad days) experiences in PE. The negative experiences were related to social isolation, competence questioned due to disability (i.e., students perceived as different), and restricted participation in class. Specifically, negative attitudes of peers without disabilities contributed to unhappy feelings toward PE. Classmates' rejection (i.e., calling names or laughing) and lack of attention (i.e., little or no communication) were reported by the participants. Moreover, the participants felt that their bodies were seen as objects of attention or curiosity, and their competence to perform in PE was compared to "normalize" standards. Students with physical disabilities who were perceived to be incapable of meeting performance standards had their ability to participate in the class questioned by their peers. Students with physical disabilities also experienced restricted class participation due to a lack of commitment and willingness from classmates that doubted their skill level, and consequently excluded them during PE activities (Goodwin & Watkinson, 2000). On the other hand, participants also reported meaningful experiences in PE, and peers once more had an important contribution to the establishment of a positive class environment. The students with physical disabilities developed a sense of belonging due to supportive interactions with classmates who provided physical support, encouragement, and companionship. Finally, the participants also reported positive PE experiences when they had the opportunity to show their skills (e.g., wheelchair basketball) and proficiency receiving attention and admiration by the classmates (Goodwin & Watkinson, 2000).

Similarly, positive and negative peers' behaviors where reported in the Hutzler et al. (2002) study about the impact of PE as a potential mediator for inclusion and empowerment of children with physical disabilities. Peers emerged as a mediated factor with a two-fold impact on empowerment (i.e., limiting as well as supporting). Most of the participants reported being teased, ridiculed, and excluded by their peers, which led to negative emotional reactions toward PE (e.g., afraid) and help-seeking reactions (e.g., asking PE teacher to handle the situation). A few participants identified peers as facilitators of inclusion (e.g., encouragement and help during the activities), which led to feelings of satisfaction and participation toward PE (Hutzler et al., 2002).

Finally, Goodwin (2001) also highlighted that students with physical disabilities can perceive helping interaction with peers without disabilities (e.g., peer tutoring) as positive and self-supporting (i.e., instrumental, caring, and consensual support), but also negative and self-threatening. Self-threating peer interactions were characterized by a loss of independence (i.e., help is unnecessary or interfere with independent task completion) by a threat to self-esteem (i.e., inappropriate support that made the students doubt their abilities), by incompetent help (i.e., putting the participant in potential physical risk mostly due to the lack of knowledge to help effectively), and by interfering help (e.g., getting in the way; Goodwin, 2001).

Thus from the exposed, peers' attitudes are a crucial factor for a successful inclusion of children with physical disabilities during PE classes. Placement alone does not guarantee that the children with a disability are accepted, valued, and truly included in the class. This is crucial because it is well-known that children with disabilities who are victims of social exclusion suffer the biopsychosocial consequences of prejudice (e.g., low self-esteem, depression, anxiety) and do not receive equal opportunities to reach their full potential (Gini & Pozzoli, 2009; Pittet, Berchtold, Akré, Michaud, & Surís, 2010; Vreeman & Carroll, 2007). Positive social, physical, and academic interactions between students with and without disabilities must exist side-by-side. This is why peer tutoring and cooperative learning are important strategies to enhance inclusive PE (Qi & Ha, 2012). When the children have the opportunity to enjoy equal-status relationships with peers during PE and sport, leadership and empowerment may occur. According to Hutzler and Sherrill (1999), an empowered child gains control over his or her life and assumes responsibility for changes that will lead to a healthy and active lifestyle as well as positive mental health.

DESIGNS OF EFFECTIVE DISABILITY–ABILITY AWARENESS PROGRAMS IN PE

The implementation of disability awareness programs is not a recent practice (Safran & Safran, 1986; Wilson & Alcorn, 1969). It is a common approach to try to modify the attitudes toward people with disabilities by placing people without disabilities in similar situations. The goal is to raise social awareness, providing a positive image about individuals with disabilities, and improving knowledge about disability itself. Lindsay and Edwards (2013) conducted a systematic review about disability awareness interventions in educational settings (i.e., targeting children and youth) and identified 42 papers between 1980 and 2011. The authors concluded that disability awareness interventions can effectively enhance children's attitudes, acceptance, and knowledge about people with disabilities. In particular, when a well-designed multiple components approach combining social contact (i.e., direct contact to an individual with a disability), simulation activities (e.g., to move using a wheelchair or blindfolded), and multi-media based curriculum activities (i.e., classroom activities such as presentations, videos, games and stories about people with disabilities) are used. In the PE setting, Hutzler (2003) conducted a systematic review on the attitudes toward the participation of individuals with disabilities and identified 16 awareness programs implemented between 1985 and 2003 aiming to improve the attitudes of peers and professionals in PE.

Lieberman and Houston-Wilson (2009) underlined that disability awareness programs can be structured in three levels of awareness of understanding disability-ability. In Level 1, exposure, is where children are exposed to people with disabilities through direct contact with invited speakers who have disabilities or by way of research activities in newspapers, books, and web sites with contents about people with disabilities. In addition, definitions about the different types of disabilities and specific characteristics are presented and explained to children. Focus should be given to the abilities of people with disabilities and to the common characteristics shared between children with and without disabilities. Teachers should encourage children to share their feelings and thoughts about disability and use an age-appropriate approach (e.g., language and examples used; Lieberman & Houston-Wilson, 2009). Level 2, experience, is where children are placed in situations of daily living or sport activities to experience what is like to have a disability and to become sensitive about the barriers that individuals with disabilities may face. Teachers should present activities in a comfortable, informative and no-negative-emotions (e.g., pity, regrets) environment, and encourage children to reflect, ask questions, or express their concerns about these experiences. It is highly recommended that disability awareness activities include Paralympic sports (e.g., sitting volleyball, goalball) in the general PE curriculum (Lieberman & Houston-Wilson, 2009). Level 3, ownership, is reached when attitudes and behaviors of children express acceptance toward difference and diversity and when children became advocates for the rights of individuals with disabilities in school (e.g., peer tutoring) and community settings (e.g., sighted guides, fundraisers groups). This is also true for children with disabilities. Lieberman and Houston-Wilson (2009) also argue about the importance of developing ongoing awareness activities in the course of the school year and not only during a limited period.

Additionally, Block (2007) pointed out two more strategies to include in awareness activities. First, to involve children without disabilities in group discussions about sport rules in order to make suggestions about rules' adaptations needed to include all students. When children are called to a sport rules discussion, they are more likely to demonstrate acceptable behaviors. Second, to use famous people with disabilities (e.g., actor, singer, and politician) whose importance is socially acknowledged due to their individual talents and abilities.

Inclusion of Paralympic Education in PE

One of the most recommended approaches to disability awareness programs is the use of Paralympic values and disability sport within general PE curriculum to raise social awareness and promote positive attitudes toward people with disabilities (e.g., physical disability and visual impairment). Nowadays, it is generally acknowledged that the PE curriculum has the responsibility of promoting an attitude of respect and appreciation toward individual differences and diversity among all students. Davis et al. (2012) argued about the importance of disability sport in general PE curriculum as a mean to promote equal status among all students, and, therefore inclusion. When disability sport and adapted physical activities are threaded throughout the general PE curriculum, they can be accepted as regular activities and not as an "add-on" (Stevenson, 2009). Disability sports are an opportunity for students without disabilities to experience new skills, rules, equipment, and, therefore, new learning situations that can expand their sporting interests (Davis et al., 2012).

PE teachers must present disability sport as a sport for everyone and for all abilities, which means that everyone can participate (Davis et al.,

2012). Consequently, Paralympic educational programs must encourage children's constructions of disability under the edge of the social model. Therefore, it is argued that restrictions that may occur in sport participation for individuals with disabilities are due to societal practices (i.e., attitudinal, organizational, and accessibility barriers) that negatively impact disability perceptions (Grenier, 2007). The social model perspective represents a way to mediate negative responses to differences in sport contexts (Grenier, Collins, Wright, & Kearns, 2014).

According to the International Paralympic Committee (IPC; Paralympic, n.d.), Paralympic education is rooted in the following goals: (a) to increase knowledge and awareness about Paralympic sport; (b) to create a better understanding of practical application of inclusion in PE settings; (c) to inform about the different concepts in disability sport; (d) to increase participation in disability sport for reverse-integration; (e) to facilitate the change of perception and attitude toward persons with a disability; and (f) to promote scholarly research activities and studies about Paralympic education. The IPC has gathered a group of practical suggestions and guidelines to help practitioners and researchers all over the world to implement Paralympic education activities (Paralympic, n.d.). In this context, Greece was a leading country not only in developing Paralympic educational material, but also in implementing an extra PE hour within school curriculums to introduce children to the Olympic and Paralympic values due to Athens 2004 Paralympic Games (Evaggelinou, 2006).

The Paralympic School Day (PSD), promoted by the educational committee of the International Paralympic Committee, is the educational program more developed worldwide. The PSD program aims to promote among school children the Paralympic values, educating youth about Paralympic sport, individual differences, and disability issues in a fun and playful environments. The IPC website provides a PSD manual and activity cards related with the following topics: (a) respect for sporting achievement, (b) respect and acceptance for individual differences, (c) sport as a human right, and (d) empowerment and social support in sport (IPC, n.d.).

In the past 20 years, several intervention studies using typically Paralympic and disability-sport activities in PE curriculums have been published specifically in the United States (Ellery & Rauschenbach, 2000; Grenier et al., 2014; McKay, Block, & Park, 2015; Wilhite, Mushett, Goldenberg, & Trader, 1997), Czech Republic (Liu, Kudlacek, & Jesina, 2010; Lucas, Kudlácek, Jesina, Machová, Janecka, & Wittmannová, 2006; Xafopoulos, Kudlacek, & Evaggelinou, 2009;), Greece (Panagiotou, Evanggelinou, Doulkeridou, Mouratidou, & Koidou, 2008), Israel (Hutzler, Fliess-Douer, Avraham, Reiter, & Talmor, 2007), Spain (Reina, López, Jiménez, García-Calvo, & Hutzler, 2011), and Portugal (Campos, Ferreira, & Block, 2014). The previously mentioned studies aimed to assess the impact of awareness of Paralympic educational programs on children's attitudes toward peers with a disability and will serve as reference scheme for the following sections of this chapter.

Globally, the awareness activities derived from the PSD curriculum consisted of disability simulation sport activities (e.g., Xafopoulos et al., 2009); information about Paralympic games, sports, rules, sport adaptations, sport equipment, and athletes through videos and group discussions (e.g., Panagiotou et al., 2008); structured contact with an athlete/person with disability narrating his/her life story; and group discussions (e.g., Wilhite et al., 1997) or reverse-integration demonstration events (e.g., Hutzler et al., 2007). Most authors targeted the attitudes of elementary (Ellery & Rauschenbach, 2000; Grenier et al., 2014; Lucas et al., 2006) and middle school aged children (McKay et al., 2015; Panagiotou et al., 2008; Xafopoulos et al., 2009). Other authors used mixed samples of middle and high school aged children (Campos et al., 2014; Hutzler et al., 2007; Reina et al., 2011; Wilhite et al., 1997).

The results about the attitudinal change toward inclusion in PE after an awareness Paralympic educational program are open to discussion due to a mix of positive, neutral, and negative findings. For example, McKay et al. (2015) reported positive significant changes on all attitudes subscales (e.g., inclusion subscale and sport-modification subscale) after a randomized control trial PSD program. In a qualitative approach, Grenier et al. (2014) also reported a positive impact of a disability sport program in the perceptions about disability (e.g., knowledge of the Paralympics, inclusion in a variety of sporting venues) of elementary-aged students. On the other hand, Ellery and Rauschenbach (2000) verified a decline of attitudes (e.g., increased awareness of the limitations that occur when using a wheelchair) toward the inclusion of students who use wheelchairs in PE after a group of awareness activities focusing on games and simulation activities, on a video about Paralympic games and sport, and on a presentation by a Paralympic athlete. Both Panagiotou et al. (2008) and Campos et al. (2014) reported positive significant changes on the general attitudes subscale, but neutral results on the sport-specific subscale. Liu et al. (2010) even stated a negative change of attitude toward changing sport rules for people with a disability (i.e., sport-specific attitudinal subscale) after a one-day PSD program.

As a result of a PSD awareness program, a similar research trend was reported when examining the differences in specific variables that can act as moderators of attitudes toward children with a disability (i.e., gender, previous contact to disability). Attitudes toward inclusion were reported to be more favorable in girls (e.g., Reina et al., 2011), but not always with a significant effect (e.g., Panagiotou et al., 2008). Campos et al. (2014) found significant positive perceptions in students who had had previous contact with a person with a disability in family and PE settings in all the attitudes subscales (i.e., overall, general physical education, and sport specific subscales). However, Hutzler et al. (2007) only partially confirmed these findings in behavioral and affective attitudes subscales.

This lack of agreement regarding the generalization of the findings about the impact of educational Paralympic programs on children's attitudes toward disability may be due to the high level of variation and flexibility in the planning and execution of the awareness activities (McKay, et al., 2015), as well as a poor methodological evidence base for intervention outcomes (Hutzler, 2003).

METHODOLOGICAL ISSUES AND SUGGESTIONS FOR FUTURE RESEARCH

Despite the growing research, several important issues about the design of Paralympic educational programs in the general PE curriculum need further enlightenment. One important issue is the lack of agreement on which methodological recommendations are more suitable to bring out more positive and long-lasting results. In order to identify potential gaps and suggest new research concerns, a detailed analysis about methodological issues will be conducted as follows.

Research Design

First, there is a clear lack of research using a true experimental design. We could only identify one study (McKay et al., 2015) using a randomized control and experimental group. Preventing a group of children to participate in an intervention that is expected to have positive effects on children's development raises, ethical and pedagogical issues, however. It is recommended that researchers consider in their experimental studies the possibility of conducting post-Paralympic education programs with the children who acted as the control group in the course of the investigation.

Moreover, it is possible to argue whether or not researchers guarantee the control group does not suffer contamination effects during the intervention phase when both experimental and control groups are recruited from the same school. Usually, Paralympic education programs have a major impact in schools since they extend beyond the scope of the PE setting and the children directly involved. The whole school community is aware that different activities are being conducted. Therefore, researchers must consider the possibility of matching a control group from another school.

Second, quantitative design predominates in Paralympic educational programs research. The only exception was the Grenier et al. study (2014), which used a triangulation of data from focus group interviews, fieldnotes, and documents (e.g., lesson plans) to assess the effectiveness of a disability sport unit in modulating students' perception of disability. Qualitative approaches are a resource clearly underused. Thus, the theoretical and applied context would profit with a mix methods approach, which can represent an important step to overcoming the limitations of quantitative research (e.g., access to representative samples, lack of control group). Moreover, qualitative methods could represent a valuable tool to give voice to both students, with and without disabilities, involved in Paralympic educational awareness programs, and consequently gather their perceptions on the topic. For example, information about the impact of these interventions in children with disabilities is scant. Wilhite et al. (1997) evaluated the Paralympic day in the schools model in five middle schools and three high schools and found that students with disabilities were less likely to agree that it was important for them to participate in PSD activities with their peers without disabilities. Further research should explore the children's involvement in the development of awareness activities and identify children's perceptions about how interventions make them feel and on how they are being treated by their peers.

Third, no follow-up studies have been conducted to determine if attitudes remain unchanged, decline or improve over time. For example, Reina et al. (2011) suggested a follow-up assessment one month after the completion of the intervention to identify long-term outcomes of exposure to disability. In our opinion, this is of crucial importance because today children represent the next generation of leaders, decision makers, and advocates of inclusion. To know their later attitudes toward people with disabilities can help to understand Paralympic educational programs legacy on the construction of a more inclusive society. Moreover, such programs can positively influence children and youth with disabilities about their sports choices, and therefore inspire new Paralympic athletes.

Participants Setting

Research conducted over the edge of Paralympic education in PE curriculums occurred in several European countries and in the United States, which means that interventions were developed in different cultural contexts. Consequently, participants were raised in a particular social context, spoke different languages, and were educated according to different values by their families, friends, and teachers, which may have led to different views of disabilities. Although Xafopoulos et al. (2009) found that children from different socioeducational backgrounds (i.e., United Kingdom, Canada, Korea, United States, and the Czech Republic) attending an international school were able to positively improve their attitudes toward peers with a disability after the implementation of a PSD program; no specific attitudes' analysis was made according to the cultural background. Future studies need to assess the influence of cultural background (e.g., social class, ethno-cultural status, geographic location) in the development of awareness activities.

Another important element for future programs to consider is the influence of impacting sport events (e.g., Paralympic Games) previously hosted by the countries where the awareness programs are developed. Panagiotou et al. (2008) stated that overall positive baseline attitudes of both the experimental and control group in a Paralympic education program may be due to the exposure of Greek children to the organization of the 2004 Paralympic Games in Athens and to the implementation of a Paralympic educational curriculum in Greek primary schools. Consequently, suggestions can be made about the need to conduct similar research in countries that have not organized Paralympic Games (Panagiotou et al., 2008). In this vein, we recommend a more active research activity in countries hosting the Paralympic Games as, with the exception of the Greek example, we did not found any study analyzing the impact of Paralympic Games on children's attitudes toward disability of the hosted countries.

There is a dearth of information about the influence of the type of school/class setting where the awareness intervention occurred. Not all the analyzed studies reported if the research was developed in an inclusive or noninclusive school/class setting. Grenier et al. (2014) stated that 15% of the school population where the disability sport unit was implemented had a disability, but none of the participants in the study. In a more detailed description, McKay et al. (2015) reported that 29.4% of the sample had or had had a classmate with a disability in one of their education classes, and 15.4% had or had had a classmate with a disability in one of their PE classes. Wilhite et al. (1997) only mentioned that the rate of students with physical or visual disabilities participating in their research was low. The type of setting where the students are enrolled can be a key factor in determining the type of social interactions previously developed between students with and without disabilities; for example, if students who went to "exposure disability" activities have (or not) peers with disabilities in their actual classes, or if they were exposed to disability casually. Further research could also analyze other important variables related to the school setting, such as public versus private school, class versus whole-school based, and active versus nonactive inclusive school policies.

In sum, it is possible to conclude that educational Paralympic programs should be context specific and take into consideration cultural environment, educational inclusive policies, and the type of school/class setting.

Research Variables

The major focus of Paralympic educational programs is to promote a positive attitudinal change by peers toward the inclusion of children with disabilities in PE settings. Most of the studies analyzed the general and sport-specific attitudes using Children's Attitudes Toward Inclusion in Physical Education questionnaire (CAIPE-R; Block, 1995). In this context, several attitude bias can be pointed as followed. Children can perceive social pressure to report favorable attitudes toward disability or to interact with peers with disability in structured settings when they are encouraged to do so (i.e., social desirability bias). Therefore, children may report what they think it is socially expected rather than report their actual attitudes toward disability. Besides that, attitudes are measured by self-reported instruments that can represent a barrier to accurately measure attitudes toward disability. As a result, positive attitudes toward disability may not transform into inclusive behaviors. Researchers have to apply specific measures to assess actually behavioral intentions. For example, implicit tests can be a useful method to obtain a more automatic and spontaneous measure of attitude. In these tests, researchers can obtain information about participants' attitudes by assessing reaction time. Reaction time is measured using a keyboard, joystick, microphone, or other input device, according to how the participants respond to stimulus items in different trial conditions (De Houwer, 2006).

Future research should also pay close attention to the predictor role of specific variables in shaping attitudes. For example, we could only identify one study (Campos et al., 2014) focusing on the participant's age and competitive level (i.e., no competitive, more or less competitive, and very competitive). The authors reported that younger students had significantly more positive attitudes on both the overall scale and general PE subscale. More competitive students had less positive attitudes toward inclusion of students with disabilities in PE. Clearly, more studies comparing children and youth from different age groups and competitive levels are needed to provide a gender and competitiveness-based pattern influencing attitudes.

Characteristics of the Intervention Design

Regarding the type of disability, most of the studies focused the effect of sport-specific disability awareness activities in the attitudes of peers toward the inclusion of students with a physical disability using a wheelchair (e.g., Ellery & Rauschenbach, 2000). Additionally, wheelchair basketball is the most representative sport (e.g., Campos et al., 2014). Exception was made in the study of Reina et al. (2011), who specifically measured the impact of awareness interventions on children's attitudes toward peers with visual impairment focusing on 5-a-side soccer game. Thus, generalizations of the findings are limited to a specific type of disability or sport. Further research should explore the attitudes toward the inclusion of students with different disabilities, and specifically with severe disabilities.

A second important topic is the type of program. Reina et al. (2011) compared the effects of two awareness programs (six-day versus one-day programs) on children's attitudes toward visual impairment. The six-day program consisted of a lecture and video on visual impairment and five-a-side soccer, simulation activities about visual impairment, training and competing in a five-a-side soccer game, and a sport event with soccer players with a visual impairment where the students had the opportunity to connect with athletes and get to know their life stories. The one-day program only considered the five-a-side soccer event followed by direct contact with the players. The authors concluded that both programs were effective in attitudinal change, but the six-day program had a higher effect in the attitude's cognitive domain. Similarly, Hutzler et al. (2007) compared the intervention effects of a one-hour disability simulation experience (e.g., eyes covered, sitting in a wheelchair) followed by a discussion about individuals with a disability versus the observation of a wheelchair basketball game in a reverse-integration context. The authors reported that both designs (i.e., active simulation versus demonstration events) successfully improved the children's attitudes toward disability. To our knowledge, the two previously mentioned studies were the only attempts to determine which length of time is ideal and which awareness activities are more effective in promoting attitudinal changes.

An extensive literature analysis suggests that intervention designs in Paralympic educational settings are very homogenous ranging in the duration, frequency, contact time, and type of the awareness activities. However, it appears that there is a consensus about the need to include long-term programs in the PE curriculum. Ideally, intervention should run during the whole school year.

PRACTICAL RECOMMENDATIONS
FOR PHYSICAL EDUCATION TEACHERS

Paralympic educational programs can be positive, and impacting interventions offer knowledge and increased contact with disability. However, a wrong or unprepared approach may lead to erroneous attitudes and misconceptions about disability. For example, Liu et al. (2010) reported feelings of frustration in children participating in a wheelchair basketball session. This was because the equipment used (i.e., wheelchairs) was not age appropriate and children were not able to shoot from a sitting position.

Ellery and Rauschenbach (2000) conducted a group of disability awareness activities during PE classes based on games and simulation activities, on a video presentation about the Paralympic Games and on a presentation by a wheelchair athlete about his disability experience, which lead to an attitudinal decrease. The authors did not report any structured group discussion or reflection moments about those experiences. Possibly, due to children's erroneous feelings or perceptions about disability that were improperly developed, wrongly interpreted, or clarified after the end of each activity. Ellery and Rauschenbach (2000) argued that the negative impact of the program was associated with an increased awareness of the limitations that occur when children use a wheelchair. Possible, these results occurred due to an inappropriate approach to the disability-ability concepts.

Wilhite et al. (1997) called attention to another important issue related to the use of Paralympic athletes in social contact activities. According to the previously mentioned authors, by presenting information about the Paralympics Games and athletes solely, and by including very capable and positive role models, Paralympic educational programs may lead to an excessive emphasis on elitism. Consequently, if children with disabilities are not as skillful as the models presented, students without disabilities may react with ambivalence or rejection. Therefore, equal status between children with and without disabilities is reached when role models are represented by peers with a disability (e.g., junior athletes or a child with a disability assuming a speaker role; Wilhite et al., 1997).

Therefore, in an attempt to guide PE teachers about the implementation of effective Paralympic educational programs focusing on peers' interactions, we gathered a group of practical suggestions supported on the above-mentioned rationale.

- Paralympic educational programs need to be planned and sustained over time. Take into consideration the specific needs of your students and the nature of your classroom (i.e., age, gender, disability contact, level of competitiveness, and cultural background; e.g., Lieberman & Houston-Wilson, 2009).
- Decide how you will intersperse disability sport in the PE curriculum (i.e., disability sport unit or part of a general sport unit; e.g., Davis et al., 2012).
- Prepare yourself for intervention. Improve your knowledge on disability sport (e.g., rules, equipment, and classification). Get familiar with specific skills and strategies to be taught (e.g., Davis et al., 2012).
- Work together with your students. Get all the students actively involved in the preparation of the awareness activities. Allow them to choose which activities will be part of the program and to decide

which rules modifications are needed to make activities accessible to all abilities (e.g., Davis et al., 2012).

- Put ability first. Focus should be given to what people with disabilities can do and not what they cannot do.
- Put similarities first. Focus should be given to common characteristics shared by people with and without disabilities. Despite individual differences we are all more alike than different (e.g., Lieberman & Houston-Wilson, 2009).
- Use age-appropriated language, examples and explanations to approach disability (e.g., Lieberman & Houston-Wilson, 2009).
- Be aware: Do not emphasize the "exceptional" or "superscript" discourse, and do not emphasize elite competition. Adopt a simple and factual approach to disability and disability sports that may be representative of children with disabilities (e.g., Wilhite et al., 1997).
- Contribute to the development of a specific disability sport culture among students with and without disabilities. Get students familiar with disability sport rules, athletes, major events and results at both the national and international levels.
- Simulation activities (activities of daily living and sport activities) must be carefully planned. Focus should be given to the participants' strengths and children must feel safe and comfortable (e.g., Panagiotou et al., 2008).
- Develop small-sided games with a small proportion of children without disabilities to children with disabilities. Students will benefit from more opportunities to engage in positive social interactions (e.g., Wilhite et al., 1997).
- Provide opportunities for children with disabilities to help and support children without disabilities during sport activities. Reverse-integration activities (e.g., boccia, goalball) allow a more equitable participation, and children with disabilities have the opportunity to assume leadership roles in sport and socialization.
- Use children with disabilities as mentors and role models in social exposure activities (i.e., equal-status relationship). Invite junior athletes with disabilities to perform demonstration events or act as invited speakers to share their personal story (e.g., Wilhite et al., 1997).
- Provide an equal representation of athletes participating in different sports (not only wheelchair sports) and with different abilities. Give equal focus to athletes with severe disabilities (e.g., boccia, table-cricket; e.g., Wilhite et al., 1997).
- Provide an equal representation of male and female athletes with disabilities.
- Allow students to reflect about their experiences after the end of each activity. Provide a structured setting where children are invited

to share their thoughts, emotions, doubts, and dilemmas. Teachers need to ensure that both children with and without disabilities fully understand and appreciate the importance of the intervention (e.g., Hutzler et al., 2007).

- Provide children information about competitions and games developed by clubs in the community for disability sport. Encourage children to become engaged in disability sport (e.g., sighted guide, boccia sport assistant) and to attend sport events (e.g., Davis et al., 2012).
- Never forget, PE teachers' attitudes are the key to successfully implementing Paralympic educational programs in PE curriculum.

REFERENCES

Block, M. E. (1995). Development and validation of the Children's Attitudes Toward Integrated Physical Education–Revised (CAIPE-R) inventory. *Adapted Physical Activity Quarterly, 12*(1), 60–77.

Block, M. E. (2007). *A teacher's guide to including students with disabilities in general physical education* (3rd ed.). Baltimore, MD: Paul H. Brookes Publishing Co.

Campos, M., Ferreira, J., & Block, M. (2014). Influence of an awareness program on Portuguese middle and high school students' perceptions of peers with disabilities. *Psychological Reports, 115*(3), 897–912. doi: 10.2466/11.15.PR0115 c26z7

Davis, R., Rocco-Dillon, S., Grenier, M., Martinez, D., & Aenchbacker, A. (2012). Implementing disability sports in the general physical education curriculum: A theory to practice approach. *Journal of Physical Education, Recreation & Dance, 83*(5), 35–41. doi:10.1080/07303084.2012.10598778

De Houwer, J. (2006). What are implicit measures and why are using them? In R. W. H. J. Wiers and A. W. Stacey (Eds.), *Handbook of implicit cognition and addiction* (pp. 11–28). Thousand Oaks, CA: SAGE.

Ellery, P. J., & Rauschenbach, J. (2000). Impact of disability awareness activities on nondisabled student attitudes toward integrated physical education with students who use wheelchairs. *Research Quarterly for Exercise and Sport, 71* (Suppl. 1), A 106.

Ellis, D. N., Wright, M., & Cronis, T. G. (1996). A description of the instructional and social interactions of students with mental retardation in regular physical education settings. *Education and Training in Mental Retardation and Developmental Disabilities, 31*(3), 235–242.

Evaggelinou, C. (2006). *Creating a school for all in Greece: The model of Paralympic education.* Proceedings of the 8th European Conference of Adapted Physical Activity. Palacky University, Olomuc, Czech Republic. Retrieved January 6, 2015, from http://www.eufapa.eu/index.php/eucapa/proceedings/eucapa-2006.html

Gini, G., & Pozzoli, T. (2009). Association between bullying and psychosomatic problems: A meta-analysis. *Pediatrics, 123*(3), 1059–1065. doi: 10.1542/peds .2008-1215

Goodwin, D. L. (2001). The meaning of help in PE: Perceptions of students with physical disabilities. *Adapted Physical Activity Quarterly, 18*(3), 289–303.

Goodwin, D. L., & Watkinson, E. J. (2000). Inclusive physical education from the perspective of students with physical disabilities. *Adapted Physical Activity Quarterly, 17*(2), 144–160.

Grenier, M. (2007). Inclusion in physical education: From the medical model to social constructionism. *Quest, 59*(3), 298–310. doi: 10.1080/00336297.2007.10483554

Grenier, M., Collins, K., Wright, S., & Kearns, C. (2014). Perceptions of a disability sport unit in general physical education. *Adapted Physical Activity Quarterly, 31*(1), 49–66. doi: http://dx.doi.org/10.1123/APAQ.2013-0006

Hutzler, Y. (2003). Attitudes toward the participation of individuals with disabilities in physical activity: A review. *Quest, 55*(4), 347–373. doi: 10.1080/00336297.2003.10491809

Hutzler, Y., & Sherrill, C. (1999). Disability, physical activity, psychological well-being and empowerment: A life-span perspective. In R. Lidor & M. Bar-Eli (Eds.), *Sport psychology: Linking theory and practice* (pp. 281–300). Morgantown, WV: Fitness Information Technology.

Hutzler, Y., Fliess-Douer, O., Avraham, A., Reiter, S., & Talmor, R. (2007). Effects of short-term awareness interventions on children's attitudes toward peers with a disability. *International Journal of Rehabilitation Research, 30*(2), 159–161.

Hutzler, Y., Fliess-Douer, O., Chacham, A., & Van den Auweele, Y. (2002). Perspectives of children with physical disabilities on inclusion and empowerment: Supporting and limiting factors. *Adapted Physical Activity Quarterly, 19*(2), 300–317.

Lieberman, L. J., & Houston-Wilson, C. (2009). *Strategies for inclusion: A handbook for physical educators* (2nd ed.). Champaign, IL: Human Kinetics.

Lieberman, L. J., James, A. R., & Ludwa, N. (2004). The impact of inclusion in general physical education for all students. *Journal of Physical Education, Recreation & Dance, 75*(5), 37–41.

Lindsay, S., & Edwards, A. (2013). A systematic review of disability awareness interventions for children and youth. *Disability and Rehabilitation, 35*(8), 623–646.

Liu, Y., Kudlacek, Y., & Jesina, O. (2010). The influence of Paralympic school day on children's attitudes toward people with disabilities. *Acta Universitatis Palackianae Olomucensis. Gymnica, 40*(2), 63–69.

Lucas, S., Kudláček, M., Jesina, O., Machová, L., Janecka, Z., & Wittmannová, J. (2006). Effect of an intervention program on attitudes of elementary school children toward the inclusion of children with a disability. *Acta Facultatis Educationis Physicae Universitatis Comenianae, 46*, 77–85.

Mauerber-DeCastro, E. (2005). *Actividade física adaptada* [Adapted physical activity] (1st ed.). Ribeirão Preto, São Paulo, Brazil: Tecmedd Editora.

McKay, C., Block, M., & Park, J. Y. (2015). The impact of Paralympic school day on student attitudes toward inclusion in physical education. *Adapted Physical Activity Quarterly, 32*(4), 331–348. Retrieved from http://dx.doi.org/10.1123/APAQ.2015-0045

Morley, D., Bailey, R., Tan, J., & Cooke, B. (2005). Inclusive physical education: Teachers' views of including pupils with special educational needs and/or disabilities in physical education. *European Physical Education Review, 2*(2), 84–107. doi: 10.1177/1356336X05049826

Panagiotou, A., Evanggelinou, C., Doulkeridou, A., Mouratidou, K., & Koidou, E. (2008). Attitudes of 5th and 6th grade Greek students toward the inclusion of children with disabilities in physical education classes after a Paralympic education program. *European Journal of Adapted Physical Activity, 1*(2), 31–43.

Paralympic Movement. (n.d.). *The IPC—What we do: Paralympic school day.* Retrieved January 5, 2015, from http://www.Paralympic.org/the-ipc/Paralympic-school -day

Pittet, I., Berchtold, A., Akré, C., Michaud, P. A, & Surís, J. C. (2010). Are adolescents with chronic conditions particularly at risk for bullying? *Archives of Disease in Childhood, 95*, 711–716. doi:10.1136/adc.2008.146571 711

Place, K., & Hodge, S. R. (2001). Social inclusion of students with physical disabilities in general physical education: A behavioral analysis. *Adapted Physical Activity Quarterly, 18*(4), 389–404.

Qi, J., & Ha, A. S. (2012). Inclusion in physical education: A review of literature. *International Journal of Disability, Development and Education, 59*(3), 257–281. doi:10.1080/1034912X.2012.697737

Reina, R., López, V., Jiménez, M., García-Calvo, T., & Hutzler, Y. (2011). Effects of awareness interventions on children's attitudes toward peers with a visual impairment. *International Journal of Rehabilitation Research, 34*(3), 235–242. doi: 10.1097/MR R.0b013e3283487f49

Safran, S. P., & Safran, J. S. (1986). Videotaped presentations by blind speakers as attitudinal change agents. *Rehabilitation Counseling Bulletin, 29*(4), 251–257.

Stevenson, P. (2009). The pedagogy of inclusive youth sport: Working toward real solutions. In H. Fitzgerald (Ed.), *Disability and youth sport* (pp. 145–131). London, England: Routledge.

United Nations Educational, Scientific and Cultural Organization. (2008). *Conclusions and recommendations of the 48th session of the International Conference on Education* (IBE document ED/BIE/CONFINTED48/5).Geneva, Switzerland.

Vreeman, R. C., & Carroll, A. E. (2007). A systematic review of school-based interventions to prevent bullying. *Archives of Pediatrics and Adolescent Medicine, 161*(1), 78–88. doi:10.1001/archpedi.161.1.78

Wilhite, B., Mushett, C. A., Goldenberg, L., & Trader, B. R. (1997). Promoting inclusive sport and leisure participation: Evaluation of the Paralympic day in the schools model. *Adapted Physical Activity Quarterly, 14*(2), 131–146.

Wilson, E. D., & Alcorn, D. (1969). Disability simulation and development of attitudes toward the exceptional. *The Journal of Special Education, 3*(3), 303–307.

Xafopoulos, G., Kudlacek, M., & Evaggelinou, C. (2009). Effect of the intervention program "Paralympic School Day" on attitudes of children attending international school toward inclusion of students with disabilities. *Acta Universitatis Palackianae Olomucensis. Gymnica, 39*(4), 63–71.

CHAPTER 6

STRATEGIES TO MAXIMIZE SOCIAL PARTICIPATION AND INCLUSION OF STUDENTS WITH DISABILITIES IN PHYSICAL EDUCATION

Martin E. Block
University of Virginia

Michelle Grenier
University of New Hampshire

Yeshayahu "Shayke" Hutzler
Academic College at Wingate

Inclusion of students with disabilities in public schools is understood as a comprehensive, schoolwide effort that encourages teachers to provide high expectations for all students and ensures flexible groupings in the development of appropriate curricula (Villa & Thousand, 2000). It is a philosophy that supports diversity through the active participation of students within

Inclusive Physical Activities, pages 109–132
Copyright © 2017 by Information Age Publishing

the school culture (Kugelmass, 2004). At the heart of inclusionary philosophy is the assumption that students with a wide range of abilities and skills can contribute to classroom learning. Inclusionary scholars call for an ongoing analysis of the ways in which teachers create and sustain practices to confront the inequities within the school culture that marginalize students with disabilities.

As a result of years of legislation, advocacy, and support from international organizations, including the United Nations, the practice of including children with disabilities in general education classrooms is becoming an international movement (Pecora, Whittaker, Maluccio, & Barth, 2012). For example, the right for children with disabilities to be included in general physical education (as well as sport, recreation, and play activities) has been mandated in Article 30 of the International Convention on Rights for Persons with Disability (CRPD; United Nations, 2006). More recently, Article 1.3 of the revised International Charter of Physical Education (UNESCO, 2015) states, "Inclusive, adapted and safe opportunities to participate in physical education, physical activity and sport must be available to all human beings, notably children of preschool age, women and girls, the aged, persons with disabilities and indigenous people" (p. 2).

Unfortunately, research via interviews with students with disabilities who participated in inclusive general physical education classes has yielded mixed results, with studies finding both positives (e.g., skill improvement, feelings of acceptance, and opportunities to make friends) and negatives (e.g., negative feelings, feeling different, social isolation and being excluded by peers, and not being accommodated by physical educators) (Asbjørnslett & Hemmingsson, 2008 [Norway]; Blinde & McCallister, 1998 [United States]; Bredahl, 2013 [Norway]; Fitzgerald, 2005 [United Kingdom]; Fitzgerald & Stride, 2012 [United Kingdom]; Goodwin & Watkinson, 2000 [Canada]; Hutzler, Fliess, Chacham, & van den Auweele, 2002 [Israel]; and Spencer-Cavaliere & Watkinson, 2010 [Canada]).

These observations raise the question of what can be done to help children with disabilities have a more positive experience in general physical education. The purpose of this chapter is to provide evidence-based practices that can promote social acceptance and social inclusion of children with disabilities in general physical education. Three main suggestions will be presented. First, suggestions will be presented for preparing peers without disabilities to communicate, understand, accept, and appreciate classmates with disabilities. Two international disability awareness programs will be presented along with research that supports the use of these programs: Paralympics School Day created by the International Paralympics and SO Get Into It created by Special Olympics International to help peers better. In addition, peer tutoring will be presented as another model for fostering interactions between students with and without disabilities. Second, suggestions to help GPE teachers improve self-esteem and develop skills needed to include students will be presented including new ways to prepare future physical education teachers and practicing physical education teachers. Finally, models to modify physical education activities to allow children with disabilities to participate will be presented including differentiation skills and the inclusion spectrum.

PREPARING PEERS WITHOUT DISABILITIES: DISABILITY AWARENESS AND PEER TUTORING

Disability Awareness

Many have noted the critical role that peers without disabilities play in the experiences of students with disabilities (Block, Klavina, & McKay, 2016; Hutzler, 2003; Tripp, French, & Sherrill, 1995). As noted earlier, peer rejection can limit social learning opportunities and can negatively impact the experience of students with disabilities. In fact, peers without disabilities were found to be the most significant support system for students with disabilities in a study by Hutzler, Fliess, Chacham, and Van den Auweele (2002). Peer education, or preparing peers without disabilities for the inclusion of peers with disabilities, has been suggested as one key factor in a successful inclusion practice (Block et al., 2016; Lieberman & Houston-Wilson, 2009). The manner in which students without disabilities are prepared for the inclusion of their peers with disabilities is essential. Blinde and McCallister (1998) emphasized that sensitivity and empathy toward the needs of others should be covered. In addition, Murata, Hodge, and Little (2000) emphasized that diversity appreciation and disability awareness should be addressed. Block, Klavina, and McKay (2016) note that specific training is needed for children without disabilities in order for them to interact with peers with disabilities in a positive and age-appropriate manner.

Conceptualizing disability in a social, rather than a medicalized, view has been endorsed by advocates of those with disabilities (Evans, 2004; Oliver, 1990). The social model of disability advances the notion that restriction in sport and physical activity is not simply a result of individual impairment, but the societal practices that limit those with disabilities (Fitzgerald, 2006; Grenier, 2007). Wilhite, Mushett, Goldenberg, and Trader (1997) emphasize the ability of individuals with disabilities can result in positive and practical outcomes for students taking part in awareness education training activities.

Disability awareness programs are one means for preparing peers without disabilities for inclusion and can be effective in educating children about and positively influencing attitudes toward people with disabilities (Lindsay & Edwards, 2013). There are several key components of effective disability awareness programs. Contact with a person with a disability and providing information are two critical factors in most disability awareness programs (IPC, 2006; McKay, Block, & Park, 2015; Peck, Donaldson, & Pezzoli, 1990; Special Olympics, n.d.). In the physical education setting, recent research on intervention activities indicates that combining structured contact, knowledge acquisition, and awareness activities constitute an effective method for changing attitudes (Liu et al., 2010; McKay et al., 2015; Panagiotou et al., 2008; Reina, Lopez, Jimenez, Garcia-Calvo & Hutzler, 2011; Xafopoulos et al., 2009).

Research supports the use of disability awareness programs to promote positive attitudes of children without disabilities toward peers with disabilities (e.g., Grenier, Collins, Wright, & Kearns, 2014; Lindsay & Edwards, 2013; Kalyvas & Reid, 2003; McKay et al., 2015; Papaioannou, Evaggelinou, Barkoukis, & Block, 2013). Several authors have suggested ways to help peers without disabilities learn how to view peers with disabilities in a positive manner, become more knowledgeable about disability to avoid stereotypes, and learn how to interact with peers with disabilities during general physical education. (e.g., Auxter, Pyfer, Zittel & Roth, 2010; Block et al., 2016; Getskow & Konczal, 1996; Lieberman & Houston-Wilson, 2009). Suggestions include guest speakers who have disabilities (ideally athletes), playing disability sports to help students rethink the concept of ability through the challenges required for participation, discussion of the concept of "handicapping" to make sports fair, lead a discussion on differences and similarities between those with and without disabilities, talk about and show video clips of famous people (ideally athletes) who have disabilities, explain how to interact with specific students with disabilities, and finally provide ongoing information and encouragement to peers without disabilities.

A disability awareness program that includes many of the components of these programs is the Paralympic School Day (PSD) published by the International Paralympic Committee (IPC, 2006). The program was designed by specialists in Paralympic sport, pedagogy, and disability to create an educational opportunity for schools to increase awareness about and understanding of disability and disability sport. Similar to the components of Allport's (1954) contact theory, PSD is founded on the overall belief that youth without disability will increase their awareness and understanding when they are informed about the lives and actions of persons with a disability, experiencing a realistic and holistic portrayal of disability sport and athletes who participate in disability sport (IPC, 2006). Goals of PSD include increasing knowledge and awareness of Paralympic sport, becoming informed about the different concepts in disability sports, and facilitating the change of perception and attitude toward persons with a disability (http://www.paralympic.org/TheIPC/WWD/Education).

The impact the PSD awareness program has on attitude change has been measured in three published studies conducted in Europe (Liu, Kudlacek, &

Jesina, 2010; Panagiotou, Evaggelinou, Doulkeridou, Mouratidou, & Koidou, 2008; Xafopoulos, Kudlacek, & Evaggelinou, 2009) and most recently in a study in the United States (McKay et al., 2015). These studies have measured the attitudes of peers without disabilities toward the inclusion of peers with disabilities in physical education. Results were mixed, as attitudes toward inclusion showed positive changes (Liu et al., 2010; McKay et al., 2015; Panagiotou et al., 2008; Xafopoulos et al., 2009) as a result of PSD, but not always at a significant level. In some cases, attitudes toward inclusion showed positive change, but attitudes toward modifying sport rules did not show change (Panagiotou et al., 2008; Xafopoulos et al., 2009) or tended to decrease (Liu et al., 2010). The impact gender had on attitude change was also mixed, as attitudes were shown to be more positive in females as a result of the PSD awareness intervention (Xafopoulos et al., 2009), yet gender differences in attitude were not found to be significant in the McKay et al. (2015), Panagiotou et al. (2008), or the Liu et al. (2010) studies.

Another disability awareness program that includes many of the key concepts of a quality disability awareness program is Special Olympics–Get Into It. Get Into It is an interactive, age-appropriate, service-learning curriculum that is designed to advance student's civic knowledge and skill development, promote acceptance and understanding of people's differences to motivate them to become advocates for and with all people. The program provides resources that can be used by educators across all subject areas in order to incorporate character education into their classrooms, and help implement meaningful service-learning projects that can have a lasting impact among students (Myśliwiec & Damentko, 2015; Special Olympics, n.d.). Specific goals of the program are presented herein. Note that since Special Olympics is an organization dedicated to sports for individuals with ID, the goals of the program specify people with intellectual disabilities. However, the concepts could be applied to disability awareness programs for other disability groups.

1. Educate, motivate, and activate young people to better understand the issue of diversity as it relates to people with intellectual disabilities
2. Demonstrate the similarities and differences among people with and without intellectual disabilities
3. Promote better understanding and acceptance of individuals with intellectual disabilities
4. Foster participation in Special Olympics
5. Motivate sustainable change among students and activate them as champions of an important social movement

The web-based program includes interactive activities, inspiring athlete stories, tools for antibulling/teasing campaigns, and experiential role-play activities all with a service-learning focus. Types of activities include self-reflecting on their own attitudes and behaviors toward those with intellectual disabilities, evaluating levels of tolerance and inclusion within their school and community, developing and delivering messages of support to athletes, creating a product that models inclusion and acceptance, and involvement as a coach, playing partner, or fan in the Special Olympics movement (Special Olympics, n.d.).

Peer Tutoring

Peer tutoring is another way to foster interactions between peers with and without disabilities. Peer tutoring involves students without disabilities providing one-to-one instruction and increased practice and reinforcement to students with disabilities rather than relying only on assistant teacher or paraprofessional assistance (Lieberman & Houston-Wilson, 2009). Peer tutoring has been successfully applied in inclusive physical education settings with students with mild and moderate disabilities (e.g., DePaepe, 1985; Houston-Wilson Dunn, van der Mars, & McCubbin 1997; Lieberman Newcomer, McCubbin, & Dalrymple, 1997; Lieberman, Dunn, van der Mars, & McCubbin, 2000; Webster, 1987), and also with students with severe and multiple disabilities (Klavina & Block, 2008). Many argue that peers provide more natural supports, increase social interactions and communication skills, and maintain or enhance students' academic engagement (Block et al., 2016; Lieberman & Houston Wilson, 2009).

There are different types of peer tutoring the teacher can use.

One-on-one peer tutoring is the most commonly used in physical education settings. With one-on-one tutoring a peer is selected to provide support to a student with a disability. In many cases multiple peers are selected and take turns supporting the student with a disability. Support includes providing extra instructions, ensuring increased practice, and providing increased reinforcement/feedback on progress (Klavina & Block, 2008). In addition to providing support on skill development, one-on-one tutoring provides an opportunity for more social interactions for a student with disabilities with different classmates. It also should be noted that some research suggests that serving as a peer tutor improves academic performance of students who have problems paying attention, problems learning and who are at risk or who their parents and teachers worry will start to fail in school (Kalkowski, 2001).

Classwide peer tutoring (CWPT) was developed by special education professionals in the early 1980s in order to support the inclusion of students with diverse abilities within the general education setting (Greenwood, Maheady, & Delaquadri, 2002). In CWPT all students in the class are paired up and work together in tutor-tutee dyads. The tutor demonstrates the skill and provides feedback to the tutee, or assists in accomplishing the task. Students then change roles at some point during the session (based on a set time or teacher's instruction). Students with mild or moderate disabilities can take on the role of tutor independently or with support from a peer. Ayvazo and Ward (2010) and Ward and Ayvazo (2006) presented successful CWPT in a physical education setting teaching striking and catching skills with students with autism spectrum disorder. Similarly, Klavina, Jerlinder, Kristén, Hammar, & Soulie (2013) implemented a type of CWPT approach across three elementary school classes in Sweden involving 42 students, including four students with moderate and mild disabilities. Teachers reported that students gained knowledge about disability and learned positive peer perception, students stated that they had become a better friend and had made a great effort to interact with and compliment peers with disabilities.

Small group tutoring (four to six students per group) is typically a mix of students with and without disabilities. Groups are formed based on skill work, such as a few groups practicing basketball skills while other groups participate in fitness activities. A child without a disability could be the leader of a small group and make sure all members of the group are active and participating successfully and appropriately. Or one child in the group could be assigned to help the child with a disability to participate successfully and appropriately with the group. Small group peer tutoring also increases opportunities for social interactions with classmates and helps the student with a disability feel belonging to the group or being part of the team. Small group peer tutoring is recommended when including a student with severe and multiple disabilities. Klavina and Block (2008) indicated that peer tutoring intervention promoted physical and social affiliation of the student with severe and multiple disabilities with a group of classmates including trained tutors as well as nontutors. Also, peer tutors felt confident and comfortable being in a group rather than one-on-one with the peer, who might have multiple health and behavior issues.

In cross-age peer tutoring, older students from another class or another school come to physical education to provide support to a student with a disability. Studies in physical education using cross-aged peer tutors suggest that these tutors needed extra time to get adjusted to the new class setting and adjust to their roles (Lieberman et al., 2000). Student pairings may include a variety of combinations such as high school students without disabilities helping elementary students with disabilities, or older elementary students without disabilities with younger elementary students with disabilities. Tutors become models of appropriate skill performance, encouraging social interaction, and/or facilitating the academic success of a tutee (Miller, Miller, & Armentrout, 1995). Cross-age tutoring can enhance self-esteem in the tutors who provide individualized instruction to tutees, result in friendly relationships outside class, and an improved school atmosphere (Kalkowski, 2001). Some schools allow peer tutoring to count toward required community service. Other schools have peer tutoring clubs in which students go through training and meet on a regular basis to discuss tutoring. One advantage is that older peers often are more reliable and focused than same-age classmates, and older peers often can handle more responsibility. In addition, some students with disabilities behave better with an older peer rather than a classmate. However, it may be difficult to free up older students from their academic classes to come and help in physical education.

Regardless of the model used, training peer tutors is critical for success (Klavina & Block, 2008; Lieberman & Houston-Wilson, 2009). Training can be formal or informal and part of the general physical education class. Training can take several days or can be conducted in two or three general physical education class sessions. Training program should include disability awareness concepts (i.e., information about the disability, improving attitudes toward and acceptance of those with disabilities), and instructional strategies on how to use cues and provide prompts, feedback, and physical assistance (Block et al. 2016; Houston-Wilson, et al., 1997; Lieberman et al., 1997, 2000). The teacher is vitally important in helping maintain peers' confidence and enjoyment, especially when tutoring a tutee with severe and multiple disabilities (Cole, 1988; Logan et al., 1998). Also, immediate and ongoing feedback should be provided to individual peer tutors during or after PE sessions to correct interaction behaviors and improve the ways they provide teaching instructions during peer tutoring.

A distinction should be made between peer tutors who provide instruction and peer mentors who mediate behavior through prompting and cueing due to the difficulty assessing nonverbal communication (Grenier & Miller, 2015). This is particularly relevant to students with severe disabilities. Peer mentors function in a more supportive role to facilitate communicative behaviors through the use of scripts and planned behavioral sequences. It is also important to recognize that mentoring relationships are reciprocal in nature and both parties receive benefits from the development of the relationship (Jacobi, 1991; Strayhorn & Terrell, 2007). Peer mentors also provide a unique experience for both the mentor and mentee because of the nature of these relationships (Colvin & Ashman, 2010). As Goodwin (2008) points out, positive perceptions of help in physical education for students with severe disabilities are dependent on whether or not the students personally retain a sense of autonomy and independence. If students perceive assistance to be unequal, this may potentially deprive the student of a sense of autonomy (see Table 6.1 for a summary of programs to prepare peers).

TABLE 6.1 Strategies to Prepare Peers			
	Key Reference	Pros/con	Empirical Support
Paralympics School Day Created by IPC to create an educational opportunity for schools to increase awareness about and understanding of disability and disability sport.	IPC, 2006; McKay et al., 2015; Liu, Kudlacek, & Jesina, 2010	Nice introduction to Paralympics; different versions for different ages; research shows program improves attitudes. Does take a lot of organization to implement	Yes
SO Get Into It is an interactive service-learning curriculum designed to advance student's civic knowledge and skill development, promote acceptance and understanding of people's differences to motivate them to become advocates for and together with all people.	Myśliwiec & Damentko, 2015; Special Olympics, n.d.	Complete program with online resources for educators; different versions for different ages; Can be implemented in health education and civics classes	No
Peer tutoring Use of peers to support and teach children with disabilities in general physical education settings.	Block et al., 2016; Klavina & Block, 2008; Lieberman & Houston-Wilson, 2009	Relatively simple way to foster interactions between children with and without disabilities; training peer tutor	Yes

PREPARING GENERAL PHYSICAL EDUCATORS

Although there are many benefits to inclusion, there also are many challenges faced by physical educators in providing students with disabilities access to the general physical education curriculum. While mostly supporting the inclusion principle in general, physical education teachers have voiced many concerns in their ability to actually include students safely and successfully in their programs (Ammah & Hodge, 2005; Hardin, 2005; Hodge, Ammah, Casebolt, Lamaster, & O'Sullivan, 2004; Obrusnikova, 2008; Qi & Ha, 2012). Most often cited concerns included the lack of in-service training, inadequate preparation, inadequate support, and the type and severity of the disabilities of students, which vary across disabilities. For example, in a study in Britain, physical education teachers said it was more difficult to teach students with behavioral disorders than children with other disabilities (Morley, Bailey, Tan, & Cooke, 2005), while a study in the United

States found the level of severity influenced teachers' attitudes toward inclusion (Block & Rizzo, 1995). Teachers also reported concerns that children with disabilities may not meet their educational needs in an inclusive class (Smith & Green, 2004), and expressed lower expectations of students with disabilities, which results in overall lower challenge and participation (Hutzler, Zamir, & Fliess-Douer, 2004). General physical education teachers' negative perceptions toward inclusion and their lack of understanding in how to create an accommodating, welcoming environment for students with disabilities can impact the overall class climate, contribute to negative peer attitudes, and foster social isolation of students with disabilities (Block & Obrusnikova, 2007; Goodwin & Watkinson, 2000; Place & Hodge, 2001).

Infusion Approach to Teacher Preparation

One of the biggest complaints voiced by general physical education teachers was that they did not feel their educational training prepared them to make adaptations and changes to accommodate students with disabilities into their programs (Ammah & Hodge, 2005; Hardin, 2005; LaMaster, Gall, Kinchin, & Siedentop, 1998; Lienert, Sherrill, & Myers, 2001). The Infusion approach represents a potentially more comprehensive approach for preparing teachers toward inclusion (DePauw & Goc Karp, 1994a, 1994b). Within this approach, knowledge of disability and appropriate methods for addressing these disabilities during curricular implementation are implemented (or infused) across and throughout the physical education teacher education curriculum. This approach occurs at three different levels: (a) adding information about individuals with disabilities to a course, (b) integrating the inclusion context within the assessment of student and faculty knowledge, and (c) integrating disability issues as a natural component of each course. A similar approach has been recommended more recently for enhancing mental health literacy among educators in general (Whitley, Smith, & Vaillancourt, 2013). However, no report on any practical implementation of the infusion approach exists, so its practicability is questionable.

A more systematical approach for promoting inclusion within the academic framework of physical education teacher preparation has been proposed by Jin, Yun, and Wegis (2013), who developed a theory-based approach for restructuring the PE teacher education curriculum. This model follows the transtheoretical model of change (TTM) developed by Prochaska and DiClemente (1983). The TTM-based PE teacher education curriculum was described as a three-stage process addressing various processes of change toward inclusion across lecture-focused courses, lectures combined with practicum, and internship focused practice. The authors of this approach have described how both cognitive and behavioral strategies of the TTM could be utilized. Again, no information is available about the utility of this approach.

Practical Experiences

There have been recommendations and efforts to add more practical experiences and content to physical education teacher preparation programs (e.g., Block, 2015; Folsom-Meek, Nearing, Grotheluschen, & Krampf, 1999; Rizzo & Vispoel, 1992). Participation in practical experiences has been shown to be an important contributor in enhancing inclusion knowledge and skills (e.g., Hodge, Davis, Woodward, & Sherrill, 2002; Hodge, Tannehill, & Kluge, 2003; Taliaferro, Hammond, & Wyant, 2015). For example, physical education majors who participated in a nine-week, on-campus physical education practicum with students with disabilities reported that they felt more comfortable around students with disabilities and had a more favorable attitude toward teaching and interacting with students with disabilities (Hodge, Tannehill, & Kluge, 2003). However, in certain cases, off-campus practicum sessions occurring within the "real" school context (e.g., observing at a public school) did not improve attitudes (Folsum-Meek et al., 1999; Hodge & Jansma, 1999). One reason for this may be limited hands-on opportunities or serving as an assistant as opposed to being the leader teacher, which in both cases reduces the degree of success necessary for developing self-efficacy.

Decision-Making Approach

Another method for enhancing teachers' exposure within an inclusionary setting has been recommended by Hutzler and Bar-Eli (2013) within a judgment and decision-making approach. These authors described group sessions where participants are reviewing case vignettes and proposing and discussing various reaction options to these vignettes. Allowing respondents to rate different choices within the vignettes and discuss those ratings and their potential reasons in a focus group could be helpful in (a) changing stereotyped attitudes, and (b) providing the "how to" required while adapting for inclusion. Sharing experiences and entering into debates with regard to individuals' strengths and weaknesses relative to particular tasks, as well as providing personal stories and insiders' perspectives on the similar tasks among focus groups participants, should be encouraged and is likely to balance the emotional bias and enhance informed decision making.

Use of Web-Based Instruction

Another recent strategy is providing web-based materials and instruction as a supplement to traditional preservice teacher training programs, and to provide in-service support to practicing physical educators. Materials are provided as information modules or episodes, videos, tips, TED-talks and other formats. Various resources are available to facilitate web-based instruction such as Theinclusionclub.com, a web-based portal of resources; PECentral.com; and Adaptip.com. Web-based learning has many benefits, particularly for in-service physical educators, including greater flexibility than traditional face-to-face teaching (the learner can adapt online course work to fit their schedules and preferences), the ability to focus on small concepts such as using visual supports for children with autism or implementing a peer tutoring program, being able to share and learn from others through discussion boards, the ability of the instructor to continually update and refine the content in real time, and access to a university professor or practicing adapted physical educator who facilitates the course (Healy, Judge, & Block, 2014; Lloyd & Duncan-Howell, 2010).

Two recent adapted physical education studies have demonstrated the positive effects of web-based learning. Kwon (2015) examined the effects of an e-learning supplement on self-efficacy and content knowledge of preservice physical educators related to including students with intellectual disabilities. Participants were divided into two groups: one group received the e-learning supplement, and the other group received traditional handouts with information. Results found that preservice teachers' perceived self-efficacy improved after taking the e-learning supplement; however, there was no significant difference in the level of content knowledge. In addition, those taking the e-learning supplement showed significantly higher satisfaction levels than the traditional group did in usability and content quality. In a similar study, Healy (2015), using a randomized control-group model, examined the effectiveness of a web-based short course designed to teach in-service physical educators how to implement a peer tutoring program in their classes. Results found that those who participated in the web-based course had a significant increase in knowledge related to peer tutoring compared to those who did not take the course. In addition, almost 70% of participants in the web-based course completed all or part of the activities needed to implement a peer tutoring program in their physical education class. More research is needed, but results of these preliminary studies suggest web-based instruction has potential with both preservice and in-service physical educators (see Table 6.2 for a summary of models for preparing physical educators).

TABLE 6.2 Strategies to Prepare Physical Educators			
	Key Reference	Pros/con	Empirical Support
Infusion Infuse concepts of disabilities throughout teacher education curriculum	DePauw, Goc, & Karp, 1994a; 1994b	Ensures future PE teachers have learned about disability throughout the curriculum; difficult to implement	Limited
Practicum/Internships Campus or off-campus, hands-on experiences working with children with disabilities in PE/ movement settings	Hodge, Davis, Woodward, & Sherrill, 2002; Hodge, Tannehill, & Kluge, 2003; Taliaferro, Hammond, & Wyant, 2015	Hands on experiences can help future PE teachers feel more comfortable and understand how to teach children with disabilities; could be difficult to create	Yes
Decision Making Approach Group sessions where participants review case vignettes, propose and discuss various reaction options to these vignettes.	Hutzler & Bar-Eli, 2013	Can promote thinking and problem solving; present real-life vignettes; theoretical and not sure if it translates to teaching	No
Web-based modules Presentation of strategies to include children with disabilities in general PE via videos and online discussions	Healy, Judge, & Block, 2015; Lloyd & Duncan-Howell, 2010	Allows infusion of disability in practical PE courses (e.g., team sports class). Can be difficult to create modules	Limited

MODELS TO MODIFY PHYSICAL EDUCATION

Even when physical education teachers have not acquired comprehensive knowledge and skills to cope with the inclusion of students with disability in their classes, it is still possible for them to utilize a variety of nonspecific, but effective, educational practices. When teachers consider how inclusion impacts students with disabilities, it is best to examine the ways in which the individual student thinks, moves, behaves, and communicates within the environment. Equally as important is an understanding of the barriers and societal structures that limit participation. The remaining portion of this paper describes several principles and strategies that emphasize how the physical and social environment can be structured to create opportunities for skill development, as well social engagement and the valued expression of physical activity for all students, including those with disabilities.

Universal Design

Navigating the diversity of student learning can be complex. While many physical educators are experienced at adapting and accommodating for their students, there remain several instructional strategies that may be utilized. Although universal design is not specifically a teaching strategy, it is a planning approach that considers how the learning environment can be used by as many students as possible (Scott, McGuire, & Shaw, 2001). Building on this architectural principle, UDL is a strategy for eliminating barriers to students' learning and participation. Within the physical education setting, universal design is achieved by a careful consideration of the teaching practices in order to meet every child. First and foremost it requires teachers to plan for all their students by reflecting on methods of instruction equipment, the task, and the way the student responds to his or her environment (Moriarty, 2007; Orr & Bachman Hamming, 2009). For example, a universal design for serving in a volleyball game would allow all children to choose a ball to serve and distance to stand. This way the accommodation is not just of the child with a disability, but a universal design for all students allowing more skilled students to stand farther away and use regulation volleyballs and less skilled students to use lighter, larger balls and stand closer to the net.

The Inclusion Spectrum

The inclusion spectrum is another teaching strategy for considering ways to address the diverse learning needs in physical education (Black & Williamson, 2011). As a general rule, physical educators typically consider the use of adaptations and accommodations when teaching students with disabilities. An adaptation is a change in spatial needs, instructional methods or the task requirements. An accommodation can also include changes to equipment, but the fundamental premise underlying an accommodation is best appreciated in how the task is structured to accommodate the individual's particular learning needs in relation to the overall goals of the class. The spectrum utilizes an inclusive design that enables teachers to understand, within context, how to address the learning needs of each student using both adaptation and accommodation as tools for instructional delivery. A unique facet of the inclusion spectrum is that it gives teachers flexibility when considering how best to manage and instruct large groups of students. The spectrum allows you to weigh the needs of students with disabilities against the considerations of the general physical education population.

Each of the five components of the inclusion spectrum interacts with and complements the other to provide an optimum environment for learning. Everyone Can Play activities are activities that require little or no modifications in order to include all students. Modified activities include everyone with modifications or supports. Parallel activities parcel abilities into grouping that allow everyone to do the same skill or activity according to level of ability. Separate, also known as different activities, are purposely planned for individuals or groups that require alternative skill development different from the general curriculum. Disability sports are activities specifically designed for disability populations. However, most disability sports can be played and enjoyed by everyone (Grenier & Kearns, 2012). When utilizing the spectrum, consider the class, the skill to be taught and the skills of the individual student. Determine what works and then "coach" them in ways that support learning. Careful planning and curriculum differentiation are essential skills for creating an inviting environment in which students feel safe and supported, as well as one that encourages active participation.

When utilizing the modified component of the spectrum, the STEP process should be applied as a way to consider the task structure of the activity (Black & Williamson, 2011). STEP is an acronym for space, task, equipment and people, and it is a mechanism for manipulating variables that may enhance the participation levels of all students. Space can be manipulated by adjusting the size of the playing area, distances from targets, and adding special zones or boundaries. The task can be manipulated by modifying, removing, or adding rules in a way that promotes the lesser skilled children, while challenging more skilled children. Equipment can be manipulated so that each student is matched with equipment that will allow the greatest success (e.g., different size balls and different size targets). People can be manipulated by allowing a greater/fewer number of players on teams, choosing teams, pairing based on ability, and allowing assistance by a peer or teacher assistant.

Cooperative Learning

Another feasible model for instruction is cooperative learning. It is equally effective for students lacking social skill competencies who may not always pick up on environmental or physical cues that direct learning. Within a well-developed program of instruction, cooperative learning nourishes a climate of support (Johnson & Johnson, 1989). Cooperative learning is both reciprocal and inclusive offering students the opportunity to be contributing members of the learning community by providing a safe environment for students of all abilities (Putnam, 1998). Whether identified as typical, at-risk, or gifted, cooperative learning encourages respect and learning (Sapon-Shevin, Ayres, & Duncan, 2002). Studies involving students with moderate to severe disabilities demonstrated significantly higher levels of positive verbal interactions and academic gains than those achieved in traditional methods of instruction (Putnam, 1998; Wilcox, Sbardellati, & Nevin, 1987). As an instructional strategy, cooperative learning fosters conditions that require students to engage with each other. A shared commitment to learning through the achievement of group goals invests students in ways that differ from more traditional styles of teaching. Five essential components seem to be necessary for cooperative learning to be effective: positive interdependence, individual accountability, face-to-face interaction, cooperative skills, and group processing (Putnam, 1998). These elements combine to capitalize on students' skills by promoting a positive climate of learning through active engagement of the students, encouraging a conceptual shift from the individual student capabilities to a cooperative construction of learning between students in their groups.

Positive interdependence is contingent on the dependence of all group members for the completion of tasks. Students are accountable for their learning through the completion of peer or teacher evaluation. Face-to-face interactions naturally occur through the designation of small groups, verbally and nonverbally. These negotiations between students encourage students to listen and work with classmates of varying abilities. Because of this, adaptations and individualized criteria for success are more easily incorporated into the group goals. Putnam (1998) notes that higher achieving students are sensitive to the efforts of their peers and tend to value their peers in multidimensional and dynamic ways. Responsive peers reinforce social skills as a direct result of the task structure, interactions between the students are frequent.

Why does cooperative learning work for students with disabilities? Principally, the implementation of cooperative learning requires a commitment to student-directed learning and a teaching philosophy that guides behavior (Grenier, 2006; Grenier, Dyson, & Yeaton 2005). Secondly, small groups increase the level of interaction through face-to-face engagement between peers (Dyson, 2001, 2002). In all likelihood, students with disabilities will require some degree of modified skill outcomes that ensure the successful participation of group members. This serves as the catalyst for the adaptation of motor skills between students as they negotiate the task. In this way, cooperative learning has been found to improve both motor and social skill development (see Table 6.3 for a summary of models to modify physical education).

CONCLUSION

The trend toward inclusive practices has spurred an examination of teacher practices, accessibility, and instructional models. As we have demonstrated

TABLE 6.3 Models to Modify PE Curricular and Presentation

	Key Reference	Pros/con	Empirical Support
Universal Design Planning approach that considers how the learning environment can be used by as many students as possible	Scott, McGuire, & Shaw, 2001	Focuses on all making the environment accessible and accommodates all students and not just child with disability	No
Inclusion Spectrum The spectrum utilizes an inclusive design that enables teachers to understand, within context, how to address the learning needs of each student using both adaptation and accommodation as tools for instructional delivery.	Black & Williamson, 2011	Practical ideas to modify space, task, equipment and people to accommodate students with disabilities in GPE; need to train PE teachers in the model	No
Cooperative Learning Children working together to solve a problem rather than competing against each other	Putnam, 1998; Johnson & Johnson, 1989	Promotes interactions and inclusion of diverse learners; promotes working together and problem solving	Limited

in this chapter, the extent to which this occurs is dependent on a number of factors including preparing peers without disabilities and teachers' beliefs and attitudes. Creating a support structure through teaching practices that include universal design, cooperative learning, and the inclusion spectrum are just a few of the instructional strategies in which the environment features prominently into student learning. Utilizing peers as natural supports further limits the social isolation many students experience (Place & Hodge, 2001). It can be further argued that these practices not only impact students with disabilities, but also the way in which teachers can tackle inherent prejudices regarding disability and "being disabled" (Beckett, 2009).

More so, understanding the instrumental role a physical education teacher can play in the active engagement of students with disabilities should be an integral part of teacher preparation programs. Simply providing one course in adapted physical education, which in many cases adopts a categorical approach, does little to move the inclusive discourse beyond inclusion as a placement rather than a process. We have argued for implementation of an infusion approach to physical education teacher education training programs as well as the use of supplemental training in the form of web-based courses for both preservice and in-service physical educators.

What we should begin to identify in our teacher training programs is that preservice teachers' work within the curriculum connects with contemporary issues and pedagogical concerns. Discussions on disability sport activities will enrich teachers' ability to address the needs of all students. If and when teacher-training programs give serious consideration to the disability literature, the most notable achievement is that they may challenge myths and the stereotypes associated with having a disability. This will require flexibility, creativity, and patience in identifying the required accommodations. More importantly, it can validate the disability experience and legitimize that ability is a multifaceted concept.

REFERENCES

Allport, G. W. (1954). *The nature of prejudice.* Reading, MA: Addison-Wesley.

Ammah, J. O., & Hodge, S. R. (2005). Secondary physical education teachers' beliefs and practices in teaching students with severe disabilities: A descriptive analysis. *High School Journal, 89,* 40–54.

Asbjørnslett, M., & Hemmingsson, H. (2008). Participation at school as experienced by teenagers with physical disabilities. *Scandinavian Journal of Occupational Therapy, 15,* 153–161.

Auxter, D., Pyfer, J., Zittel, L., & Roth, K. (2010). *Principles and methods of adapted physical education and recreation* (11th ed.). New York, NY: McGraw Hill.

Ayvazo, S., & Ward, P. (2010). Assessment of classwide peer tutoring for students with autism as an inclusion strategy in physical education. *Palaestra, 25*(1), 5–7.

Beckett, A. (2009). Challenging disabling attitudes, building an inclusive society: Considering the role of education in encouraging non-disabled children to develop positive attitudes toward disabled people. *British Journal of Sociology of Education, 30,* 317–329.

Black, K., & Williamson, D. (2011). Designing inclusive physical activities and games. In A. Cereijo-Roibas, E. Stamatakis, & K. Black (Eds.), *Design for sport* (pp. 195–224). Farnham, England: Gower.

Blinde, E. M., & McCallister, S. G. (1998). Listening to the voices of students with physical disabilities. *Journal of Physical Education, Recreation and Dance, 69,* 64–68.

Block, M. E. (2015, June). Preparing future physical educators for inclusion: Changing physical education teacher training programs. Keynote presentation at the *International Symposium of Adapted Physical Activity.* Netanya, Israel.

Block, M. E., Klavina, A., & McKay, C. (2016). Facilitating social acceptance and inclusion. In M. E. Block (Ed.). *An inclusive approach to adapted physical education: A teacher's guide to including students with disabilities in physical education and sports* (4th ed.; pp. 271–288). Baltimore, MD: Paul H. Brookes.

Block, M. E., & Obrusnikova, I. (2007). A research review on inclusion of students with disabilities in general physical education. *Adapted Physical Activity Quarterly, 24,* 103–124.

Block, M. E., & Rizzo, T. L. (1995). Attitudes and attributes of physical education teachers toward including students with severe and profound disabilities into regular physical education. *Journal of the Association for Persons With Severe Handicaps, 20,* 80–87.

Bredahl, A-M. (2013). Sitting and watching the others being active: The experienced difficulties in PE when having a disability. *Adapted Physical Activity Quarterly, 30,* 40–58.

Cole, D. A. (1988). Difficulties in relationships between non-handicapped and severely mentally retarded children: The effect of physical impairments. *Research in Developmental Disabilities. 9,* 55–72.

Colvin, J. W., & Ashman, M. (2010). Roles, risks, and benefits of peer mentoring relationships in higher education. *Mentoring & Tutoring: Partnership in Learning, 18,* 121–134.

DePaepe, J. (1985). The influence of three least restrictive environments on the content, motor-ALT and performance of moderately mentally retarded students. *Journal of Teaching in Physical Education, 5,* 34–41.

DePauw, K. P., & Goc Karp, G. (1994a). Integrating knowledge of disability throughout the physical education curriculum: An infusion approach. *Adapted Physical Activity Quarterly, 11,* 3–13.

DePauw, K. P., & Goc Karp, G. (1994b). The role of higher education for curriculum infusion of disability. *Journal of Health, Physical Education, Recreation, and Dance, 65,* 51–53.

Dyson, B. (2001). Cooperative learning in an elementary physical education program. *Journal of Teaching in Physical Education, 20,* 264–281.

Dyson, B. (2002). The implementation of cooperative learning in an elementary physical education program. *Journal of Teaching in Physical Education, 22,* 69–86.

Evans, J. (2004). Making a difference? Education and "ability" in physical education, *European Physical Education Review, 10,* 95–108. doi: 10.1177/1356336 X04042158

Fitzgerald, H. (2005). Still feeling like a spare piece of luggage? Embodied experiences of (dis)ability in physical education and school sport. *Physical Education and Sport Pedagogy, 10,* 41–59.

Fitzgerald, H. (2006). Disability and physical education. In D. Kirk, D. Macdonald, & M. O'Sullivan (Eds.), *The handbook of physical education* (pp. 752–765). London, England: Sage.

Fitzgerald, H., & Stride, A. (2012). Stories about physical education from young people with disabilities. *International Journal of Disability, Development and Education, 59,* 283–293.

Folsom-Meek, S. R., Nearing, R. J., Grotheluschen, W., & Krampf, H. (1999). Effects of academic major, gender, and hands-on experience on attitudes of pre-service professionals. *Adapted Physical Activity Quarterly, 16,* 389–402.

Getskow, V., & Konczal, D. (1996). *Kids with special needs.* Santa Barbara, CA: Learning Works.

Goodwin, D. (2008). Self-regulated dependency: Ethical reflections on interdependence and help in adapted physical activity. *Sport, Ethics and Philosophy, 2,* 172–184.

Goodwin, D. L., & Watkinson, E. J. (2000). Inclusive physical education from the perspective of students with physical disabilities. *Adapted Physical Activity Quarterly, 17,* 144–160.

Greenwood, C. R., Maheady, L., & Delaquadri, J. (2002). Classwide peer tutoring programs. In M. R. Shinn, H. M. Walker, & G. Stoner (Eds.), *Interventions for academic and behavior problems II: Preventive and remedial approaches* (pp. 611–649). Bethesda, MD: National Association of School Psychologists.

Grenier, M. (2006) A social constructionist perspective of inclusion. *Adapted Physical Activity Quarterly, 23,* 245–260.

Grenier, M. (2007). Inclusion in physical education: From the medical model to social constructionism, *Quest, 59,* 298–310.

Grenier, M., Collins, K., Wright, S., & Kearns, C. (2014). Perceptions of a disability sport unit in general physical education. *Adapted Physical Activity Quarterly, 31,* 49–66.

Grenier, M., Dyson, B. P., Yeaton, P. (2005). Cooperative learning that includes students with disabilities. *Journal of Health, Physical Education, Recreation and Dance, 76,* 29–35.

Grenier, M., & Kearns, C. (2012). The benefits of implementing disability sport into physical education: A model for success. *Journal of Physical Education, Recreation, and Dance, 83,* 24–27.

Grenier, M., & Miller, N. (2015). Using peers as natural supports for students with severe disabilities in general physical education, *Palaestra, 29*(1), 22–26.

Hardin, B. (2005). Physical education teachers' reflections on preparation for inclusion. The *Physical Educator, 62,* 44–56.

Healy, S. (2015). *The impact of online professional development on physical educators' knowledge and implementation of peer tutoring.* [Unpublished doctoral dissertation]. University of Virginia, Charlottesville, VA.

Healy, S., Judge, J., & Block, M. E. (2014). APE teacher perceptions on advantages and disadvantages of online teacher development. *Palaestra, 28,* 14–16.

Hodge, S. R., Ammah, J. O. A., Casebolt, K., Lamaster, K., & O'Sullivan, M. (2004). High school general physical education teachers' behaviors and beliefs associated with inclusion. *Sport Education and Society, 9,* 395–419.

Hodge, S. R., Davis, R., Woodard, R., & Sherrill, C. (2002). Comparison of practicum types in changing preservice teachers' attitudes and perceived competence. *Adapted Physical Activity Quarterly, 19,* 155–172.

Hodge, S. R., & Jansma, P. (1999). Effects of contact time location of practicum experiences on attitudes of physical education majors. *Adapted Physical Activity Quarterly, 16,* 48–63.

Hodge, S. R., Tannehill, D., & Kluge, M. (2003). Exploring the meaning of practicum experiences for PETE students. *Adapted Physical Activity Quarterly, 20,* 381–399.

Houston-Wilson, C., Dunn, J. M., van der Mars, H., & McCubbin, J. (1997). The effects of peer tutors on the motor performance in integrated physical education classes. *Adapted Physical Activity Quarterly, 14,* 298–313.

Hutzler, Y. (2003). Attitudes toward the participation of individuals with disabilities in physical activity: A review. *Quest, 55,* 347–373.

Hutzler, Y., & Bar-Eli, M. (2013). How to cope with bias while adapting for inclusion in physical education and sports: A judgment and decision making perspective. *Quest, 65,* 57–71.

Hutzler, Y., Fliess, O., Chacham, A., & van den Auweele, Y. (2002). Perspectives of children with physical disabilities on inclusion and empowerment: Supporting and limiting factors. *Adapted Physical Activity Quarterly, 19,* 300–317.

Hutzler, Y., Zamir, G., & Fliess-Douer, O. (2004). Inclusion of the child with physical disability in physical activity: Supporting and limiting factors. *Issues in Special Education and Rehabilitation, 19,* 5–18.

International Paralympic Committee (IPC). (2006). *Paralympic School Day manual.* Retrieved August 14, 2012, from https://www.paralympic.org/the-ipc/paralympic-school-day

Jacobi, M. (1991). Mentoring and undergraduate academic success: A literature review. *Review of Educational Research, 61,* 505–532.

Jin, J., Yun, J., & Wegis, H. (2013). Changing physical education teacher education curriculum to promote inclusion. *Quest, 65,* 372–383.

Johnson, D. W., & Johnson, R. (1989). *Cooperation and competition: Theory and research.* Edina, MN: Interaction Book Company.

Kalkowski, P. (2001). *Peer and cross-age tutoring.* Portland, OR: Education Northwest.

Kalyvas, V., & Reid, G. (2003) Sport adaptation, participation and enjoyment of students with and without disabilities. *Adapted Physical Activity Quarterly, 20,* 182–199.

Klavina, A., & Block, M. E. (2008). The effects of peer tutoring on interaction behaviors in inclusive physical education. *Adapted Physical Activity Quarterly, 25,* 132–158.

Klavina, A., Jerlinder, K., Kristén, L., Hammar, L., & Soulie, T. (2013). Cooperative oriented learning in inclusive physical education, *European Journal of Special Needs Education, 28,* 1–16.

Kugelmass, J. W. 2004. *The inclusive school: Sustaining equity and standards.* New York, NY: Teachers College Press.

Kwon, E. (2015). *Implementing blended E-learning supplement into physical education teacher education program.* (Unpublished doctoral dissertation). University of Virginia, Charlottesville, VA.

LaMaster, K., Gall, K., Kinchin, G., & Siedentop, D. (1998). Inclusion practices of effective elementary specialists. *Adapted Physical Activity Quarterly, 15,* 64–81.

Lieberman, L. J., Dunn, J. M., van der Mars, H., & McCubbin, J. (2000). Peer tutors' effects on activity levels of deaf students in inclusive elementary physical education. *Adapted Physical Activity Quarterly, 17,* 20–39.

Lieberman, L. J., & Houston-Wilson, C. (2009). *Strategies for inclusion: A handbook for physical educators* (2nd ed.). Champaign, IL: Human Kinetics.

Lieberman, L. J., Newcomer, J., McCubbin, J., & Dalrymple, N. (1997). The effects of cross-aged peer tutors on the academic learning time of students with disabilities in inclusive elementary physical education classes. *Brazilian International Journal of Adapted Physical Education Research, 4,* 15–32.

Lienert, C., Sherrrill, C., & Myers, B. (2001). Physical educators' concerns about integrating children with disabilities: A cross-cultural comparison. *Adapted Physical Activity Quarterly, 18,* 1–17.

Lindsay, S., & Edwards, A. (2013). A systematic review of disability awareness interventions for children and youth. *Disability & Rehabilitation, 35,* 623–646.

Liu, Y., Kudlacek, Y., & Jesina, O. (2010). The influence of Paralympic school day on children's attitudes toward people with disabilities. *Acta Universitatis Palackianae Olomucensis. Gymnica, 40,* 63–69.

Lloyd, M., & Duncan-Howell, J. (2010). Changing the metaphor: The potential of online communities in teacher professional development. In J. O. Lindberg & A. D. Olofsson (Eds.), *Online learning communities and teacher professional development: Methods for improved delivery.* Hershey, NY: IGI Global.

Logan, K. R., Jacobs, H. A., Gast, L. L., Murray, A. S., Daino, K., & Skala, C. (1998). The impact of typical peers on the perceived happiness of children with profound multiple disabilities. *Journal of the Association for Persons with Severe Handicaps, 23,* 309–318.

McKay, C., Block, M. E., Park, J. Y. (2015). The impact of Paralympic school day on student attitudes toward inclusion in physical education. *Adapted Physical Activity Quarterly, 32,* 331–348.

Miller, S. R., Miller, P. F., & Armentrout, J. A. (1995). Cross-age peer tutoring: A strategy for promoting self-determination in students with severe emotional disabilities/behavior disorders. *Preventing School Failure, 39,* 32–37.

Moriarty, M. A. (2007). Inclusive pedagogy: Teaching methodologies to reach diverse learners in science instruction. *Equity & Excellence in Education. 40,* 252–265.

Morley, D., Bailey, R., Tan, J., & Cooke, B. (2005). Inclusive physical education: Teachers' views of including pupils with special educational needs and/or disabilities in physical education. *European Physical Education Review, 11,* 84–107.

Murata, N., Hodge, S., & Little, J. (2000). Students' attitudes, experiences, and perspectives on their peers with disabilities. *Clinical Kinesiology, 54,* 59–66.

Myśliwiec, A., & Damentko, M. (2015). Global initiative of the Special Olympics movement for people with intellectual disabilities. *Journal of Human Kinetics, 45,* 253–259.

Obrusnikova, I. (2008). Physical educators' beliefs about teaching children with disabilities. *Perceptual and Motor Skills, 106,* 637–644.

Oliver, M. (1990). *The politics of disablement.* New York, NY: St. Martin's Press.

Orr, A. C., & Bachman Hammig, S. (2009). Inclusive postsecondary strategies for teaching students with learning disabilities: A review of the literature. *Teaching Disabilities Quarterly, 32,* 181–196.

Panagiotou, A. K., Evaggelinou, C., Doulkeridou, A., Mouratidou, K., & Koidou, E. (2008). Attitudes of 5th and 6th grade Greek students toward the inclusion of children with disabilities in physical education classes after a Paralympic education program. *European Journal of Adapted Physical Activity, 1,* 31–43.

Papaioannou, C., Evaggelinou, C., Barkoukis, V., & Block, M. (2013). Disability awareness program in a summer camp. *European Journal of Adapted Physical Activity, 6,* 19–28.

Peck, C.A., Donaldson, J., & Pezzoli, M. (1990). Some benefits nonhandicapped adolescents perceive for themselves from their social relationships with peers who have severe handicaps. *Journal of the Association for Persons with Severe Handicaps, 15,* 211–230.

Pecora, J. K., Whittaker, J. K., Maluccio, A. N., & Barth, R. P. (2012). *The child welfare challenge: Policy, practice and research* (3rd ed.). New Brunswick, NJ: Aldine Transaction.

Place, K., & Hodge, S. R. (2001). Social inclusion of students with physical disabilities in GPE: A behavioral analysis. *Adapted Physical Activity Quarterly, 18,* 389–404.

Prochaska, J., & DiClemente, C. (1983) Stages and processes of self-change in smoking: Toward an integrative model of change. *Journal of Consulting and Clinical Psychology, 5,* 390–395.

Putnam, J. A. (1998). *Cooperative learning and strategies for inclusion.* Baltimore, MD: Brookes.

Qi, J., & Ha, A. S. (2012). Inclusion in physical education: A review of literature. *International Journal of Disability, Development and Education, 59,* 257–281.

Reina, R., Lopez, V., Jimenez, M., Garcia-Calvo, T., & Hutzler, Y. (2011). Effects of awareness interventions on children's attitudes toward peers with a visual impairment. *International Journal of Rehabilitation Research, 34,* 243–248.

Rizzo, T. & Vispoel, W. P. (1992). Changing attitudes about teaching students with handicaps. *Adapted Physical Activity Quarterly, 9,* 54–63.

Sapon-Shevin, M., Ayres, B., & Duncan, J. (2002). Cooperative learning and inclusion. In J. Thousand, R. Villa, & A. Nevin (Eds.), *Creativity and collaborative learning: The practical guide* to *empowering students, teachers, and families.* Baltimore, MD: Paul H. Brookes.

Scott, S. S., McGuire, J. M., & Shaw, S. F. (2001). *The principles of universal design for instruction.* Storrs, CT: University of Connecticut, Center on Postsecondary Education and Disability. Retrieved from http://udi.uconn.edu/index.php?q=node/12

Smith, A., & Green, K. (2004). Including pupils with special educational needs in secondary school physical education: A sociological analysis of teachers' views. *British Journal of Sociology of Education, 25,* 593–607.

Special Olympics. (n.d.). *Get into it.* Retrieved from https://getintoit.specialolympics.org

Spencer-Cavaliere, N., & Watkinson, J. E. (2010). Inclusion understood from the perspectives of children with disability. *Adapted Physical Activity Quarterly, 27,* 275–293.

Strayhorn, T. L., & Terrell, M. C. (2007). Mentoring and satisfaction with college for black students. *The Negro Educational Review, 58,* 69–83.

Taliaferro, A. R., Hammond, L., & Wyant, K. (2015). Pre-service physical educators' self-efficacy beliefs toward inclusion: The impact of coursework and practicum. *Adapted Physical Activity Quarterly, 32,* 49–67.

Tripp. A., French, R., & Sherrill, C. (1995). Contact theory and attitudes of children in physical education programs toward peers with disability. *Adapted Physical Activity Quarterly, 12,* 323–332.

UNESCO. (2015). *International charter of physical education, physical activity and sport.* Retrieved from http://unesdoc.unesco.org/images/0023/002354/235409e.pdf

United Nations. (2006). *Convention on the rights of persons with disabilities.* New York, NY: NY: Author.

Villa, R., & Thousand, J. (2000). *Restructuring for caring and effective education.* Baltimore, MD: Brookes.

Ward, P., & Ayvazo, S. (2006). Classwide peer tutoring in physical education: Assessing its effects with kindergartners with autism. *Adapted Physical Activity Quarterly, 23,* 233–244.

Webster, G. E. (1987). Influence of peer tutors upon academic learning time-physical education of mentally handicapped students. *Journal of Teaching in Physical Education, 6,* 393–403.

Whitley, J., Smith, J. D., & Vaillancourt, T. (2013). Promoting mental health literacy among educators: Critical in school-based prevention and intervention. *Canadian Journal of School Psychology, 28,* 56–70.

Wilcox, J., Sbardelati, E., & Nevin, A. (1987). Cooperative learning groups aid integration. *Teaching Exceptional Children, 20,* 61–63.

Wilhite, B., Mushett, C. A., Goldenberg, L., & Trader, B. R. (1997). Promoting inclusive sport and leisure participation: Evaluation of the Paralympic day in the schools model. *Adapted Physical Activity Quarterly, 14,* 131–146.

Xafopoulos, G., Kudlacek, M., & Evaggelinou, C. (2009). Effect of the intervention program "Paralympic School Day" on attitudes of children attending international school toward inclusion of students with disabilities. *Acta Universitatis Palackianae Olomucensis. Gymnica, 39,* 63–71.

CHAPTER 7

UNDERSTANDING INCLUSION IN PHYSICAL EDUCATION FROM THE CHILD'S PERSPECTIVE

Janine Coates
Loughborough University

"We've GOT to make noises in greater amounts!
So, open your mouth, lad! For every voice counts!"
Thus he spoke as he climbed. When they got to the top,
the lad cleared his throat and he shouted out, "Yopp!"
And that Yopp . . . That one small extra Yopp put it over!
Finally, at last! From that speck on that clover
their voices were heard! They rang out clear and clean.
And the elephant smiled. "Do you see what I mean?
They've proved they ARE persons, not matter how small.
And their whole world was saved by the Smallest of ALL!"
"How true! Yes, how true," said the big kangaroo.
"And, from now on, you know what I'm planning to do?
From now on, I'm going to protect them with you!"

Horton Hears a Who—Dr. Seuss (Geisel, 1954)

Inclusive Physical Activities, pages 133–160
Copyright © 2017 by Information Age Publishing
All rights of reproduction in any form reserved.

Successful inclusive practice depends on our ability to consult with and listen to the experiences of the individuals we aim to include. Too often in research (and in practice), those voices are absent (Smith, 2007). Having spent much of my late teenage and early adult years working with children and adults who have special educational needs and/or disabilities (SEND; for the purpose of this chapter, I use SEND and disability interchangeably), I was always struck by how little their viewpoints were accommodated. Decisions were made for them, not by them, and stories and experiences were shared on their behalf. To me this seemed bizarre. Why do we rely on secondhand accounts, when we could have a firsthand account from the person living those experiences? More importantly, why are other people having more say about the specific needs of an individual than that individual? Surely that person knows his or her disability and needs better than any other. This is what led me toward academic research. I wanted to find out what the experiences were of individuals who have SEND, and I wanted to know how understanding those experiences could help us to be more inclusive in educational practice. I was specifically interested in physical education (PE) and how children with a variety of different SEND experienced this curriculum area. Physical education, according to the National Curriculum in England (Department for Education, 2013) aims to inspire pupils to succeed in competitive sport and other physically demanding activities; provides opportunities to become physically confident, and opportunities to compete in sport and other activities; and to embed values such as fairness and respect. These aims highlight the importance of PE in the development of children's psychological, social, and emotional well-being (Bailey, 2006).

This chapter aims to provide an overview of inclusion in PE from the child's perspective based within the education system in the United Kingdom. It will first draw on theory and research that explores the importance of consulting with children who have SEND, applying this to PE settings. Second, findings will be presented from a large qualitative study that explored the experiences of PE for primary, secondary, and special school pupils in England. These findings explore some of the facilitators and barriers to inclusion in PE drawn from my own research with children. It will conclude with a number of key recommendations for improving the experiences of children with SEND in PE lessons.

RATIONALE FOR SEEKING AND LISTENING TO CHILDREN WHO HAVE SEND

Over the last decade, the inclusion of children with SEND in education has been brought to attention through national and international children's and education policy. Much of this has been driven by the 1994 Salamanca

Statement (UNESCO, 1994). The Salamanca Statement advanced a number of policy changes in the international arena, ensuring that all children have fair and equal access to education. In the United Kingdom, Australia, and the United States this has resulted in policy changes to promote inclusion in education for children with SEND.

For example, in the United Kingdom, the physical education and school sport for young people (PESSYP) strategy (DCSF, 2008) was developed to promote high quality, inclusive PE teaching to improve social, psychological, and academic outcomes for children. These aims were also included in the revised National Curriculum for PE (DfE, 2013). In addition, the SEND Code of Practice (DfE/DfH, 2014), has been developed to provide guidance to schools and education practitioners about how to best include, assess, and provide for children with SEND. A fundamental part of this policy guidance is the promotion of consultation with children and young people with disabilities about their needs and how these needs can be met. These changes to policy are important as they highlight that all children should be receiving high quality PE that provides them with the opportunity to learn and develop physically, mentally, and socially; and that children should have the opportunity to discuss their needs, and have these discussions listened to and acted upon in order to facilitate their inclusion in education. This relates to a shift in thinking about how we conceptualize disability.

THE MEDICAL AND SOCIAL MODELS

There are two prevailing, although polarized, models that have been used to understand disability: the medical model and the social model.

The Medical Model

The medical model conceptualizes disability as a number of deficits and functional limitations resulting in disadvantages that can only be rectified through treatment (Farrell, 2004). The model is reductionist and pathologizes disability by explaining SEND in terms of etiology, diagnosis, and cure (Bailey, 2005; Reed & Watson, 1994). Using this model, individuals with SEND are compared against a set of norms that results in them being perceived as "abnormal" (Brisenden, 1986; Shakespeare, 2012). Moreover, the categorization of individuals using a medical model suggests that difficulties or problems exist within that individual: the disability is owned by them and any challenges they face must therefore be overcome by changes that come from within. In this sense, the medical model is considered to be a framework for disablement. It places responsibility for change on the individual, and in doing so, ignores social experiences that might create barriers for that individual to functioning in a social world (Farrell, 2001; Shakespeare, 2012).

The Social Model

The medicalized view of disability started to change in the 1970s as disability reformist groups (e.g., the Union of Physically Impaired Against Segregation [UPIAS]) started to campaign for the rights of people with disabilities and the promotion of social understanding surrounding disability (Shakespeare, 2012). Conceptions of disability shifted from disability as "personal tragedy" toward the creation of social theory explaining disability as social restriction (Oliver, 1990). This model sees disability as a social construction by nondisabled people such that disability is created by the physical, material, or economic barriers present in society resulting in people with disabilities being unnecessarily isolated or excluded (Anastasiou & Kauffman, 2013; Armstrong, 2005; Connors & Stalker, 2007). Social models challenge traditional explanations and instead argue that disability must be understood in terms of exclusion from social norms (Evans 2004; Shakespeare & Watson, 1997). Unlike the medical model, the social model proposes that problems exist in society, not in the individual (Low, 2007). Thus "disability is becoming a social phenomenon, owned by society as a group rather than an individual person" (Jones, 2005, p. 378). The emergence of a social theory about disability has resulted in an international drive to promote inclusion.

Implications

Given this shift in thinking about disability, we have moved away from pathologizing disability (in social policy at least) toward recognizing that as a society, we have created notions of disability. By understanding that social structures and attitudes might in fact serve to exclude rather than include some people, policymakers are able to drive forward change. However, changes to policy, while important, do not necessarily represent change in practice (although do drive forward changes in inclusive practice). For example, when exploring PE research, it is evident that the perceptions of children with SEND are not as frequently accounted for (Fitzgerald, 2005), and that PE quite often excludes, rather than includes, children with SEND (e.g., Penney & Evans, 2013). The literature exploring perceptions about inclusion in PE will now be considered.

INCLUDING CHILDREN WITH SEND IN PE:
AN OVERVIEW OF THE LITERATURE

The relationships children have with others during their school years are a driving force in their later psychological development and well-being. These relationships are also fundamental for fostering inclusion. Research demonstrates that children's relationships with their teachers and peers at school can positively or negatively impact on school adjustment (Baker, 2006), social competence with peers (Howes, 2000), behavioral adjustment, and prosocial behavior (Birch & Ladd, 1998).

While teacher–child relationships are well-researched for typically developing children (Baker, 2006), relatively little research has explored these relationships for children with SEND and their PE teachers. Nevertheless, research suggests that children with SEND are at higher risk of peer rejection and victimization than their typically developing peers (Farmer, Hall, Leung, Estell, & Brooks, 2011; Siperstein, Norins, & Mohler, 2007; Weiner & Schneider, 2002). They also tend to have poorer quality relationships with teachers (Baker, 2006).

It is worth considering the impact of these relationships in PE lessons. PE lessons tend to focus on peer collaboration, team games, and peer support, which provides opportunity for children to interact with their peers less formally than in classroom-based subjects (Smith, 2003). PE also provides a forum to interact with teachers, which differs from other classroom settings. Indeed, Bailey (2006), in a review of the benefits of PE for children, indicated that PE has vast social benefits for children including providing an opportunity for children to develop their moral reasoning, co-operative play skills, and personal responsibility. Bailey also emphasized that teachers can foster development as PE lessons allow for situations to arise naturally through activities which can be mediated through questioning and modeling of appropriate behavior and responses. While the benefits of PE are well-documented, there is a dearth of research investigating the significance of school relationships for children with SEND in PE settings.

Research shows that children with SEND's perceptions of PE are closely linked to the relationships they have with their PE teachers (e.g., Blinde & McCallister, 1998; Fitzgerald, 2005; Goodwin & Watkinson, 2000; Hutzler, Fliess, Chacham, & Auweele, 2002; Qi & Ha, 2012). In particular, children often do not feel lessons are differentiated enough to meet their needs, excluding them from some or all aspects of the lesson (Blinde & McCallister, 1998; Goodwin & Watkinson, 2000). This can result in children having poor experiences of and expectations for PE. Conversely, positive relationships in PE can foster positive experiences of and expectations for PE. Goodwin and Watkinson explain this in their research with children with physical disabilities. Their participants are described as having "good days" and "bad days" in PE, and much of this is determined by the interactions they have with others in their PE lessons. Goodwin and Watkinson's framework of good and bad days in PE can underpin much of the research, which has explored children with SEND perceptions of inclusive PE, and so this will be used as a basis to explore the literature.

"Good Days" in PE

According to Goodwin and Watkinson (2000), good days in PE are a result of supportive interactions with peers and teachers, acknowledgement of the health benefits relating to physical activity, and the opportunity to demonstrate their skills, as well as having these skills acknowledged by others. This is supported by other research that explores children with SEND experiences of PE. For example, Fitzgerald (2005) shows that some children with SEND have positive experiences of PE teachers. She notes that when PE teachers differentiate lessons according to the needs of the individual child, this encourages participation and promotes positive attitudes toward PE. In many cases, positive experiences of PE are centered on inclusive practice by PE teachers. Where PE teachers act in ways which promote participation, positive experiences were more frequently reported in the literature (Coates & Vickerman, 2010; Fitzgerald, 2005; Goodwin & Watkinson, 2000; Hutzler et al., 2002).

Peer relationships are also important for positive engagement in PE for children with SEND. Seymour, Reid, and Bloom (2009) show the important role that friends play in promoting self-efficacy amongst children with disabilities in PE lessons. Their study of experiences of friendship during physical activity for children with and without disabilities demonstrates the role peers and teachers play in facilitating engagement. One participant states:

> [My friend] Anne understands that I can do some things better than them because they'll say, "Wow you're actually very good at that!" like rock climbing or horseback riding.... But sometimes I can do more than my friends and sometimes I can do less than them, but I also think because it's adapted for me I can do it. (Seymour, Reid, & Bloom, 2009, p. 212)

Statements such as this highlight that both friends and teachers are key stakeholders in inclusive PE practice. This participant indicates that a friend's encouragement is a source of positive affect, and acknowledges that the ability to participate skillfully is a result of the activity being adapted to her needs. Further research has also demonstrated the supporting role peers can have in promoting inclusion in PE (Coates & Vickerman, 2010; Goodwin & Watkinson, 2000; Goodwin, 2001; Healy, Msetfi, & Gallagher, 2013). For example, Goodwin (2001) in a study relating to peer support in PE, found that when help and assistance from peers did not hinder independence, perceptions of peers was positive and boosted PE experiences. Additionally, Coates and Vickerman (2010) identified that the opportunity to learn alongside friends in a supportive environment was a valued characteristic of PE lessons for children with SEND. Similarly, Hutzler et al. (2002) found that when peers are supportive and encouraging, children with SEND felt like they were part of the group and felt better included in PE lessons.

Smith (2003) argues that peers contribute to quality physical activity experiences, and while literature on the role of friendship in PE for children with SEND is scarce, what is available appears to corroborate this (Qi & Ha, 2012). Of particular importance, however, is the impact that these supportive relationships might have on the child's self-efficacy or confidence to participate skillfully. Hagger, Chatzisarntis, and Biddle (2001) indicate that self-efficacy influences children's intentions to engage in physical activity. In a large study of adolescent physical activity intentions, they found that positive attitudes and high self-efficacy were significant predictors of intention to engage in physical activity. They concluded that the development of an environment that promotes personal improvement and competence was crucial for continued engagement in physical activity. If, as research exploring children with SEND perceptions of PE might indicate, positive relationships with others in PE help to promote self-efficacy in children with SEND, then building these positive relationships should be a focus for inclusive PE development, particularly if the intention of inclusive PE is to develop lifelong physically active individuals. Nevertheless, research also indicates that while teachers and peers can be supportive and promote positive experiences, they can also be key agents in excluding children with SEND from PE. These feelings of exclusion relate to Goodwin and Watkinson's conception of bad days in PE.

"Bad Days" in PE

Goodwin and Watkinson (2000) argue that bad days in PE are a result of children with SEND having their competence questioned, feeling socially isolated from their peers, and being restricted from participating in PE activities. In particular, research indicates that children with disabilities often have poor perceptions of PE when they are subject to exclusionary practice by teachers and when they are discriminated against or bullied by their peers (Blinde & McCallister, 1998; Connors & Stalker, 2007; Coates & Vickerman, 2010; Fitzgerald, 2005; Hutzler et al., 2002). These negative experiences of PE tend to center on the child feeling excluded, whether fully or partially, because of the behavior of others.

Alarmingly, negative experiences of PE and experiences of exclusion are more frequently reported in literature exploring children with SEND's perceptions of PE than positive experiences. Blinde and McCallister (1998), for example, found that their participants with physical disability experiences of PE were minimal to nonexistent. When exclusion of these children from PE lessons did occur, it was often attributed to teacher practice. Children reported that some of their PE teachers did not modify their lesson plans accordingly to include them, which often resulted in negative experiences and/or complete exclusion from lessons (Blinde & McCallister, 1998). Equally, where children were present in lessons, they were not given the opportunity to take part and instead became an audience for other pupils participation (e.g., "I just sit and watch them and clap and stuff"; Blinde & McCallister, 1998, p. 65). Similarly, Goodwin and Watkinson (2000) found that some children were asked to undertake menial tasks relating to the PE lesson, without an opportunity to participate in the lesson itself. One child in their study states: "[The teacher]'s, like, go pump up the balls in the storage room. And they're playing volleyball and I'm, like, —grrrr!" (p. 152). It is worth noting that perceptions such as these are not limited to Canada and the United States where these two studies were carried out. Studies by Hutzler et al. (2002) in Israel and Fitzgerald (2005) in the United Kingdom report similar findings.

Academics have suggested that these experiences are a result of PE teachers lacking the necessary training to prepare and deliver PE lessons inclusively (Morley, Bailey, Tan, & Cooke, 2005; Vickerman & Coates, 2009). Further, available training programs are either inaccessible to teachers or are ineffective in fully preparing and training teachers for inclusive education (Hutzler et al., 2002). Research has also indicated that teachers are not fully aware of how to achieve inclusion (Hodge, Ammah, Casebolt, LaMaster, & O'Sullivan, 2004; Morley et al., 2005; Smith, 2004). Interestingly, recent research by Fitzgerald (2012) in which she asked PE stakeholders (including teachers, sport development officers, and researchers) to analyze children's drawings about PE, showed that while some children with SEND do still experience exclusion in PE, there are inconsistencies in how PE teachers understand and implement inclusive practice. This, she argues, highlights that policy frameworks designed to promote inclusion, do little more than focus attention away from how and why children should learn in PE and instead, result in a box-ticking exercise with little understanding of what inclusion actually "looks like." Nevertheless, stakeholders in Fitzgerald's (2012) study did believe that children with SEND should be having better experiences of PE, which is a step in the right direction.

In addition to the breakdown in the relationship between teacher and child, children with SEND also report negative experiences of other children in their PE lessons due to poor self-esteem, discrimination, and bullying. This is exacerbated by teachers ignoring the child's needs, resulting in children feeling invisible to PE teachers, particularly teachers with a lack of SEND experience (Fitzgerald, 2005). Inevitably, these children compared themselves to others who were treated more positively by their teachers, and often attributed deficit within themselves to the treatment they received from others (Fitzgerald, 2005). This results in children questioning their own competence, impacts negatively on their self-esteem, and jeopardizes the quality of the relationships they form with other children and with their teachers.

Differential treatment of children in PE lessons may contribute to discrimination against children with SEND in PE lessons, particularly those with physical disabilities (Blinde & McCallister, 1998; Connors & Stalker, 2007; Fitzgerald, 2005; Goodwin & Watkinson, 2000). Goodwin and Watkinson state that children with SEND report feeling socially isolated by their classmates, which is characterized by rejection, neglect, and bullying by peers in the lesson. Instances of discriminatory behaviors include peers laughing and criticizing the child's performance; physical bullying, such as tripping the child up; and communicatory discrimination, such as ignoring the child. They suggest that bullying in PE, particularly for children with physical disabilities, can be attributed to their inability to disguise their impairment.

Fitzgerald (2005) suggests that it is not only children with physical disabilities who are subject to discrimination in PE. In her study, children with more diverse SEND, including learning disabilities, reported feeling discriminated against in PE by peers. Discriminatory behavior included not being passed the ball, name calling, and not feeling welcome in lessons. As a result, children compared themselves to implicit class norms to try to understand the reasons behind their exclusion.

These findings are indicative of the kinds of discrimination and bullying children with SEND are sometimes subject to in their PE lessons. While children do and will develop coping mechanisms to deal with these types of negative experience (Fitzgerald, 2005), Slininger, Sherrill, and Jankowski (2000) indicate that discriminatory behavior can be reduced by increasing children's contact with others who have varying and complex SEND in mainstream schools. They show that sensitizing children without SEND to those who do have SEND through facilitated peer interaction can result in more positive attitudes toward peers with SEND. An alternative to increased contact is to provide children without disabilities the opportunity to experience sport from the perspective of someone with a disability. Evans, Bright, and Brown (2015) did this and showed that providing children with an embodied experience of what it might be like to have a disability—in this case through a disability sport education program—can lead to changes in attitudes toward disability. They showed that following a wheelchair basketball experience, the nondisabled participants had a better appreciation for the demand of playing sport with a disability and were more able to relate to individuals with a disability. Moreover, Townsend and Hassall (2007) found that younger children have more positive attitudes toward peers with SEND. Taken together, these studies support the argument for early inclusion for children with SEND and the need to facilitate positive social interactions between children with and without SEND.

The research exploring children with SEND's perceptions of PE highlights that the relationships children have with those around them in PE lessons are of fundamental importance in determining whether they have positive or negative experiences. Yet it is apparent that little research exists that explores this from the perceptions of the child, particularly children with a range of different SEND. The present study aims to contribute to the literature base in this respect.

THE PRESENT INVESTIGATION

Aims

This study aimed to explore the PE experiences of children aged 7-14 with diverse SEND with a view to better understanding the barriers and facilitators to engaging in PE. This was to understand more broadly whether the experiences highlighted in previous literature were applicable only to those children who might require additional practical support for PE lessons (i.e., those with physical and/or sensory disabilities), or if perhaps there were universal experiences shared by children who experience additional challenges in education.

This chapter presents findings from my PhD research. Some of the findings from this study are reported in Coates and Vickerman (2010) and Coates (2011), but this chapter will focus on the unpublished findings. For the purpose of my research, SEND refers to any child who has difficulties "which call for special educational provision to be made for them" (DfE/DfH, 2014, p. 15). Essentially, what this translates to is any child considered by their school to have SEND and who thus receives additional support for some or all of that child's studies.

Participants

In the United Kingdom, mainstream (general education) schools keep a SEND register, which identifies children who require additional provisions for their learning. For this study, mainstream schools with SEND populations of more than 10% were invited to participate as well as a number of special schools specifically catering to children with SEND. Children from two mainstream primary, two mainstream secondary (high) schools, two special schools (catering for children 11–18 years of age), as well as one SEND base unit at a participating primary school took part in the research. The special schools included one for children with moderate to profound learning difficulties; and one for children with social, emotional, and behavioral difficulties (SEBD) who had been excluded from mainstream education.

Thirty children with SEND took part in this study, including 14 males and 16 females. The average age of the children was 10. Children had a range of different SEND including moderate learning difficulties, motor-coordination difficulties, SEBD, physical disability, sensory impairment, and specific learning difficulties. The majority had some difficulty with cognition and learning (73%). See Table 7.1 for participant information.

Written consent was given by each child and their parents/caregiver before participating in the research. This was consistent with British Educational Research Association (BERA, 2004) ethical guidelines. All participants were also made aware of their right to withdraw from the study.

Research Design

I was interested in understanding children's lived experiences of PE, and wanted to provide children with the opportunity to reflect on their own experiences. Thus, I followed a phenomenological research design, which places emphasis on understanding lived experience from the participants' point of view (Smith, Flowers, & Larkin, 2009).

TABLE 7.1 Participant Information					
School	Participant identifier	Gender	Age	SEND as stated on school SEN register	Interview, focus group or both?
A (mainstream primary)	LA	Female	8	Dyslexia	Focus group
	OA	Female	11	Emotional, behavior and social development needs (EBSD), Global Learning Difficulties (GLD)	Both
	AA	Female	9	GLD, Medical needs	Focus group
	KA	Female	9	Dyslexia	Focus group
	MA	Male	11	Dyslexia	Both

(continued)

TABLE 7.1 Participant Information (continued)

School	Participant identifier	Gender	Age	SEND as stated on school SEN register	Interview, focus group or both?
B (mainstream primary)	SB	Male	10	Cerebral Palsy (CP), Medical (epilepsy)	Focus group
	MB	Male	9	Specific Learning Difficulties (SpLD) (Literacy)	Both
	BB	Male	9	Concentration difficulties, possible dyslexia	Focus group
	DB	Male	9	Literacy difficulties, Gross and fine motor skill difficulty	Focus group
	FB	Female	8	Literacy difficulties	Both
	AB	Male	8	Medical, Learning delay	Interview
	NB	Female	10	Dyslexia	Interview
C (mainstream secondary)	AC	Male	12	SpLD (Dyslexia)	Both
	NC	Female	13	SpLD (Dyslexia), Visual Impairment	Both
	DC	Female	12	Moderate Learning Difficulties (MLD)	Focus group
D (mainstream secondary)	JD	Male	12	Speech and Language difficulties	Both
	MD	Male	12	Autistic Spectrum Disorder (ASD), Dyspraxia	Both
	LD	Female	14	GLD	Focus group
E (SEND base unit at school A)	PE	Female	10	MLD	Both
	AE	Male	10	ASD	Both
	CE	Male	9	MLD	Focus group
	DE	Male	10	MLD	Focus group
	SE	Male	7	MLD	Focus group
F (special school)	AF	Female	12	Developmental Delay (DD)	Both
	KF	Female	13	DD	Focus group
	AAF	Male	13	CP	Both
G (special school)[a]	CG	Female	12	EBSD	Interview
	LG	Female	14	EBSD	Interview
	TG	Male	13	EBSD, Medical needs	Interview
	JG	Male	13	EBSD	Interview

[a] School G is a hospital school that caters to children excluded from mainstream education due to their social, emotional, and behavioral difficulties.

To do this, I used interviews and focus groups. To ensure my methods were accessible to a wide range of children with SEND, a pilot study was carried out (Coates & Vickerman, 2010). This highlighted that using standard interview and focus group techniques (i.e., simply following an interview schedule in a question–answer format) would not yield high quality data, nor was it motivating for the child participants. Based on the findings of the pilot study, the focus group methods were adapted to incorporate participatory elements allowing participants to have more control over data collection. Children were encouraged to choose how to capture the data ranging from data collection being researcher-led through to participants having free choice to determine how the focus groups should run. Children in each school unanimously chose one method: the "ping-pong ball" method. This involved presenting participants with a bag filled with ping-pong balls, each with a topic relating to PE and/or sport written on it. Children were asked to randomly select balls in turn and decide whether to keep and discuss the topic or discard it (if deemed unimportant to their experiences of PE). Additionally, a range of activities were presented in the focus groups including worksheets, drawing activities, and role play. These were included on ping-pong balls and indicated by gold stars. Again, children had freedom to choose whether or not they completed activities. This gave children who felt less confident or less able to communicate verbally the opportunity to engage in the research.

The aim of the focus groups was to understand the shared experiences of PE for a group of children with SEND. Interviews consisted of an eight-item interview schedule where the aim was to better understand children's personal experiences of PE.

Key themes from across the focus group and interview data were drawn out and analyzed paying particular attention to participants' reflections on their experiences in PE lessons. There were four stages to the data analysis in which the interpretive phenomenological analysis processes outlined by Smith et al. (2009) were followed. First, data were continually reflected upon during the data collection period, including keeping detailed fieldnotes. This allowed for initial ideas about the data to be drawn out. This is what Smith et al. (2009, p. 82) termed "active engagement with the data." Next, all data were transcribed verbatim. The transcripts were read individually and then grouped by school type and read again. Summaries of the transcripts were produced to develop a succinct understanding of the key messages within the data. Finally, a full detailed analysis of the data was undertaken, where transcripts were coded and key themes were developed from these codes. In the next section, the key themes identified will be presented.

RESULTS

Facilitators

Findings show that there are a number of core facilitators in PE, which not only result in children with SEND feeling included in PE lessons, but also prompt positive perceptions about PE. These are: differentiation in PE lessons, positive teacher–child relationships, and peer support. Each of these themes will be discussed in turn.

Differentiation in PE

Children with SEND had positive perceptions about PE when their teachers differentiated lessons to meet their specific needs. Children acknowledged that having their work differentiated made them feel different from the other children in their lessons. However, difference was associated with positive feelings, particularly when differentiation came from their ability to do something well, rather than an inability to participate. Differentiation related to modified work and learning objectives, adapted assessment techniques, and individual support during lessons. The following excerpts demonstrate how differentiation can lead to feelings of pride:

> **OA:** Erm, I did, I do dancing [outside school] . . . It's good to get, to be able to do something else cos if you do like say you learn to do the splits in dancing, that'd be good for you also in gymnastics, cos then you don't have to practice for the next thing [in PE], you can say I know how to do that. You show it to them [PE teachers] so you don't have to take longer, and then you miss like most of the lessons, like you don't, you could spend one week trying to do the splits when you could have been doing other things.
>
> **I:** So if you'd learnt the splits in [extracurricular] dance tonight and tomorrow in gymnastics [PE], they were teaching you the splits, what would you say to your teacher?
>
> **OA:** I can do them and then I'd have to show them and maybe do the thing that we're supposed to do next week, maybe they'd teach me that week, so I could practice while they were doing the splits.
>
> **I:** How does that make you feel?
>
> **OA:** Proud.   (Interview with OA)

> **AE:** They [other children in the class] don't do the same because they're younger and they're not tall. [Classmates do]

easy ones like roll over and like do cartwheels and on the mats.

I: Would you like them to do the same things as you?

AE: No, because they're younger and they might hurt themselves because their legs are not that tall and they like break their backs. They fall over.

I: So would you like to do the same things that they do on the mats?

AE: Uh-uh. It's too easy. I done it before when I was in year two . . . [I feel different from others in PE] because I know more than them because I go to mainstream classes. So they do different work and, and I get different work. [I feel] quite good because I've got different work and the work's harder. (Interview with AE)

This kind of differentiation, where children's skills are acknowledged and acted on by teachers, can lead to children having a greater sense of achievement in PE. This supports Goodwin and Watkinson's (2000) findings that showed children had good days in PE when they felt that they had skillfully participated in lessons. Differentiation in PE lessons can empower children to participate (Hutzler et al., 2002); and by promoting positive difference in PE lessons, children are able to challenge themselves to develop their skills further. In addition, differentiation was also used to encourage children to participate in activities they were not confident about, resulting in increased participation in those activities. This is illustrated by NC below when reflecting on her dance PE assessment, which caused anxiety for her due to a physical disfigurement:

NC: On Wednesday we had PE and because the other group is doing dance, Miss said, "Just sit down and remember the beginning of the dance" and, you know, and when, I went, "Do I have to show it to anyone," she went "No, just as long as I can assess you on it." So it wasn't like, I didn't have to go on the DVD that the others have to go on and all that. . . . I feel better about it [not going on the DVD] because I don't show anyone up, and no one shows me up.

Earlier in her interview, NC had discussed feeling inferior to other children, particularly in dance, much of this resulting from her self-perceptions relating to her SEND. Yet, adapting the way that she was assessed helped her to overcome some of her anxieties and prompted engagement where previously she would have refused to take part. Differentiated assessment is an important element of inclusive PE. It encourages children to progress at their own pace and set goals which meet their specific needs (Sherrill, 2004). This was particularly important for secondary school children in this study who were formally assessed during PE lessons, where their younger counterparts were not.

These findings support previous literature, which indicates that differentiation in PE lessons is fundamental for promoting positive experiences of PE (Goodwin & Watkinson, 2000; Hutzler et al., 2002). Additionally, the findings demonstrate that differentiation and inclusive practice is happening for some children with SEND. Researchers exploring teacher perceptions of inclusion (Fitzgerald, 2012; Morley et al., 2005; Slininger et al., 2000; Vickerman, 2002) and children's perceptions of PE (Blinde & McCallister, 1998; Fitzgerald, 2005; Goodwin & Watkinson, 2000) often suggest that differentiation is not well-understood by teachers and does not happen frequently enough for children with SEND, yet these findings show the positive impact differentiation can have for children when done appropriately.

Positive Teacher–Child Relationships

Children in this study, despite their different SEND, age, and educational setting, shared very similar views in relation to their experiences of PE teachers. Positive relationships with teachers stemmed from children's perception that their PE teachers were different from teachers of other subjects at school (especially more academic subjects). Many children used words such as *helpful, funny,* and *friend* to describe their teachers. This was often related to support the teacher gave the child in lessons, and the informal manner in which they approached teaching. In particular, children had positive perceptions of the help they received from their PE teachers:

> **FB:** They [PE teachers] tell you what we're going to be doing, how you play and what sort of things you play with. They're good and they're helpful, because if we, if we're struggling, then they help us, um, carry on.
>
> **AC:** Like in rock climbing when you don't know how to, like cos we're learning how to do a double figured reef knot, I couldn't do that, they helped me, teach me how to do it.... They give you more confidence in doing some stuff.... They cheer you on and, and let you, let you go at your own pace.

Statements like these were common in this study. Children were generally very positive about the support they received from PE teachers, and this contributed to children's perceptions that they were being included in the lessons. Supportive PE teachers were often associated with increased confidence, as well as encouraging participation and facilitating an environment where all children felt equal.

LG: It's nice to be taught by them. Um, we know them other than just for PE, like he'll talk to us, and he will treat us like a student but as a friend as well, you know, like pally teacher, it's nice to be taught by someone you know and can trust. He's fair with everyone and he treats everyone the same.

This is further substantiated by Goodwin and Watkinson (2000), Fitzgerald (2005), and Coates and Vickerman (2010), who indicate that support received from a PE teacher can enhance children's perceptions of PE lessons. This has been shown to help children feel included, promoting positive experiences in PE. Similarly, findings from this study demonstrated the important role teachers have in facilitating positive experiences in PE. Children who discussed the positive relationship they had with teachers, also used words such as fun, exciting, and good to describe PE lessons.

Previous studies, however, have demonstrated that PE teachers are sometimes not perceived positively, and are often perceived as stakeholders responsible for the exclusion of children with SEND in lessons (Blinde & McCallister, 1998; Goodwin & Watkinson, 2000; Hutzler et al., 2002). These studies did focus upon the perceptions of children with physical disabilities, whereas this research considered SEND more broadly. However, it is worth noting that positive perceptions were also held by children in this study who had physical disabilities. Thus, it is wholly possible, as demonstrated here, that when supported in lessons and given the opportunity to develop positive relationships with teachers, children with SEND can feel included in PE and have positive experiences, regardless of their SEND. As Fitzgerald (2005) states, PE teachers "can nurture a more positive disposition toward participating in PE" (Fitzgerald, 2005, p. 54), and so should nurture their relationships with pupils to build trust, so children feel confident enough to approach them for support.

Peer Support

Like their teachers, children with SEND in this study reported positive relationships with some peers in PE lessons, and the positive relationships they had with these children resulted in better experiences of PE. Children often referred to their classmates as "friends" and explored the different ways they helped them to participate in and enjoy PE.

School E Focus Group: They [classmates] make me feel happy because when I'm left out they always cheer me up.

AC: If you do something good, then all your mates will cheer you and clap you and help you.

FB: If I'm struggling and they see me they come over to help and I think that's really nice. If we're playing tennis they

would help me like, tell me, um, which way to hold the rac-
quet and stuff, and um how like Mrs. E or Miss P said to do,
they tell me again, just so, just to make sure I know ... If you
didn't have anybody in PE with you, then you would struggle
a very lot.

Classmates played an important role in including children in lessons by
ensuring they were aware of the rules of play, assisting them with participation, and providing support and encouragement. These findings are supported by Seymour et al. (2009), who illustrate that children with disabilities often consider classmates to be friends. This relates to what Goodwin
and Watkinson (2000, p. 151) refer to as having a "sense of belonging,"
where the child considers classmates to be companions who contribute
to the supportive PE environment. Promoting positive relationships with
peers can therefore be an important contributor to successful inclusive
practice (Slininger et al., 2000).

It is worth noting that within this study, even for children who have physical disabilities, experiences of classmates were generally positive, and did
not reflect the negative experiences found by other researchers (Blinde
& McCallister, 1998; Fitzgerald, 2005; Hutzler et al., 2002; Place & Hodge,
2001). This could be explained by Seymour et al. (2009) who state that
the development of friendships can be an outcome of inclusive education.
Moreover, they argue that friendship in PE can improve children's perceptions of themselves, the support and guidance they receive, and their en-
thusiasm for the subject (Seymour et al., 2009). This further supports the
fundamental role peers play in supporting inclusion.

The findings that pertain to positive experiences of PE illustrate that the
relationships children with SEND have with their teachers and peers play
a fundamental role in improving perceptions of and participation in PE.
However, like previous research, experiences of PE were not all positive.
Children highlighted specific barriers that resulted in negative experiences
of PE, and in some instances exclusion from PE.

Barriers

Findings from this study showed that barriers to PE related to: the prescriptive nature of the PE curriculum, as well as discrimination and bullying
by peers and teachers. Each of these barriers will be considered in turn.

Experiences of the PE curriculum

Children with SEND in this study tended to discuss their experiences of
PE in relation to specific PE activities. They explored their feelings toward

different activities and reflected on how this impacted on their general experiences of the subject. In particular, dance and gymnastics activities were often related to poorer experiences in PE. For primary school children, especially boys, dance, and gymnastics were referred to as "girls" activities, which reduced their enjoyment and participation in these activities:

> **I:** So what kinds of things don't you like doing in PE?
>
> **BB and MB (together):** Gymnastics!
>
> > **DB:** Dance
> >
> > **BB:** I don't like dance
> >
> > **SB:** It's for girls. I watched Boogie Beebies one time and there was belly-dancing and I saw a boy doing belly-dancing
> >
> > **MB:** I get embarrassed
> >
> > **SB:** I hate ballet! I'd sort of do it if I had a sister. I don't know why girls just do ballet all the time.
> >
> > **FB:** I don't like playing football because it's for boys.
> >
> > **DB:** I don't like gymnastics, because, um, I don't know.
>
> Interview with MA

> > **MA:** We do football, some, like, games to warm us up, um, some exercise, and sometimes dance.
> >
> > **I:** Why do you pull that face when you say dance?
> >
> > **MA:** I'm a boy and I don't like dance!
> >
> > **I:** You don't like dance? Why not?
> >
> > **MA:** It's more of a girly thing.   (School B Focus Group)

For these children, dance and gymnastics inherited gendered stereotypes, resulting in boys feeling embarrassed during lessons. This was similar for boys in the secondary schools who disliked dance because they wanted to be more active in PE lessons. This supports research with typically developing children that showed children preferred activities which they believed fit with their gender (Frömel, Formánková, & Sallis, 2002; Lee, Fredenburg, Belcher, & Cleveland, 1999). These socially constructed conceptions of masculinity and femininity play a part in motivating children to participate in particular activities, and so it is important that these stereotypes are stripped away to improve children's perceptions of these activities. This could be achieved by making dance and gymnastics activities more desirable for boys, by offering the opportunity to participate in less gendered forms, like break dancing (Coates & Vickerman, 2010), or by teachers using different language to break down these stereotypes (Lee et al., 1999).

For secondary school girls, dance and gymnastics were activities that threatened self-esteem. Participants made comments relating to their physical appearance, the perceptions of others about them, and how these activities made them feel as reasons for disliking participating in these activities. The comments below illustrate this:

> **CG:** I was like the tallest and like, I wasn't the fattest, like but I am fat and like I'd notice that and like they'd point it out to me like, "Oh my God why can't you dance, is it 'cause you're fat?" And I was, like, "No, it's just that I'm not joining in 'cause I don't want to."
>
> **NC:** I'm really sporty and I can do all the things. It's like, I hate netball but I'll do netball any day instead of dance, because it's different when you go out with your mum and dad on holiday, and you know, you're doing all those weird dances when everyone's up, but it's just some of the things they want, like, it's like when you're not comfortable with how you look and that and you can see yourself in the mirror, and you look, like, how the other girls are doing it, you know you just don't feel comfortable doing it . . . I've got webbed toes and the first time when you go in there with bare feet, "Eeeeee, look at her toes," and you're just like, "I can't help it." So I don't feel comfortable with that and then you just feel really awkward with everything, because the other girls, like the popular ones in a way, you know, they can, they'll have their friends with their laugh and all that and then you see us, and there's the middle group and all that, and you just think, I can't do that, because I know I can't because I don't feel comfortable and I tell myself, "You can't do it" because I don't want to get made a fool of in front of them.

Self-perceptions impacted on their motivation to participate in these types of activities. Female participants were particularly concerned with the reactions of others and the ways in which they perceived themselves. Dance, and for some gymnastics, made girls feel uncomfortable about themselves and this restricted their willingness to participate–sometimes resulting in a refusal to take part. Research has shown that children with SEND do sometimes feel self-conscious in PE lessons and attribute these feelings of difference and social isolation to having SEND (Fitzgerald, 2005; Goodwin & Watkinson, 2001). While the girls in this study had similar feelings, this tended to stem from body consciousness rather than directly from their SEND, and this was limited to experiences of dance and gymnastics. Nevertheless, on closer inspection of the experiences of some participants, it was apparent that self-perceptions as a result of having SEND did play a role in negative experiences of dance and gymnastics.

I: Why didn't you want to be a part of it [dance]?

NC: Because I reckon it just makes you feel stupid in a way, and I feel stupid as it is, so there's no point in me making myself feel worse.

I: Why do you feel stupid as it is?

NC: I'm dyslexic and I have Irlen Syndrome, and English

I: So is it just in English that you feel that way or...

NC: Most of my classes ... I just sit out [of dance] because it's like I feel stupid anyway, I don't like dancing, it's a stupid dance so it just makes me feel like I look retarded basically.

MD: I, I don't like, like gymnastics and that ... Well like I dunno like it might be hard cos I've got like dyspraxia and it might be hard I dunno just cos like dunno it's just, just hard.

(Interview with NC and MD)

This is similar to the experiences of children in previous research (Blinde & McCallister, 1998; Fitzgerald, 2005; Goodwin & Watkinson, 2000) where they reported lower self-confidence in PE because of their SEND. However, for this study it was only in dance and gymnastics where children seemed to feel the wider impact of their SEND in relation to taking part in PE. Goodwin and Watkinson (2000) noted that often the competence of children with SEND was questioned by others in lessons, and the child would use self-appraisal to determine whether or not he or she feel able to participate as a result. These negative perceptions about dance and gymnastics may stem from internalizing labels relating to SEND that causes feelings of inferiority in some, but not all, contexts. Interestingly, Penney (2002) argues that the prescriptive nature of the PE curriculum in the United Kingdom, alongside teacher preference for competitive games, results in children with SEND being less able to access the curriculum. While findings from this study showed that competitive games were the most common PE activities participated in by children, they were also the activities that children enjoyed most. However, Penney (2002) suggests that children with SEND are more easily included in activities that are frequently being marginalized within the PE curriculum, like dance. Smith (2004) further suggests that dance and gymnastics are activities more conducive to inclusion. He states that these types of activities focus upon the individual, embracing their personal abilities through moderate, rhythmic physical activity. Yet, findings from this study indicate that dance, and to a lesser degree gymnastics, were the least preferred activities, particularly for mainstream school children, and seemed to have a negative impact on a child's self-esteem. The use of effective goal-setting, differentiated activities and the use of a personalized curriculum (Cabral & Crisfield, 1996; Sampson, Karagiannidis, & Kinshuk,

2002) may therefore benefit children with SEND who have lower self-confidence in certain activities.

Discrimination/Bullying

While many children in this study had positive experiences of their PE teachers and peers, children discussed some interactions that led children to feel bullied and discriminated against. Participants from School G in particular, reflected on specific interactions with their teachers in their previous mainstream schools that resulted in them feeling less confident, belittled, and bullied.

> **CG:** I didn't really do PE [at the mainstream school], cos the PE teacher used to bully me, used to call me fat and that to make me feel bad, and that happened at primary school as well... In mainstream school, like the [PE] teachers, they'll get away with saying anything to you, because they just like call you fat and that, pass comments about your weight and how you look and everything, when you were doing PE. And like if you'd say anything they'd be like yeah but we're trying to make you better at PE but it doesn't, it just hurts your feelings more than anything... I didn't want to do PE anymore because I just felt embarrassed and insecure because like everyone'd laugh when the teacher would do that.
>
> **LG:** The [mainstream PE] teachers were nasty and because of my size very nasty about that... when I went and told the teacher [about a situation in the changing rooms] and the PE teacher was horrible to me over everything in the changing rooms and then she was making a show of me in front of the group who were in and stuff like that so that was my worst PE lesson.

Poor experiences of PE teachers resulted in children feeling discouraged from participation, feeling angered and upset, and lacking confidence to participate in PE. For the two participants just quoted, these events were experienced in the mainstream school they attended before being moved into special education, and interestingly were not related to their SEND (behavioral and emotional difficulties). Instead, they were attributed to physical appearance. In fact, these two participants blamed negative relationships with PE teachers as a factor in the development of their difficulties, and their subsequent move into special education.

This further emphasizes the need for teachers to nurture their relationships with the children they teach, carefully selecting the language they use around children, and considering the ways their interactions might impact on the experiences of the child. Moreover, these findings also relate to children who do not have SEND (Groves & Laws, 2000).

Children also reported feeling discriminated against and bullied by their peers in PE lessons.

> **LD:** [Classmates say] like, "Oh my god you just thick, you done it wrong," "Oh god, get off the team" and all that.
>
> **I:** How does it make you feel when they say that?
>
> **LD:** "Miss I'm not playing" and I sit on the bench.
>
> **CG:** Well once I got me pants robbed...and they were all standing on one side of the changing room laughing at me, and I was running round crying, and they was horrible, so I hated that. (School D Focus Group)

While generally perceptions of peers were positive, bullying was still a barrier, which was detrimental to positive experiences of PE, and in some cases led children to voluntarily exclude themselves from participating. Bullying and discrimination came in the form of verbal name-calling, and physical acts, including aggression. These findings are similar to those presented by previous researchers (Blinde & McCallister, 1998; Fitzgerald, 2005; Goodwin & Watkinson, 2000; Hutzler et al., 2002).

Interestingly, bullying was discussed by female participants more so than male. Glover et al. (2000) indicate the females are more likely to become victims of bullying, due to their non-retaliatory nature, and this may explain why incidences of bullying were more common for the female participants. Additionally, Glover, Gough, Johnson, and Cartwright (2000) found in their study that being different accounted for 13% of bullying, which goes some way to understanding why children with SEND experience bullying. In particular, children in this study indicated they were bullied for "being stupid," "dressing differently," or "being fat." Fitzgerald (2005) highlights that children with SEND are aware of their perceived difference from other children, and this difference may well be a contributing factor to the discriminatory behavior they experienced. Teachers should be tactful in their approach to dealing with bullying in the classroom to reduce its impact. This requires sensitivity in order to reduce feelings of otherness among children who may already be feeling different from their peers (Fitzgerald, 2005; Goodwin & Watkinson, 2001).

DISCUSSION AND IMPLICATIONS

This chapter has highlighted a number of key facilitators and barriers to inclusive PE from the perspectives of children with a range of SEND. While the research reported here has considered the experiences of children with a number of different challenges and difficulties–ranging from specific learning difficulties to complex physical and intellectual disabilities–previous literature has tended to only focus on children with physical disabilities or complex intellectual disabilities. Nevertheless, the findings have illustrated a number of similarities with previous research: Children have better experiences of PE when they have good relationships with their teachers and their peers, and when the activities and expectations are adapted to suit the needs of the individual child; while barriers to inclusion include bullying and discrimination from teachers and peers.

In addition, some areas of the PE curriculum, particularly those which focus on the individual such as dance and gymnastics, might threaten their identity, confidence, and self-esteem. This implies inclusion could be achieved through the development of practices and curricula that are adaptable to the needs of individual children, and by nurturing a supportive environment that promotes the development of positive relationships between children, their teachers, and their peers. Importantly, for this to happen, there is the need for PE teachers to embrace change and to develop strategies to ensure that all children, not just those with aptitude in PE, are able to become physically literate and achieve to the best of their individual ability. Taking this into account, some key recommendations can be made.

First, PE teacher education needs to be improved. Research (e.g., Coates, 2012; Morley et al., 2005) has shown that PE teachers require better training and support to teach inclusively, yet this study has shown that when done well, differentiation can improve children's perceptions of PE and promote inclusion. Therefore, initial teacher education and continued professional development courses should include compulsory elements that provide teachers with the practical know-how about strategies to adapt lessons appropriately so that children's specific needs are accounted for.

Second, teachers should work toward building supportive, trusting relationships with their pupils to promote positive experiences in PE and buffer against children's feelings of low self-confidence and self-esteem, which might be an inherent result of having SEND. This can also promote engagement in lessons. In addition, the development of a supportive PE environment should also include elements of peer mentoring. Peers play an important role in improving self-esteem and confidence in lessons; and at the opposing end can also be stakeholders in children having poor experiences and feeling isolated and excluded. Teachers should be mindful of the role that peers can play in inclusion and work toward helping children behave toward each other in ways that promote engagement.

Flexibility should also be built into the PE curriculum so that activities that are less favorable for children can be adapted in such a way that they do not threaten self-esteem or confidence. For this to work, children need to be consulted with about curriculum design. Empowering children to engage in curriculum/lesson design can promote engagement. Equally, teachers could work toward developing physically literate children who have developed the skills necessary for being lifelong participants of physical activity. Thus curriculum and teaching should be skills-based rather than activity-based (Coates, 2011; Whitehead, 2010). This also builds in room for successful differentiation in lessons.

There is one final, important point: We should be consulting with children who have SEND about their experiences and their needs. Who better to learn from than the individuals we are seeking to include?

REFERENCES

Anastasiou, D., & Kauffman, J. M. (2013). The social model of disability: Dichotomy between impairment and disability. *Journal of Medicine and Philosophy, 38*(4), 441–459. DOI:10.1093/jmp/jht026

Armstrong, D. (2005). Reinventing 'Inclusion': New Labour and the Cultural Politics of Special Education. *Oxford Review of Education, 31*(1), 135–151.

Bailey, J. (2005). Medical and psychological models of special educational needs. In C. Clark, A. Dyson, & A. Millward (Eds.), *Theorising Special Education* (pp. 44–60). London, England: Routledge.

Bailey, R. (2006). Physical education and sport in schools: A review of benefits and outcomes. *Journal of School Health, 76*(8), 397–440. doi:10.1111/j.1746-1561.2006.00132.x

Baker, J. (2006). Contributions of teacher–child relationships to positive school adjustment during elementary school. *Journal of School Psychology, 44*, 21–229. doi:10.1016/j.jsp.2006.02.002

BERA. (2004). *Revised ethical guidelines for educational research.* Nottingham, England: BERA.

Birch, S., & Ladd, G. (1998). Children's interpersonal behaviors and the teacher–child relationship, *developmental psychology, 34*(5), 934–946. doi:10.1037/0012-1649.34.5.934

Blinde, E. M., & McCallister, S. G. (1998). Listening to the voices of students with physical disabilities. *Journal of Physical Education, Recreation, and Dance, 69*(6), 64–68.

Brisenden, S. (1986) Independent living and the medical model of disability. *Disability, Handicap and Society, 1*(2), 173–178.

Cabral, P., & Crisfield, P. (1996). *Motivation and mental toughness.* Leeds, England: National Coaching Foundation.

Coates, J. (2011). Physically fit or physically literate? Children with special educational needs understanding of physical education. *European Physical Education Review, 17*(2), 167–182. doi:10.1177/1356336X11413183

Coates, J. (2012). Teaching inclusively: Are secondary physical education student teachers sufficiently prepared to teach in inclusive environments? *Physical Education and Sport Pedagogy, 17*(4), 349–365.

Coates, J., & Vickerman, P. (2010). Empowering children with special educational needs to speak up: Experiences of inclusive physical education. *Disability and Rehabilitation, 32* (18), 1517–1526. doi:10.3109/09638288.2010.497037

Connors, C., & Stalker, K. (2007). Children's experiences of disability: Pointers to a social model of childhood disability. *Disability and Society, 22*(1), 19–33. doi:10.1080/09687590601056162

Department for Children Schools and Families (DCSF). (2008). *Physical education and sport strategy for young people (PESSYP)*. London, England: HMSO.

Department for Education (DfE). (2013). *National curriculum in England: Physical education programmes of study*. Retrieved November, 1, 2016, from https://www.gov.uk/government/publications/national-curriculum-in-england-physical-education-programmes-of-study/national-curriculum-in-england-physical-education-programmes-of-study

Department for Education & Department for Health (DfE/DfH). (2014). *Special educational needs code of practice: 0–25 Years*. London, England: HMSO.

Evans, A. B., Bright, J. L., & Brown, L. J. (2015). Non-disabled secondary school children's lived experiences of a wheelchair basketball programme delivered in the East of England. *Sport, Education and Society, 20*(6), 741–761. doi:10.1080/13573322.2013.808620

Evans, J. (2004). Making a difference? Education and 'ability' in physical education. *European Physical Education Review, 10*(1), 95–108. doi:10.1177/1356336X04042158

Farmer, T. W., Hall, C. M., Leung, M-C., Estell, D. B., & Brooks, D. S. (2011). Social prominence and the heterogeneity of rejected status in late elementary school. *School Psychology Quarterly, 26*, 260–274, doi:10.1037/a0025624

Farrell, M. (2004). *Special educational needs: A resource for practitioners*. London: Paul Chapman.

Farrell, P. (2001). Special education in the last twenty years: Have things really got better? *British Journal of Special Education, 28*(1), 3–9.

Fitzgerald, H. (2005). Still feeling like a spare piece of luggage? Embodied experiences of (dis)ability in physical education and school sport. *Physical Education and Sport Pedagogy, 10*(1), 41–59. doi:10.1080/1740898042000334908

Fitzgerald, H. (2012). 'Drawing' on disabled students' experiences of physical education and stakeholder responses. *Sport, Education and Society, 17*(4), 443–462. doi:10.1080/13573322.2011.609290

Frömel, K., Formánková, S., & Sallis, J. F. (2002). Physical activity and sport preferences of 10 to 14 year old children: A 5 year prospective study. *Acta Universitatis Palackianae Olomucensis. Gymnica, 32*(1), 11–16.

Geisel, T. G. (1954). *Horton hears a who*. New York, NY: Random House.

Glover, D., Gough, G., Johnson, M., & Cartwright, N. (2000). Bullying in 25 secondary schools: Incidence, impact and intervention. *Educational Research, 42*(2), 141–156.

Goodwin, D. L. (2001). The meaning of help in PE: Perceptions of students with physical disabilities. *Adapted Physical Activity Quarterly, 18*(3), 289–303.

Goodwin, D., & Watkinson, J. (2000). Inclusive physical education from the perspectives of students with physical disabilities. *Adapted Physical Activity Quarterly, 17*, 144–160.

Groves, S., & Laws, C. (2000). Children's experiences of physical education. *European Journal of Physical Education, 5*(1), 19–27.

Hagger, M. S., Chatzisarantis, N., & Biddle, S. J. (2001). The influence of self-efficacy and past behavior on the physical activity intentions of young people. *Journal of Sports Sciences, 19*(9), 711–725.

Healy, S., Msetfi, R., & Gallagher, S. (2013). Happy and a bit nervous: The experiences of children with autism in physical education. *British Journal of Learning Disabilities, 41*(3), 222–228. doi:10.1111/bld.12053

Hodge, S., Ammah, J., Casebolt, K., LaMaster, K., & O'Sullivan, M. (2004) High school general physical education teachers' behaviors and beliefs associated with inclusion. *Sport, Education and Society, 9*(3), 395–420.

Howes, C. (2000). Social-emotional classroom climate in child care, child-teacher relationships and children's second grade peer relations. *Social Development, 9*(2), 191–204. doi:10.1111/1467-9507.00119

Hutzler, Y., Fliess, O., Chacham, A., & Auweele, Y. (2002). Perspectives of children with physical disabilities on inclusion and empowerment: Supporting and limiting factors. *Physical Activity Quarterly, 19*(3), 300–317.

Jones, P. (2005). Teachers' views of their pupils with profound and multiple learning difficulties. *European Journal of Special Needs Education, 20*(4), 375–385. doi:10.1080/08856250500274195

Lee, A. M., Fredenburg, K., Belcher, D., & Cleveland, N. (1999). Gender differences in children's conceptions of competence and motivation in physical education. *Sport, Education and Society, 4*(2), 161–174.

Low, C. (2007) A defence of moderate inclusion. In R. Cigman (Ed), *Included or excluded? The challenge of the mainstream for some SEN children* (pp. 15–23). Oxford, England: Routledge.

Morley, D., Bailey, R., Tan, J., & Cooke, B. (2005). Inclusive physical education: Teachers' views of teaching children with special educational needs and disabilities in physical education. *European Physical Education Review, 11*(1), 84–107. doi:10.1177/1356336X05049826

Oliver, M (1990). *The politics of disablement.* London, England: Palgrave

Penney, D. (2002) Equality, equity and inclusion in physical education and school sport. In: A. Laker (Ed.), *The sociology of sport and physical education* (pp. 110–128). London, England: Routledge.

Penney, D. & Evans, J. (2013) Who is physical education for? In S. Capel & M. Whitehead (Eds.), *Debates in physical education* (pp. 164–165). London, England: Routledge.

Place, K., & Hodge, S. (2001) Social inclusion of students with physical disabilities in general physical education: A behavioral analysis. *Adapted Physical Activity Quarterly, 18*, 389–404.

Qi, J., & Ha, A. S. (2012). Inclusion in physical education: A review of literature. *International Journal of Disability, Development and Education, 59*(3), 257–281. doi:10.1080/1034912X.2012.697737

Reed, J., & Watson, D. (1994). The impact of the medical model on nursing practice and assessment. *International Journal of Nursing Studies, 31*(1), 57–66.

Sampson, D., Karagiannidis, C., & Kinshuk. (2002). Personalised learning: Educational, technological and standardisation perspectives. *Interactive Educational Multimedia, Special Issue on Adaptive Educational Multimedia, 4,* 24–39.

Seymour, H., Reid, G., & Bloom, G. (2009). Friendship in inclusive physical education. *Adapted Physical Activity Quarterly, 26*(3), 201–219.

Shakespeare, T. (2012). *Disability rights and wrongs.* London, England: Routledge.

Shakespeare, T., & Watson, N. (1997). Defending the social model. *Disability and Society, 12*(2), 293–300.

Sherrill, C. (2004). *Adapted physical activity, recreation and sport: Psychosocial perspectives on inclusion, integration and participation* (6th ed.). New York, NY: McGraw-Hill

Siperstein, G. N., Norins, J., & Mohler, A. (2007). Social acceptance and attitude change. In J. W. Jacobson, J. A. Mulick, & J. Rojahn (Eds). *Handbook of intellectual and developmental disabilities* (pp. 133–154). New York, NY: Springer.

Slininger, D., Sherril, C., & Jankowski, C. (2000). Children's attitudes toward peers with severe disabilities: Revisiting contact theory. *Adapted Physical Activity Quarterly, 17,* 176–198.

Smith, A. (2004). The inclusion of pupils with special educational needs in secondary school physical education. *Physical Education & Sport Pedagogy, 9*(1), 37–54. doi:10.1080/1740898042000208115

Smith, A. B. (2007). Children and young people's participation rights in education. *The International Journal of Children's Rights, 15*(1), 147–164.

Smith, A. L. (2003). Peer relationships in physical activity contexts: A road less travelled in youth sport and exercise psychology research. *Psychology of Sport and Exercise, 4*(1), 25–39.

Smith, J., Flowers, P., & Larkin, M. (2009). *Interpretive phenomenological analysis: Theory, method and research.* London, England: SAGE.

Townsend, M., & Hassal, J. (2007). Mainstream student's attitudes to possible inclusion in unified sports with students who have an intellectual disability. *Journal of Applied Research in Intellectual Disabilities, 20,* 265–273.

United Nations Educational, Scientific and Cultural Organization (UNESCO). (1994). *The Salamanca statement and framework for action.* Salamanca, Spain: Ministry of Education and Science.

Vickerman, P., & Coates, J. K. (2009). Trainee and recently qualified physical education teachers' perspectives on including children with special educational needs. *Physical Education and Sport Pedagogy, 14*(2), 137–153.

Whitehead, M. (Ed.). (2010). *Physical literacy: Throughout the life course.* London, England: Routledge.

Wiener, J., & Schneider, B. H. (2002). A multisource exploration of the friendship patterns of children with and without learning disabilities. *Journal of Abnormal Child Psychology, 30*(2), 127–141. doi:10.1023/A:1014701215315

PART III

EFFECTIVE PHYSICAL EDUCATION STRATEGIES
TO ENHANCE BIOPSYCHOSOCIAL OUTCOMES FOR
CHILDREN AND ADOLESCENTS WITH SPECIAL NEEDS

CHAPTER 8

PLAY FIGHTING AS A STRATEGY TO COPE WITH AGGRESSIVE BEHAVIORS AMONG YOUTH WITH SOCIAL DISADVANTAGES IN ITALY

Erica Gobbi and Attilio Carraro
University of Padua

YOUTH FROM SOCIALLY DISADVANTAGED BACKGROUNDS WITHIN THE ITALIAN CONTEXT AND EDUCATIONAL SYSTEM

Social Fabric of Italian Youth

Modern society is marked by complexity and rapid changes, which have resulted in local, national and international political, social, and religious turmoil. Many scholars and commentators consider today's youth to be highly vulnerable to these changing times (Kelly, 2001). A parallel phenomenon that has affected Italy since the end of the 1960s is the demographic

Inclusive Physical Activities, pages 163–182
Copyright © 2017 by Information Age Publishing
All rights of reproduction in any form reserved.

reduction in the younger population. Numerous disadvantages have been reported for young people. Due to having less demographic weight, they experience disadvantages in the political, social, and economic domains both in relation to previous generations and to young people in other developed countries (Ambrosi & Rosina, 2009; Boeri & Galasso, 2007).

In this context, young foreigners represent a further element of transformation in the development of contemporary Italian society. Regardless of the political prominence and the media emphasis on the urgent situation of migrants landing on Italian shores, to date incoming migratory flows represent a regular feature of this country (Ambrosini, 2014). Youths with a migrant background are considered to be those who have arrived to join their families, or who were born in Italy from foreign parents. Each has a different story: some have reached Italy alone, others accompanied by their families; some were forced to leave their countries for economic reasons or due to war or political or religious persecution; some arrived in Italy because it represents a country of transit to reach other countries; and others are suffering due to mistreatment and human trafficking. Underage foreigners in Italy are a growing population, which according to the last report of the Istat (the Italian National Statistics Agency) on January 1, 2013, amounted to 908,539. The presence of this relatively new segment of young people brings about major demographic and cultural transformations in Italian society. Moreover, the growing number of children and adolescents from immigrant families attending school is, on the one hand, an indicator that migration is becoming rooted in Italy (Santagati, 2015); and on the other hand, it represents a sociodemographic challenge because Italy has yet to acquire a consolidated position on the management of multiethnic groups in education (Cesareo, 2014). Many variables can affect the school life of a youth with a social disadvantage, like children and adolescents with an immigrant background. Among the causes of disadvantages in educational settings are primarily the lower socioeconomic background from which many of these children stem, language problems that youths with an immigrant origin experience, and cultural differences and differing systems of education existing in the country of origin (Dronkers, de Heus, & Levels, 2012). These variables can contribute toward generating a risk situation. Departing from these difficult conditions, other variables can further compromise school achievement among youths with social disadvantages linked to an immigrant background: relations with peers and teachers may affect attitudes toward learning, alter the classroom environment and affect the teachers' pedagogical style and effort (Contini, 2013). Recent findings have shown how the disadvantages of immigrant youth need to be urgently addressed with effective policies of inclusion aimed at ensuring equality of opportunity to all youth, and with intervention strategies aimed at fostering social cohesion (Contini, 2013).

The Italian Inclusive Educational System

The process of inclusion is strongly linked to the educational system of a country. Schools and teachers alike are uniquely placed to teach the knowledge, skills, and attitudes that underpin responsible citizenship as they provide early and sustained access to the future citizenry who are now challenged with the inclusion of numerous children of diverse origins and different social backgrounds.

In Italy, the educational system responds to the principle of equality prescribed also in Article 3 of the Constitution of the Italian Republic:

> All citizens have equal social dignity and are equal before the law, without distinction of sex, race, language, religion, political opinion, personal and social conditions. It is the duty of the Republic to remove those obstacles of an economic or social nature which constrain the freedom and equality of citizens, thereby impeding the full development of the person. (Senato della Repubblica, 2012, pp. 8–9)

The process of integration in the educational system started in 1971, when education for all had to take place in regular classes with the exception of students with severe impairments. In 1977, special education teachers were introduced into the school system with the role of providing special support to promote the integration of students with a disability into the school system. The process of constituting an inclusive educational system continued in the final years of the last century, and in 1992 the Law n.104 prescribed the removal of any barriers (architectural and sensorial), and set out to introduce appropriate aids and tools to support students with disabilities in education and training. New ways of teaching were prescribed under Law n. 170 in 2010, when all students were to be considered from a pedagogical and not from a clinical viewpoint, i.e., as individuals with different potentialities that required different teaching methods in accordance with their way of learning. Starting from the fact that inclusion is not only a matter of disability, in 2012, the term *special educational needs* (SEN) was introduced as an umbrella term to address all kinds of difficulty that a student can experience within the school setting (Ministerial Directive of 27, 2012). This had the effect of ensuring more inclusive practices in the classroom through individualized and personalized educational plans, and thereby addressing a wide range of difficulties ranging from disabilities, socioeconomic/cultural/linguistic disadvantages, learning disorders, or any other condition that can prevent students from full inclusion in the educational process. In this context, a youth with a disadvantaged background has had to be considered as a minor with special needs, especially when aiming to include them in the education system, and in the health and societal system of the country.

If, on one hand, Italy adopts an inclusive educational model so that general education and regular classes are organized so that they focus on the enrichment derived from cultural diversity; on the other hand, a lot of work still remains to be done to effectively include youths with special needs, whereby positive outcomes and the successful involvement of these youths in educational, sport, health, and social practices are maximized.

Maintaining an intercultural and inclusive perspective in educational strategies, and paying particular attention to the recognition of the individual differences appear to be the most suitable way of addressing the needs of a multicultural society. It is clear that such a transformation in the educational system calls for action among different actors, starting from the institutions responsible for managing the system, for teacher training and further education, and increasing the involvement of families in their children's education. Nowadays, actions aimed at improving the school life of all students are desirable, and all institutions and bodies (not forgetting universities) are key players in the challenge of building an effective inclusive educational system.

AGGRESSION AS A PROBLEM FOR YOUTH

Effective policies of inclusion aimed at ensuring the equality of opportunity in all domains of life are urgently needed; however, the school in particular is asked to provide young people with an ideal setting where they can be supported in their harmonious self-actualization. In this period of transformation, the schools are facing a particular challenge in fully adhering to their educational role and training. Youths who have behavioral difficulties often characterize school life, and disturb themselves and others during classes hampering social development of the group and compromising the overall growth process.

According to the last national report on *Aspects of Daily Life* (Istat, 2015), it was shown that real vexatious actions among youths range from insults to derision, from threats to aggression with hard pushes, kicks, and punches. Other actions are directed to damage or steal things owned by peers; the defamation, lies with the intention to discredit, and social exclusion are also mechanisms through which antisocial behavior is displayed among youth in high schools. The most common forms of bullying consist of offenses with ugly nicknames or insults (12.1%), derision for the physical appearance and/or how one talks (6.3%), defamation (5.1%), exclusion for the point of view (4.7%), and physical attack with hard push, blows, kicks, and punches (3.8%; Istat, 2015).

In 2014, more than 50% of youths aged from 11 to 17 reported having been a victim in some offensive, disrespectful and/or violent episodes in the previous 12 months; 19.8% reported having been a victim of bullying, with a frequency of one or more times per month; and 9.1% reported having been the victim of acts of bullying, with weekly frequency (Istat, 2015).

Aggressive behaviors represent a serious problem among Italian youths, especially for some categories of them. As registered in the national report, girls are more at risk than boys of being victims (with 55% of girls aged 11–17 reported having been a victim of some prevarication acts in the previous year compared to 49.9% of the boys). Secondly, antisocial behavior is more frequent among youths aged 11–13 (22.5% reported suffering from one or more vexatious actions monthly compared to 17.9% of youths aged 14–17). Territorial differences in the phenomenon do also exist: in the north part of Italy, especially in the northeast part (24.5%), the assiduous victims of abuse are more than in the central and south part of Italy. Moreover, the highest rates of antisocial and disrespectful or violent behavior are reported among youths living in disadvantaged areas: 23.3% of youths living in this areas reported having been a victim in the last year, compared to 17% of youths living in non-disadvantaged areas (Istat, 2015).

Evidence showed the size of the urgent need for action to stop antisocial behavior and prevent its repetition among youths. Innovative and cost-effective strategies are needed to support teachers' work in this challenging setting.

PLAY FIGHTING

Play Fighting to Fight Aggression: The Conception of the Idea

The authors of this chapter have long been involved in physical education teacher education and were themselves physical education teachers and sport coaches for some years. Starting from this perspective, we have been able to observe and directly experience how teachers struggle with the question of how to manage and reduce behavioral problems that compromise the process of inclusion in schools. Inspired by our personal experience and by the literature, it has been clear that innovative and cost-effective interventions to cope with aggressive behaviors among youths are necessary. The challenging social situation of our living and working area strengthened the idea that the school context, especially physical education lessons, can provide an ideal setting to recognize and address socioemotional and behavioral problems among children and adolescents. The conception of the idea was based on empirical results identified among children by means of teaching play fighting in schools. Students involved in this activity were always happy and enjoyed it a lot, and time after time it was possible to recognize behavioral improvements among students both through analyzing anecdotal observations collected during regular lessons and gathering opinions from other teachers and by collecting the results of the first controlled trials organized in primary and middle schools.

Therefore, teaching preservice teachers how to implement and manage play fighting in school, and how to identify the effects of play fighting on antisocial behaviors and aggression among children and early adolescents, became an integral part of our interest and a regular topic of debate and discussion during our university classes. Different research projects involving physical education teachers and students with different backgrounds were carried out, and a summary of the results is shown in the following paragraphs. Generally, among teachers there are many fears and misperceptions surrounding the idea of rough, big-body play. Nonetheless, providing children and adolescents the right environment in which to play fight without injury is a prerogative for the teacher to understand how to offer this type of activity in a safe and supportive context. Teaching play fighting does not mean allowing it to go unsupervised: the best accident prevention comes from adequate adult supervision, but the best action in curbing adolescents' aggression during the play goes hand in hand with sharing rules and guidelines with the class. Therefore, the first step of the authors' research has been to teach physical education teachers how to manage play fighting, and to arrive at the research question that is to evaluate the effect of teaching this particular form of activity in physical education and extra-curricular sessions with the hypothesis that it could be an effective strategy for reducing aggression in youth.

Current Understandings of the Functional Significance of Play Fighting

Rough-and-Tumble Play

Children and adolescents' play has been extensively studied in its different forms, functions and consequences. Often in childhood, play has a vigorous physical component, and physical play has been defined as playful activities that require a metabolic expenditure well above the resting metabolic rate (moderate-to-vigorous physical activity; Simons-Morton et al., 1990). Rough-and-tumble (R&T) play is part of these activities that include a wide range of behaviors from running and chasing to tagging, grappling, and kicking. R&T play may resemble fighting, but it is distinctly different from it (Humphreys & Smith, 1987). R&T play has been repeatedly confused with direct aggression, despite a large body of evidence that shows that they have different antecedents, components, and consequences (Pellegrini & Smith, 1998). Overall, it has the greatest impact in the social domain, facilitating the encoding and the decoding of social signals

(Bjorklund & Brown, 1998). This play also requires children to alternate and change roles, and these successful social conversations and interactions can provide children with social knowledge, cognitive performance, and emotional development (Pellegrini & Smith, 1998). Due to its features, play fighting may be an important prelude for more elaborate associative play that involves pretend play and the imaginative dramatizations of older children. Two suggestions contribute toward distinguishing the functional significance of R&T play: it peaks during the mid-childhood period (10% of free play behavior), and it is a distinct form of behavior, similar to real fighting, but uncorrelated with it, with no escalation to high levels of aggression for most children (Pellegrini & Smith, 1998). Even for parents and teachers who recognize the features of R&T, there is often a concern that, if allowed to continue, the play will transform to real fighting. The reality is that R&T play digresses into real fighting less than 1% of the time for preschoolers (Scott & Panksepp, 2003). The factors that distinguish R&T play from real fighting may be summarized in distinctive behaviors. Primarily, children's facial expressions are often characterized by smiles, whereas in real fighting children's expressions are characterized by frowns and tears. Moreover, in R&T play the children involved are willing participants and remain so as long as the play carries on, but in fighting one participant is usually dominating another. At the end of R&T play, children keep returning for more, whereas as soon as an episode is resolved in real aggression, the unwilling participants often flee (Humphreys & Smith, 1987).

In reality, due to its specific features, R&T is a spontaneous form of play that offers children positive effects on social, emotional, and physical developmental areas (Carlson, 2011). In childhood, R&T play is a dimension of social play composed of physically vigorous behaviors in a friendly context; in adolescence, it may become more intense and more often related to aggression and struggles for dominance. Looking at this issue closer, for adolescent boys, R&T play is related to physical aggression and may be used as a way of establishing peer status in the form of dominance; whereas, adolescent girls play at wrestling with boys like an early and relatively low-risk form of heterosexual interaction (Pellegrini, 2003). For this reason, physically vigorous episodes in early adolescence may be associated with a poor, socially flexible attitude due to a lack of adequate social play opportunities in childhood. When trying to explain this phenomenon, Flanders, Leo, Paquette, Pihl, & Seguin (2009) showed that the quality of father–child R&T play may help young children learn to regulate aggressive emotions in their future life.

Since R&T play increases until later childhood (having a peak around 8 to 10 years), and then decreases in the early adolescence and further decreases in adolescence (Pellegrini & Smith, 1998), during these periods the type of sport, and particularly the level of physical contact and opposition, has been studied in relation to aggressive behavior and the socioemotional competence of youths.

Sports Features and Aggressive Behaviors

Does sport increase or reduce aggression in youths? Does sport build character? These questions have been tackled using different approaches, leading to conclusions that sometimes seem irreconcilable. There is evidence to suggest that sport has the power to educate people promoting positive values (Knijnik & Tavares, 2012); however, empirical studies have provided mixed results: on one hand, some studies seem to find an inverse relationship between sport and behavioral problems in children and adolescents (Miller, Melnick, Barnes, Sabo, & Farrell, 2007); other studies have found no link whatsoever (Reynes & Lorant, 2001); while some others have reported increased aggression for practitioners in some sports activities (Endresen & Olweus, 2005).

In general practice, physical activity provides situations where youths learn to engage in more socially accepted goal-oriented behavior, ultimately preventing and reducing aggression and other antisocial behavior (Fite & Vitulano 2011). It has been demonstrated that sport can increase youths' levels of empathy (Brunelle, Danish, & Forneris 2007) with positive consequences on their normative beliefs, and consequently on aggressive behaviors (Carlo et al., 2012). In particular, physical activities involving a significant amount of physical contact, like martial arts, have been considered effective in coping with aggressiveness (Vertonghen & Theeboom 2010) and also in developing moral values (Cynarski & Lee-Barron, 2014). In fact, most studies investigating the sociopsychological aspects of attending martial arts and combat sports reported negative correlations between practicing martial arts and aggressiveness and antisocial behaviors (Lamakre & Nosanchuk, 1999; Steyn & Roux, 2009; Ziaee, 2010). Furthermore, various experimental studies analyzed the effect of martial arts designed as specific intervention aimed at reducing youths' aggressive behaviors (Delva-Tauiliili, 1995; Lakes & Hoyt, 2004; Twemlow et al., 2008; Zivin et al., 2001). These studies reported that youths who practiced martial arts activities exhibited a decrease in the frequency of aggressive behaviors.

In spite of these considerations on the positive role of sport participation, sport is also related to antisocial and unhealthy behaviors. For example, it has been pointed out that participants of sports that involve physical contact between athletes are more aggressive than their peers who play sports without contact (Shields & Bredemeier, 2006). Moreover, those players involved in a high competitive level displayed more instrumental aggression than players competing at a low level (Kavussanu, 2008).

Regarding youths from a disadvantaged background, literature reported how they are a population at risk because of the difficulty of involving them in educational pathways and sports activities (La Torre et al., 2006). However, young people from these backgrounds, especially males, are particularly attracted to sports where physical contact is emphasized (Endresen & Olweus, 2005). For this reason, play fighting seems to be a good way not only of obtaining a reduction in levels of aggression, but mainly of involving youth from socially disadvantaged backgrounds, who would normally have refused to be involved in other kinds of activities.

Play Fighting

Play fighting could be considered to be a structured form of the R&T play that is spontaneous during childhood (Lillard et al., 2013), and that according to Jarvis (2006) is an integral part of "lessons in life." Men of all cultures around the globe have engaged in physical fighting for centuries, not only to overcome enemies and rivals, but also to celebrate rituals, to play, and to have fun. Aggressiveness, of which the fight is permeated, is a key instinctual component in humans. According to Freud (1949), the fight is a primary instinct, and Lapierre and Aucouturier (1982, 2001) defined it as the motivation and the primary instinct of all human activity. Humankind aggressive instinctual drives cannot be eliminated, but they ought to be controlled and expressed in socially acceptable behaviors. To play fight, players have to assume inherently fair behavior: they can play rough without injury only when they are able to control excessive physical aggression, and must respect the opponent and the rules of the game (Olivier, 1994). Educating and taming the expression of these feelings gives students the chance to behave consciously in a regulated and safe environment, and this teaches them to control their aggressive impulses, and to have respect for others (Carraro & Bertollo, 2005).

In play fighting, participants constantly establish bodily contacts and are given the opportunity to reflect on the problem of fair play, because if the violence is not excluded from the game, participants can endanger their and others' safety. Becoming violent and being hurt during play fighting means not only breaking the rules and disrespecting playmates, but also exposing oneself to receiving the same violence in return from one's opponent. Play fighting requires participants to establish a relationship of mutual confidence and self-control in order not to exceed the safety limits. Increasing the opportunities for both collaborative and opposition play in the school environment responds to concerns about a perceived deterioration in the socialization and mental health of youth (Jarvis, 2006). Moreover, play fighting provides an excellent setting for developing and refining various motor skills and physical qualities (e.g., movement speed, agility, flexibility and coordination) and for supporting vigorous physical activity practice and meeting the recommendations and guidelines for physical activity and health promotion (Carraro & Bertollo, 2005).

Due to its peculiar physical and psychological features, play fighting in structured and supervised settings may be an effective activity to promote social and emotional skills. This can, in turn, be helpful in preventing self-perceived aggression among young adolescents from a socially disadvantaged background, thereby meeting the aims of inclusive physical activity programs (Carraro & Gobbi, 2016).

Effects of Play Fighting Interventions Within the Italian Context

The Method of Play Fighting in Physical Education

As previously noted, play fighting is intended to provide students with experiences of bodily contact, feelings, and emotions that facilitate the process of becoming aware of themselves and of others, by combining physical contact with caution, with an emphasis on safeguarding personal safety. Important recommendations and guidelines have to be observed to develop an effective teaching of play fighting (Carraro & Bertollo, 2005; Olivier, 1994; Sigg & Tauber-Gioiella, 1998):

a. It is important that the educator sets up a suitable environment using mats or other equipment to minimize the risk of injury.

b. It is necessary to establish a positive and motivational climate in which participants are invited to take part in all the activities, however participation has to be not mandatory, educators should sustain and support youths' involvement.

c. It is better to start the lesson with a noncompetitive activity that allows students to experience bodily contact by chance. All proposals have to respond to the principle of gradual progression in exercise complexity.

d. In the central part of the lesson, it may be helpful to introduce fighting play where bodily contact is not immediately directed, but is mediated by an object like a ball or a tag, so emotional reactions are reduced. Then continue with activities involving direct and intentional bodily contact.

e. It must be clear that violations of the rules are not allowed. In this regard, the educator has a key role in explaining the rules, that must be few and clear, and in keeping the play safe, intervening as a referee whenever there is a violation.

f. Similarly to combat sports and martial arts that are rich in rituals such as greeting or bowing to the opponent and acts of respect toward the jury or the referees, it is important to transfer these habits even in play fighting. Behaviors like a greeting ceremony before the fight, help extended to the defeated opponent at the end of the play, and a high five can represent rituals that contribute to building a positive climate and establishing good relationships within the class.

g. It is useful to establish an emergency signal at which all the participants have to stop the activities immediately and remain calm until the situation has returned to normal, and it is important that the signal is unambiguous.

h. The strength, height and body weight of participants have to be considered in order to ensure positive experiences for all. Among children, boys and girls can play fight together and without the need for particular precautions.

i. Plan a conclusive activity that includes both a calm down play (breathing exercises and bodily contact with others) and a circle time discussion on the lesson just experienced (reflection on the emotions felt during the games).

All the previous recommendations were considered when planning the interventions in the research projects discussed in this chapter. Moreover, a standard protocol of an eight-week program was defined in order to have comparable results in different groups and with different teachers. All procedures performed in the studies presented in the following paragraphs were in accordance with the ethical standards of the institutional research committee and with the 1964 Helsinki declaration and its later amendments. All participants and their parents volunteered to participate and provided written informed consent prior to their enrollment in the studies. A description of the specific contents of the play fighting protocol is reported in Table 8.1 where the physical and socioemotional commitment of the students becomes gradually more complex as the lessons progress. Obviously, the plan has a flexible structure allowing for modifications aimed at adapting the contents to the special needs of the participants.

In our research, we have observed the aggressive behavior of children and young adolescents as the most interesting outcome, because the area in which we live is characterized by a high density of students from a socially disadvantaged background and a high rate of youth aggression. In this community, there is frequent antisocial and aggressive behavior toward peers. Teachers are challenged by the urgent situation, which in addition to hampering the teaching/learning process, reduces the feasibility of inclusive education and the development of positive relationships (prosocial behaviors) within and beyond the school gates.

Primary Schools

Research in primary schools started in 2011 when a play fighting intervention was implemented in the physical education curriculum of 4th and

	Games and exercise key contents	Teaching Goals
	TABLE 8.1 Play Fighting Progression of Contents and Teaching Goals	
1	Contact mediated by objects between participants, e.g., balls, cones, foam discs.	Cooperation, shortening of interpersonal distance.
2	Games involving physical contact and touch between participants, e.g., "the mosquitoes": each student has a clothes peg and tries to hang it on to the classmates' clothes.	Social interaction, acceptance of physical contact, emotional regulation, responding appropriately to participants' ethical and unethical behavior during physical activity by using rules and guidelines for resolving conflicts.[a]
3	Paired balance games; e.g., "partner hopping": partners coordinate hopping in different positions (hold right hands and hop on the left leg). During both group and paired activities, opponents meet by chance (e.g., the colour of their t-shirt or of their socks) or according to their own preferences.	Strength regulation, cooperation, emotional regulation.
4	Games of physical opposition in pairs; e.g., "duel on the bench": in pairs on a bench pupils try to pull the partner to the ground with the use of a pillow.	Social and emotional regulation, respect the rules.
5	Partner support stunts, in groups of two, three or four; e.g., "dead person lift": one pupil lies down facing the ceiling, two helpers stand one on each side and working together lift the "dead" person.	Cooperation with a small group of classmates during team-building activities, acceptance of differences among classmates in physical development and maturation.[a]
6	Preliminary acrogym activities with pyramid formation.	Cooperation, strength regulation, exhibition of responsible personal and social behavior that respect self and others in PA.[a]
7	Games involving physical opposition in groups; e.g., "the carrots": the pupils are carrots lying down on the ground holding each other's hand; others are farmers that try to separate them by dragging them by their feet.	Cooperation with multiple classmates on problem-solving initiatives including large-group initiatives and game play.[a]
8	Play fighting in pairs, e.g., pushing, pulling chasing in pairs trying to pull the partner to the ground.	Respond appropriately to participants' ethical and unethical behavior during physical activity by using rules and guidelines for resolving conflicts.[a]

Source: Carraro, Gobbi, & Moè, 2014

Note: PA = physical activity

[a] American Alliance for Health, Physical Education, Recreation and Dance (2013)

5th grade children in a low-income community school with high rates of disruptive behaviors. The project lasted three months; at the baseline teachers were asked to identify the most aggressive students and data regarding the exhibition of aggressive behaviors were collected among children before and after the intervention using the 12-item version of the aggression questionnaire (AQ-12; Bryant & Smith, 2001). This is a self-report instrument that investigates the phenomenon according to four dimensions: physical aggression, verbal aggression, anger, and hostility. These four figures represent the instrumental or motor component of aggression (physical and verbal aggression); the affective or emotional component of aggression is represented by the anger subscale; and the cognitive component of aggression is evaluated with the hostility factor.

The data collected on the 42 children seemed to confirm the hypothesis that play fighting activities reduce aggressive behavior in children: in particular, the physical component of aggression (-12.9%) and hostility (-13.5%) were reduced more than the other two dimensions. Another element that emerged from the analysis was related to the higher effect of play fighting on children who have a baseline level of aggression higher than the average value of the group. For these children, decreases of 39%, 14.3%, 25%, and 14% were found for physical aggression, verbal aggression, anger, and hostility respectively. A general conclusion seems to emerge whereby the more physically aggressive the children, the greater the benefits from a play fighting intervention (Carraro, Cucchelli, Gobbi, Ferri, & Greguol, 2013).

It is also important to note that as the project progressed, the children's behavior gradually improved. The off-task behaviors during physical education involving play fighting were almost completely eliminated, and the children who displayed more difficulties in controlling their aggression improved as the intervention progressed in time. In the final part of each lesson, a relaxation activity was proposed and students appeared to be better at relaxing, speaking to one another in a lower tone of voice together in the gym, even though the lesson was long over.

Junior High Schools

A first exploratory study was conducted in 2006 in junior high schools involving a total of 39 students of 11–12 years of age in eight-week play fighting interventions during curricular physical education. They, and a control group of 137 students, were observed by teachers before and after the program and the frequency of disruptive behaviors per classroom were recorded by using an ad hoc observation checklist (Carraro, Mauro, & Ventura, 2006). This was the first experience implementing play fighting in a school with high rates of antisocial behavior, and results showed a reduction of 20% in students displaying disruptive behavior among those participating in play fighting and a small change of 4% in the control group (Carraro et al., 2006).

In the wake of these promising results, another research project was conducted a few years later in 2010. A junior high school with students from different cultural backgrounds and displaying antisocial behavior was selected, and the study was carried out in collaboration with the physical education teachers of 10 classrooms. A total of 213 students participated in the research project: 90 girls and 123 boys with an average age of 13.3 years (SD = 12.4) and with a rate of 7% from an immigrant background (coming from Morocco, China, Moldova and Romania). The classes were randomly divided into a control group ($n = 109$), who played eight volley-ball lessons; and in a play fighting group ($n = 104$), who participated in a program of eight lessons. The AQ-12 (Bryant & Smith, 2001) was used before and after the intervention to test changes in self-reported aggression among early adolescents. According to the baseline assessment, students that were placed above the 75th percentile, and those with a higher value of aggression amounted to 64 and were selected to investigate the effects of the intervention. At the end of the experience, among the students with higher aggression that participated in the play fighting ($n = 34$) a statistically significant decrease ($p < .001$) on the scores of all the AQ-12 subscales was reported (physical aggression –28.6%, verbal aggression –19.9%, anger –18.9% and hostility –17.5%); whereas in the control group, participants with higher aggression ($n = 30$) did not report any changes (Gobbi, Ferri, & Carraro, 2012).

Similar to this project, in 2012 another play fighting intervention was implemented in two suburban middle schools during the physical education class. That project involved a total of 210 8th-grade students who were reported as being at risk socially due to the particular area in which they lived. Many of the students came from a densely populated immigrant and low-income suburban community. Play fighting was offered to an experimental group of 103 students and the remaining 107 were involved in volleyball activities. The AQ-12 self-reported questionnaires on aggression was used and data analysis confirmed the hypothesis of the study: students involved in the play fighting activities showed significantly reduced scores of all the AQ-12 subscales (physical aggression –23%, verbal aggression –19%, anger –16% and hostility –18%). In the physical aggression subscale, there was a marked reduction and similar effects on boys and girls were shown (Carraro, Gobbi, & Moè, 2014). Therefore, findings showed that providing play fighting in a safe and supportive environment with adequate supervision, clear rules and policies to guide the play can be effective in curbing aggression among early adolescents characterized by disruptive behavior and social disadvantages.

Extracurricular Intervention

A play fighting project was implemented in 2015 in eight youth recreation centers, known as *dopo scuola* (after school meeting). In these centers, youths received help with their homework and spent their time in free play or in various activities proposed by educators for three afternoons per week after school. In order to be admitted to a youth recreation center, students had to be recommended by schoolteachers or by welfare workers as young adolescents with behavioral problems. Most of them came from low-income urban communities and had an immigrant background. The participants in this research project were made up of 98 young adolescents (66 boys and 32 girls with a mean age of 13.4 ±1.2 years), 76.5% of whom had an immigrant background. Participants were invited to take part in play fighting activities and 33 volunteered to participate, while the rest did not attend any extra activities and constituted the control group for our analysis. Pre and post intervention, all the participants filled out the reactive proactive aggression questionnaire (Raine et al., 2006). During the period of the intervention, a total of 22 youths dropped out (two youths from the intervention group and 20 youths from the control group), so results refer to 31 early adolescents that participated in a 12-week play fighting intervention compared to 45 students serving as controls. At the end of the inclusive physical activity program, proactive and reactive aggression significantly decreased (–59.7% and –25% respectively) among adolescents that participated in the play fighting in comparison with the control group (with changes of –21.9 and –4.2% respectively) (Cucchelli, Gobbi, Marino, & Carraro, 2015).

The sample involved in this study was a group of young adolescents coming from a low-income urban community, the majority of whom had an immigrant background and showed considerably higher levels of aggressive behavior than peers from the general population. Findings on the effect of play fighting on both proactive and reactive aggression are encouraging. Moreover, even if the present research did not directly investigate other aspects related to enjoyment and motivation among the involved youth, the rate of attendance and the low dropout rate in the play fighting group (two participants) suggests how this kind of activity could effectively respond to the special needs of youth from a socially disadvantaged background, especially boys, and probably stimulate further motivation to exercise.

IMPLICATIONS AND FUTURE DIRECTIONS
FOR RESEARCH AND PRACTICE

According to the results presented, we would suggest some future research and best practice examples to understand more in-depth the potential of play fighting as a strategy to reduce antisocial behaviors, and in turn to promote inclusion especially in those schools with a high density of students from a socially disadvantaged background.

The exploratory studies presented have some limitations that do not allow for generalization of the findings. Nonetheless, they could serve as a stimulus for implementing future educational interventions within school physical education programs aimed at managing aggressive behaviors in children and adolescents from a socially disadvantaged background. These practices can be further compared with other physical activities and best practice examples to promote inclusion and prosocial behavior. Schools and teachers may benefit highly from interventions such as those described in this chapter because they come at a low cost, and physical education teachers can easily plan play fighting interventions that may also evidence improved behavior for participants. Such improvements in behavior will, in turn, enhance the quality of school life and of interpersonal relationships among peers and between peers and teachers. Students from a socially disadvantaged background can gain benefits in global health and at the same time improve their motivation toward physical activity.

Future research should be conducted to investigate more in depth which variables may be strongly associated with a reduction in aggression and follow-up measures should be carried out to evaluate the maintenance over time of the effects of the physical activity interventions.

The goal of the physical education interventions aimed at improving the health of youths experiencing disadvantages should not be only to inhibit aggression, but to teach them how to manage and control aggression positively, and to transform negative emotions into actions marked by initiative, creativity, and desire.

Future studies may also look for a confirmation of the hypothesis that sports with high levels of physical contact are more attractive for young people from disadvantaged backgrounds, which include low-income urban and/or immigrant communities. Moreover, the study of mediating factors in the reduction of aggressive behavior through physical activity can be further investigated in order to implement effective strategies.

Research into the effects of play fighting or inclusive physical activity on aggressive behavior in youths from socially disadvantaged backgrounds is still scant. The current findings provide some initial insight into play fighting as part of a physical education curriculum to increase the social and emotional learning of young adolescents with behavioral problems. The results so far are highly encouraging; and in the future, interventions beyond school physical education would hopefully be implemented on a wider scale to support physical activity practice among those youths who display aggressive behaviors and originate from socially disadvantaged backgrounds.

ACKNOWLEDGMENTS

We would thank very much all the young people, the educators, the primary school teachers, and the physical education teachers who kindly cooperated in the described research projects.

REFERENCES

Ambrosi, E., & Rosina, A. (2009). *Non è un paese per giovani. L'anomalia italiana: una generazione senza voce* [It is not a country for youngsters. The Italian anomaly: A generation without voice]. Venice, Italy: Marsilio.

Ambrosini, M. (2014). Better than our fears? Refugees in Italy: Between rhetoric of exclusion and local projects of inclusion. In S. Kneebone, D. Stevens, & L. Baldassar (Eds.), *Refugee protection and the role of law: Conflicting identities* (pp. 235–250). London, England: Routledge.

American Alliance for Health, Physical Education, Recreation and Dance. (2013). *Grade-level outcomes for K-12 physical education.* Reston, VA: Author.

Bjorklund, D. F., & Brown, R. D. (1998). Physical play and cognitive development: Integrating activity, cognition and education. *Child Development, 69*, 604–606.

Boeri, T., & Galasso, V. (2007). *Contro i giovani. Come l'Italia sta tradendo le nuove generazioni* [Against the youngsters. How Italy is deceiving the new generations]. Milano, Italy: Mondadori.

Brunelle, J., Danish, S. J., & Forneris, T., (2007). The impact of a sport-based life skill program on adolescent prosocial values. *Applied Developmental Science, 11*(1), 43–55.

Bryant, F. B., & Smith, B. D. (2001). Refining the architecture of aggression: A measurement model for the Buss-Perry aggression questionnaire. *Journal of Research in Personality, 35*, 138–167.

Carlo, G., Mestre, M. V., McGinley, M. M., Samper, P., Tur, A., & Sandman, D., (2012). The interplay of emotional instability, empathy, and coping on prosocial and aggressive behaviors. *Personality and Individual Differences, 53*(5), 675–680.

Carlson, F. M. (2011). *Big body play: Why boisterous, vigorous, and very physical play is essential to children's development and learning.* Washington, DC: NAEYC.

Carraro, A., & Bertollo, M. (2005). *Le scienze motorie e sportive nella scuola primaria* [Sport sciences in primary school]. Padova, Italy: Cleup.

Carraro, A., Cucchelli, M., Gobbi, E., Ferri, I., & Greguol, M. (2013). *Rough-and-tumble play to cope with physical aggression in primary school.* Paper presented in AIESEP International Conference "Physical Education and Sport: Challenging The Future." Warsaw, Poland, July 4–7, 2013.

Carraro, A., & Gobbi, E. (2016). *Muoversi per stare bene. Una guida introduttiva all'attività fisica* [Move yourself to feel good. An introduction to physical activity]. Rome, Italy: Carocci.

Carraro, A., Gobbi, E., & Moè, A. (2014). Brief report: Play fighting to curb self-reported aggression in young adolescents, *Journal of Adolescence, 37*, 1003–1007.

Carraro, A., Mauro, L., & Ventura, L., (2006). Giochi di lotta e aggressività: un'esperienza nella scuola [Play fighting and aggressiveness: aschool-based approach]. *Giornale Italiano di Psicologia dello Sport, 1*(1), 53–58.

Cesareo, V. (2014). Twenty years of immigration. In V. Cesareo (Ed.), *Twenty years of migrations in Italy: 1994–2014* (pp. 1–18). Milan, Italy: McGraw-Hill Education.

Contini, D. (2013) Immigrant background peer effects in Italian schools. *Social Science Research, 42*(4), 1122–1142.

Cucchelli, M., Gobbi, E., Marino, M., & Carraro, A. (2015). Play fighting to cope with reactive and pro-active aggression in young adolescents from low-income urban communities. *Sport Sciences for Health, 11* (Supplement 1), S101.

Cynarski, W. J., & Lee-Barron, J., (2014). Philosophies of martial arts and their pedagogical consequences. *Ido Movement for Culture. Journal of Martial Arts Anthropology, 14*(1), 11–19.

Delva-Tauiliili, J., (1995). Does brief Aikido training reduce aggression of youth? *Perceptual and Motor Skills, 80*(1), 297–298.

Dronkers, J. M., de Heus M., & Levels M. (2012). *Immigrant pupils' scientific performance: the Influence of educational system features of countries of origin and destination.* Center for Research and Analysis of Migration (Working paper no.12/12). Retrieved from http://www.cream-migration.org/publ_uploads/CDP_12_12.pdf

Endresen, I. M., & Olweus, D. (2005). Participation in power sports and antisocial involvement in preadolescent and adolescent boys. *Journal of Child Psychology and Psychiatry, 46*(5), 468–478.

Fite, P. J., & Vitulano, M. (2011). Proactive and reactive aggression and physical activity. *Journal of Psychopathology and Behavioral Assessment, 33*(1), 11–18.

Flanders, J. L., Leo, V., Paquette, D., Pihl R. O., & Seguin, J. R. (2009). Rough-and-tumble play and regulation of aggression: An observational study of father–child play dyads. *Aggressive Behavior, 35*, 285–295.

Freud, S. (1949). *Il disagio della civiltà* [Civilization and its discontents]. Rome, Italy: Scienza moderna.

Gobbi, E., Ferri, I., & Carraro, A. (2012). I giochi di lotta in Educazione Fisica. Effetti sull'aggressività degli adolescenti. [Play fighting in physical education. Effects on adolescents' aggressiveness]. *Giornale Italiano della Ricerca Educativa, 5*, 64–70.

Humphreys A. P., & Smith P. K., (1987). Rough and tumble, friendships, and dominance in schoolchildren: Evidence for continuity and change with age. *Child Development, 58*, 201–212.

Istat (2015). *Il bullismo in Italia: Comportamenti offensivi e violenti tra i giovanissimi* [Bullying in Italy: offensive and violent behaviours among early teens]. Retrieved from http://www.istat.it/it/files/2015/12/Bullismo.pdf?title=Bullismo++tra+i+giovanissimi+-+15%2Fdic%2F2015+-+Testo+integrale+e+nota+metodologica.pdf

Jarvis, P. (2006). "Rough and tumble" play: LESSONS in life. *Evolutionary Psychology, 4*, 268–284.

Kavussanu, M. (2008). Moral behavior in sport: A critical review of the literature. *International Review of Sport and Exercise Psychology, 1*(2), 124–138.

Kelly, P. (2001). Youth at risk: Processes of individualisation and responsibilities in the risk society. *Discourse, 22*(1), 23–33.

Knijnik, J., & Tavares, O. (2012). Educating Copacabana: A critical analysis of the "second half", an Olympic education program of Rio 2016. *Educational Review, 64*(3), 352–367.

La Torre, G., Masala, D., De Vito, E., Langiano, E., Capelli, G., & Ricciardi, W. (2006). Extra-curricular physical activity and socioeconomic status in Italian adolescents. *BMC Public Health, 6*(1), 22.

Lakes, K. D., & Hoyt, W. T., (2004). Promoting self-regulation through school based martial arts training. *Applied Developmental Psychology, 25*, 283–302.

Lamakre, B. W., & Nosanchuk, T. A. (1999). Judo the gentle way: A replication of studies on martial arts and aggression. *Perceptual And Motor Skills, 88*(3), 992–996.

Lapierre, A., & Aucouturier, B. (1982). *Il corpo e l'inconscio in educazione e terapia* [The body and the subconscious in education and therapy]. Rome, Italy: Armando Editore.

Lapierre, A., & Aucouturier, B. (2001). *La simbologia del movimento* [The symbolism of the movement]. Cremona, Italy: Edipsicologiche.

Lillard, A. S., Lerner, M. D., Hopkins, E. J., Dore, R. A., Smith, E. D., & Palmquist, C. M. (2013). The impact of pretend play on children's development: a review of the evidence. *Psychological Bulletin, 139*(1), 1–34.

Miller, K. E., Melnick, M. J., Barnes, G. M., Sabo, D., & Farrell, M. P. (2007). Athletic involvement and adolescent delinquency. *Journal of Youth and Adolescence, 36*(5), 711–723.

Ministerial Directive 27 (2012, December). *Strumenti d'intervento per alunni con bisogni educativi speciali e organizzazione territoriale per l'inclusione scolastica* [Interventional instruments for special education needs students and local organization for inclusion in the school]. Retrieved from http://hubmiur.pubblica.istruzione.it/alfresco/d/d/workspace/SpacesStore/8d31611f-9d06-47d0-bcb7-3580ea282df1/dir271212.pdf

Olivier, J. C. (1994). *La lutte a l'ecole* [The fight in the school]. Paris, France: Nathan.

Pellegrini, A. D. (2003). Perception and function of play and real fighting in early adolescence. *Child Development, 74*, 1522–1533.

Pellegrini, A. D., & Smith, P.K., (1998). Physical activity play: The nature and function of a neglected aspect of play. *Child Development, 69*, 577–598.

Raine, A., Dodge, K., Loeber, R., Gatzke-Kopp, L., Lynam, D., Reynolds, C., ... & Liu, J. (2006). The reactive–proactive aggression questionnaire: Differential correlates of reactive and proactive aggression in adolescent boys. *Aggressive Behavior, 32*(2), 159–171.

Reynes, E., & Lorant, J. (2001). Do competitive martial arts attract aggressive children? *Perceptual and Motor Skills 93*, 382–386.

Santagati, M. (2015). Researching integration in multiethnic Italian schools. A sociological review on educational inequalities. *Italian Journal of Sociology of Education, 7*(3), 294–334.

Scott, E., & Panksepp, J. (2003). Rough and tumble play in human children. *Aggressive Behavior, 29*, 539–551.

Senato della Repubblica (2012). *Costituzione della Repubblica Italiana* [The Constitution of the Italian Republic]. Rome, Italy: Tipografia del Sanato. Retrieved from https://www.senato.it/documenti/repository/istituzione/costituzione.pdf

Shields, D. L. L., & Bredemeier, B. J. L. (2006). Sport and character development. *Research Digest Series, 7*, 1–8

Sigg, B., & Tauber-Gioiella, Z. (1998). Meno violenza grazie agli sport giovanili [Less violence thanks to young sports]. *Mobile, 2*, 1–8.

Simons-Morton, B. G., O'Hara, N. M., Parcel, G. S., Huang, J. W., Baranowski, T., & Wilson, B. (1990). Children's frequency of participation in moderate to vigorous physical activities. *Research Quarterly for Exercise and Sport, 61*, 307–314.

Steyn, B. J. M., & Roux, S. (2009). Aggression and psychological well-being of adolescent tae kwon do participants in comparison with hockey participants and a non-sport group. *African Journal for Physical, Health Education, Recreation and Dance, 15*(1), 32–43.

Twemlow, W. S., Nelson, T. D., Vernberg, E. M., Fonagy, P., & Twemlow, S. W. (2008). Effects of participation in a martial arts-based anti-bullying program in elementary schools. *Psychology in the Schools, 45*(10), 947–959

Vertonghen, J., & Theeboom, M. (2010). The social-psychological outcomes of martial arts practise among youth: A review. *Journal of Sports Science & Medicine, 9*(4), 528.

Ziaee, V., Lotfian, S., Amini, H., Mansournia, M. A., & Memari, A. H. (2012). Anger in adolescent boy athletes: A comparison among judo, karate, swimming and non athletes. *Iranian Journal of Pediatrics, 22*(1), 9–14.

Zivin, G., Hassan, N. R., DePaula, G. F., & Monti, D. A. (2001). An effective approach to violence prevention: Traditional martial arts in middle school. *Adolescence, 36*(143), 443.

CHAPTER 9

PROMOTING SOCIAL INCLUSION AND PHYSICAL ACTIVITY FOR STUDENTS WITH SPECIAL EDUCATIONAL NEEDS THROUGH ADVENTURE EDUCATION

Daniel Tindall
University of Limerick

Jack Neylon
Coláiste Muire, Ennis, Ireland

Melissa Parker and Deborah Tannehill
University of Limerick

Over the past 20 years, educational provision for students with special educational needs (SEN) worldwide has made substantial developments. These developments started in 1994 with the Salamanca World Conference on Special Needs Education and its endorsement of the idea of inclusive education (UNESCO, 1994). The Salamanca Statement is considered a key

Inclusive Physical Activities, pages 183–202
Copyright © 2017 by Information Age Publishing
All rights of reproduction in any form reserved.

document calling for inclusion to be the norm globally (Ainscow, 2005). Created as a framework for thinking about how to shape policy and practice, it stated that mainstream schools with an inclusive orientation are the most effective and best positioned to build an inclusive society: one that suppresses biased attitudes and promotes education for all (UNESCO, 1994).

Taking its lead from the Salamanca Statement, Europe began to embrace the tenets of inclusion from an educational perspective with the passing of the European Disability Action Plan for 2010–2020. With this plan, students with disabilities were ensured that benefit from an accessible education system and lifelong learning programs would be one of the key areas within the strategy. The plan looked to build on other policy documents such as the Guidelines for Inclusion: Ensuring Access to Education for All (UNESCO, 2005), the United Nations Convention on the Rights of Persons with Disabilities (UN General Assembly, 2007), Europe 2020 (the European Union's strategy for smart, sustainable and inclusive growth), as well as the European Charter of Fundamental Rights contained within the Lisbon Treaty (European Union, 2007).

As a result of this worldwide shift in educational policy, European Union (EU) member countries began to embrace a more inclusive approach toward children and young people with SEN. Ireland, though yet to fully ratify the document, was one of the first to sign the resolution put forth by the UN General Assembly. Likewise, it was one of the first countries within the EU to draft legislation geared specifically toward educational provision for students with SEN. This document, the Education for Persons with Special Educational Needs (EPSEN) Act (Government of Ireland, 2004), mandated that a child with SEN shall be educated in an inclusive environment appropriate for the child. According to Shelvin and his colleagues, though there has been a significant shift in policy toward the provision of inclusion for children and young people with SEN, both within special and mainstream education, this provision has yet to fully occur within Irish schools (Shevlin, Kenny, & Loxley, 2008; Shevlin, Winter, & Flynn, 2013). While the introduction of inclusion in mainstream Irish schools was supported "in principle," it was for the most part perceived as a way to develop the socialization skills of students rather than a means to develop the student from a holistic perspective.

Definition of Inclusion

In their report to the Research and Development Committee of the Department of Education and Skills (DES), Travers and colleagues (2010) identified various definitions and views regarding inclusion, none of which is explicitly defined in either the Education Act (Government of Ireland, 1998) or

ESPEN Act (Government of Ireland, 2004) of Ireland. For example, Bailey (1998) refers to inclusion as students being in a school setting with their peers following the same curriculum at the same time, in a way that makes the student feel no different from their classmates. Others see it as a continuing process of increasing the participation and interaction of students in both mainstream school and community settings (Booth, 1996). Within physical education, Block (2007) defines inclusion as having individually determined goals/objectives met and accommodations provided within the general physical education setting by trained professionals, rather than students receiving services externally. He emphasizes that an inclusive environment allows students with disabilities to work together and learn from their peers, while forming friendships and ensuring they receive an appropriate education.

Though many definitions of inclusion exist throughout the literature, until recently, most students with disabilities in Ireland were not fully included, but rather educated in segregated special schools. Today, children with SEN are predominantly enrolled in mainstream primary and secondary school settings supported as needed by resource teachers, special needs assistants (SNAs), and other learning provisions. Students with disabilities requiring more specific consideration are themselves placed in full-time special units (e.g., autism) offered within mainstream schools or in special schools as identified under the ESPEN Act. It should be noted that in Ireland, special schools cater for children up to the age of 18 years and fall under the Primary Branch of the Department of Education and Skills (Shevlin, Kenny, & Loxley, 2008).

While research suggests that a significant number of students with SEN are socially included in mainstream schools, there is a notable amount of research suggesting that some of these students continue to face social isolation, bullying, and difficulty in forming friendships in such settings (Frostad & Pijl, 2007; Maïano, Aimé, Salvas, Morin, & Normand, 2016; Symes & Humphrey, 2010). From the perspective of inclusive education, this is troubling for two reasons: (a) the idea of social inclusion reinforces the overall idea and philosophy of inclusion, and (b) the quality of a person's life is very much reliant on the quality of their social relationships with others. Specifically, a lack of friendship or exclusion by peers has been recognized as having a direct link to the loneliness, unhappiness, rejection, and ultimately the inability of these students to develop meaningful social skills (Frostad & Pijl, 2007).

FOCUS OF THE CHAPTER

In 2007, results of a National Disability Authority (NDA) survey revealed that 52% of respondents believed that persons with SEN did not receive equal opportunities within the Irish education system (NDA, 2007). When asked if those polled would be open to having children with SEN attending the same school as children without SEN, 75% expressed acceptance of children with physical disabilities, and 36% expressed acceptance of children with mental health difficulties. However, 21% percent noted that they would object to having children with mental health difficulties attending the same school as children without SEN. Given these findings, how can the inclusion of persons with SEN be fully realized within the Irish education system? One way is through alternative and inclusive approaches within the learning environment where teachers have the ability to shape the attitudes, perceptions, and practices of all their students in relation to social inclusion within and beyond the educational setting (Shevlin et al., 2013; Travers et al., 2010).

Unfortunately, at present there is no agreed approach for teaching social skills to students with SEN. Although research exists on the use of physical education and physical activity to improve the motor functioning of people with SEN, there is a scarcity of information in regards to its use to improve social and psychological deficits. Yet, recent information on the positive effects of outdoor adventure experiences on social skills from a nonacademic context provides some interesting alternatives (Gibson, 2000; Sutherland & Stroot, 2009, 2010). This chapter shares how the implementation of an outdoor adventure education learning experience in a physical education setting can help to foster the development of students with SEN: those at-risk physically, intellectually, socially, and psychologically. The interdisciplinary concept of sport pedagogy (Armour, 2011), as it relates to the development of evidenced-based and practice-focused effective teaching toward the promotion of physical activity for students with disabilities and SEN, serves as the basis for this chapter. It is designed to support physical education teachers and teacher educators, as well as others in physical activity settings, by providing examples that can be used to meet the needs of diverse learners. As such, the purpose of this chapter is to share how curriculum models are used as part of the postprimary curriculum in Ireland and justify the particular use of one model of outdoor adventure education in promoting the social inclusion of students with SEN through physical activity. As the chapter progresses, the reader will understand how the curricular model framework is utilized within the Irish educational system with a particular focus on adventure education and its application for students with SEN. Finally, through a case study approach framed using a constructivist theoretical perspective, the authors offer an example of how to maximize involvement, social participation, and the inclusion of students with SEN both within and beyond the physical education setting.

Enhancing Student Engagement in Physical Activity Through a Curriculum Model Framework

In Ireland, the National Council for Curriculum and Assessment (NCCA) prepares all curriculum documents (including syllabi) and the DES has responsibility for their implementation in schools. Curriculum implementation at the primary school level (ages 4–11) consists of 8 years of schooling spread over four levels providing education to junior infants up to sixth class (grade). Secondary education comprises a 3-year junior cycle followed by a 2- or 3-year senior cycle. Students may opt to take a 1-year transition year between their junior and senior cycle education.

At the primary school level, the physical education syllabus includes six activity strands: athletics, adventure, aquatics, dance, gymnastics, and games to which all children are to be introduced during weekly one hour physical education classes. The junior cycle physical education (JCPE) syllabus is based on the recommendation that all students 11 to 17 years of age should be provided two hours of physical education each week and includes seven physical activity strands: athletics, adventure, aquatics, dance, gymnastics, games (divided between invasion games and net/wall/fielding games), and the addition of a health related activity. It should be noted that teacher adherence to teaching the seven strands is, however, voluntary (Tannehill, van der Mars, & MacPhail, 2015).

Curricular issues are currently being considered in Ireland by the NCCA's design of senior cycle physical education (SCPE) and are composed of two distinct courses: a nonexamination curriculum framework and an examination syllabus. The nonexamination framework, the focus of our attention here, is to be accessible to all students and open to student choice through an innovative set of instructional models that will guide learning. After gaining insight from students, physical education teachers select a physical activity area, a curriculum model, and instructional models informed by their beliefs and philosophy regarding what will be most effective for the students they teach.

The framework is built on a model-based approach (Metzler, 2005) to teaching and learning in physical education. There are two types of models that frame teaching and learning: curriculum models and instructional models. Curriculum models are focused, theme-based, and reflect a specific philosophy. They define a clear focus around content, and aim toward specific, relevant, and challenging outcomes. Once a curriculum model has been chosen to develop the learning goal, then determining which instructional model will best guide instruction and learning must be made. An instructional model, however, organizes instruction and determines how students will interact with and practice content. Each instructional model includes a number of strategies, methods, styles, and skills that are used to plan, design, and implement instruction to meet selected learning goals. In a few instances, curriculum models are linked directly to an instructional model to most effectively reach the intended outcomes. For example, problem solving and cooperative learning are most closely linked to outdoor and adventure education; whereas, teaching through questions is often associated with teaching games for understanding.

Six curriculum and instruction models that have a strong research basis and history in practice have been chosen by the NCCA (2013). Each one includes a rationale, aims, objectives, teaching and learning approaches, and assessment strategies. They are described as:

- Health-related physical activity: Developing learners' understanding of health-related physical fitness now and in the future.
- Sport education: Providing learners with an enjoyable and authentic sport experience as they perform playing and nonplaying roles.
- Contemporary issues in physical activity: Encouraging learners to critically reflect on their own and others' experience in physical activity and sport.
- Teaching games for understanding: Developing learners' tactical awareness and decision making skills in a variety of games.
- Personal and social responsibility: Learners taking responsibility for themselves and their learning in physical education class including respecting the rights and feelings of others.
- Adventure education: Encouraging learners to challenge themselves and cooperate with others as they learn to solve physical activity challenges.

ADVENTURE EDUCATION

Within the Irish physical education curriculum, adventure education is a combination of adventure and outdoor education and includes a wide range of physical activities, including cooperative activities, trust activities and problem-solving initiatives based on one or more of the following concepts: challenge, cooperation, risk, trust, and problem solving. Through this strand of the curriculum, students are provided with the opportunity to develop personally, socially, and physically by presenting them with elements of adventure in a safe, challenging, and controlled environment (Government of Ireland, 2003). Doing so can lead to student development of self-reliance, self-confidence, responsibility, regard for others, and respect for the environment. Though not defined within the Irish curriculum, social skills can be identified as specific behaviors that result in positive social interactions and encompass both verbal and nonverbal behaviors necessary for effective interpersonal communication (Heatherton & Walcott, 2009). Thus social skills form part of the adventure education strand of Irish physical education. While the content of adventure education can range from outdoor activities such as hiking, kayaking, and cycling to artificially developed initiatives and problem solving activities in a nonwilderness environment, the latter reflects the most prominent teaching model for Irish schools.

Each model has a set of unique practices or characteristics referred to as nonnegotiables, as they are deemed central to providing learners with an authentic and worthwhile experience of that particular model. The nonnegotiables of adventure education are that it is experiential (students are actively engaged, they reflect on their experience, and they transfer what was learned to new settings), that members share commitment (members commit to one another through respectful and responsible personal and group behavior), and that students actively choose the level of challenge (students choose at what level they are willing and able to participate knowing that nonparticipation is not a choice).

In practice, choice of curriculum model should be based on the intent of students' learning and achievement. For students to acquire the capacity to cooperate with others while solving group challenges and negotiating their way in the outdoors, then adventure education might be an effective choice of model. If the intent of learning is for students to acquire competence in sport skills by participating as a member of a team in authentic sport experiences, then sport education might be the most effective choice. If the focus however is to understand what to do, when to it, and how to do it, then perhaps Teaching Games for Understanding would be more appropriate. When students are striving toward a level of fitness that allows them to participate in a chosen activity or to develop and maintain an active and healthy lifestyle then Health-Related Physical Activity would be a logical choice.

In any event, teachers must consider their context, their students and students' needs, age group, and developmental level when determining if employing a curriculum model as a framework is appropriate. For example, it might be that framing learning within a curriculum model in the early primary level is not in the best interests of children while framing learning around basic motor skills and movement themes is more appropriate. This suggests that teachers at all levels need to first consider the learning outcomes for which they are designing the instruction, and determine if the first step is to select a curriculum model to frame learning or to directly move to the choice of instructional models. The same is true when designing instruction and selecting curricular and instructional models for students with SEN.

Students with SEN

In Ireland, there have been significant developments in promoting the inclusion and service provision of students with SEN in physical education (Meegan & MacPhail, 2006). While students with disabilities and SEN may need assistance to enable them to participate in physical activities, the NCCA (2005b) encourages teachers to take special care in designing appropriate experiences for these young people. The NCCA suggests that it is essential for every student to have access to a wide range of curriculum experiences in movement, physical education, and physical activity. When engaging in these experiences, students should do so safely and to their fullest capacity using a wide range of stimulating equipment and receiving assistance when needed (NCCA, 2005a). With this in mind, each of the curriculum and instruction models can be adapted to enhance the learning of all children and youth.

The NCCA indicates that continuity and progression are important features of the educational experience of all students, and for students with SEN they are particularly important. They suggest that students with mild general learning disabilities can access the curriculum through differentiated approaches and methodologies allowing them access to all strands of the physical education curriculum. By adapting to the talents, strengths, and needs of individual students (whether those with special needs or not) the teacher can facilitate student progression within a physical education/ activity program. When planning for teaching and learning in the area of physical education, a variety of teaching strategies need to be considered. These are intended to respond to and aid in facilitating growth in the potential areas of difficulty that students with mild general learning disabilities may experience.

Theoretical Perspective

Constructivist learning is the theoretical framework guiding the evidence-based and practice-focused teaching strategies in this chapter. Adventure education adheres to an experiential education model reflecting constructivist learning tenets posed by Dewey (1938) who believed that genuine education comes through experience and that the learner should be at the center of that experience. Itin (1999) suggests experiential education is a process that blends experience with the environment resulting in students making discoveries and testing new knowledge, instead of reading or hearing about such knowledge from others (Kraft & Sakofs, 1988). As a result students develop new skills and attitudes. Such an educational environment supports pedagogies that reflect a constructivist view of learning, which implies that learners are constructors of their own knowledge gained by interacting with their sociocultural environment (Vygotsky, 1978). Learning from a constructivist perspective is a "process of active adaptation" (Quay, 2003).

Constructivism assumes that learners are not empty vessels to be filled, rather, they are actively attempting to create meaning. This type of learning is messy and complex (Siemens, 2005). As such, the task of the teacher is to provide opportunities and incentives to build up knowledge rather than be a simple dispenser of knowledge (Fosnot, 2005). Three major constructivist tenets (Rovegno & Dolly, 2006) have implications here. First, learning is an active process where learners are viewed as agents in their knowledge construction and understanding through decision making, critical thinking, and problem solving. Both the learner and the environment are important, as it is the interaction between the two that creates knowledge (Ertmer & Newby, 2013). In this manner knowledge is coproduced through the activity as learning tasks are fully integrated within multiple domains of learning. Second, learners construct knowledge in relation to their prior knowledge and experiences. Acknowledging the role of past experiences in the learning process, constructivism suggests that to be useful, knowledge must be situated in a relevant or "authentic" context. When students experience adventure education designed to focus on learning about compassion and caring for one another, an activity such as making a safe and secure nest for an egg so that it will not break would demonstrate the principles to be understood. Third, knowledge is a social product and knowledge creation is a shared experience. Group settings provide experiences in which child development and social processes of knowledge construction occur concurrently and interactively (Borko, Mayfield, Marion, Flexer, & Hiebert, 1997). Ultimately, these pedagogies and instructional models that support constructivist learning allow students to be engaged in self-directed learning over which they have control.

Constructivist pedagogies may afford individuals with disabilities and SEN greater autonomy and authority in defining and directing their own learning (Gallagher, 2004). In fact, disability studies encompass a range of theoretical positions (Williams, 2001) with many being behavioral in nature. In turn the pedagogies that support constructivist learning also challenge the behavioristic view of learning to which the education of learners with SEN has traditionally adhered. From the behaviorist perspective, the learning process is characterized as the learner being reactive to the conditions in the environment as opposed to taking an active role in discovering the environment (Ertmer & Newby, 2013). From this standpoint learning is viewed as external to the learner (Siemens, 2005): an input/output process where a learner finds information rather than creates it. Our thoughts align with those of Gallagher (2004) who contends that constructivism and constructivist pedagogies, are "consistent with the aim of disability studies to confront the oppression and marginalization of people with disabilities, particularly with regard to their right to define who they are and their liberty to speak for themselves" (p. 2). At the same time, we acknowledge that the wide range of characteristics of various "disabilities" makes generalizations about appropriate learning theories extremely difficult.

What follows is a case study describing how adventure education, through a constructivist approach, was employed to focus on the social skill development of students with autism spectrum disorders (ASD). ASD are defined in terms of qualitative impairments in social interaction and communication, as well as restricted, repetitive, and stereotyped patterns of behaviors, interests, and activities (APA, 2011). It is the limitations in social cognition that are often most devastating for individuals with ASD (Tantam, 2003). In Ireland, students with ASD are entitled to additional educational support structures through the July Provision Programme, provided for by the Department of Education and Skills. This support offers funding for an extended school year for students with ASD, engaging them in a more balanced curriculum, focusing on holistic development. This means the students have mathematics, English, Irish (Gaeilge), science, home economics, art, music, and physical education. From a physical education perspective, the use of curriculum models as a means of promoting the inclusion of students with SEN has yet to be fully explored. The case study presented below is a first step in examining the use of adventure education focusing on the interpersonal and intrapersonal development of students with SEN from a social skills perspective through the adventure education curriculum model.

Case Study

Jack has worked in the July Provision Programme for the past 2 years, both as an SNA and as a resource teacher. During this time, Jack learned about ASD, and social interaction and social skills education for these students. The students experienced a subject called "social" that focused on developing their social skills through role playing and social stories. These classes attempted to teach students social skills through real-life situations, such as making appointments or calling a friend. While the students did show development in terms of these structured situations, there was little development in terms of their social cognition throughout the day (between themselves and the teaching staff). Coming from a physical education background, Jack identified adventure education as holding potential for increasing the students' social development. His understanding was that the adventure education curriculum combined psychosocial and experiential methods of teaching social skills, with a strong emphasis on learning in groups and from each other (Stuhr, Sutherland, Ressler, & Ortiz-Stuhr, 2016). Through discussions with the resource teachers in the school, it appeared that all involved were interested in using adventure education and investigating whether or not this curriculum model and selected teaching methods would increase the student's social skills throughout the day.

As they began to collaborate on introducing adventure education in the SEN context, it seemed difficult to accurately define social skills. Therefore, the iLAUGH framework for social cognition was used as the main framework to guide their work. Smith-Myles (2007) explains that the framework takes an abstract concept, such as social thinking, and breaks it down into more salient, observable components. In fact, it provides a more specific lens through which to evaluate and understand the strengths and weaknesses of students who have social cognitive difficulties. The iLAUGH framework consists of six different social components: initiation, listening with one's eyes and brain, abstract and inferential, understanding the perspectives of others, getting the big picture, and humor/human relatedness. Therefore, these six lenses were used to represent the social skills of these students.

Before the July Provision Programme, Jack met with the resource teachers who were organizing the provision. They all agreed that four adventure classes a week would be appropriate for these students. The resource teachers were also interviewed to gain a base level for each student in the group. From this interview, it was clear that a social skills deficit existed within the group, with students struggling on all six components of the iLAUGH framework.

Ten teenage male students aged 13–18 (M = 15, SD = 1.93) with ASD participated in the program. The group experienced four classes a week, for the duration of the four week program. Each class followed a standard sequence of activities: (a) recap on previous lesson; (b) introduction to current lesson, including the key aim of the lesson, as well as the activities that would be experienced; (c) students engage in the activities, while constantly being reminded of the key aim/skill of the lesson; and (d) a final debriefing, where the lesson was summarized and students allowed to answer or ask any questions.

The classes were led by Jack, a qualified physical education teacher, and supported by two qualified SNAs. Many of the activities included in the adventure education classes were adapted from Tannehill and Dillon's (2007) resource, *A Handbook of Ideas: Teaching Adventure Education*. This handbook was developed for physical education teachers, containing various adventure education lessons. The following was the layout of themes for the four weeks: Week 1–communication and cooperation; Week 2–trust and problem-solving; Week 3–teamwork and introduction to orienteering; and Week 4–orienteering. The pace of the adventure education content was flexible and dependent on the students' reactions and progress during various activities.

As part of the project the SEN teachers, SNAs, and Jack kept separate reflective logs containing observations of the students' social interactions during each day. This was particularly useful as these individuals were in constant contact with the students, including critical moments such as school trips and lunchtime. The SEN teachers and Jack also observed the physical education classes, in order to see if what was being taught and learned in this context was transferring to other contexts.

During the first week, the social skills deficits of the students were highlighted through the communication and cooperation activities; for example, a lack of eye contact. As the students learned more about what communication and cooperation were, they became more comfortable using the particular skills. While skills were being developed in the adventure education class, there was little to no transfer outside the classroom. Students still sat alone at lunch and still struggled to understand the perspectives of their classmates and the teachers. It was difficult to see if they had developed any key social skills and if adventure education was helping social improvement.

During the second week, it became apparent to the teachers that some development was being made in regards to the students' social ability. The focus of this week was on trust and problem solving, which effectively forced the students to interact and communicate with each other (which most of them did successfully). The students began using their communication skills from the previous week, such as hand gestures and facial expressions, to effectively communicate with each other. In fact, during the last activity, the students collectively completed the "human knot" challenge. This is an activity requiring the students to hold hands and "untie the human knot" that they have created with their bodies joined by holding hands. Before the lesson, the resource teacher mentioned that she thought they would struggle. However, all students were involved, with some challenging themselves by holding hands and others holding a small rope instead. This proved to be an important moment for the whole group, and it was after this lesson that transfer was noted outside of the physical education setting when students began playing together at lunchtime. Although they were not necessarily communicating verbally, they were still interacting, and for the first time not isolating themselves. This was a significant step, as before social cognition can occur, individuals must learn to be social with each other to some extent.

The third week was where Jack and the SEN teachers started to apply the communication, cooperation, trust, and problem-solving skills previously learned. During this week the idea of a team was emphasized as the students were introduced to orienteering. The adventure education classes this week went really well, and Jack, the teachers, and the SNAs all began to see the students more confident in their ability to ask questions during the class, something with which they would have previously struggled. As part of the class, students had to create a nest for an egg, so that when an egg was dropped into the nest it wouldn't break. During this activity, the students really displayed increased awareness of social cognition, interacting with their group, and also helping other groups. Outside the classroom, the students continued to display improved social awareness. For example, the students coped well with timetable changes and changes to the teaching personnel during the week. As well, they began displaying an understanding of the perspectives of others, offering advice to a particular student who was upset due to an illness to a family member.

In the final week, the students focused solely on orienteering, with the group going on a school trip. During the adventure education classes, the students seemed accustomed to working together and there was little need for prompts or assistance from the SNAs. This was predominantly evident in the school orienteering course, which was completed by all the students; fully communicating and working together in a group of three with little assistance. In fact, the resource teacher mentioned that she was proud of the students' development after seeing them interact with each other on the bus during a school trip. Personally, Jack too was proud and extremely satisfied with the work that the staff, as a team, had put in and the effort and participation of the students. At the end of the four weeks, everyone agreed that the students definitely learned some valuable social skills through their participation in the adventure education program. These skills were reflected in the adventure classes, and also throughout the week outside the physical education program. The students grew to enjoy and look forward to the adventure education classes, and saw them as a place where they could actually challenge themselves both personally and physically.

Overall, there were a number of significant results from this work. The first was improvement in the social skills of the students. This was apparent in the adventure education classes where one could see the students learn key social skills, such as eye contact, and actually apply them in an activity. In fact, it appeared that the skills most developed by the students were initiation of social interaction and understanding the perspectives of others. These skills showed the biggest increase during the extent of the July Provision Programme. There were also noted improvements in the social cognition of the students outside of the physical education context. These contexts included break times, school trips, and other curricular subjects taken by the students. For example, on a particular trip to a local historic site, the resource teacher mentioned that she was "proud of the way they [students] initiated conversation with the guide." One of the SNAs noted in her diary that during group work activities, the students seemed more and more comfortable working with each other as the weeks went on demonstrating that the social skills learned could be transferred to other contexts.

Finally, it became apparent from speaking with the SEN teachers that they believed adventure education was an effective, useful resource for fostering social skill development for students with ASD. Initially, the SEN teachers highlighted the lack of a physical education curriculum provided for the students. At the end of the program, however, the teachers expressed their interest in adventure education as an appropriate and effective method for teaching social skills to the students. One teacher said that she hoped "to continue with the adventure style social skills activities, as these lessons were far more valuable for learning and team-building than reading from a social skills program." Similarly, the other teacher mentioned that she thought "the adventure classes definitely helped to bring on the boys' social skills and teamwork," and she would like to see "specific physical education classes for the students with ASD." These comments from the teachers were particularly useful in advocating for an adventure education program for students with SEN.

After the success of the first implementation of the project, it has been decided that the adventure education classes would again be implemented as part of the July Provision Programme for next year. The SEN teachers expressed their desire for the students to experience adventure education as part of their physical education curriculum in their mainstream classroom; however, to date that has not happened. This year, the focus will again be on developing the students' social skills outside the classroom through their engagement and involvement in the experiential adventure education curriculum.

Limitations of the Case Study

It must be recognized that the findings of the present case study are limited. The absence of female participants and the small sample size mean the results could be sample specific. However, the prominence of male participants was expected, given that according to the Centers for Disease Control and Prevention, ASD are five times more common in males than females (CDC, 2014). To increase the reliability of the results, the adventure education classes could be implemented for a longer period of time; for example, a whole academic year instead of a four-week block period. This would allow for the examination of the long-term impact of this curriculum model on the students' social skills. Furthermore, it would be beneficial to examine the students' social skills development in a context unrelated to school. This would require support and assistance from parents and family members. Despite some of these limitations, the findings provide important and meaningful information regarding the social skill development of students with ASD through AE. Results support an evidence-based strategy for the teaching of social skills to students with ASD, in the form of adventure education.

CONCLUSIONS AND IMPLICATIONS

The purpose of this chapter was to share and promote the usefulness of curriculum and instructional models in the Irish post-primary physical education curriculum as a means of promoting the social skills and inclusion of students with SEN. Over the past decade, various theories have been discussed noting the problems that individuals with SEN possess. There is, however, divergence among these theories, as each highlights different factors to explain the difficulties individuals with SEN may experience and the different ways of responding to them. From the perspective of inclusive education, social and interpersonal skill deficits can have major direct and indirect consequences for people with SEN; specifically, feelings of isolation, bullying, unhappiness, and rejection. Although there is a desire for peer interaction among students with SEN, this is often met with poor social support and increased loneliness when compared to their typically developing peers (Bauminger & Kasari, 2000). This comes as individuals begin to understand their own social difficulties and their differences with respect to others, as well as the consequences they face as a result of their behavior choices (Capps, Sigman, & Yirmiya, 1995). This disability awareness can cause embarrassment, frustration, and social isolation, which may lead ultimately to psychiatric issues such as anxiety, and depression, as well as difficulty in forming friendships (Frostad & Pijl, 2007; Maïano et al., 2016; Symes & Humphrey, 2010; Vaughn, Bos, & Schumm, 2011).

Currently, there appears to be no common approach for teaching social skills to children and young people with SEN by parents, teachers, or other service providers. This is primarily due to the fact that no one intervention is deemed suitable for individuals with various disabilities or disorders. Despite this, numerous interventions to teach social skills have been developed over the years (Carter & Hughes, 2007; Laugeson, Frankel, Gantman, Dillon, & Mogil, 2012; Walton & Ingersoll, 2013). Although many of these methods do not meet the requirements for evidence-based practice, some approaches have been shown to improve the social skills of individuals with SEN. Therefore, in general, there is agreement that additional pedagogical strategies are needed that would allow students with and without disabilities to learn and understand social skills and social situations, while at the same time promote physical activity. These strategies include behavior modification, peer-mediated training, social stories, and the implementation of a buddy system (Matson, Matson, & Rivet, 2007). It is unclear how successful these various interventions are when implemented on a large and long-term scale. While there is evidence of a number of effective practices, there is not one specific, evidence-based intervention in place or recommended. Yet, one method in particular that has shown promise as a way to improve social skills and promote social inclusion among students with SEN, particularly those with ASD, is the adventure education curriculum model and its corresponding instructional models.

Using constructivism as the theoretical framework, the instructional approaches contained within adventure education have been shown to be a unique and effective pedagogical method that is useful in promoting the social skills of students with SEN. For example, using an ethnographic case study approach, Sutherland and Stroot (2009, 2010) examined the impact of participation in an inclusive three-day rock climbing trip on the group dynamics of 10 to14-year-olds that included a 13-year-old male diagnosed with high functioning autism ("Brad"). Findings from these two studies suggest that the group dynamics changed over the course of the trip, and that participants became a more cohesive group for all involved, especially Brad.

Though first introduced primarily in the United States in the 1980s and 1990s, adventure education is still an emerging curricular model internationally. It is one that focuses on the learning that we as physical education teachers, teacher educators, coaches, and other professionals within various physical activity settings want all students to acquire. As described earlier in the chapter, constructivism assumes that learners do not enter the learning environment without knowledge or skills, but rather they are learners actively attempting to create meaning. Our job as teachers and coaches is to provide opportunities and encouragement as a means of building knowledge and shaping behaviors. This is particularly relevant when teaching students with SEN. From Jack's case study presented earlier, introducing students with SEN (specifically ASD) to elements of adventure education resulted in a slow but noticeable increase in their social skills and overall interactions with others, both within and outside the educational setting. These findings were similar to those presented in the work of Sutherland and Stroot (2009, 2010), where students were observed working together and cooperating more during and after the program than before suggesting its positive effects. For example, students demonstrated improvement in key social skills, such as eye contact, as well as the initiation of social interaction and understanding the perspectives of others during various activities. This has future implications for teaching and learning as the ultimate goal is to find ways to create more inclusive environments for students with and without SEN in both physical education and physical activity settings.

According to Kearns and Shevlin (2006) and Crawford (2011), preservice training for preparing teachers to work with children with SEN in Ireland is inadequate at best. Information in this chapter provides a step toward addressing this issue: integrating a theoretical perspective (constructivism) with an immediate and prolonged practical experience (adventure education). In this controlled and structured environment, students with SEN were able to develop a deeper understanding of how to engage others through the adventure education curriculum model. For many, through this "lived" learning experience, the unknown became known as students were able to create meaning through decision making, critical thinking, and problem solving. Such skills are critical for students with SEN in building relationships with their peers.

These conclusions add to the present literature supporting the continued implementation of this type of learning experience to better prepare preservice teachers and assist current teachers as well as other professionals in providing an inclusive environment for students with SEN. The benefits of using the adventure education model are clearly identified (Stuhr et al., 2016). As such, additional examination of this pedagogical approach as a means of further informing professionals working in the field is suggested. By identifying, strengthening, and utilizing the factors that influence positive change for children with SEN, physical education and physical activity in Ireland and abroad can move us as professionals closer to safer and more supportive practices in creating inclusive environments. Doing so reflects a more social model approach toward disability (Connors & Stalker, 2007; Shakespeare, 2013) allowing for the philosophy of inclusion to further develop among all involved: students, parents, teachers, and service providers.

REFERENCES

Ainscow, M. (2005). Developing inclusive education systems: What are the levers for change? *Journal of Educational Change, 6,* 109–124.

American Psychiatric Association (APA). (2011). *Diagnostic and statistical manual of mental disorders* (5th ed.). Washington, DC: Author.

Armour, K. M. (2011). What is 'sport pedagogy' and why study it? In K. Armour (Ed.), *Sport pedagogy. An introduction for teaching and coaching* (pp. 11–23). London, England: Pearson.

Bailey, J. (1998). Australia: Inclusion through categorization? In T. Booth & M. Ainscow (Eds.), *From them to us: An international study of inclusion in education* (pp. 171–185). London, England: Routledge.

Bauminger, N., & Kasari, C. (2000). Loneliness and friendship in high-functioning children with autism. *Child Development, 71,* 447–456.

Block, M. E. (2007). *A teachers' guide to including students with disabilities in general physical education* (3rd ed.). Baltimore, MD: Brookes.

Booth, T. (1996). A perspective on inclusion from England. *Cambridge Journal of Education, 26,* 87–99.

Borko, H., Mayfield, V., Marion, S., Flexer, M.D., & Hiebert, E. (1997). Teachers' developing ideas and practices about mathematics performance assessment:

Successes, stumbling blocks, and implications for professional development. *Teaching & Teacher Education, 13*, 259–278.

Capps, L., Sigman, M., & Yirmiya, N. (1995). Self-competence and emotional understanding in high functioning children with autism. *Development & Psychopathology, 7*, 137–149.

Carter, E., & Hughes, C. (2007). Social interaction interventions: Promoting socially supportive environments and teaching new skills. In S. Odam, R. Horner, M. Snell, & J. Blancher (Eds.) *Handbook of developmental disabilities* (pp. 310–328). New York, NY: Guilford.

Centers for Disease Control and Prevention. (2014). *Autism spectrum disorder (ASD): Research.* Retrieved from http://www.cdc.gov/ncbddd/autism/data.html

Connors, C., & Stalker, K. (2007). Children's experiences of disability: Pointers to a social model of childhood disability. *Disability & Society, 22*, 19–33.

Crawford, S. (2011). An examination of current adapted physical activity provision in primary and special schools in Ireland. *European Physical Education Review, 17*, 91–109.

Dewey, J. (1938). *Experience and education.* New York, NY: Collier Books.

Ertmer P. A., & Newby, T. J. (2013). Behaviorism, cognitivism, constructivism: Comparing critical features from an instructional design perspective. *Performance Improvement Quarterly, 26*, 43–71.

European Union. (2007, December 3). Treaty of Lisbon amending the treaty on European Union and the treaty establishing the European community. *Official Journal of the European Union, C 306*.

Fosnot, C. T. (2005). *Constructivism: Theory, perspectives, and practice.* New York, NY: Teachers College Press.

Frostad, P., & Pijl, S. J. (2007). Does being friendly help in making friends? The relation between the social position and social skills of pupils with special needs in mainstream education. *European Journal of Special Needs Education, 22*, 15–30.

Gallagher, D. (2004). The importance of constructivism and constructivist pedagogy for disability studies in education. *Disability Studies Quarterly, 24*, 1–18.

Gibson, J. (2000). Fred outdoors: An initial report into the experiences of outdoor activities for an adult who is congenitally deafblind. *Journal of Adventure Education & Outdoor Learning, 1*, 45–54.

Government of Ireland. (1998). *Education act.* Dublin, Ireland: The Stationery Office.

Government of Ireland. (2003). *Junior cycle physical education syllabus.* Dublin, Ireland: The Stationery Office.

Government of Ireland. (2004). *Education for persons with special educational needs act.* Dublin, Ireland: The Stationery Office.

Heatherton, A., & Walcott, V. (Eds.) (2009). *Handbook of social interactions in the 21st century.* New York, NY: Nova Science.

Itin, C. (1999). Reasserting the philosophy of experiential education as a vehicle for change in the 21st century. *Journal of Experiential Education, 22*, 91–98.

Kearns, H., & Shevlin, M. (2006). Initial teacher preparation for special educational needs: Policy and practice in the North and South of Ireland. *Teacher Development: An International Journal of Teachers' Professional Development, 10*, 25–42.

Kraft, D., & Sakofs, M. M. (Eds.). (1988). *The theory of adventure education.* Boulder, CO: Association of Experiential Education.

Laugeson, E. A., Frankel, F., Gantman, A., Dillon, A. R., & Mogil, C. (2012). Evidence-based social skills training for adolescents with autism spectrum disorders: The UCLA PEERS program. *Journal of Autism & Developmental Disorders, 42,* 1025–1036.

Maïano, C., Aimé, A., Salvas, M. C., Morin, A. J. S., & Normand, C. (2016). Prevalence and correlates of bullying perpetration and victimization among school-aged youth with intellectual disabilities: A systematic review. *Research in Developmental Disabilities, 49/50,* 181–195.

Matson, J., Matson, M., & Rivet, T. (2007). Social-skills treatments for children with autism spectrum disorders an overview. *Behavior Modification, 31,* 682–707.

Meegan, S., & MacPhail, A. (2006). Inclusive education: Ireland's education provision for children with special educational needs. *Irish Educational Studies, 25,* 53–62.

Metzler, M. W. (2005). *Instructional models for physical education.* Scottsdale, AZ: Holcomb Hathaway.

National Council for Curriculum and Assessment. (2005a). *Physical education (primary) guidelines for severe and profound general learning disabilities.* Dublin, Ireland: NCCA.

National Council for Curriculum and Assessment. (2005b). *Physical education (primary) guidelines for mild general learning disabilities.* Dublin, Ireland: NCCA.

National Council for Curriculum and Assessment. (2013). *Senior cycle physical education: Draft curriculum framework.* Dublin, Ireland: NCCA.

National Disability Authority. (2007) *Public attitudes to disability in Ireland.* Dublin, Ireland: NDA.

Quay, J. (2003). Experience and participation: Relating theories of learning. *Journal of Experiential Education, 26,* 105116.

Rovegno, I., & Dolly, P. (2006). Constructivist perspectives on learning, In D. Kirk, D. Macdonald, & M. Sullivan (Eds.), *The handbook of physical education* (pp. 226–241). London, England: Sage.

Shakespeare, T. (2013). The social model of disability. In L. J. Davis (Ed.), *The disability studies reader* (4th ed.; pp. 214–221). New York, NY: Routledge.

Shevlin, M., Kenny, M., & Loxley, A. (2008). A time of transition: Exploring special educational provision in the Republic of Ireland. *Journal of Research in Special Educational Needs, 8,* 141–152.

Shevlin, M., Winter, E., & Flynn, P. (2013). Developing inclusive practice: Teacher perceptions of opportunities and constraints in the Republic of Ireland. *International Journal of Inclusive Education, 17,* 1119–1133.

Siemens, G. (2005). Connectivism: A learning theory for the digital age. *Instructional Technology and Distance Learning, 2,* 1–8.

Smith-Myles, B. (Ed.). (2007). *Autism spectrum disorders: A handbook for parents and professionals.* Westport, CT: Greenwood.

Stuhr, P. T., Sutherland, S., Ressler, J., & Ortiz-Stuhr, E. M. (2016). The ABC's of adventure-based learning. *Strategies, 29,* 3–9.

Sutherland, S., & Stroot, S. (2009). Brad's story: An exploration of an inclusive adventure education experience. *Therapeutic Recreation Journal, 43,* 27–29.

Sutherland, S., & Stroot, S. (2010). The impact of participation in an inclusive adventure education trip on group dynamics. *Journal of Leisure Research, 42*, 153–176.

Symes, W., & Humphrey, N. (2010). Peer-group indicators of social inclusion among pupils with autism spectrum disorders (ASD) in mainstream secondary schools: A comparative study. *School Psychology International, 31*, 478–494.

Tannehill, D., & Dillon, M. (2007). *A handbook of ideas: Teaching adventure education.* Limerick, Ireland: Physical Education Association of Ireland.

Tannehill, D., van der Mars, H., & MacPhail, A. (2015). *Building effective physical education programs.* Burlington, MA: Jones & Bartlett.

Tantam, D. (2003). The challenges of adolescents and adults with Asperger syndrome. *Child Adolescents & Psychiatric Clinics of North America, 12*, 143–163.

Travers, J., Balfe, T., Butler, C., Day, T., Dupont, M., McDaid, R., . . . Prunty, A. (2010). *Addressing the challenges and barriers to inclusion in Irish schools.* Report to Research and Development Committee of the Department of Education and Skills. Dublin, Ireland: Department of Education and Science.

United Nations Educational, Scientific and Cultural Organization. (1994). *The Salamanca statement and framework for action on special needs education.* Paris, France: UNESCO.

United Nations Educational, Scientific and Cultural Organization. (2005). *Guidelines for inclusion: Ensuring access to education for all.* Paris, France: UNESCO.

United Nations General Assembly. (2007, January 24). *Convention on the rights of persons with disabilities:* Resolution adopted by the General Assembly, A/RES/61/106, New York, NY: UN General Assembly.

Vaughn, S., Bos, C., & Schumm, J. (2011). *Teaching students who are exceptional, diverse, and at risk in the general educational classroom.* Upper Saddle River, NJ: Pearson.

Vygotsky, L. (1978). *Mind in society: The development of higher psychological processes.* Cambridge, MA: Harvard University Press.

Walton, K. M., & Ingersoll, B. R. (2013). Improving social skills in adolescents and adults with autism and severe to profound intellectual disability: A review of the literature. *Journal of Autism & Developmental Disorders, 43*, 594–615.

Williams, G. (2001). Theorizing disability. In G. L. Albrecht, K. D. Seelman, & M. Bury (Eds.), *Handbook of disability studies* (pp. 123–144). Thousand Oaks, CA: Sage.

CHAPTER 10

UNDERSERVED URBAN MINORITY CHILDREN

Overcoming the Challenges and Enhancing the Benefits of Engaging in Physical Activity

Alex C. Garn
Louisiana State University

Jeffrey Martin, Brigid Byrd, and Nate McCaughtry
Wayne State University

Children and adolescents living in poverty is a social problem that dramatically increases secondary health risks. In 2011, 18% or 16.7 million American children lived in poverty, a 35% increase from 2007. In the United States, a disproportionate number of children in urban communities face the difficult task of living in poverty. In addition minority citizens, especially Hispanic and African Americans, are far more likely to live in urban centers and experience poverty. For example, in 2014, 24% of Hispanic and 26% of African Americans lived in poverty; whereas, only 10% of Caucasian

Inclusive Physical Activities, pages 203–221

Americans were affected by poverty (United States Census Bureau, 2016). This suggests that the issue of poverty is both a widespread epidemic in urban communities, and is stratified by race and ethnicity making it a glaring example of inequity.

Some of the primary consequences of urban poverty are health disparities. Residents in low income areas of urban centers have higher rates of nearly every chronic disease and negative health markers than residents in more affluent communities. Factors contributing to this include lack of access to quality healthcare, high quality foods, physical activity (PA) supportive contexts, as well as many urban stressors (e.g., community violence, transportation, harmful air quality, sanitation).

In particular, poverty produces barriers to PA such as reduced green spaces, safety concerns, crime, less community PA program opportunities, and limited financial resources to cover PA costs. In turn, inner city populations are significantly less physically active than suburban and more affluent groups. Moreover, these diminished rates of PA are one of a number of contributors to higher rates of overweight and obesity in urban communities, which are, in turn, underlying catalysts for many of the health disparities in those communities.

Taken together, a range of health related inequities and disparities position low income urban residents in the United States as less active and less healthy than their counterparts in different geographic locations and socioeconomic categories. Specific to the role of PA, the national conversation in the United States has shifted to changing the activity landscape for all Americans. The National Physical Activity Plan (www.physicalactivityplan.org), for instance, has been developed linking together needed PA interventions across many different spheres of social life. Specific to children, the plan focuses heavily on the role that schools and education settings might play in helping to get children more active and teach them to value an active lifestyle. The plan has gained traction through the development of Let's Move, Active Schools led by Michelle Obama, and positions statements by the Institute of Medicine (2013). Never before has there been a stronger focus on utilizing the anchor institutions of schools to accomplish public health agendas, like the promotion of PA and healthy eating.

The Centers for Disease Control and Prevention (CDC) have been pioneers in the conceptualization of models for health promoting schools in the United States. Since 1987, their coordinated school health approach has been the blueprint for integrating programs across entire schools and districts. Their newest iteration—Whole School, Whole Community, Whole Child, (www.cdc.gov/healthyyouth/wscc)—includes 10 components of integrated school wellness: health education; physical education (PE) and PA; nutrition environment and services; health services; counseling, psychological, and social services; social and emotional climate; physical environment; employee wellness; family engagement; and community involvement. Models like this unite best practices across school systems to advance a universal format for enhancing the health of school environments irrespective of sociocultural contexts.

While comprehensive models such as Whole School, Whole Community, Whole Child provide an ideal conceptual model for school wellness, the reality is that reform initiatives often emerge in a much more grassroots progression and embrace pieces of reform initiatives that are valued by stakeholders, manageable under organizational constraints, and fundable outside of existing organizational operating funds. The purpose of this chapter is to describe one urban school district's collaborative partnership with its local university to design a long-term, progressive school health reform initiative, titled the Detroit Health Youth Initiative (DHYI), to address its students' health disparities. We describe the evolution of the initiative over a decade and a half. The chapter has three objectives: (a) to describe the DHYI and its evolution over 15 years, (b) to overview the breadth of research on the impact of the DHYI, and (c) to provide recommendations about how to implement successful school-based PA programs with underserved urban minority children.

DETROIT HEALTHY YOUTH INITIATIVE

The DHYI began in 2001 with a series of strategy sessions between faculty and staff at Wayne State University and the school health administrators at the Detroit Public Schools. In this chapter, we briefly summarize the context and nature in which the DHYI occurred. However, interested readers should consult McCaughtry, Krause, McAuliffe, Miotke, and Price (2012) for additional information on this extensive collaborative effort, and on the lessons learned from this initiative in terms of program implementation.

Over the previous several decades, the city of Detroit had struggled in many ways. The city plunged toward fiscal bankruptcy, crime skyrocketed, city services were eliminated, affluent citizens fled to suburbs, and the infrastructure of the city crumbled. By 2000, Detroit had become one of the poorest and racially segregated urban centers in the United States. More than 90% of city residents were minorities and 80% of school-age children qualified for free or reduced price school meals. During this time, the disparities between the health of city residents and their suburban counterparts had also escalated on many fronts (e.g., incidents of type 2 diabetes, asthma, overweight/obesity, heart disease, etc.). The Detroit Public School district was no exception. Dropout rates increased, graduation rates decreased, financial deficits mounted, and district administration and accountability shrank. For example, germane to this chapter, the district had previously employed four individuals to administer and oversee PE across the district. As of 2001, only one individual oversaw district PE, while also directing the areas of school safety, transportation, 21st century programming, and athletics. Practically, this meant that physical educators across the district received very little guidance and support from the central administration, especially in the areas of negotiating building-level politics, funds for resources and equipment, and opportunities for subject-specific professional development.

Despite these many challenges, faculty at the university and both teachers and administrators at the school district have had a long history of informal collaboration (e.g., student teacher placements, periodic professional development workshops, research projects, etc.). Both groups recognized two fundamental trends in the district: (a) students were getting unhealthier and (b) the focus on school health was eroding.

Galvanized by a common goal to address health disparities and improve school health, initial strategy sessions ensued, which in 2001 culminated in a 10-year blueprint for working progressively across the K-12 spectrum in a collaborative effort to rejuvenate health and PA programs throughout the city by diversifying curricula, facilitating teacher development, and support, and providing adequate, updated resources.

The project became known as the DHYI. The goal of the initiative was to increase the health of Detroit children by improving the quality of school health environments and programs. The district volunteered in-kind support, consensus building among all levels of district administration and schools, and program monitoring. Wayne State University offered to seek external funding, co-design programing, organize and lead professional development and at-school support, and evaluate the project outcomes.

With funding from a U.S. Department of Education Physical Education Program grant, the initiative began in earnest in 2002 with a focus on adopting the newly-developed exemplary physical education curriculum (EPEC) as the official primary curriculum and implementing it in the PE classes in all primary schools. A fundamental motor skill development curriculum, EPEC was developed by a coalition of Michigan educators, field tested in Michigan schools (www.epec4kids.com), and was widely praised by most primary PE teachers in the district. The intent was to kick-start the long-term initiative by improving the curricular foundation in more than 120 primary schools. Continuing the teachers' professional learning and building a mentoring system where developed and successful teachers learned how to mentor new primary PE teachers. After learning general mentoring skills, experienced teachers were then paired with all new primary PE teachers to the district for year-long mentoring relationships that included workshops, school exchanges, videotaped lesson exchanges, and electronic chat room correspondence (Cothran et al., 2008; Cothran et al., 2009; Kulinna, McCaughtry, Martin, Cothran, & Faust, 2008; McCaughtry,

Kulinna, Cothran, Martin, & Faust, 2005). Building a coordinated mentoring system was critical because of high teacher turnover and burnout, as well as restructuring across the district.

Undergirded by success in the primary schools and another physical education program grant, as well as by support from the U.S. Department of Agriculture, the initiative embarked on the middle school phase. In this phase, the DHYI was broadened in scope to include health education and PE program development, focusing on both PA and healthy eating. The PE component centered on supplementing middle school teachers' expertise and instruction in competitive team sports with wellness knowledge curricula (EPEC personal conditioning), more individualized, lifetime fitness activities (e.g., yoga, Pilates, TaeBo, stepping, aerobics, and functional strength training), and instructional technologies (pedometers and web-based resources). Health educators were supported in their teaching of the district's comprehensive health education curricula, Michigan Model for Health (www.emc.cmich.edu/mm/), through professional development and resources to enhance their PA and nutrition instruction.

In 2009, the initiative moved into its final phase in the Detroit high schools. Again DHYI broadened in scope to include development in PE, health education, interdisciplinary nutrition education, and the formation of after-school PA clubs. The PE education programs underwent an expansion by supplementing sport instruction with wellness knowledge curricula, health club–style functional fitness, and popular culture exercise programs (e.g., Power 90, P90X, Boot Camp Fitness, Zumba). Health educators participated in professional development in the areas of PA promotion, healthy eating, violence prevention, and character development. Each high school also established an after-school PA club that attempted to recruit typically inactive youths (those who did not regularly participate in PE classes or PA programs outside the school). The clubs were student centered, and they focused on culturally relevant, noncompetitive, lifetime fitness activities. To recruit participants, they were advertised as fun, safe, supportive places to do physical activities with friends.

Collectively, over the 10-year span, the collaborative initiative facilitated program development in 125 K-12 schools, with more than 200 teachers, and 100,000 students. In addition to the program's sheer reach, the research team at Wayne State University, along with collaborators from other universities, have published more than 40 journal articles and book chapters and given more than 100 research presentations in national and international venues. This literature base has chronicled program development, student and teacher outcomes, and important factors that facilitate or inhibit teacher development and student learning. Our objective in the next section of this chapter is to summarize selected research and the knowledge it generated as part of this extensive research partnership.

MAJOR FINDINGS FROM DHYI RESEARCH

In this section we highlight and reflect upon major findings from all three phases of the DHYI. We overview studies focusing on three main topics: (a) motivation and engagement in PE; (b) PA behaviors in and out of school; and (c) after-school PA programs. Within these areas we synthesize findings and highlight exemplar investigations. The participants across all DHYI research were mostly African Americans and youth from other ethnic minority backgrounds attending urban schools with high rates of poverty. The collaborative efforts between Detroit Public Schools and Wayne State University created an environment that produced systematic investigation of children's health in underserved and understudied segments of the population (Gochman, 2013).

Motivation and Engagement in PE

Schools are considered important intervention points for increasing youth PA for a variety of reasons (CDC, 2013). For example, a majority of youths are enrolled in schools, which creates an environment that can potentially maximize the reach of interventions. Schools are especially important intervention points for underserved urban minority children and adolescents because of complex environmental (e.g., ineffective land-use for PA) and social (e.g., safety concerns) PA barriers common in poor urban centers (Lopez & Hynes, 2006). The CDC (2013) suggests that schools that take a comprehensive approach to PA can substantially contribute to children acquiring 60 minutes of PA per day. PE is uniquely situated in the school curriculum to help facilitate healthy behaviors such as PA and enhance health-related fitness and knowledge (McKenzie & Lounsbery, 2013). Motivation and engagement in PE are both considered important outcomes for psychological health and underlying mechanisms of establishing health behaviors from an early age (Corbin, 2002; Deci & Ryan, 2000). Motivation is defined as the energy and direction of behavior (Pintrich, 2000), while engagement is described as one's proactive and persistent interaction with her or his environment (Skinner, Furrer, Marchand, & Kindermann, 2008). Investigations of students' motivation, or lack of it, and engagement in PE has been a staple of DHYI studies focusing on middle school and high school students.

Bo Shen has been at the forefront of DHYI research on student motivation and engagement in PE. He has been the primary author of a series of studies grounded in self-determination theory (Deci & Ryan, 2000) and the self-system model of motivational development (Skinner et al., 2008). SDT suggests that autonomous motivation is critical to self-determined behaviors, and thus that externally controlled activities result in poor behavioral regulation. This is very important in the context of school-based mandatory PA activities such as compulsory PE classes. Students are "forced" to attend, which can hinder self-determination. Naturally, those students who enjoy sport and exercise (intrinsic motivation) will still enjoy PE classes. But for all the others, SDT suggests the importance of encouraging the internalization of these externally determined goals. So the idea is not necessarily to help students to "love" PA, which is unlikely to work for many of the most problematic ones, but rather to focus on the ways to encourage them to internalize the importance of these activities so that they start to adopt a self-determined approach to them. A portion of Shen and colleagues' work has focused solely on African American girls' PE motivation and engagement, a segment of the population especially at-risk for physical inactivity and obesity (Barr-Anderson, Adams-Wynn, DiSantis, & Kumanyika, 2013). Historically, researchers have highlighted the inability of many urban PE programs to effectively motivate and engage African American girls (Ennis, 1999).

Shen, McCaughtry et al. (2012) have explored how African American girls' ($N = 184$) sense of relatedness with their teacher and peers predicted behavioral and emotional engagement in high school PE. Behavioral and emotional engagement data were collected from both students and their teachers and used as outcome variables in separate regression analyses. Findings revealed that feelings of relatedness with teachers was a robust predictor of both student and teacher reports of behavioral and emotional engagement in PE. Feelings of peer relatedness only predicted student reports of behavioral engagement. Regression models accounted for 26% of the variance of student reports of behavioral engagement and 14% of the variance of student reports of emotional engagement. Less variance was accounted for in models predicting teacher reports of behavioral ($R^2 = .10$) and emotional engagement ($R^2 = .06$).

In a follow-up study, Shen, Rinehart-Lee, McCaughtry, and Li (2012) revealed complementary findings with African American girls ($N = 168$) enrolled in compulsory high school PE. Utilizing a mixed-method approach, Shen, Rinehart-Lee and colleagues investigated facilitators and barriers to future enrolment and participation in elective PE courses. Although many of the participants appreciated what they viewed as short-term benefits of PE such as having fun, socializing with friends, and working out, these were often viewed as somewhat superficial. In fact, PE was often seen as a cathartic break in the school day rather than providing a context to learn about and improve one's health. Social influences (e.g., lack of family support and undervaluing PE) were prominent reasons that undermined enrollment in future PE courses. Taken together, these two studies highlight the value placed on fulfilling peer and teacher-peer relationships in PE, and they underscore the need to convey the long-term importance and benefits derived from PE to African American girls and their family members. These results from DHYI identify the need to target and change the social environment created in PE in order to improve African American girls' motivation and engagement.

Additional work by Shen and colleagues has also advanced an understanding of African American adolescents' motivation toward high school PE (Shen, Garn, McCaughtry, Martin, & Fahlman, 2013; Shen et al., 2015). These studies have generally focused on the motivational continuum posited in self-determination theory (see Deci and Ryan, 2000 for a review). Shen et al. (2015) recently published a noteworthy study that used multilevel modeling to link PE teachers' reports of burnout to high school students' autonomous motivation. Using a two-wave study design (four-month interval) with more than 1,300 students and 30 teachers, Shen and colleagues revealed the effects of different dimensions (i.e., emotional exhaustion, depersonalization, reduced personal accomplishment) of teacher burnout on students' autonomous motivation toward PE. Findings revealed that only the depersonalization dimension of teacher burnout negatively predicted students' changes in autonomous motivation. Shen and colleagues argue that student motivation is likely to deteriorate when teachers develop negative and uncaring attitudes toward work and work-related interactions. Emotional exhaustion and reduced personal accomplishment appear to affect teachers, not students' motivation. Unfortunately, many urban teachers report greater levels of burnout than peers from rural or suburban schools (Abel & Sewell, 1999). Therefore, students in urban PE contexts such as the pupils in Detroit Public Schools may face greater exposure to teachers with burnout, undermining motivational development. This may be especially problematic for establishing long-term enjoyment and engagement in PA.

PA Behaviors In and Out of School

Providing safe and enjoyable PA opportunities for all students was an overarching objective for all three phases of the DHYI. It was important to the DHYI leadership team that enhancing students' health was facilitated in a manner that was fun for the students rather than taking a sterile, bottom-line prescriptive approach. The rationale was to not only get students active and enhance their health-related fitness, but to develop positive attitudes toward PA that could stimulate chronic engagement in activities deemed enjoyable. With this conceptual rationale in mind, Martin and colleagues used the theory of planned behavior (Ajzen, 1991) as a theoretical framework in a series of studies aimed to predict PA and cardiorespiratory fitness in African American (Martin et al., 2005) and Hispanic (Martin, McCaughtry, & Shen, 2009) children in the primary phase of DHYI. Similar studies were completed in the middle school phase of DHYI by Martin and colleagues predicting PA and cardiorespiratory fitness. In these further studies, a combination of the theory of planned behavior and social cognitive theory (Bandura, 2004) was used to predict PA and cardiovascular fitness with a diverse sample of middle school students ($N = 506$; Martin, McCaughtry, Flory, Murphy, & Wisdom, 2011) and a subsample of Arab American students ($N = 348$) (Martin, McCaughtry, & Shen, 2008).

Findings across these studies revealed some theoretical limitations of using the theory of planned behavior to predict PA, especially in children. For example, African American children's ($N = 548$) attitudes toward PA did not predict their behavioral intentions, and in turn behavioral intentions did not predict PA (Martin et al., 2005). With Hispanic American ($N = 129$) children, behavioral intentions predicted subsequent PA, but only accounted for a modest amount of variance (i.e., <10%). The theory of planned behavior was originally developed for adult populations and assumed individuals made rationale and preplanned decisions (Ajzen, 1991), which likely does not reflect the decision-making processes that children use. It is also possible that the compulsory nature of school-based PA may undermine the utility value of the theory of planned behavior. Primary students have no choice in attending these classes, which may not readily represent the theoretical assumption of predicting volitional behavior in the theory of planned behavior (Ajzen, 1991).

In order to address these limitations, Martin and colleagues added a social cognitive lens with middle school students in DHYI Phase 2. Findings with middle school students revealed that students' barrier self-efficacy was a consistent predictor of PA across the two studies, but again only accounted for approximately 12% of the variance with ethnically diverse students (Martin et al., 2011), and 8% of the variance with Arab American students (Martin et al., 2008). Martin et al. (2011) concluded that a great deal of research was needed to understand and account for the main determinants of ethnically diverse children's PA behaviors.

In Phase 3 of the DHYI project with high school students, greater amounts of variance in students' PA were accounted for (Garn, McCaughtry, Shen, Martin, & Fahlman, 2013). Using tenets of achievement goal theory, Garn et al. (2013) predicted PA behaviors in underserved, ethnic minority adolescent girls ($N = 286$). Findings revealed that girls' perceived physical competence mediated the relationships between perceptions of the motivational climate in PE and PA behaviors. Specifically, a full unit of change (i.e., one standard deviation) in girls' perceived competence was associated with a half unit of change (.5 standard deviation) in PA. Overall, the model accounted for 31% of the variance in girls PA.

While DHYI studies provide meaningful insights about ethnically diverse youths' PA behaviors, it should be noted that these studies were mainly correlational in nature. Therefore, the need for more stringent research designs that provide greater confidence about the determinants of PA behaviors is needed to build on the pioneering work set forth in the DHYI. Based on the collaborative nature of the DHYI, the use of gold standard research designs (such as randomized control trials that delay or withhold programming) was not considered a feasible research approach. Maximizing PA opportunities for all students enrolled in Detroit Public Schools took precedence.

After-School Physical Activity Clubs

A critical part of DHYI Phase 3 was the implementation and evaluation of the after-school PA clubs (PACs) in high schools. Students who were physically inactive, obese, or faced health-risks were targeted for involvement in the PACs. The curriculum emphasized noncompetitive, cooperative, and structured PA that produced "student-centered opportunities to be physically active in safe, supportive environments with friends" (Garn et al., 2014, p. 115). Leaders of the PACs emphasized learning self-management skills and the improvement of personal health. Over a 2-year period, 14 urban inner-city high schools established PACs that engaged more than 15,000 student attendees. The clubs were led by PE and health teachers with assistance from other school personnel and student leaders; they met two to three times per week for 60 to 90 minutes each session. Collectively, PAC clubs met 938 times and averaged 16.5 students per meeting (Garn et al., 2014). Garn and colleagues used participant observation methodology based on a large database consisting of 115 observations of individual sessions and 404 interviews with adult leaders and student attendees to systematically investigate PACs (Garn et al., 2014; Maljak et al., 2014; Whalen et al., 2015). These studies provided firsthand participant accounts of key components needed to develop and sustain successful PACs (Garn et al., 2014), major challenges and barriers undermining PACs (Maljak et al., 2014), and student motives underlying sustained participation in PACs (Whalen et al., 2015). Themes emerged across these studies that provided valuable information about what stakeholders in urban schools reported as the necessities and common pitfalls associated with creating, delivering, and sustaining after-school PACs. Overwhelmingly, supportive interpersonal relationships arose as a critical element of effective after-school PACs. For example, emotional connections with PAC leaders and fellow participants was consistently reported by both adult leaders (Garn et al., 2014) and student participants (Whalen et al., 2015) as essential for maximizing the impact and success of individual sessions and long-term sustainability of after-school programs. The most successful adult leaders used a personal approach to recruit students into their PACs and developed bonds that kept students coming back.

Maljak et al. (2014) revealed, on the other hand, that competing school-activities in which interpersonal relationships and affiliation had previously been established provided challenges to recruiting and subsequently getting students to attend their first after-school PAC session. Garn et al. (2014) noted that some PAC leaders implemented a "bring a friend" approach to recruiting, capitalizing on the strong interconnection between interpersonal relations and student involvement. Family obligations were another example of how interpersonal relationships, in this case prioritizing family interactions and responsibilities, obstructed participation in after-school clubs. A final interpersonal barrier occurred with unsupportive school administrators. Specifically, many school administrators took a "business approach," whereby school programs with more "prestige" (e.g., basketball), and "school history," but less reach on students in need of health intervention received preferred treatment, school space, and personal attention.

Curricular programming was also identified as a vital aspect of sustaining effective PACs. Both adult leaders and student participants were adamant about the need for fun, culturally relevant, and noncompetitive activities. Almost all of the PACs provided students with responsibilities and choices in the types of activities implemented in the programs. Students discussed how culturally relevant activities viewed as "popular" (e.g., Zumba, Yoga, P90x, step dancing) were more appealing than competitive sports activities commonly used in a traditional PE curriculum. It should be noted that highly fit athletes were not the target audience of these after-school PACs, although athletes did attend PACs and seemed to enjoy the noncompetitive environment. Observational evidence demonstrated that adult leaders were quick to step in and redirect activities when they became overly competitive (Garn et al., 2014). Similarly, student participants noted on several occasions that noncompetitive, popular activities provided a good mix of social interaction and health benefits (e.g., "a workout that made me sweat"; Whalen et al., 2015).

Finally, stakeholders recounted barriers related to hunger and inadequate transportation. Specifically, if a student's need for food provisions at the start of each after-school session and safe transportation home upon completion of each session were unmet, attendance and sustainability of the after-school programs suffered (Maljak et al., 2014). Like many high schools situated in poor urban centers in the United States, fast-food restaurants and low nutritious snacks from vending machine were often the only easily accessible food options for these students (Larson, Story, & Nelson, 2009). Many students were hungry after school because of early lunch services (e.g., 10:30 a.m.) or no lunch at all, and hunger or eating fatty foods that lacked nutrition right after school prevented PAC attendance. Thus, providing students with a healthy snack at the beginning of each PAC session was an important strategy for maximizing attendance.

In many cases, safe passage home after PAC sessions was another challenge that ultimately hindered participation rates. Families either did not own cars, or parental work patterns (e.g., working multiple shifts; working late shifts) prohibited consistent transportation home after sessions according to student participants. Fear of personal harm and violence, parental safety concerns, freezing cold weather, and inconsistent time schedules (e.g., buses that never showed up) made public transportation an unappealing and ineffective option. Compounding the problem, school busing was not endorsed by school administrators, which was often a reflection of inadequate budgets. A few adult leaders helped students organize carpools, but overall transportation posed a serious threat to implementing PACs in these inner-city schools.

Garn and colleagues used qualitative methods to provide rich description of PACs associated with the DYHI, but quantitative investigation was less prevalent. An exception was Martin and colleagues (2014) investigation of the ability of PACs to promote students' physical self-concept. Martin, Garn, Shen, McCaughtry, and Nash (2014) examined the multidimensional physical self-concept (SC) of students participating in the PACs. Using a quasi-experimental design, changes in multidimensional physical self-concepts over the course of a school year were compared between students: (a) participating in PE classes and PACs ($n = 257$); (b) participating in PE classes only ($n = 548$); (c) participating in PACs only ($n = 187$), and (d) not participating in either a PAC or PE classes ($n = 501$). It was hypothesized that changes in physical self-concept would follow a linear pattern in the following manner: PE and PAC > PE or PAC > no PE or PAC. Participants completed the short version of the physical self-description questionnaire (PSDQ-S; Marsh, Martin, & Jackson, 2010), which allowed for the evaluation of global self-esteem, global physical self-concept, and nine subdomains of physical self-concept including physical activity, body fat, appearance, coordination, endurance, flexibility, health, sport, and strength. Students participating in both the PE and PAC had significantly higher global self-esteem, endurance self-concept, sport self-concept, strength self-concept, and coordination self-concept compared to the other three groups. However, the hypothesis regarding a linear relationship across the four groups for multidimensional self-concepts was only partially supported.

Despite a limited amount of DHYI research on PACs, findings provide empirical evidence and rich information on how to implement PACs in urban high schools. Capitalizing on key facilitators (e.g., caring, supportive, and non-competitive environments; culturally-relevant activities), reducing inhibitive factors (e.g., providing snacks to curb hunger; setting up car pools or school-based transportation), recognizing student participation motives (e.g., social affiliation; engaging in fun activities), and understanding meaningful participation outcomes (e.g., multidimensional physical self-concept) can provide the foundation for planning future PAC implementation and guide future PAC policies at different spheres of influence (e.g., state, regional, district, school).

RECOMMENDATIONS FOR PROMOTING SCHOOL-BASED PA

Capitalizing on DHYI research and lessons learned from extensive collaborations with Detroit Public Schools, we share a diverse set of recommendations for promoting school-based PA and reducing health inequities for underserved urban minority youth in the third and final section of the chapter. First, we generate links across all three phases of DHYI research to make evidence-based recommendations for promoting school-based PA. Finally, we discuss practical recommendations for producing school-based partnerships in urban schools serving disadvantaged students. Of central importance are strategic issues that can enhance or undermine collaborations, and ultimately determine the success of program implementation.

Evidence-Based Recommendations

Drawing on evidence gathered across all three phases of the DHYI, we make three general recommendations for promoting school-based PA: (a) emphasize social aspects of PA, (b) grow personal agency toward PA, and (c) carefully consider PA curricular content. In the following, we will elaborate in detail on what each of these recommendations look like in action.

Emphasize Social Aspects of PA
Developing close interpersonal relationships between teachers and students (Garn et al., 2014; Shen, Rinehart-Lee et al., 2012) and among students (Shen, McCaughtry et al., 2012; Whalen et al., 2015) were a key ingredients to promoting engagement and motivation in school-based PA programs. On the other hand, when PE teachers expressed feelings of relational depersonalization, their students' motivation toward school-based PA started to erode (Shen et al., 2015). Therefore, we strongly recommend school leaders involved with program development and delivery serving disadvantaged youth incorporate strategies that facilitate the relational aspects of PA. Based on hundreds of interviews with students, Garn et al. (2014) note that school-based PA programs must be highly caring and supportive toward students and create an environment of encouragement. For example, teachers must develop strategies that help them get to know their

students personally, such as becoming familiar with family backgrounds, interests and dislikes both in and out of school, and individual participation facilitators (e.g., friends) and barriers (e.g., transportation). Scheduling socialization periods into PA programing may be one tactic for creating highly personalized PA contexts.

Developing PA programs that stress care, support, and encouragement appears to be another strategy that increases student attendance, motivation, and engagement (Garn et al., 2014; Maljak et al., 2014; Shen, Reinehart-Lee et al., 2012; Whalen et al., 2015). Therefore, a combination of ongoing teacher and student learning opportunities may be one course of action to help accomplish this recommendation. For example, teacher professional learning could focus on how to provide effective feedback (Hattie & Timperley, 2007), be responsive and sensitive, and show empathy (Hellison, 2011). Embedding social skill learning into PA sessions could be a student-oriented approach for creating a caring and supportive environment (Collaborative for Academic, Social, and Emotional Learning, http://www.casel.org). PA contexts often call for students to use interpersonal skills such as active listening, communication, and cooperation. Teachers could assist students in developing competencies and value for interpersonal skills. Our experiences with DHYI suggest interpersonal learning for both teachers and students needs to be an explicit part of school-based PA programming.

Grow Personal Agency Toward PA

Our second recommendation underscores the need to create school-based PA programs that empower students and their self-beliefs about PA. Bandura (2001) highlights the importance of self-beliefs about one's capabilities to control his/her actions and produce successful outcomes in behavioral regulation. In DHYI studies, we have examined reflective self-beliefs including perceived physical competence (Garn et al., 2013) as well as prospective self-beliefs such as barrier self-efficacy for PA (Martin et al., 2008; Martin et al., 2011). Our studies support the importance of cultivating both reflective and prospective self-beliefs toward PA with underserved urban minority children.

Garn et al. (2013) revealed robust links between secondary students' perceptions of a mastery climate in PE and feelings of perceived competence, which in turn predicted PA. Promoting a mastery climate, therefore, appears to be one strategy that can boost PA-related self-beliefs. Examples of contextual characteristics of a mastery climate include focusing on personal standards of success and task mastery instead of social comparison standards, emphasizing fun and cooperation over competition, and recognizing and rewarding effort over ability or performance (Duda, 1996). Maljak et al. (2014) also confirmed the value of stressing fun and personal standards of success over competition in after-school PA programs. Martin et al. (2011) highlighted the meaningful role of barrier self-efficacy in relation to ethnically diverse middle school students' intentions for PA. Barrier self-efficacy, in this case defined as students' self-beliefs to engage in future PA despite common obstacles (e.g., lack of time, motivation, resources), can be enhanced through mastery experiences and encouraging feedback (Bandura, 1997). Therefore, we advocate for growing personal agency by using mastery climate characteristics and encouragement as core elements for school-based PA programs.

Carefully Consider PA Curricular Content

A common theme across DHYI research in both primary (e.g., McCaughtry, Barnard, Martin, Shen, & Kulinna, 2006) and secondary (e.g., Shen et al., 2013; Whalen et al., 2015) phases highlights the importance of using curricula that meets the needs of a broad variety of students, not just those who are physically talented. DHYI research has consistently revealed the inadequacies of competitive sport-based content that caters to a small percentage of athletic students. The widely popular competitive sport model often produces an environment of power inequity, dominance, and marginalization for many students who would likely benefit most from PA engagement (Ennis, 1999; Ferry & McCaughtry, 2013). Therefore, careful planning, monitoring, and evaluation of curricular content is needed to maximize the effectiveness of school-based PA programs.

DHYI projects have emphasized the need for curricular transformation toward more individualized, culturally relevant curricula that meet the PA needs of students with diverse physical abilities and interests. Moving toward a wellness model that emphasizes the integration of lifetime wellness activities (e.g., dance, aerobics, yoga, functional strength training) and wellness knowledge has been identified by both urban students and teachers as an effective strategy for making school-based PA more enjoyable and appealing to a greater breadth of students. What we have learned, however, is that teachers are often more comfortable with the traditional competitive sport model (Ferry & McCaughtry, 2013). Therefore, consistent and ongoing investments in both instructional resources and equipment geared toward lifetime wellness curricula must occur throughout planning and implementation stages. Unfortunately, funding these types of resources in poor urban schools is a major challenge that can undermine the ultimate success of PA programs needed to reduce health inequities faced by many disadvantaged urban minority children.

Practical Recommendations

As the original 10-year blueprint for PA and nutrition curriculum and environmental reform reached its culmination, stakeholders from both organizations met often to reflect on the process and outcomes of the initiative and to develop a comparable roadmap for moving forward. The group had regular opportunities to identify courses of action that helped the partnership succeed. Although many factors contributed to the success, we specifically highlight the practical importance of building collaborative relationships between university and school personnel.

Collaborative Relationships

Over the years, relationships emerged as a central feature in the success of the DHYI partnership. Naturally, a host of relationships evolved during the project, but those built around project design, those with school principals, and those that developed during the formation of project staff proved most important.

From the beginning, Detroit Public School administrators and Wayne State University project staff agreed on the need to incorporate administrators, teachers, students, and university personnel into the vision and design of the project because each group brought diverse insights, desires, and professional capacities. We knew from the outset, however, that students were central to the relationship process. In order for successful change, students would have to buy-in and see the relevance between the new PE curriculum and school-based PA opportunities, and their lives outside of school (e.g., popularity of activities in youth culture, access to opportunities outside schools, limited finances, few safe green spaces). What proved critical over time was to conduct regular meetings with each group of stakeholders, understand one another's perspectives, and design programs that were mutually beneficial for each group. This emerged as a give-and-take process where the voices of each group were heard and solutions were identified that benefited everyone.

Establishing relationships with principals also contributed to success. Over the duration of the project, the power structure in the district gradually decentralized, and the fate of the project often rested on the support of individual principals. This meant understanding principals' building-level concerns and initiatives and responding in ways that furthered our project's goals, while also meeting those of principals. Some microlevel strategies to build relationships with principals included identifying safe storage protocols for expensive equipment, presenting the project at school events and meetings (e.g., parent-teacher conferences, PTA events), and delivering project reports that principals could use in their school promotions.

As explained earlier, the district underwent dramatic downsizing during the project. This affected many district operations, but specifically it led to decreases in the teaching force either through layoffs or early retirement incentives. In many cases, seasoned and beloved teachers were left unemployed, but still wanted to remain connected to education and influence the lives of children. The project team often recruited these individuals to fill project staff positions in which they facilitated the project by acting as coordinators with schools, creating professional development workshops, presenting to parents, and serving in many other ways. In other words, the project leveraged the long-standing relationships and institutional wisdom of early retired teachers to help steer the project successfully through the district's ever-changing landscape. Based on these experiences and similar to our previous recommendations, there is a clear need to continually build relationships. Stakeholder groups must feel connected to one another in a collective way (i.e., feelings of "we"). Sharing these DHYI experiences can provide greater knowledge about important practical considerations that must be undertaken in order for school-based PA programs in poor urban schools to thrive.

REFERENCES

Abel, M. H., & Sewell, J. (1999). Stress and burnout in rural and urban secondary teachers. *The Journal of Educational Research, 92,* 287–293.

Ajzen, I. (1991). The theory of planned behavior. *Organizational Behavior & Human Decision Processing, 50,* 179–211.

Bandura, A. (1997). *Self-efficacy: The exercise of control.* New York, NY: Freeman.

Bandura, A. (2001). Social cognitive theory: An agentic perspective. *Annual Review of Psychology, 52,* 1–26.

Bandura, A. (2004). Health promotion by social cognitive means. *Health Education & Behavior, 31,* 143–164.

Barr-Anderson, D. J., Adams-Wynn, A. W., DiSantis, K. I., & Kumanyika, S. (2013). Family-focused physical activity, diet, and obesity interventions in African-American girls: A systematic review. *Obesity Reviews, 14,* 29–51.

Centers for Disease Control and Prevention (CDC). (2013). *Comprehensive school physical activity programs: A guide for schools.* Atlanta, GA: Department of Health and Human Services.

Corbin, C. B. (2002). Physical activity for everyone: What every physical educator should know about promoting lifelong physical activity. *Journal of Teaching in Physical Education, 21,* 128–144.

Cothran, D. J., McCaughtry, N., Faust, R., Garn, A. C., Kulinna, P. H., & Martin, J. (2009). E-mentoring in physical education: Promises and pitfalls. *Research Quarterly for Exercise and Sport, 80,* 552–562.

Cothran, D. J., McCaughtry, N., Smigell, S., Garn, A. C., Kulinna, P.H., Faust, R., & Martin, J. (2008). Teachers' preferences on the roles and qualities of a mentor teacher. *Journal of Teaching in Physical Education, 27*, 241–251.

Deci, E. L., & Ryan, R. M. (2000). The "what" and "why" of goal pursuits: Human need and the self-determination of behavior. *Psychological Inquiry, 11*, 227–268.

Duda, J. L. (1996). Maximizing motivation in sport and physical education among children and adolescents: The case for greater task involvement. *Quest, 48*, 290–302.

Ennis, C. D. (*1999*). Creating a culturally relevant curriculum for disengaged girls. *Sport, Education, and Society, 4*, 31–49.

Ferry, M., & McCaughtry, N. (2013). Secondary physical educators and sport: A love affair. *Journal of Teaching in Physical Education, 32*, 375–393.

Garn, A. C., McCaughtry, N., Kulik, N., Kaseta, M., Maljak, K., Whalen, L., ... Fahlman, M. (2014). Successful after-school physical activity clubs in urban high schools: Perceptions of adult leaders and students participants. *Journal of Teaching in Physical Education, 33*, 112-133.

Garn, A. C., McCaughtry, N., Shen, B., Martin, J. J., & Fahlman, M. (2013). Underserved adolescent girls' physical activity intentions and behaviors: Relationships with the motivational climate and perceived competence in physical education. *Advances in Physical Education, 3*, 103–110.

Gochman, D. S. (2013). *Handbook of health behavior research III: Demography, development, and diversity.* New York, NY: Springer.

Hattie, J., & Timperley, H. (2007). The power of feedback. *Review of Educational Research, 77*, 81–112.

Hellison, D. (2011). *Teaching personal and social responsibility through physical activity* (3rd ed.). Champaign, IL: Human Kinetics.

Institute of Medicine. (2013). *Educating the student body: Taking physical activity and physical education to school.* Washington, DC: The National Academies Press.

Kulinna, P. H., McCaughtry, N., Martin, J. J., Cothran, D. J., & Faust, R. (2008). The influence of professional development on teachers' psychosocial perceptions of teaching a health-related physical education curriculum. *Journal of Teaching in Physical Education, 27*, 292–307.

Larson, N. I., Story, M. T., & Nelson, M. C. (2009). Disparities in access to healthy foods in the U.S. *Neighborhood Environments, 36*, 74–81.

Lopez, R. P., & Hynes, H. P. (2006). Obesity, physical activity, and the urban environment: Public health research. *Environmental Health, 5*, 25–35.

Maljak, K., Garn, A. C., McCaughtry, N., Kulik, N., Martin, J., Shen, B., ... Fahlman, M. (2014). Challenges in offering inner-city after-school physical activity clubs. *American Journal of Health Education, 45*, 297–307.

Marsh, H. W., Martin, A. J., & Jackson S. (2010). Introducing a short version of the physical self-description questionnaire: New strategies, short-form evaluative criteria, and applications of factor analysis. *Journal of Sport and Exercise Psychology, 32*, 438–482.

Martin, J. J., Garn, A. C., Shen, B., McCaughtry, N., & Nash, B. (2014). Variations in multi-dimensional physical self-concept linked to physical education and physical activity clubs in underserved urban high school students. In J. H.

Borders (Ed.). *The psychology of self-esteem: New research* (pp. 11–18). New York, NY: Nova Science.

Martin, J. J., McCaughtry, N., Flory, S., Murphy, A., & Wisdom, K. (2011). Using social cognitive theory to predict physical activity and fitness in underserved middle school children. *Research Quarterly for Exercise and Sport, 82,* 247–255.

Martin, J. J., McCaughtry, N., Kulinna, P. H., Cothran, D., Dake, J., & Fahoome, G. (2005). Predicting physical activity and cardiorespiratory fitness in African American children. *Journal of Sport and Exercise Psychology, 27,* 456–469.

Martin, J. J., McCaughtry, N., & Shen, B. (2008). Predicting physical activity in Arab American school children. *Journal of Teaching Physical Education, 27,* 205–219.

Martin, J. J., McCaughtry, N., & Shen, B. (2009). Physical activity and fitness in inner-city Hispanic children. *Hispanic Health Care International, 7,* 21–29.

McCaughtry, N., Barnard, S., Martin, J., Shen, B., & Kulinna, P. (2006). Teachers' perspectives on the challenges of teaching physical education in urban schools: The student emotional filter. *Research Quarterly for Exercise and Sport, 77,* 486–498.

McCaughtry, N., Krause, J., Mcauliffe, P., Miotke, R., & Price, f. (2012). Detroit healthy youth initiative: Lessons learned in creating successful school-university partnerships. *Journal of Physical Education, Recreation, and Dance, 83,* 28–31.

McCaughtry, N., Kulinna, P. H., Cothran, D.J., Martin, J., & Faust, R. (2005). Teachers mentoring teachers: A view over time. *Journal of Teaching in Physical Education, 24,* 326–343.

McKenzie, T. L., & Lounsbery M. A. (2013). Physical education teacher effectiveness in a public health context. *Research Quarterly for Exercise and Sport, 84,* 419–430.

Pintrich, P. R. (2000). Educational psychology at the millennium: A look back and a look forward. *Educational Psychologist, 35,* 221–226.

Shen, B., Garn, A. C., McCaughtry, N., Martin, J. J., & Fahlman, M. M. (2013). Testing factorial invariance of the Amotivation Inventory-Physical Education across gender for urban adolescents. *Measurement in Physical Education and Exercise Science, 17,* 208–220.

Shen, B., McCaughtry, N., Martin, J. J., Fahlmann, M. & Garn, A. (2012). Urban high-school girls sense of relatedness and their engagement in physical education. *Journal of Teaching in Physical Education, 31,* 231–245.

Shen, B., McCaughtry, N., Martin, J. J., Garn, A. C., Kulik, N., & Fahlman, M. (2015). The relationship between teacher burnout and student motivation. *British Journal of Educational Psychology, 85,* 519–532.

Shen, B., Rinehart-Lee, T., McCaughtry, N., & Li, X. (2012). Urban African American girls' participation and future intentions toward physical education. *Sex Roles, 67,* 323–333.

Skinner, E., Furrer, C., Marchand, G., & Kindermann, T. (2008). Engagement and disaffection in the classroom: Part of a larger motivational dynamic? *Journal of Educational Psychology, 100,* 765–781.

United States Census Bureau (2016). *Current population survey annual social and economic supplement.* Retrieved from http://www.census.gov/data/tables/time-series/demo/income-poverty/cps-pov/pov-01.2014.html

Whalen, L., McCaughtry, N., Garn, A. C., Centeio, E., Kulik, N., Shen, B., & Martin, J. (2015). Why inner-city high schoolers voluntarily attend after-school physical activity clubs. *Health Education Journal.* doi: 10.1177/0017896915608885.

PART IV

ADVANCING THE PRACTICE OF EDUCATORS AND
COACHES TO CULTIVATE THE SOCIAL INCLUSION AND
PARTICIPATION IN PHYSICAL ACTIVITY OF CHILDREN
AND ADOLESCENTS WITH SPECIAL NEEDS

CHAPTER 11

THE USE OF MULTIMEDIA AND THE INTERNET IN PROVIDING GLOBAL TRAINING OPPORTUNITIES FOR COACHES IN ADAPTED SPORTS

Case of Sitting Volleyball/Volley*SLIDE*

Kwok Ng
University of Jyvaskyla

Matthew Rogers
*Volley*SLIDE

Ken Black
University of Worcester

BACKGROUND

Adapted sports has been popularized through events like the Paralympics. The Paralympics grew from values similar to the Olympics Games, and was begun through the concept of sport as a form of rehabilitation by Sir Ludwig Guttmann. Guttmann believed that there was more to life than just waiting to die for the people in the wards of the Stoke Mandeville Hospital (Guttmann, 1976). Rehabilitation gave individuals inspiration to practice in sports as well as the notion to compete against others. The competitions led to the birth of the Stoke Mandeville Games, which later became the Paralympic Games (Brittain, 2009).

An agreement between the International Olympic Committee and the International Paralympic Committee was signed in 2001, whereby game organizers needed to include both Olympic and Paralympic plans when submitting a hosting bid (Bailey, 2008). As a result, the games became more professional at all levels. These included the various actors involved in these games such as athletes, coaches, officials, managers, sponsors, delegation teams, medical staff, as well as the architects, builders, constructors, designers, and engineers that have to consider accessibility, equality, and equity for the games. As a result, the games have been so impressive that there are more demands from the spectators. There are household names that people talk about, and stadiums full of people chanting their favorite athletes' names.

Coupled with this, is the professionalization of the media on the Paralympics (Schantz & Gilbert, 2008). The growth in print media, in coverage and quality, has increased around the world. There is an increase in the number of hours of coverage on television sets, Internet channels and live broadcasts, which have demanded trained commentators as well as reported interviews and knowledge of how to use statistics. The International Paralympic Committee (IPC) has its own Paralympic TV channel that broadcasts live and recorded events. Given the relatively short history of the Paralympic Games, the increased attention is impressive. But any output levels of spectators, staff, athletes, ticket sales, worldwide coverage, and the like are still a fraction of the Olympic Games. Much more is needed in science and the understanding of the Paralympic Games before it is on par with the Olympics (Hums, Moorman, & Wolff, 2003; UN, 2010). An important issue is the comparative lack of grassroots development by national Paralympic committees, as they are partly driven from government and commercial funding at the elite end of the sport (Black, 2015).

One of the fundamental areas of growth in adapted sports is to make more opportunities for potential athletes. Coaches play a vital role in this. Many coaches involved in adapted sports do so as volunteers, which may include activities in clubs a few times a week for a few hours at a time. With this limited exposure to coaching in adapted sports, materials for basic coach education are limited. Specialist training can be found through university degrees in adapted physical activity, which can take a few years to complete. This may seem a bit excessive for a person who just helps out at the local club a few times a week. Other less formal ways of learning must be available to these volunteers. Some of these methods are presented in this chapter.

In this chapter, we will focus on the coaches and teachers of individuals who may be at a sports club trying out adapted sports with the intention of being continually active. We also target readers who are teachers who have the regular challenge of creating meaningful PE lessons for children with and without disabilities as part of their inclusive physical education classes. At times in this chapter, when we refer to both teachers and coaches, we'll use the term instructor. At other occasions, when we are trying to convey the message of a specific type of audience, the term teacher or coach is used. The teachers' audience are pupils in schools (and in schooltime activities), and coaches in organized sports settings outside of school and throughout the lifespan.

We start off by explaining some of the background about how instructors acquire the knowledge needed to run meaningful sessions. Meaningful can be associated with delivering high quality, meeting outcomes as well as having successful sessions for the individual (Armour, 2010). Athlete-centered sessions are important and have proven to be effective in both classes and clubs; therefore, we will explore why it is important to investigate principles of learning for instructors before we provide some examples of these principles that have been found useful for training instructors of adapted physical activities.

DIRECT LEARNING

Professional Development

Professional development for physical education is essential for PE teachers to stay current with the advances from sports sciences (Armour, 2010). Traditionally, teachers take a day or two off from teaching in the year to undertake staff training (Pühse & Gerber, 2004). There are many concerns about the importance and organization of training days. As part of the employment of a teacher, it occurs during the school term, which could mean that teachers need to work for extra days or pupils do not have a teacher for the day. Training may occur at a time when teachers are already saturated with other tasks (like planning and assessing), and it can become a distraction for both the current work and meeting the learning objectives from the training. With the availability of so many online resources, professional development can be done through online courses that are spread over the course of a term, and completed in time during the working hours allocated for professional development.

Here, teachers attend structured courses with the possibility of obtaining continuous professional development (CPD) hours for their ongoing learning and development. Teachers who enroll are expected to have teaching experience, and it is through this reflective practice, that teachers can benefit from these hours and CPD. Attendees who enroll in such courses can take the course at a pace that suits them. Often the teachers have little time to do much else, so to attend a course that would achieve learning outcomes that meet their needs could be difficult if organized in a traditional setup. Course structures may require attendees of the course to find out more information from other sources, such as books, the Internet, or community groups.

A key aspect is access to preservice or student teacher programs. Offering in-depth training on adapted sports before students enter the profession has many advantages, including the impact they can have by introducing the latest thinking and new ideas to in-service colleagues.

Face-to-Face Training

As inclusive activities get more professionalized, there is the need to provide training from experts. The traditional educational institutes have led the way for pre- and in-service training, which are based on the premise of the teacher telling the learners what they needed to know. Learning has been transforming toward democratic, constructive, and humanistic approaches (Dewey, 1966; Freire & Bergman Ramos, 1970; Tynjälä, 1999; Woolfolk, Rosoff, & Hoy, 1990). These changes have evolved the way people perceive face-to-face training. Particularly in the sense of practical activities like sports instruction, many learners find greater comfort in seeing with their own eyes, hearing from their own ears, and speaking from their own mouths to others during training sessions (Piletic & Davis, 2010). These types of training can be fruitful with long-lasting relationships and support groups that may be derived from such events. Mentoring between experts and coaches can commence in such environments, too; however, poorly organized face-to-face training can be worse than no training at all (TED, 2010).

Attempts to demonstrate adapted sports through simulated environments may not be consistent enough with a real environment. Some examples of these include simulating an environment with people without limbs and trying to move around the floor in an activity like sitting volleyball. Whereas it can be useful for the instructor to grasp the idea of moving on the floor, a question remains unknown: how does the experience of a person with all their limbs in place help teach, motivate, and improve a person who is limbless? In some adapted courses, learners may be forced to improvise their bodily or cognitive impairments while learning a new adapted sport. However, transfer of knowledge from self-learning in a simulated environment to actual instruction to a group with disabilities requires much experience in learning and delivery.

Another and more positive interpretation of the use of adapted sports in regular PE and sport programs is the notion of reverse integration (Hutzler, Chacham-Guber, & Reiter, 2013). This encourages the inclusion of adapted sports for *all* young people, putting the young disabled person at the center of the activity, and exposing nondisabled individuals to a wider range of activities (Black, 2011). Mechanisms to put this methodology into place require careful planning for meaningful learning experiences.

Face-to-face training can be supervised by a person with a disability and could have motivating outcomes. Attendees can see with their own eyes how disability types can function in a certain context, which can allow a stronger transfer of knowledge into the context of adapted sports. However, supervision is limited to only one individual, usually highly trained, rather than exposure to a heterogeneous group that instructors often encounter. To provide meaningful practices, the optimal training opportunity would include people with disabilities combined with supervisors with expert knowledge. Such sessions are logistically challenging to organize and opportunities are lessened, as there are few expert supervisors located nearby the instructors who seek training. Putting fundamental training through an online platform is a fruitful means of providing training.

Sainsbury Inclusive Community Training Program

Sports Coach UK is a provider for generic and sport specific coach training. Over the years, more short courses in the forms of workshops have been provided with the specific purpose of helping coaches to improve their knowledge in adapted sports. According to Sports Coach UK these courses are "Practical, bite-sized sessions for today's coaches" (Sports Coach UK, 2014). New or experienced instructors can find courses offered locally, or travel to other regions where a course is held. Courses run when a minimum number of participants have enrolled. Most workshops last between two to three hours, and attendees can take home some resources for future reference. Sports Coach UK also offers tier level membership that can then provide access to various generic and sport specific coach related resources. The purpose of these resources are to provide further guidance for coaches, illustrate good practice cases, offer more training through e-learning, and report on research and viewpoints from others in blogs. The resource bank can be a useful way of archiving materials for coaches, and requires someone to create content.

Some of the Sports Coach UK workshops have been rationalized and replaced by the Sainsbury's Inclusive Community Training Programme.[1] This three-hour workshop introduces community sports coaches, volunteers, and others to a simple inclusion framework (the inclusion spectrum) supported by the STEP adaptation tool. STEP is an acronym for space, task, equipment, and people, which represents the four elements of any activity that can be manipulated to promote inclusion. The workshop is coordinated jointly with the English Federation of Disability Sport, the umbrella organization for adapted sports in England.

The Inclusive Community Training is itself predated by another workshop, this time aimed at in-service and student teachers, and again sponsored by Sainsbury's. It's called the Active Kids for All Inclusive PE (physical education) Training Programme[2]. Inclusive PE is a four to six-hour workshop and again introduces the inclusion spectrum framework, incorporating the STEP adaptation tool. Workshop participants receive face-to-face training from experienced tutors, but also gain access to online resources specifically developed for the program.

Volunteer Learning

Adapted sports are still largely amateur in their operation, and volunteers tend to serve as the backbone of successful programs. Deeper understanding of the motivation of volunteers is a core component of the success in grassroots sports. It has been reported that if the time used in volunteering can be translated into paid work, it would be the equivalent of $400 billion annually (Salamon, Sokolowski, & List, 2004). Furthermore, volunteers who continue have often found their previous experiences have been met with satisfaction (Finkelstein, 2008). It is therefore important to be able to meet the needs, and specifically the training needs, of volunteers and to retain and recognize their efforts. Recently, the OECD (2015) has started to promote concepts that nonformal and informal learning are part of the lifelong learning process. These concepts are useful for designing and implementing strategies to improve volunteer abilities.

Formal learning takes place in schools, training centers or on the job. Formal learning may be part of an educational structure, whereby a degree in coaching is obtained. Another type of formal learning could be endorsed certification from a governing body of sport. Good formal learning programs should have learning outcomes and be assessed through formative and summative techniques.

Informal learning is different in that there is a lack of organization, it has no structure, and could be unintended. Informal learning occurs in daily work, family, or leisure activities. It is learning that is not conducted through any organized means, but happens among people or through experiences.

Nonformal learning differs from informal in that the activities are planned, but there are no learning objectives. Nonformal learning is often considered to have components of formal and informal learning. It can have outcomes, it can be structured, it can happen through the initiative of the individual, as well as a byproduct of other organized activities.

One predicament presented by nonformal learning is the lack of exposure that individuals can benefit from organized activities. In the professional sporting environment, there are plenty of practice times, competitions, and media exposure to learn more about the sport. There are the advantages of lots of people to talk with and discuss the sport, and to make the sport better. However, these types of opportunities are less in adapted sports, even eligible events for the Paralympics. This limits some people with the right skills from delivering coach training in a formal setting. It also limits the opportunities for nonformal and informal learning. With the world connected more through the Internet and social media, this does not have to be such a big problem as it used to be.

Advantages and Disadvantages of Direct Learning

Direct learning has evolved from the traditional pedagogical approaches, in that a person leads a class and the attendees are learning what is spoken. The development of interactive learning, particularly for physical educators, has followed similar principles. Volunteers can comfortably attend training from direct methods with the support of a tutor or mentor at hand. In the formal and nonformal setting, learners attempt to meet outcomes, and informal settings are accompanied by verbal support or praise once something has been achieved. The need for personnel to be available for this is a must for direct learning.

Direct learning can have many advantages, such as:

- Learners can find that they are in constant contact with someone who is qualified and can acquire support from them based on expert knowledge.
- The environment for learning may be organized, whereby equipment, resources, and the support of other learners are available to enhance learning about adapted sports instruction.
- Time available for the training is set aside without other distractions to enable attentive learning.

- Social learning habits are enhanced greatly by the act of actually doing activities, seeing others doing, being motivated to do, and reflecting on one's own feelings.
- Practical examples can be demonstrated and seen by learners. Repetition can last until sufficient mastery is achieved or recommended by the expert.
- Demonstration of equipment is available based on good practice to assist in future instructing.

People interested in working in adapted sports may find that training opportunities are thinly spread, as population density may affect the availability and range of available activities. Due to the vastness of different types of impairment groups in a local catchment area, instructors often find their sessions consist of people with many types of impairments, limitations, and abilities. The wide range of participants can make meaningful sessions challenging to implement. Successful sessions require a wide knowledge of adapting settings. The following are some examples of the disadvantages to direct learning.

- Learners may have many barriers to be physically present during the direct learning.
- The pace of the learning is guided by the course instructor and not by the learner.
- The content is provided by the course instructors and limited to their experiences and expertise, which may limit the scope of the course.
- It can be difficult to find time and availability for the expert to be the instructor at times when learners are available.
- Overly difficult tasks to do in the first place may reduce the fun and satisfaction of the learner when asked to practice it, rather than practicing on their own in their private space.
- The context of the learning may be different from the learner's own understanding and can make it hard to relate to.

DISTANCE LEARNING

Distance learning was popularized by the Open University in the 1960s. Lectures were recorded as a TV program late at night. Programs were free to watch for the TV license payer, and it encouraged people to learn about something from TV and perhaps become sufficiently interested to acquire a formal qualification, like a higher education certificate or even a bachelor's degree. Half a century later, a number of online universities around the world offer full degrees (Miller, 2000), as well as many free massive open online courses (MOOC). It is almost possible to learn about any academic subject through these MOOCs, and courses in sport sciences are slowly becoming available.

Distance learning students will need to ensure they have access to equipment, students, observers, technology, and facilities before they take part in a course. These types of requirements do not really meet the "open online" potential, not least of all does it seem possible for the course instructor to manage. There is still much more development needed for online courses in sports pedagogy that would provide equal or better learning experiences than the traditional forms.

One of the main drawbacks from a MOOC is the ability to monitor learning progress through experience. The majority of university degrees in sports pedagogy have elements of teaching practice. For some courses, preservice training involves simulated teaching experiences; and in more advanced courses, teaching practice experiences are embedded. In sports pedagogy, the learned experience of the actual teaching experience has been shown time and time again to be more effective than just learning about the theories and case studies that get transmitted from sitting in a lecture hall (Piletic & Davis, 2010). Therefore, there are challenges to creating MOOCs in sports pedagogy as the environment to set up simulations or teaching practices are extremely difficult to manage in an open online community.

Social Media

The way humans socialize has evolved through the use of technology. Social networks are arguably social ways of learning, but the levels of abstraction are different. The way others give opinions by simple thumbs up, retweeting, or placing stars can change the way people learn socially. This notion of social influence is underdeveloped in social learning theory (Prior, Mazanov, Meacheam, Heaslip, & Hanson, 2016).

Social media became popularized when technological platforms became capable of handling such interactions. These interactions include user-generated content that connects people (Ellison & Boyd, 2013). This is what is known as Web 2.0 platforms. In it, countless amounts of data are being produced in a way that makes socializing an integral part of everyday life. Companies and operators have capitalized on people's desires to share their information and connect with others through a virtual environment (Baym, 2015). Many of these companies offer free-to-use connections, and thus educational providers may find it useful to take advantage of these platforms to host their own materials.

Learning Modes

The focus on instructing in adapted sports is considerably weaker when compared to general PE. The role of higher education has been the primary consideration for young people looking to work in a field of inclusive physical education (DePauw & Goc Karp, 1994). People who may be interested in instructing adapted sports may benefit from research conducted from special education; however, studies lack coordination and are scattered across different areas in education, which makes it difficult for learners to apply knowledge to their instructing tasks (Sindelar, Brownell, & Billingsley, 2010). The recent developments in the importance of professionalizing coaching education have brought forth new journals that focus on coaching science, but hardly anything is published in relation to adapted sports.

Furthermore, learning through the experiences of working with communities has been seen to be beneficial for the learner (Langone, Langone, & McLaughlin, 2000). Literature on the professional development of existing teachers, including co-teaching, use of mentors, and regular group discussions have been seen to be beneficial for instructing adapted sports (Desimone, 2011). However, these require extra manpower and time management skills to be beneficial. In each of these situations, it requires regular contact between coach and mentor. Finding a match with someone who is available at the same time as others may limit the advancement and development of individuals. Furthermore, dyadic mentor-mentee relationships are often based on unequal power relations and old-fashioned ideas about the mentor having knowledge that is transmitted to the mentee are commonly misunderstood (Darwin & Palmer, 2009). Therefore a program for guiding the mentee requires some regulation to ensure effectiveness so that short, medium, and long-term goals can be set up and met.

The use of the worldwide connectivity through the Internet is a very real solution for connecting the right people to each other. Large organizations have been known to communicate through the Internet. In the field of disability, WHO has provided many free downloadable publications specifically to help educate and inform people about important health issues, including training. As far back as 1989, online training was provided for "training the community for people with disabilities" (WHO, 1989), including four guides and 30 training packages, with one particular guide focused on school teachers. The resources were also available in French, although they lacked specific content related to adapted sports. In a similar model, some researchers across Europe secured funding to develop a tool called the European Inclusive Physical Education Training (EIPET) resource pack (Flanagan, 2009; Kudláček, Ješina, & Flanagan, 2010). EIPET focused on addressing core competencies and the functionality of instructors in adapted sports settings. It provided generic lecture slides for educators as well as the week-by-week planning of activities. The materials were free to download and available in a number of languages. Such tools brought the expertise from around the world to be freely distributed around the world.

Delivery of these materials was left to the service providers of education. This gave institutes the freedom to change content as and when they wished, provide information at the suitable level for their learners, allow for courses to be short in duration or to be run in full throughout an academic semester, as well as give flexibility on the purpose of learning, whether it is for preservice training or for continuous professional development. There were also a few drawbacks with placing free training materials online. A continuous stream of money is needed to keep resources available online. Organizations need to continue to find financing for hosting their materials. Materials that were prepared for training were collected up until a certain point in time. Although some medical conditions may not change their diagnosis, sport science, on the other hand, does not consist of static information. New records are constantly broken, new events take place around the world, and some of adapted sports' specific science changes the sport. Between 2012 and 2016, the IPC went through several changes, including the decision to remove sailing from its sports program, introduce Tae Kwon Do, and renew the athlete classification system. Materials that may have focused on these issues would need revising, while informing those educators of the changes was a challenge to avoid misleading information. In most cases, the responsibility layed upon the educator to ensure information was up-to-date, or to specify the situation up until that point in time. Coordination through social media can assist with this new knowledge.

The Inclusion Club

An online example of a practitioner community is The Inclusion Club[3], a website launched in 2011 in Paris at the International Symposium on Adapted Physical Activity (ISAPA). The Inclusion Club, founded by Peter Downs and Ken Black, is aimed primarily at practitioners working in the area of adapted sports. The website takes the form of an interactive platform where ideas and strategies can be aired and shared. At the time of this writing, The Inclusion Club was free to join and had 2,000 regular subscribers from 35 countries. Each month a new "episode" is published (usually video-based) highlighting a specific aspect of inclusive practice or inviting comment and debate around a burning issue. The site also includes self-generated online publications that can be downloaded by users. The Inclusion Club introduces a series of short online "lessons" covering topics identified and requested by its members.

Professional development has been seen as an important area even in physical education, and AIESEP has produced a position statement on PE continuing professional development (Armour, 2010). In it, there are details about the rights and responsibilities of PE teachers to be engaged in the process of CPD. Coach education is now seen as a necessity that can take place as formal coach accreditation, coaching workshops, personal coach development sessions, as well as accessing current information (McCullick et al., 2009; Rynne, Mallett, & Tinning, 2009).

Advantages and Disadvantages of Distance Learning

Distance learning has embraced the modern advantages of computer technology. The use of educational apps has increased for all stages of learning, with nearly 50% of top-selling apps aimed at preschool children (Shuler, Levine, & Ree, 2012). Pew Research Center Report (Rainie & Smith, 2013) has revealed that 35% of students over the age of 16 own tablet computers, and 24% own e-readers. More of today's learners have grown up not knowing what it was like not to have a computer. These people are referred to as the digital natives, or the e-generation. Some of the advantages of distance learning include:

- Learners can access materials at their own convenience and complete the tasks at their own pace.
- Learners have access to connections with other learners from around the world and responses do not require people to discuss issues over time to develop critical thinking.
- The learners' own self-motivation to complete the course gives them a sense of control.
- Multiple simulations can take place with the assistance of computers and technology.
- The role of facilitator of course participation requires less expertise on the subject matter for distance learners and more soft skills that are transferable between disciplines.
- Feedback on assessments can be designed to be immediate, allowing faster improvements in correcting mistakes and knowing the correct answers.

Some of the disadvantages to distance learning currently include:

- Open access does not necessarily equate to equality for all, since the costs of acquiring equipment may not be realistic as well as the knowledge to use computers.
- Practical experiences are difficult to set up through distance learning methods in order for learners to experience the actual art of instructing and acquire feedback for deep learning.

- A physical sense of community can be missing for learners, since people complete courses at a distance from each other.
- Assessments may be restricted to the capabilities of technology rather than a holistic approach to the overall abilities that have been learned.
- Learners may get distracted by other irrelevant activities that also take place while using the Internet to either find or create information.

HYBRID PROGRAMS

The possibility of combining technology with direct learning is known as a hybrid program. Availability for instructor training in adapted sports that includes a hybrid model that combines online learning with onsite training is more popular than ever. In these models, the online learning modules can supplement the training.

TOP Sportsability

The Youth Sport Trust TOP Sportsability online resource is one such hybrid model. Prior to the expansion of the Internet, TOP Sportsability (launched in 1998) combined equipment and a set of resource cards that were initially distributed free via training, but thereafter could be purchased to help instructors plan their sessions with the purpose of providing adapted sports provisions into their lessons. Instructors attending TOP Sportsability training learned how to maximize the use of the cards. In this way, the training supplemented the materials. The site can be accessed through school networks or internationally through a training program offered by Youth Sport Trust International.[4]

When the online platform was launched in 2012, resources from 17 sports, including dedicated manuals, activity cards, and video clips became available. These included an overview of the inclusion spectrum framework and the STEP adaptation tool. The cards featured sports-specific STEP suggestions for every activity and visual examples through videos clips. Recent additions to TOP Sportsability include a section entitled "Wheelchair Skills for Sport" exploring basic manual wheelchair skills, sports-specific wheelchair skills, and some powerchair sport examples. In addition, a fifth section—"Elements" explores the inclusion of young people who have profound and complex needs in physical activity programs. Similarly, the Australian Institute of Sport has put together resource cards and uses a similar anagram (TREE) for teaching style, rules and regulations, equipment, and environment.

The TOP Sportsability resources can be mapped to the high-quality learning attributes as presented by Dee Fink (2013). Online access gives people the option of visiting the materials at anytime, anywhere, and as often as they like. The presentation of the materials draws from key models presented through the STEP principles, and links for further information are embedded. Instructors can reflect upon their own experiences and how the TOP Sportsability resources can influence their abilities. One aim of TOP Sportsability online is to provide a stand-alone resource that includes all the basic information that practitioners might need concerning a range of activities in one place.

One area that is lacking from these online resources is the ability to monitor experience. To overcome this, workshops to support these resources have been made available, although more effort is needed to make it as open and accessible as it could be. To attend a workshop, a tutor must be readily available to deliver in the area, people participating need to find the time to attend, and costs must be met for providing the training. The majority of teachers who might be interested in attending workshops have full working days, and extending their day longer may be difficult to organize. Offering the workshops during school time and finding substitute teachers for that day may limit the possibility of volunteer coaches attending because they probably have full-time jobs or studies to attend to.

Advantages

The advantages of hybrid courses are that more learners can be reached than through physical attendance of a course. Potential for unrestricted class sizes and individual learning can be achieved through courses that combine online and interactive teaching.

As a subject, inclusive physical activities can be broad. As a relatively young field, there are few specialists and they are scattered around the world. Rarely are there places where enough specialists with various backgrounds can be gathered to provide rich learning experiences in the different areas of adapted sports. To address the needs, instructors may find themselves spending much of their time traveling, when that travel time might be spent on other activities. Online learning can facilitate learning and mentoring from different parts of the world without the need for regular transportation of people to meet (Knapczyk, Hew, Frey, & Wall-Marencik, 2005). Furthermore, placing these ideas into an online platform allows access to the ideas of the mentor at any time a person may wish to get the information, and from anywhere. The potential of archiving materials allows learners to quickly access materials they want without consuming too much of their time going through materials that do not meet their needs.

MOOCs can offer more than fixed content in textbooks. Up-to-date content can be superior to traditional courses. Students can also use electronic platforms to reflect upon their learning. Without going into too much detail, high quality MOOCs will use an electronic platform that gives space for the learner to reflect through themselves as well as with other students who have also presented their reflections through the MOOC portal.

In some ways, online reflection can be advantageous to class discussions as the pace of discussions are individualized and people can feel free to discuss their own opinions on the Internet than in face-to-face. Dee Fink (2013) suggests that for online learning, there can be direct online learning through observing methods and out of classroom activities. There is also indirect learning, whereby learners use an online community to discuss case studies or simulations. The course instructor of the MOOC may have to be a bit more creative in engaging students in experiencing learning. Options for instructions could include:

- Lectures
- Slideshows
- Videos
- Group work
- Online forums
- Case studies
- Hot topics
- Reflective journal logs
- Online surveys
- Assessments

Disadvantages

There are many advantages to online learning in adapted physical activity, but practicum training is crucial and is often missing from these programs, and it is critical in developing constructive knowledge (Piletic & Davis, 2010) and improving attitudes toward instructing in an inclusive setting (Ellis, Lepore, & Lieberman, 2012). Learning by doing can reinforce the concepts covered in traditional teachings. This in turn builds up a set of experiences that prepare a person to be professional and reflective on what they do (Schön, 1983).

Students who remain focused by attending lectures and gaining moral support through personal contact may have difficulty in regulating their own paced distance learning module (Owston, Lupshenyuk, & Wideman, 2011). Learners who lack their own directed behavior can exhibit lower attention and outcomes from completing online learning modules (Sansone, Smith, Thoman, & MacNamara, 2012). These are some of the reasons for regular assessment, as well as provisions for support when devising online courses (Simpson, 2012).

Novice instructors may find it necessary to attend yearlong courses, and online courses may supplement their qualifications. Barriers to taking part in courses may be a lack of digital literacy, insufficient powered machines to run the applications, incompatible platforms, and weak Internet connections. Individuals may feel a lack of support when taking part in online courses (Simpson, 2012). Discussion forums have tried to overcome this concern. However the lack of face-to-face communication can be frustrating for some people who prefer to speak rather than to write. Instructors tend to use much more verbal and nonverbal communication when at work, and less is evident with reading and writing. Despite this flaw, online discussions are essential for any course as it allows another support mechanism, be it the only one.

Within such contexts, misunderstandings can be common: people may write with high emotions, particularly when there might be some conflicts, and often would not have escalated if they had the chance to speak to each other. Hence, a requirement for attendance in online courses is Internet etiquette in addition to digital literacy (Owston et al., 2011; Prior et al., 2016).

AN EXEMPLAR: THE VOLLEY*SLIDE* PROGRAM

With more data being transmitted over the Internet in the last two years than the total amount transmitted by mankind in its entire history, it is important that education for sports training does not fall behind. In addition to the standard coaching manuals, people can find a lot of material available to instructors in other forms through the Internet. Videos, photos, blogs, graphics, audiorecordings, and short interviews are all necessary ways to keep up with providing education and to develop sports. An Internet-based initiative named Volley*SLIDE* is one such way that offers a whole host of opportunities to engage the audience in a multitude of ways for the sport of sitting volleyball. The use of social media has accelerated in recent years, thus providing a fast updating mechanism for new trends, archiving of important moments, discussions between followers, as well as providing an archive of events in time for future use.

Volley*SLIDE* was started as an independent online platform aimed at supporting individuals who want to initiate or develop the sport of sitting volleyball. Previous to its inception, there were only a few publications that could be used to inform instructors about sitting volleyball (Ng, 2012). Sitting volleyball is considered the fastest growing inclusion sport and furthermore is attractive at all levels of the game from classroom activities through to the center stage of the Paralympics (Davis, 2002). Attendees of short four-hour workshops specific to sitting volleyball, similar to the design of the Sainsbury Inclusive Community Training, considered sitting volleyball as one of the most universal inclusion sports (Ng, 2011). Volley*SLIDE* was first to support the athletes and coaches of the sport. It originated from a coaching resource much like the TOP Sportsability cards, but with a specific focus on sitting volleyball. Since then, it has used social media platforms to publicize the availability of free resources as well as to communicate about global sitting volleyball activity.

The word "volley" shows the link with volleyball, and the "slide" emphasizes the movement, speed, energy, and fun participants experience. Volley*SLIDE* was positioned to push the sport of sitting volleyball as both inclusive and accessible and quickly these five points were decided upon as "the notion of slide":

- Simple—it is easy to play, you just need the floor, a ball and some kind of divide.
- Liberating—it provides players a sense of freedom.
- Inclusive—at club level, anyone can play.
- Different—there is no other sport like it where you are sliding around the floor on your buttocks.
- Enjoyable—it is a fast, dynamic team sport, even faster than its Olympic equivalent.

As with many other adapted sports, there has been a lack of focus on coach education or pathways for coaches at all levels. It is incredibly important that instructors get some education that fits along a pathway (Carless & Douglas, 2011). From this, instructors can track their knowledge to fit their instructor goals. A vertical ladder that goes from grassroots to world class coaching is important for people who want to represent their country and compete internationally. Until recently, a horizontal pathway had not existed for instructors who wanted to get better at what they were doing without the desire, stress, and competition to go onto international levels. This matrix of coaching education has been, at large, missing in adapted sports.

Another potential that Volley*SLIDE* has for instructors is to use the materials to assist young learners in addressing the growing presence of peer teaching and learning (Raghavendra, Newman, Grace, & Wood, 2013). Much like other learning modes, there are informal and formal routes. Young people are not exposed to income and have limited money to go on formal courses; hence, open and online activities can help their development while helping others, too. Friendships in youth sport are extremely important and peers teaching and learning can enhance this important value (Devine & Parr, 2008). Recognizing the work of a peer leader can be as beneficial as a volunteer in a club, and utilizing closeness of friendships is a strong value among sitting volleyball athletes (Vute & Krpac, 2000).

Volley*SLIDE* was quick to acknowledge this when it created its coach education for sitting volleyball. The materials and ideas have gained support from the international federation that represents sitting volleyball, namely World ParaVolley (WPV), formerly World Organization of Volleyball for the

Disabled (WOVD) as level '0' education (International Paralympic Committee, 2014). At that time, it was agreed that the Volley*SLIDE* mission should be: "To support World ParaVolley with the growth of Sitting Volleyball, by providing a resource for developing programmes that focuses on the inclusive and accessible nature of the sport" (See volleyslide.net).

As Volley*SLIDE* has grown, it has attracted more and more people to join its team. As well as the original founder and leader, there are now six coordinators and 22 translators, all from across the world who do their work as volunteers.

Currently, Volley*SLIDE* offers a template for an introductory workshop covering all aspects of the sport, which can be self-led by people or organizations. Along with a short resource (which has been translated into 16 languages) a full resource (in English and Portuguese) is available. Here, the resources supplement a face-to-face type of education. The resources are freely available to download, and opportunities for other languages to be translated remain open. In addition to the card resources, other initiatives are available on the site for coach education materials. These include infographics that explain the four main differences between volleyball and sitting volleyball, 10 that attempt to dispel some of the common misconceptions about the sport, and seven where some of the leading players talk through their own views on their favorite sitting volleyball skills.

As well as offering the resources, Volley*SLIDE* liaises with those in areas of the world with no other form of support to activate or develop the sport. Since January 2015, Volley*SLIDE* has been in contact with people from almost 95 countries and has provided remote support regularly to around 50.

Regarding social media, Volley*SLIDE* is regularly active on six different platforms: Facebook, Twitter, Instagram, Flickr, YouTube, and Tumblr. Each one has a different focus, but all look to promote the availability of Volley*SLIDE* resources and communicate about any and all sitting volleyball development activity that takes place around the world. In a new way of examining the technological changes that have occurred since the origins of social learning theories, the use of social media is seen to help with what has been called a personal learning environment (PLE; Dabbagh & Kitsantas, 2012).

The Volley*SLIDE* platform engages with users' content for educational purposes. This can come in the form of a simple tweet or photo as well as materials that could highlight certain aspects of the sport through videos, discussions, or interviews. Instructors may find this PLE is related to the informal learning; while at the backend of Volley*SLIDE*, statistics offered by these platforms are used to determine future material along with requests from those out there working at ground level. Social media is not uncommon to share and disseminate findings from sport sciences (Williams, 2011).

Prior to technologically assisted virtual learning, instructors would learn best through practice, experience, and reflection (Dee Fink, 2013). Upon given specific instructions of what to do to utilize active learning, reflections would differ vastly among different instructors. Through videos pinpointing certain aspects to the pedagogy; through slow motion, camera angles, commentary, and other prompts that highlight areas for reflections; more common outcomes among instructors is expected. This could strengthen online learning and its potential to provide sufficient cognitive abilities to increase self-efficacy to attempt instructing without prior experiences.

The Volley*SLIDE* social media channels are the second most popular in the sport, behind only the International Federation. One positive outcome is that the pure existence and activity of Volley*SLIDE* has instigated a large number of teams, players, and national federations to become a lot more active on social media. User-generated content can be used in many ways for many types of learning as well as acting as reminders for fans to be aware of events that take place. After a few years of being a resource for social media, it has become evident that visual information is much more powerful than written materials. The content of athletes through blogs is enhanced through videos and interviews, much like events that take place in postmatch interviews.

Twitter feeds may provide a live string of observations; for example, during the 2015 African Championships there were 141 twitter posts and 90 retweets (Ng, 2015). Many of these retweets were by Volley*SLIDE*. These championships served as the qualifying tournament for Rio in 2016. In this tournament, the winning women's team gained the first ever African women's team place for the sitting volleyball competition at the Paralympics.

Everything done or produced by Volley*SLIDE* is done on a voluntary basis. In fact the annual budget is 108 Euros, which is for the website platform and domain name. The next step for Volley*SLIDE* is to start to produce some more professionally looking resources, possibly with the support of a sponsor, and to focus more on education via videos, rather than words and pictures. World ParaVolley is looking to build upon the first ever Level 1 Coaching Course in Sitting Volleyball (held May 2016) into which Volley*SLIDE* has been contributing to ensure that it flows nicely on from Volley*SLIDE*. So as you can see, Volley*SLIDE* really is part of all workforce pathways for sitting volleyball, but most importantly coaching.

Future Assessment of VolleySLIDE

It is identified that the biggest challenge for Volley*SLIDE* at present is having the available time to suitably develop more materials. It is run by a team of volunteers and that means the platform is rarely the highest priority. Additionally, as the resource has grown significantly beyond what was first imagined, there are evident signs of this growth in the products' layout, structure, and resource presentation. A review is needed to simplify some parts, most notably the main website, which now contains so much that first time users have claimed "getting lost" with all that is offered. Furthermore, scientific evaluations of sports pedagogy through the avenues available through Volley*SLIDE* would be useful to direct other international federations training programs.

CONCLUSION

In this chapter, the underlying principles of learning, and examples of how multimedia and the Internet have been used as teaching tools have been discussed. Examples of the various formal, nonformal, and informal routes were presented to give an overview of inclusion. Particular highlights were also included from the examples, led by Volley*SLIDE* as a sport specific avenue to push the boundaries of adapted sports education. It exemplifies a shift in learning opportunities for other disability sport specific educators.

NOTES

1. http://www.sportscoachuk.org/site-tools/workshops/sainsburys-active-kids-all-inclusive-community-training-ak4a-ict
2. http://www.efds.co.uk/resources/sainsbury_s_active_kids_for_all/active_kids_for_all_inclusive_pe
3. www.theinclusionclub.com
4. http://theinclusionclub.com/YSTi/

REFERENCES

Armour K. M. (2010). *AIESEP position statement on PE-CPD*. Retrieved from http://aiesep.org/wp-content/uploads/2014/11/2009-AIESEP-Position-Statement-on-Continuous-Professional-Development.pdf

Bailey, S. (2008). *Athlete first: A history of the Paralympic movement*. Chichester, England: Wiley.

Baym, N. K. (2015, May 11). Social media and the struggle for society. *Social Media + Society*. doi: 10.1177/2056305115580477

Black, K. (2011). Coaching disabled children. In I. Stafford (Ed.), *Coaching children in sport* (pp. 197–212). London, England: Routledge.

Black, K. (2015, June). Joining the dots: Connecting practice from grassroots to performance. *International Symposium of Adapted Physical Activity 2015*. Netanya, Israel.

Brittain, I. (2009). *The Paralympic games explained*. London, England: Routledge.

Carless, D., & Douglas, K. (2011). Stories as personal coaching philosophy. *International Journal of Sports Science & Coaching, 6*(1), 1–12.

Dabbagh, N., & Kitsantas, A. (2012). Personal learning environments, social media, and self-regulated learning: A natural formula for connecting formal and informal learning. *The Internet and Higher Education, 15*(1), 3–8. doi: 10.1016/J.Iheduc.2011.06.002

Darwin, A., & Palmer, E. (2009). Mentoring circles in higher education. *Higher Education Research & Development, 28*(2), 125–136. doi: 10.1080/07294360902725017

Davis, R. W. (2002). *Inclusion through sports.* Champaign, IL: Human Kinetics.

Dee Fink, L. (2013). *Creating significant learning experiences: An integrated approach to designing college courses.* San Francisco, CA: Jossey-Bass.

Depauw, K. P., & Goc Karp, G. (1994). Integrating knowledge of disability throughout the physical education curriculum: An infusion approach. *Adapted Physical Activity Quarterly, 11*, 3–13.

Desimone, L. M. (2011). A primer on effective professional development. *Phi Delta Kappan, 92*(6), 68–71.

Devine, M. A., & Parr, M. G. (2008). "Come on in, but not too far": Social capital in an inclusive leisure setting. *Leisure Sciences, 30*(5), 391–408. doi: 10.1080/01490400802353083

Dewey, J. (1966). *Democracy and education: An introduction to the philosophy of education.* New York, NY: Free Press.

Ellis, M. K., Lepore, M., & Lieberman, L. (2012). Effect Of practicum experiences on pre-professional physical education teachers' intentions toward teaching students with disabilities in general physical education classes. *Revista Brasileira De Educação Especial, 18*, 361–374.

Ellison, N., & Boyd, D. (2013). Sociality through social network sites. In W. Dutton (Ed.), *The Oxford handbook of internet studies* (pp. 151–172). Oxford, England: Oxford University Press.

Finkelstein, M. A. (2008). Predictors of volunteer time: The changing contributions of motive fulfillment and role identity. *Social Behavior and Personality, 36*(10), 1353–1364.

Flanagan, P. (2009). *EIPET model.* Retrieved From http://eipet.eu/index.php/eipet-model

Freire, P., & Bergman Ramos, M. (1970). *Pedagogy of the oppressed.* New York, NY: Herder & Herder.

Guttmann, L. (1976). *Textbook of sport for the disabled.* Aylesbury, England: HM+M.

Hums, M. A., Moorman, A. M., & Wolff, E. A. (2003). The inclusion of the Paralympics in the Olympic and amateur sports act: Legal and policy implications for integration of athletes with disabilities into the United States Olympic Committee and national governing bodies. *Journal of Sport and Social Issues, 27*(3), 261–275. doi: 10.1177/0193732503255480

Hutzler, Y. S., Chacham-Guber, A., & Reiter, S. (2013). Psychosocial effects of reverse-integrated basketball activity compared to separate and no physical activity in young people with physical disability. *Research in Developmental Disabilities, 34*(1), 579–587. doi: 10.1016/J.Ridd.2012.09.010

International Paralympic Committee. (2014). *World paravolley joins forces with volley SLIDE*. Retrieved From http://www.paralympic.org/news/world-paravolley -joins-forces-volleyslide

Knapczyk, D. R., Hew, K. F., Frey, T. J., & Wall-Marencik, W. (2005). Evaluation of online mentoring of practicum for limited licensed teachers. *Teacher Education and Special Education, 28*(3), 207–220.

Kudláček, M., Ješina, O., & Flanagan, P. (2010). European inclusive physical education training. *Advances in Rehabilitation, 3*(1), 14–17. doi: 10.2478/ V10029-010-0003-6

Langone, J., Langone, C. A., & McLaughlin, P. J. (2000). Analyzing special educators' views on community-based instruction for students with mental retardation and developmental disabilities: Implications for teacher education. *Journal of Developmental and Physical Disabilities, 12*(1), 17–34.

McCullick, B., Schempp, P., Mason, I., Foo, C., Vickers, B., & Connolly, G. (2009). A scrutiny of the coaching education program scholarship since 1995. *Quest, 61*(3), 322–335.

Miller, I. (2000). Distance learning: A personal history. *The Internet and Higher Education, 3*(1/2), 7–21. doi: 10.1016/S1096-7516(00)00030-0

Ng, K. W. (2011). *Implementing sitting volleyball workshop in an inclusive setting: A pilot study focusing on self-efficacy teachers and coaches* (Unpublished thesis). University Of Jyväskylä, Jyväskylä, Finland.

Ng, K. W. (2012). *When sitting is not resting: Sitting volleyball*. Bloomington, IN: Author House.

Ng, K. W. (2015). *Reports from African championships 2015*. Retrieved from https:// sittingvolleyball.wordpress.com/2015/07/29/reports-from-african-championships -2015/

OECD. (2015). *Recognition of non-formal and informal learning*. Retrieved from http://www.oecd.org/edu/skills-beyond-school/recognitionofnon-formal- andinformallearning-home.htm

Owston, R., Lupshenyuk, D., & Wideman, H. (2011). Lecture capture in large undergraduate classes: Student perceptions and academic performance. *The Internet and Higher Education, 14*(4), 262–268. doi: 10.1016/J.Iheduc.2011.05.006

Piletic, C. K., & Davis, R. W. (2010). A profile of the introduction to adapted physical education course within undergraduate physical education teacher education programs. *ICHPER-SD Journal of Research, 5*(2), 26–32.

Prior, D. D., Mazanov, J., Meacheam, D., Heaslip, G., & Hanson, J. (2016). Attitude, digital literacy and self-efficacy: Flow-on effects for online learning behavior. *The Internet and Higher Education, 29*, 91–97. doi: 10.1016/J. Iheduc.2016.01.001

Pühse, U., & Gerber, M. (2004). Editors' preface: Global concerns about the situation of physical education. In U. Pühse, & M. Gerber (Eds.), *International comparison of physical education: Concepts, problems, prospects* (pp. 32–49). Aachen, Germany: Meyer & Meyer Sport.

Raghavendra, P., Newman, L., Grace, E., & Wood, D. (2013). "I could never do that before": Effectiveness of a tailored Internet support intervention to increase the social participation of youth with disabilities. *Child: Care, Health and Development, 39*(4), 552–561. doi: 10.1111/Cch.12048

Rainie, L., & Smith, A. (2013). *Tablet and e-reader ownership update*. Retrieved from http://www.pewinternet.org/2013/10/18/tablet-and-e-reader-ownership -update/

Rynne, S. B., Mallett, C. J., & Tinning, K. (2009). A review of published coach education research, 2007–2008. *International Journal of Physical Education, 46*(1), 9–16.

Salamon, L. M., Sokolowski, S. W., & List, R. (2004). Global civil society: An overview. In L. M. Salamon, & S. W. Sokolowski (Eds.), *Global civil society: Dimensions of the nonprofit sector* (Vol. 2; pp. 3–60). Bloomfield, CT: Kumarian Press.

Sansone, C., Smith, J. L., Thoman, D. B., & Macnamara, A. (2012). Regulating interest when learning online: Potential motivation and performance trade-offs. *The Internet and Higher Education, 15*(3), 141–149. doi: 10.1016/J. Iheduc.2011.10.004

Schantz, O. J., & Gilbert, K. (2008). Reconceptualizing the Paralympic movement. In K. Gilbert, & O. J. Schantz (Eds.), *The Paralympic Games: Empowerment or sideshow* (pp. 8–16). Aachen, Germany: Meyer & Meyer.

Schön, D. A. (1983). *The reflective practitioner: How professionals think in action*. New York, NY: Basic Books.

Shuler, C., Levine, Z. & Ree, J. (2012). *iLearn II: An analysis of the education category of Apple's app store*. New York, NY: Hoan Ganz Cooney Center at Sesame Workshop. Retrieved from http://joanganzcooneycenter.org/upload_kits/ ilearnii.pdf

Simpson, O. (2012). *Supporting students for success in online and distance education*. London, England: Routledge.

Sindelar, P. T., Brownell, M. T., & Billingsley, B. (2010). Special education teacher education research: Current status and future directions. *Teacher Education and Special Education, 33*(1), 8–24. doi: 10.1177/0888406409358593

Sports Coach UK. (2014). *About our workshops*. Retrieved from http://www.sports coachuk.org/workshops/about-our-workshops

TED Talk (Producer), & Mitra, S. (Director). (2010, September 10). *The child-driven education*. [Video]. Available at https://www.ted.com/talks/sugata_mitra_the _child_driven_education?language=en

Tynjälä, P. (1999). *Learning in the construction of knowledge: Constructivist learning theory justification*. Helsinki, Finland: Kirjayhtymä.

UN. (2010). *United Nations, sports and the Paralympic Games: Promoting human rights, development and the ideals of humanity*. Retrieved from https://www.un.org/ development/desa/disabilities/united-nations-sports-and-the-paralympic- games-promoting-human-rights-development-and-the-ideals-of-humanity. html

Vute, R., & Krpac, F. (2000). Sportovni hodnoty mezi evropskymi vrcholovymi hraci sitting volejbalu. [Sporting values among Europe's elite sitting-volleyball players]. *Acta Universitatis Palackianae Olomucensis.Gymnica, 30*(1), 33–39.

WHO. (1989). *Training in the community for people with disabilities*. Retrieved from http://www.who.int/disabilities/publications/cbr/training/en/index.html

Williams, J. H. (2011). Use of social media to communicate sport science research. *International Journal of Sports Science & Coaching, 6*(2), 295–300.

Woolfolk, A. E., Rosoff, B., & Hoy, W. K. (1990). Teachers' sense of efficacy and their beliefs about managing students. *Teaching and Teacher Education, 6*(2), 137–148.

CHAPTER 12

A HOLISTIC APPROACH TO TRAINING FOR INCLUSION IN PHYSICAL EDUCATION

Policy, Practice, Challenges, and Solutions

Philip Vickerman
Liverpool John Moores University

Anthony Maher
Edge Hill University

The U.K. government's 2015 Special Educational Needs (SEN) and Disability Code of Practice provides statutory guidance for organizations working with and supporting children and young people who have special educational needs or disabilities (SEND). The code suggests schools must develop high quality provisions to meet the needs and capitalize on the capabilities of all its children (Department for Education and Department of Health, 2015). This somewhat ambitious target can only be achieved if all those involved in the education of children with SEND are adequately trained.

Inclusive Physical Activities, pages 249–267
Copyright © 2017 by Information Age Publishing
All rights of reproduction in any form reserved.

While gaps in school staff knowledge, competence, and confidence to teach children with SEND have been identified across all curriculum subjects, physical education (PE) in the United Kingdom has been identified as a particular subject of concern (see Maher, 2016; Maher & Macbeth, 2013).

Much of the available research emphasizes a perceived failure of the U.K. Government to develop educational policies to ensure teachers are provided with training that enables them to include children with SEND in PE (Vickerman, 2007). Further concerns have also been raised about the PE and SEND training of other key facilitators of inclusion; namely, SEN coordinators (SENCOs) (Maher & Macbeth, 2013) and learning support assistants (LSAs) (Maher, 2016). Consequently, children with SEND have been found to participate less frequently and in a narrower range of physical activities than their age-peers (Fitzgerald, 2005, 2012).

It is in light of these issues of concern that this chapter proposes to provide a holistic analysis of the training and practices of those involved in facilitating inclusion in PE in mainstream schools in the United Kingdom; namely, training providers, PE teachers, SENCOs, and LSAs. In order to achieve this, the chapter will,

1. Analyze U.K. policy relating to the inclusion training of key stakeholders and, where relevant, link this to a broader international context.
2. Analyze the views and experiences of key stakeholders vis-à-vis inclusion training.
3. Analyze the impact of inclusion training on the practices of key stakeholders.
4. Identify strategies as solutions to some of the key challenges to inclusion in mainstream PE.

Consequently, the chapter will connect with the theme of the monograph by redressing the paucity of SEND and physical activity research, and by identifying strategies that facilitate success in maximizing the involvement in, and the positive biopsychosocial outcomes associated with physical activity practices.

HOW HAS CURRENT KNOWLEDGE AND UNDERSTANDING OF CHILDREN WITH SEND EMERGED IN THE U.K.?

Historically within the United Kingdom, the passing of the Education Act (Department for Education, 1844) gave central government limited powers to be able to form school districts. However, in doing so, the government was not allowed to stipulate that a particular district had to build a school, nor were they allowed to advise the parents of children in the area to send their children, as this was seen by certain groups of individuals as undermining their right to choose what was best for their child. While this act was seen as the beginning of what is now the current U.K. mainstream education system, many children with SEND were still being educated away from their peers in schools that specialized in vocational skills, until several commissions published their findings in relation to the perceived academic ability of children with SEND (Heward & Lloyd-Smith, 1990).

Prior to the publication of the Warnock Report (Department for Education and Science, 1978), children with SEND were educated in separate institutions away from those without SEND, as they were viewed by many as ineducable and thus more suitable for the workhouse (Lacom, 2005). Various legislation and reports were commissioned to investigate both the conditions that individuals were expected to work in as well as their levels of education.

The establishment of the Welfare State in Britain in the 1940s had a significant impact upon the way in which people with SEND were viewed by the wider society. Many of the policy changes that took place during this time resulted in the removal of vulnerable children from the exploitative conditions of the workhouses to more caring humanitarian environments. Community care also became very important, when in 1961 the government announced it was planning to halve the number of beds in mental hospitals. This meant many people with SEND would become reliant upon the "kindness of strangers." According to Towned, Ryan, and Law (1990), the World Health Organization developed the International Classification of Impairments, Disabilities and Handicaps (ICIDH), which provided a broad definition of disability by listing three overall categories, each encompassing multiple subcategories. However, in the intervening years between the mid-1900s and the present, subsequent U.K. governments have successfully reduced the number of categories of disability so much so that it is now one all-encompassing conceptual framework (Barnes & Sheldon, 2010). It cannot and should not be assumed that all people with SEND fit neatly into distinct categories of convenience because needs and capabilities can be extremely complex and diverse. Instead, needs and capabilities should be viewed on a continuum and considered in relation to the varying degrees of support and autonomy required and desired by each person with SEND, something that was not previously possible because of rigid classifications systems that tended to view people with SEND as part of homogenous groupings.

The Impact of the 1994 Salamanca Statement on U.K. Policy and Practice

On account of the U.K. government signing up to abide by the Salamanca Statement (UNESCO, 1994), the first Code of SEN was published. While consecutive conservative governments may have laid the foundation for a more inclusive education system, it was the aspirations of the Labour Party that made the current education system what it is today. During the 1997 election campaign, the then opposition leader Tony Blair made a speech that would prove crucial to the party's eventually coming to power in 1997. In this speech, he stated his three priorities were "education, education, education." And after he was elected to power, Blair's government set about developing a series of initiatives designed to promote better inclusion of children and young people with SEND in order that they could be educated alongside their peers.

One of the most important pieces of legislation of the 21st century in this regard was the adoption of the Dakar Statement (World Education Forum, 2000), a more wide-ranging extension of the Salamanca Statement of 1994, urging governments worldwide to improve early childhood education for all vulnerable and disadvantaged children. It also advocated the elimination of gender inequality and endeavored to ensure that all children worldwide had access to good quality, free compulsory education. In addition, the framework also recommended that all adults and young people have access to an equitable education, especially in English, science, and mathematics.

As a direct result of the Labour government adopting the Dakar Framework, a new piece of legislation was passed entitled SENDA (Her Majesty's Stationery Office, 2001), which in turn led to the publication of a new code of practice (Department for Education and Skills, 2001). Following the publication of this document, the Labour government continued to strengthen their ideology behind inclusion both with the enactment of further legislation (Education Act [Her Majesty's Stationery Office, 2002], the Disability Discrimination Act, 2005 [Her Majesty's Stationery Office, 2005], and the Disability Discrimination Act, 2008 [Her Majesty's Stationery Office, 2008]); and also with the introduction of new educational initiatives, which as stated earlier were designed to improve the academic outcomes of children and young people with SEND and their peers.

All the recent policy changes culminated in a piece of legislation addressing the rights of individuals with disabilities and other vulnerable groups who may be susceptible to discrimination (Equality Act [Her Majesty's Stationery Office, 2010]). The enforcement of this act has meant the United Kingdom has seen the most radical changes in terms of individuals' attitudes and responsibilities toward minority groups since the beginning of the new millennium. Under the Equality Act (Her Majesty's Stationery Office, 2010), you are identified as having a disability if you have a physical or mental impairment that has a substantial and long term negative effect on your ability to carry out normal daily activities. The legislation has also updated the disability equality duty as well as contributed toward the most recent educational reforms for children with SEND. The latest code of practice (Department for Education and Department of Health, 2015), has also made significant changes in regards to how children with SEND are taught in mainstream schools, and has also increased the responsibilities of SENCOs.

Unlike the previous code of practice, which was published in 2001, the new document extends the age range from 0–18 to 0–25 years. There is a clearer focus on the views of children and young people, and it takes account of the importance of their role in the decision making process. It includes guidance on the joint planning and commissioning of services to ensure close cooperation between education, health services, and social care. For children and young people with more complex needs, a coordinated assessment process and the new education, health and care plans (EHCPs) replace statements and learning difficulty assessments.

Access and Entitlement to PE for Children with SEND

According to the World Education Forum (2000), adopting inclusive approaches to teaching and learning are a high priority and are rooted within the context of the United Nations (2008) promotion of "Education for All." The intention of such approaches is to increase the participation and learning of children who are perceived to be vulnerable to marginalization and/or barriers to learning. The World Education Forum (2000) continues that the aim of inclusive education is to eliminate social exclusion and promote diversity of opportunity for children, with a particular focus upon issues of race, social class, ethnicity, religion, gender, and ability. Thus according to Bailey (2005), equality of opportunity in PE should focus upon the celebration of difference and diversity among children that is matched by a commitment to treat people differently but fairly according to their individual needs.

Internationally, many educational authorities have adopted a philosophy of inclusion to address their social and moral obligations to educate all children. In attempting to accommodate the diverse range of needs, this has led to a plethora of philosophies, policies, and practices for promoting entitlement and accessibility to PE. Norwich (2002, p. 483), for example, suggests, "There is no logical purity in education," rather there is "ideological impurity" in which no single value or principle encompasses all of what is considered worthwhile. As a result, there needs to be recognition of a range of "multiple values" (Norwich, 2002, p. 483) through which a series of interrelated concepts, ideologies, learning, teaching, and assessment practices are recognized as contributing to the removal of barriers to learning.

Creating a precise definition of what constitutes inclusive education can be problematic due to the complexity of children it refers to. Booth, Ainscow, Black-Hawkins, Vaughan, and Shaw (2000, p. 12) suggest

> inclusion is a set of never ending processes. It involves the specification of the direction of change. It is relevant to any school however inclusive or exclusive its current cultures, policies and practices. It requires schools to engage in a critical examination of what can be done to increase the learning and participation of the diversity of students within the school locality.

In contrast, Ballard (1997, p. 244) suggests

> inclusive education means education that is non-discriminatory in terms of disability, culture, gender or other aspects of students or staff that are assigned significance by a society. It involves all students in a community, with no exceptions and irrespective of their intellectual, physical, sensory or other differences, having equal rights to access the culturally valued curriculum of their society as full-timed valued members of age-appropriate mainstream classes. Inclusion emphasises diversity over assimilation, striving to avoid the colonisation of minority experiences by dominant modes of thought and action.

The location and causation of barriers to learning in PE have been the subject of much debate by authors such as Farrell (2000), Fredrickson and Cline (2002), and Lloyd (2000). In support of developments in models of inclusion, Fredrickson and Cline (2002) suggest a combination of individual differences; environmental demands and interactional analyses have contributed to differing perspectives on inclusion. In relation to individual models of inclusion, barriers to learning are viewed as being owned by the individual child. Thus if a Muslim girl cannot access mixed swimming because of her cultural and religious beliefs, the problem is considered as hers, rather than the schools to be proactive in responding to address her needs by offering alternative activities, facilitating single sex lessons, or enabling the child to swim in full length swimwear (See Jandaghi, Khanifar, Moghimi, & Memar, 2008). Another example may be where a boy with SEND cannot access a gymnastics lesson because of a lack of adapted equipment, which is seen as a barrier that has been created by his disability rather than the school developing alternative and/or modified equipment and activities to meet his particular needs. Thus, individual models of inclusion tend to advocate barriers to learning are created by children's diversity and as such the causation of exclusion is owned by them rather than the school or PE teacher.

According to Burchardt (2004), environmental models in contrast adopt a situation rather than a person-centered focus to inclusive PE. Cole (2008) suggests barriers to learning and access to high quality inclusive teaching and learning can only be defined in terms of relationships between what a child can do, and what a teacher must do to enable success in any given environment. Thus, the limiting factor for a child being included effectively rests with the PE teacher and school to adopt flexible approaches to learning, teaching, and assessment rather than the child being expected to fit into pre-existing structures. Thus barriers to learning, teaching, and assessment are considered to be created by teachers and schools' lack of flexibility, rather than any "deficit" the child may bring to the activity. Frederickson and Cline (2002, p. 40) support this view by suggesting, therefore, that "at one extreme then, the environmentally focused approach holds that there are no children with learning difficulties, only adults with teaching difficulties."

National Curriculum for Physical Education: Setting High Standards in Learning, Teaching and Assessment of Inclusive PE

PE teachers are expected to establish a set of core values within their learning, teaching and assessment styles and strategies that celebrate difference and diversity. Indeed, PE particularly offers many opportunities for children to learn mutual understanding and respect for each other, which fulfils many broader aspects of government citizenship agendas of fostering mutual understanding and respect for diversity. Moreover, the National Curriculum (DfES, 2014) within the United Kingdom has set out to suggest how this can be addressed via three principles.

- Setting suitable learning challenges: PE teachers should recognize that in order to reflect diversity of children, they should develop different objectives for children based upon their individual needs and differences. For example, a child who has a learning difficulty may be set a task of creating a dance routine with five sequences in contrast to their age-peers who may be asked to develop more (See Vickerman, 2007).
- Responding to the diverse needs of children: This places a requirement on teachers to acknowledge difference and diversity of children in PE, while embracing interactional models of inclusion (noted earlier) and as such modify activities as required (See Coates & Vickerman, 2008, 2013).
- Differentiating assessment and learning to meet individual needs of children: This recognizes that if PE teachers are to set appropriate objectives and recognize children are all on a continuum of learning, then they should also offer alternative methods of assessment that maximize opportunities for children to demonstrate their knowledge and understanding. For example, a child may be asked

to verbally describe rather than physically demonstrate the principles of a forward roll in gymnastics if they have a physical disability.

THE ROLE AND INCLUSION TRAINING OF KEY STAKEHOLDERS

Physical Education Teachers

PE teachers have a fundamental responsibility to maximize the learning of all children. Teachers must, therefore, be trained to work flexibly and creatively to design environments that are conducive to learning for all. This involves identifying potential barriers to learning, teaching, and assessment, while being able to use strategies that offer full access and entitlement to PE. As part of this process, teachers must be trained to develop strategies for working in partnership with children, parents, teachers, and external agencies to ensure equality of opportunity in PE. A central aspect of this involves active consultation with the children themselves and listening to their views, opinions and perceptions of PE (Coates, 2011).

In recent years within the United Kingdom, notions of inclusion and diversity have risen up the agenda to such an extent that there is a plethora of policies, legislation, and statutory guidance, all of which influence teacher training programs. The National Curriculum states teachers should "set high expectations for every pupil. They should plan stretching work for pupils whose attainment is significantly above the expected standard. They have an even greater obligation to plan lessons for pupils who have low levels of prior attainment or come from disadvantaged backgrounds" (Department for Education, 2014, p. 9).

This requirement is supported by other statutory and policy directives such as SEN and the Disability Rights Act (Department for Education and Skills, 2001), and the Equality Act (Her Majesty's Stationery Office, 2010). Currently, the Children and Families Act (Her Majesty's Stationery Office, 2014) has focused its attention on reforming services for vulnerable children in order to give every child an equal chance—whatever their start in life—to make the very best of themselves. These acts all intend to tackle entrenched inequalities, with the contribution of all children and groups now being signaled as an important part of a modern society. Naturally, this has significant implications for PE teachers in ensuring they are trained to meet the full diversity of childrens' needs (Vickerman & Blundell, 2012).

Runswick-Cole (2011) asserts that inclusion has become part of the global agenda and is part of a modern society whereby equality of opportunity in all aspects of life is a social and moral right for all citizens. They propose schools offer ideal opportunities to learn mutual understanding and respect for diversity. In order for teachers of PE to consider planning for inclusion, it is essential first to clarify that children have a fundamental right to an inclusive education, supported in the United Kingdom through statutory legislation and guidance. In beginning to interpret this though, it is critical that all key stakeholders recognize that success depends largely on PE teachers having an open mind, a positive attitude, and the ability through appropriate training to modify and adapt learning, teaching, and assessment strategies and practices (Morley, Bailey, Tan, & Cooke, 2005).

It is crucial to appreciate this does not involve trying to support all children in the same way though. As Rogers (2007) indicates, in order to facilitate full access to the PE curriculum, PE teachers need to develop skills to identify individual children's needs, and then devise plans appropriate to their particular circumstances. As such, Mouratidis, Vansteenkiste, Lens, and Sideris (2008) and Vickerman (2007) support this view, suggesting that training relating to equality of opportunity and inclusiveness should focus on celebrating difference while creating systems in which children are treated equally but differently. This ensures their particular needs are met through gaining access to all aspects of PE and school sport.

Training on Planning for Inclusion in PE

When it comes to planning for inclusion, Goodley, Lathom, and Runswick-Cole (2014) support the promotion of the social model of disability (Watermeyer, 2012) as a means of moving the emphasis away from children with SEND, focusing rather on the roles teachers and other children can play. The social model of disability recognizes that often the greatest restrictive factor to a barrier-free PE curriculum is not the child who is being perceived as different, but the lack of flexibility and commitment to modifying current practices by schools and teachers. Similarly, according to Capel and Whitehead (2010), the move toward a fully inclusive education will require cultural and flexible shifts in ideologies and practices in schools. For example, if a child in a wheelchair struggles to shoot netballs into a high hoop, schools should consider purchasing alternative shooting rings that move up or down. Another example may be where children, because of their cultural beliefs, cannot take part in strenuous physical activity when fasting; PE teachers should consider involving them in an officiating or coaching role in order to ensure they can participate in the lesson. In order to develop an inclusive PE curriculum, teachers should therefore consider strategies that respect difference (Rink & Hall, 2008) and offer other children opportunities to value and celebrate diversity.

Planning for inclusion requires responsive and flexible approaches that recognize all children are on a continuum of learning in PE (Vickerman &

Coates, 2009). Vickerman and Blundell (2012) and Coates (2011) also advocate training that considers new ways of involving all children, drawing on the teacher's skills of experimentation and reflection as well as collaborating with other colleagues and external agencies to maximize learning potential.

Special Educational Needs Coordinators

A SENCO is an educational specialist, whose *proposed remit* involves liaising with and advising teachers, parents, senior management, and external agencies in relation to inclusion issues for children with SEND. They are also involved in managing LSAs, staff inclusion training, assessing children with SEND, and managing the records and statements of children with SEND (Department for Education and Skills, 2001).

The role of SENCO was created and is maintained to enable all teachers to include children with SEND in their lessons. Much of the albeit limited research available suggests that the ability of PE teachers to include children with SEND has been constrained, to some extent, by the propensity of many SENCOs to neglect PE teachers in terms of support, resources, and information, especially when it comes to the allocation of learning support assistants and the guidelines included in statements of SEND, prioritizing English, math, and science (Morley et al., 2005; Maher & Macbeth, 2013). Many statements of SEND, which report the child's specific learning needs and the support they should receive to ensure they are included in mainstream education (DfES, 2001), relate more to classroom-based subjects such as English, math, and science, and thus do little to advise teachers about the learning needs and capabilities of children in PE (Maher, 2013). The onus, therefore, is often on PE teachers to judge the abilities of these children, and in turn try to develop suitable provision to meet their particular needs and optimize their capabilities. The existing whole-school process of identifying and assessing children with SEND thus may need to be changed because of the different type and level of challenges that PE teachers must attempt to overcome vis-à-vis teachers of other subjects.

According to Cowne (2005, p. 67), "The modern SENCO has to be master of many trades," possibly because of the wide and diverse nature of SEND policy, processes, and practice. Training, together with professional experience, can help to equip SENCOs with the knowledge, skills, experience, and confidence that their role demands. In this respect, Maher and Macbeth (2013) researched the appropriateness of SENCO training for supporting the inclusion of children with SEND in PE. Of the 135 SENCOs surveyed in their study, 93 had not received any PE-specific training for their role. While these findings are perhaps not surprising, they do bring into question the ability of SENCOs to advise PE teachers, provide staff inclusion training, and manage the records and statements of children, at least in a PE context. It cannot be assumed that the generic classroom-based training that many SENCOs, and for that matter learning support assistants (LSAs), undertake (Vickerman & Blundell, 2012) will be relevant to a more physically-orientated subject such as PE, especially when some of those children who have a SEND in PE may not necessarily have one in classroom-based subjects because of its contextual nature (DfES, 2001).

Given that "the modern SENCO has to be master of many trades" (Cowne, 2005, p. 67), because of the wide and diverse nature of SEND policy and practice, it does not seem unreasonable to expect that SENCO training programs should focus on PE as a comparatively unique learning environment. When asked why they had not undertaken any PE-specific training, more than half (57%) of SENCOs suggested that they did not think it was relevant to their role (Maher & Macbeth, 2013). It could be argued that such a response does not take account of PE being a physically-oriented, dynamic, and interactive subject, as well as the challenges this may pose in terms of including some children with SEND. So some SENCOs believed that it is LSAs, not themselves, who should undertake PE-specific training. The potential issue here is that, without engaging in PE-specific training themselves, SENCOs are unlikely to appreciate fully the distinct challenges that PE may pose in terms of inclusion.

The Role of Learning Support Assistants

Research by Farr (2010) considered how learning support assistants (LSAs) construct their role when supporting children with SEND in PE. A key focus was whether LSAs consider themselves to be "teachers-in-waiting" (Kessler, Bach, & Heron, 2007) or whether there was a more humanistic aspect to their role in schools. According to Farr (2010), LSAs in a large scale study in one school in southern England suggested that they did indeed have a bifurcated role, but that the caring, more holistic nature of the job had been suppressed by the drive to professionalize and standardize their terms of employment.

The role of the LSA is not only one with, increasingly, a set of prescribed skills, attributes, and competencies, but one whose existence is at odds with a social model, placing them between a rock and a hard place. The very nature of the role of the LSA, which is presented here, is grounded in a notion that in order to be included in mainstream education, a child with SEND needs some sort of additional assistance.

If the "new" professionalism of supporting children with SEND in PE embraces the concepts outlined by Thorburn (2006), such as more professional dialogue, creating environments of trust (Frowe, 2005) and restructuring time and space, the multidisciplinary approach of a range of professionals does offer a multiservice approach. Indeed, Sachs (2003) notes the requirement for the activist (or reflective) teacher to work collectively and collaboratively with others. Using Wenger's (2000) concept of mutual engagement, Sachs (2003) notes the contribution and knowledge of others is deemed significant in promoting an activist PE profession that is both effective and builds on social capital. In supporting this transformation and moving toward communities of practice, Sachs (2003) challenges the whole notion of teacher identity and thus provides PE with a tangible model on which to build successful partnerships with every professional body or individual with an interest in physically educating young people with SEND.

Additionally, the LSA's relationship may be with the subject as much as the child and the teacher of PE, and therefore the LSA's understanding of the nature of that subject might also be important. Furthermore, it may be that the child's learning is directly affected by the ability of the LSA to engage fully with the subject knowledge in situations where the teacher devolves responsibility for delivery to the LSA.

Studies by Kerry (2005) and Kessler, Bach, and Heron (2007), attempt to create a typology of "assistant roles," the former for LSAs specifically, the latter for assistants across education and social welfare. These typologies appear hierarchical in construction: in the case of Kerry (2005, p. 376), from "dogsbody" incorporating the infamous phrase "pig-ignorant-peasant," to mobile paraprofessional and teacher-support staff. Kessler et al. (2007) identify an "apprentice" who as an assistant is preparing for a move into the "profession." The assumption here, of course, is that this is an upward move with higher status. This hierarchical system applied to evolving professions is likely to ensure that the subject of assisting (the child with SEND) is at the bottom of the pile rather than being a central focus.

A similar perspective is gleaned from Wilson and Bedford's (2008) research into relationships between teachers and LSAs. According to the authors, the perception of terms such as support staff is that they have negative connotations. This reinforces a them-and-us relationship where the qualities inherent in one profession seem to be of higher value (professionally) than those of someone in a supporting or assisting role.

The Growth of the Learning Support Assistant Profession

Giangreco and colleagues (1997, 1999, 2001, 2002, 2004, 2005) used both qualitative and quantitative data over a period of time to assess the growth and impact of the role of people who support children with SEND. In particular, Giangreco, Edelman, Broer, and Doyle's (2002) extensive review of the U.S. literature and Pivik, McComas and Laflamme's (2002) in

Canada, revealed that it was case law and parental choice that had originally determined the need for paraprofessional support in North America as far back as 1975. Biklen and Kliewer (2000) trace the work of the parents' movement in this regard as far back as the 1940s; the latter's efforts to secure improved educational opportunities and conditions in care were unmatched by equivalent moves in science and medicine, with their focus remaining on eugenics and their perception that a child with SEND was "not capable of being educated" (Kennedy, 1942, in Biklen & Kliewer, 2000).

In the United Kingdom, however, central government policy has determined the rise in LSA deployment. Since 1997, figures presented in Morris (2001) show the rapid growth of support staff in schools in a variety of roles, mostly to support or release teachers from administrative tasks. In a 4-year period, by 2003, the number of LSAs had risen by more than 50% (Kessler et al., 2007).

According to the literature, LSAs in the United Kingdom appear to play an increasingly instructional role in the classroom, and there is some evidence to suggest that the training and job descriptions, for example, do in fact reinforce that an instructional role is the appropriate one, particularly in regards to PE. Palladino, Cornoldi, Vianello, Scruggs, and Mastropieri (1999) reported that in Italian schools, where inclusion has prevailed for more than 30 years (a similar length of time to both the United States and United Kingdom), instruction is exclusively the remit of the teacher; whereas matters of personal care or mobility, for example, are the domain of the LSA, a clearer delineation of roles that appears not to be so straightforward in the United Kingdom. Indeed, increasingly there is a notion that the LSA is reimaged as a teacher in all but name (Quicke, 2003).

FUTURE DIRECTIONS FOR THEORY, RESEARCH, AND PRACTICE GLOBALLY

This chapter has set out to provide a holistic overview of the training and practices of those involved in facilitating inclusion in PE in mainstream schools in the United Kingdom, namely training providers, PE teachers, SENCOs, and LSAs. The chapter analyzed U.K. policy relating to the training of key stakeholders and where relevant internationally. It also reviewed the views and experiences of key stakeholders, alongside considering the impact of training on the practices of how to include children with SEND in PE.

In relation to how practice can be moved forward in relation to children with SEND in PE, Vickerman (2007) suggests there are four key principles to consider that will maximize the full potential of all children regardless of their disability. These are entitlement, accessibility, inclusion, and integrity. In relation to entitlement, the premise is to acknowledge the fundamental right of all children to access PE, and this is of particular relevance with the emergence of national and international inclusive legislation. Secondly, accessibility refers to the responsibility of PE teachers to devise strategies to ensure all children gain their full entitlement to the curriculum. This involves adopting flexible approaches to learning, teaching, and assessment with teachers recognizing their responsibility, rather than the children's responsibility, to modify and adapt activities.

With reference to the third principle of inclusion, teachers of PE should start with recognizing that in any class there will be a continuum of learning needs. As such, teachers should work upon the premise of planning for full inclusion (Vickerman, 2007), then work backwards to alternative and/or separate activities. It is also important to recognize here, though, that for some children separate activities may be the best way of achieving inclusion in PE. For example, it may be more appropriate for a child with learning difficulties to take part in an alternative activity if the rest of the class is performing an activity requiring relatively complex cognition. What is important here, though, is that the child has been consulted and is happy with any alternative offered. This links to the final principle of integrity (Vickerman, 2007), which suggests that whatever the nature of learning, teaching and/or assessment strategy utilized, it must be of equal worth and in no way tokenistic or patronizing.

DEVELOPING A FRAMEWORK FOR INCLUSIVE PE

This chapter has also attempted to provoke thought about how PE teachers can think flexibly and openly about the diversity of methods to minimize barriers to learning for all children with SEND. Vickerman (2007) also proposes an Eight P Inclusive Framework encouraging those facilitating inclusive PE to take a full and detailed review of what needs to be considered to meet the full continuum of learning needs teachers are likely to be presented with in PE.

In considering this framework, the first feature is a need to appreciate the philosophy of inclusive PE and its relationships to basic and fundamental human rights. This requires consideration of how human rights are supported as a society through statutory and nonstatutory guidance and principles of the international Salamanca Statement (UNESCO, 1994). It therefore requires those involved in facilitating inclusive PE to understand the philosophical basis and principles of inclusion, as well as buying into the notion that all children have a fundamental entitlement to learn. Consequently, if you do not get this first belief system in place, the potential to realize it in practice will be severely constrained.

In order to acknowledge the philosophical complexities of inclusion, a purposeful approach to fulfilling the requirements of inclusive PE should be considered to initially examining various philosophical standpoints in order to gain a clear appreciation of the rationale and arguments behind inclusive PE.

In order to achieve this, you must be proactive in the development, implementation, and review of inclusive PE and be prepared to work in partnership and consult actively with children and professionals in order to maximize an appreciation of how to minimize barriers to learning. Additionally, inclusive PE does necessitate a commitment to modify, adapt, and change existing teaching, learning, assessment strategies, policies, and practices in order to facilitate full access and entitlement to the curriculum. This must be recognized as part of a process model that evolves, emerges, and changes over time, and as such needs regular review and reflection.

Inclusive PE is also now reflected internationally within policy and legislative documentation. This sets out to publicly state how agencies are going to respond to inclusive practice, while also being used as a means of holding people to account (Lloyd, 2000). However, PE teachers ultimately must recognize the need to move policies through into their pedagogical practices in order to ensure they have the necessary skills to deliver inclusive PE. Consequently, while philosophies and processes are vital, they must in due course be measured in terms of effective and successful inclusive practice that values person-centered approaches to the education of children.

CONCLUSION

In summary, issues related to children with SEND have risen up the political, statutory, policy, and practice arenas over recent years. It is evident from the discussion in this chapter that key ingredients to successful inclusion are centered upon PE teachers adopting flexible approaches to their learning, teaching, and assessment. Critical to successful inclusion is also the training PE teachers may have had via their initial teacher training and/ or continuing professional development. It is also evident from discussion in this chapter that the role of SENCOs and LSAs can also play a role in successfully inclusive PE. Taking all this into account, what is critical is the willingness of PE teachers to be ready to differentiate their teaching and use the statutory duties of the curriculum and society at large to ensure children with SEND receive their full entitlement and accessibility to schooling.

REFERENCES

Bailey, R. (2005). Evaluating the relationship between physical education, sport and social inclusion. *Educational Review, 57*(1), 71–90.

Ballard, K. (1997). Researching disability and inclusive education: Participation, construction and interpretation. *International Journal of Inclusive Education, 1*(3), 243–256.

Barnes, C., & Sheldon, A. (2010). Disability, politics and poverty in a majority world context. *Disability & Society, 25*(7), 771–782.

Biklen, D., & Kliewer, C. (2000). Democratising disability inquiry. *Journal Of Disability Policy Studies, 10*(2), 186–206.

Booth, T., Ainscow, M., Black-Hawkins, K., Vaughan, M., & Shaw, L. (2000). *Index for inclusion: Developing learning and participation in schools.* Bristol, England: Centre for Studies on Inclusive Education.

Burchardt, T. (2004). Capabilities and disability: The capabilities framework and the social model of disability. *Disability and Society, 19*(7), 735–751.

Capel, S., & Whitehead, M. (2010). Developing your knowledge, skills and understanding for teaching PE. In S. Capel & M. Whitehead (Eds.), *Learning to teach physical education in the secondary school: A companion to school experience* (pp. 288–299). London, England: Routledge.

Coates, J. (2011). Teaching inclusively: Are secondary physical education teachers sufficiently prepared to teach in inclusive environments? *Physical Education and Sport Pedagogy, 17*(4), 349–365.

Coates, J., & Vickerman, P. (2008). Let the children have their say: Children with special educational needs and their experiences of physical education: A review. *Support for Learning, 23*(4), 168–175.

Coates, J., & Vickerman, P. (2013). A review of methodological strategies for consulting children with special educational needs in physical education. *European Journal of Special Needs Education, 28*(3), 333–347.

Cole, R. (2008). *Educating everybody's children: Diverse strategies for diverse learners, association for supervision and curriculum development.* Google Books, http://books.google.co.uk/books?id=ixmw-porsoac

Cowne, E. (2005). What do special educational needs coordinators think they do? *British Journal of Learning Support, 20*(2), 61–68.

Department for Education. (1844). *The education act.* London, England: HMSO.

Department for Education. (2014). *The physical education national curriculum: Key stages 1–4.* London, England: HMSO.

Department for Education and Department for Health. (2015). *Special educational needs (SEN) and disability code of practice.* London, England: HMSO

Department for Education and Science. (1978). *Special educational needs: The Warnock report.* London, England: HMSO.

Department for Education and Skills. (2001). *The special education needs and disability act (SENDA).* London, England: HMSO.

Department for Education and Skills. (2014). *The special educational needs and disabilities code of practice.* London, England: HMSO.

Farr, J. (2010). Between a rock and a hard place? Teaching assistants supporting physically disabled children in mainstream secondary school physical education: The tensions of professionalising the role (Unpublished doctoral thesis). London, England: University of Greenwich.

Farrell, P. (2000). The impact of research on developments in inclusive education. *International Journal of Inclusive Education, 4*(2), 153–164.

Fitzgerald, H. (2005). Still feeling like a spare piece of luggage? Embodied experiences of (dis)ability in physical education and school sport. *Physical Education and Sport Pedagogy, 10*(1), 41–59.

Fitzgerald, H. (2012). The Paralympics and knowing disability. *International Journal of Disability, Development and Education, 59*(3), 243–255.

Fredrickson, N., & Cline, T. (2002). *Special educational needs, inclusion and diversity,* Birmingham, England: Open University Press.

Frowe, I. (2005). Professional trust. *British Journal of Educational Studies, 53*(1), 34–53.

Giangreco, M. F. (1997). Key lessons learned about inclusive education: Summary of the 1996 Schonell memorial lecture. *International Journal Of Disability, 44*(3), 193–206.

Giangreco, M. F., & Broer, S.M. (2005). Questionable utilization of paraprofessionals in inclusive schools: Are we addressing symptoms or causes? *Focus on Autism and Other Developmental Disabilities, 20*(1), 10–26.

Giangreco, M. F.; Broer, S. M. & Edelman, S. (1999). The tip of the iceberg: Determining whether paraprofessional support is needed for students with disabilities in general education settings. *The Journal of the Association for Persons With Severe Handicaps, 24*(4), 280–290.

Giangreco, M. F., Edelman, S., & Broer, S. M. (2001). *A guide to schoolwide planning for paraeducator supports: Center on disability and community inclusion.* University of Vermont, Burlington, VT: Office of Special Education Programs.

Giangreco, M. F., Edelman, S., Broer, S. M., & Doyle, M. B. (2002). Paraprofessional support of students with disabilities: literature from the past decade. *Exceptional Children, 68*(1), 45–63.

Giangreco, M. F., Halverson, A. T., Broer, S. M., & Doyle, M. B. (2004). Alternatives to overreliance on paraprofessionals in inclusive schools. *Journal of Special Education Leadership, 17*(2), 82–90.

Goodley, D., Lawthom, R., & Runswick-Cole, K. (2014). Dis/Ability and austerity: Beyond work and slow death. *Disability & Society, 29*(6), 980–984.

Her Majesty's Stationery Office. (2014). *The children and families act.* London, England: Author.

Her Majesty's Stationery Office. (2001). *The special educational needs and disability act.* London, England: Author.

Her Majesty's Stationery Office. (2002). *The education act.* London, England: Author.

Her Majesty's Stationery Office. (2005). *The disability discrimination act.* London, England: Author.

Her Majesty's Stationery Office. (2008). *The disability discrimination act* (Revised). London, England: Author.

Her Majesty's Stationery Office. (2010). *The equality act.* London, England: Author.

Heward, C., & Lloyd-Smith, M. (1990). Assessing the impact of legislation on special education policy: An historical analysis. *Journal of Education Policy, 5*(1), 21–36.

Jandaghi, G., Khanifar, H., Moghimi, S. M., & Memar, S. A. (2008). Ethical considerations in physical education. *Online Journal of Health Ethics, 5*(1).

Kerry, T. (2005). Towards a typology for conceptualizing the roles of teaching assistants. *Educational Review, 57*(3), 373–384.

Kessler, L., Bach, S., & Heron, P. (2007). Comparing assistant roles in education and social care: Backgrounds, behaviors and boundaries. *International Journal of Human Resource Management, 18*(9), 1648–1665.

Lacom, C. (2005). "The time is sick and out of joint": Physical disability in Victorian England. *PMLA, 120*(2), 547–552.

Lloyd, C. (2000). Excellence for all children: False promises! The failure of current policy for inclusive education and implications for schooling in the 21st century. *International Journal of Inclusive Education, 4*(2), 133–152

Maher, A. (2013). Statements of special educational needs and mainstream secondary physical education in north-west England. *British Journal of Special Education, 40*(3), 130–136.

Maher, A. (2016). Special educational needs in mainstream secondary school physical education: Learning support assistants have their say. *Sport, Education and Society, 21*(2), 262–278.

Maher, A., & Macbeth, J. (2013). Physical education, resources and training: The perspective of special educational needs coordinators working in secondary schools in north-west England. *European Physical Education Review, 20*(2), 90–103.

Morley, D., Bailey, R., Tan, J., & Cooke, B. (2005). Inclusive physical education: Teachers' views of including children with special educational needs and/or disabilities in physical education. *European Physical Education Review, 11*(1), 84–107.

Morris, E. (2001, November 12). *Professionalism and trust: The future of teachers and teaching.* DfES speech to the Social Market Foundation, London, England.

Mouratidis, A., Vansteenkiste, M., Lens, W., & Sideris, G. (2008). The motivating role of positive feedback in sport and physical education: Evidence for a motivational model. *Journal of Sport and Exercise Psychology, 30*(2), 240–268.

Norwich, B. (2002). Education, inclusion and individual differences: Recognising and resolving dilemmas. *British Journal of Education Studies, 50*(4), 482–502.

Palladino, P., Cornoldi, C., Vianello, R., Scruggs, T., & Mastropieri, M. (1999). Paraprofessionals in Italy: Perspectives from an inclusive country. *Journal of The Association for People With Severe Handicaps, 24*(4), 254–258.

Pivik, J., McComas, J., & Laflamme, M. (2002). Barriers and facilitators to inclusive education. *Exceptional Children, 69*(1), 97–107.

Quicke, J. (2003). Teaching assistants: Students or servants? *Forum, 45*(2) 71–74.

Rink, J., & Hall, T. (2008). Research on effective teaching in elementary school physical education. *The Elementary School Journal, 108*(3), 207–218.

Rogers, C. (2007). Experiencing an inclusive education: Parents and their children with special educational needs. *British Journal of Sociology of Education, 28*(1), 55–68.

Runswick-Cole, K. (2011). Time to end the bias towards inclusive education? *British Journal of Special Education, 38*(3), 112–119.

Sachs, J. (2003). *The activist teaching profession.* Maidenhead, England: Open University Press.

Thorburn, M. (2006). The loneliness of the long-distance Scottish physical education teacher: How to provide effective in-service for experienced teachers' implementing new curricula. *Journal of In-Service Education, 32*(3), 359–373.

Townsend, E., Ryan, B., & Law, M. (1990). Using the World Health Organization's international classification of impairments, disabilities, and handicaps in occupational therapy. *Canadian Journal of Occupational Therapy, 57*(1), 16–25.

Townsend, P. (2014). *International analysis poverty.* London, England: Routledge.

United Nations. (2008). *Education for all: Overcoming inequality: Why governance matters.* Oxford, England: Oxford University Press.

United Nations Educational, Scientific and Cultural Organization (UNESCO). (1994). *The Salamanca statement and framework for action on special needs education.* Salamanca, Spain: Author.

Vickerman, P. (2007). Training physical education teachers to include children with special educational needs. *European Physical Education Review, 13*(3), 385–402.

Vickerman, P., & Blundell, M. (2012). English learning support assistants' experiences of including children with special educational needs in physical education. *European Journal of Special Needs Education, 27*(2), 143–156.

Vickerman, P., & Coates, J. (2009). Trainee and recently qualified PE teachers perspectives on including children with special education needs. *Physical Education & Sport Pedagogy, 14*(2), 137–153.

Watermeyer, B. (2012). *Towards a contextual psychology of disablism.* London, England: Routledge.

Wenger, E. (2000). Communities of practice and social learning systems. *Organization, 7*(2), 225–246.

Wilson, E., & Bedford, D. (2008). New partnerships for learning: Teachers and teaching assistants working together in schools: The way forward. *Journal of Education for Teaching, 34*(2), 137–150.

World Education Forum. (2000). *Inclusion in education: The participation of disabled learners.* Dakar, Senegal: UNESCO.

PART V

CHALLENGING THE MEANING
AND IMPLEMENTATION OF INCLUSIVE PRACTICES
IN PHYSICAL EDUCATION GLOBALLY

CHAPTER 13

REFLECTIONS ON PROFESSIONAL PRACTICE IN ADAPTED PHYSICAL ACTIVITY THROUGH A SOCIAL JUSTICE LENS

Donna L. Goodwin
University of Alberta

The ideas expressed in this chapter bridge the interdisciplinary, ideological, and theoretical perspectives of social justice, education, disability studies, ethics, and adapted physical activity in an effort to reflect upon and bring awareness to widening understandings of disability experiences within physical activity contexts. Adapted physical activity is dedicated to the advancement of well-being and physically active lifestyles of people with impairments (Sherrill & DePauw, 1997). This is accomplished through knowledge creation, dissemination, and mobilization in the areas of parasport, adapted physical activity and physical education, creative arts, and recreation and leisure (International Federation for Adapted Physical Activity, 2016).

Inclusive Physical Activities, pages 271–286
Copyright © 2017 by Information Age Publishing
All rights of reproduction in any form reserved.

The aims of the chapter are (a) to delve into the experiences of disability through a social justice lens, and (b) engage with an epistemology that forefronts alternate embodiments. The critical question guiding the development of the chapter was, "Is the rhetoric of enlightened ableism masking the continuation of ableistic practices and thinking in our conceptualization of disability?" I explore the question, not as a disabled person,[1] but as a privileged, educated White woman. By my own admission, I am providing a "voiceover" of the disability experience (Titchkosky, 2003, p. 43). The biases I bring are mine alone and I engage with them as a way of addressing my moral discomfort with the deficient understanding of disability I bring to my research and teaching.

I wish to be clear from the outset that lingering with ideas about how we have come to understand disability, prepare practitioners, and engage in professional practice in adapted physical activity is not to disparage the meaningful work we have achieved to date and the positive impacts that committed professionals and researchers have had on knowledge creation and translation toward enhancing opportunities for engagement in physical activity. The intent of the chapter is to *think* about professional practice and sit with the insecurity it creates to potentially cultivate an expanded understanding of the disability experience (Standal, 2008). Due to space confines, the perspectives shared in this chapter pertain primarily to literature pertaining to people who experience physical impairment. Although very imperfect, delimiting the discussion in this manner acknowledges that disability and disablement are experienced differently across contexts and life circumstances, with no one being more important than another. Finally, it is not my intention to displace or replace current practices with new ones, but rather to reflect on actions and strategies that may inadvertently exclude, marginalize, normalize, or discount.

The Social Injustice of the Ideal

"Social justice is about equality" (Bickenbach, 2009, p. 110). Fundamental to Rawls' (2004) idealized conceptualization of justice is the notion that society is a well-organized and fair system of social cooperation over time, and that citizens are free and equal persons. Inequality persists, however, as citizens' prospects for a complete life are contingent upon social class at birth, native endowments, and opportunities to develop endowments given social class of origin, good or ill fortune, or good and bad luck over time (Rawls, 2001). In other words, being born into different social circumstances, availability of access to opportunities, and or experiencing different fortunes can create deep inequalities. If our freedom is limited by social structures, then society is unjust (Ikäheimo, 2009). "It is these inequalities, presumably inevitable in the basic structure of any society, to which the principles of social justice must in the first instance apply" (Rawls, 2004). Social justice then is assessed by the distributive aspects of the basic structures of society.

When structures of society hinder our abilities, then our freedom is also hindered (Hull, 2009). In its broadest sense then, social justice issues arise when the freedom of individual and groups is affected by differential distributions of benefit and burdens (Clayton & Williams, 2004). Impairment is not viewed by Rawls (2001) as an impediment to freedom, and justice is fulfilled if freedom is not violated by others. This view was expressed earlier by Tawney (1931) when he purported that inequality does not flow from natural differences (e.g., disability) among people, but rather the manner in which society is organized. Ethically objectionable inequality is "not inequality of personal gifts, but of the social and economic environment" (Tawney, 1931, p. 50). Rawls' (2001) view of disability and justice has been criticized as it is a mistake to treat abstract rights, opportunities, and duties as objects for distribution. It presumes that identities and capacities are stable, while overlooking notions such as oppression and domination, representation of groups in deliberation and decision making, and available means of communication.

To experience equality of fairness, people must be recognized for their full humanness, individuality, desire for a full-blown inner life, and membership in society. Furthermore, for freedom to be part of a human wellbeing, it must be worthwhile and realizable. Access to education, leisure, social affiliation, and employment is not realizable if the physical space (e.g., parking lot, washrooms, building access, and swimming pool access) is not accessible (Titchkosky, 2011). Protesting against unfairness can only be recognized when the full human status of those protesting is recognized (Kuusela, 2011). In an alternative to Rawls' theory of justice, Sen (2009) suggests that enhancing justice entails removing injustice through comparative judgments of justice rather than identification of the ideal. Sen (2009) promoted a practical point of view of social justice brought about by reflecting on behavioral transgressions rather than institutional failings, asking the question: What would reasonable people do?

Wasserman (1996, 1998) remarked that impairment is about social justice in two ways: functional deficit and social markers. Functional deficits call up the need for accommodation, services, and resources. Harm marked by the social markers of stigma, marginalization, and exclusion, calls up the need for corrective and/or procedural justice (Bickenbach, 2009). Corrective social justice action has focused on equality by providing resources (experts) to modify the individual (individual deficiencies) to maximize functionality, appearance, and capacity toward productivity. Another response to the harm of social markers has been exceeding disability limitations through hyper-prostheticization (technologically supplemented bodies) or other forms of "able-disabled" overcompensation such as is apparent in runner blades for those with amputations (Mitchell & Snyder, 2015, p. 12), further segmenting disability embodiment and identity. Normalized and able-disabled bodies may have little to teach about the everyday struggles of those who do not identify with disabled athleticism or the "less able disabled" (p. 59). The real work involved in being disabled is the work required to negotiate socially imposed perceptions of bodies and their political arrangements, or the map of disability as a complex set of social and discursive interactions (Titchkosky, 2011).

In summary, social justice and disability can be conceptualized two ways. First, social justice is aimed at the fair distribution of resources (social and economic) thereby enhancing freedom and humanness, a full-blown inner life, and equal access to education, leisure, and social affiliation. The burdens of social and cultural structures are the focus of action. Second, social justice is conceptualized as a means to reduce social stigma and marginalization (negative social markers) by providing experts and resources (accommodation, services, and resources) to maximize individual functionality and capacity. Alleviating individual difference toward social norms is the focus.

Each view of social justice brings strong implications for professional practice. Social justice aimed at the fair distribution of resources creates a political pedagogy that problematizes professional beliefs and attitudes, and external impediments to the benefits afforded all members of society. The pedagogical focus is inward reflectivity and reflexivity. Social justice aimed at normalizing the individual through reliance on expert resources creates an intervention pedagogy aimed at improving the person through professional measurement, assessment, and instructional techniques. The pedagogical focus is on normalizing the individual through functional change.

An Embodied Disability Ethic

"The notion of justice is of great importance to ethics. Any account of morality that ignores it seems substantially incomplete" (Kuusela, 2011, p. 51). Updale (2008) reminds us that every day professional practice requires ongoing ethical reflection by each of us; it is not just the realm of bio and medical ethicists (Standal & Rugseth, 2016). Philosophers and ethicists have largely been interested in disability questions of eugenics, euthanasia, prenatal screening, and levels of care, taking less interest in the larger social, cultural, or politically contextualized factors central to the phenomenon of disability embodiment (Asch, 2001; Vehmas, Kristiansen, & Shakespeare, 2009; Wendell, 1989).

Researchers and those in professional practice should expand upon Sen (2009) by asking not only what would reasonable people do, but how is the world experienced based on the consequences of our actions? The lives of people experiencing disability have been researched and theorized at some length (Goodley & Runswick-Cole, 2011). Much less work has been done on increasing our understanding of how people experience their bodies in various physical activity contexts, such as the school, sport, recreation, and leisure contexts (Goodwin, Johnston, & Causgrove Dunn, 2014). Embodiment means "all the way we have to sense, feel, and move in the world as these are mediated by the interests of social environment" (Titchkosky, 2011, p. 3). As such, thought is not distinct from the body as the body makes thinking possible. The body and its actions constitute a form of knowledge in-and-of-itself due to sensation, perceptions, and motion. This knowledge explains how to be a particular kind of person in particular social and cultural settings. Disability then, is a relational phenomenon that exists between natural properties and the surrounding physical and social world (Vehmas & Mäkelä, 2009).

The very act of classifying and objectifying (through measurement) a person as disabled, based upon an embodied presence presupposes an ethical decision, exemplifying the place of values in disablement discussions (Nordenfelt, 2000). According to Titchkosky (2003), disability as object has given rise to measurement as a social and political taken-for-granted practice of control, intervention, and change.

> The social practice of measurement always needs to measure some *thing*. Through measurement, disability can be made into a thing, a reality ion and of a person's body. This conceptual map of disability begins with the assumption that disability is readily observable easily quantifiable, impervious to interpretation, set in stone. (Titchkosky, 2003, pp. 55–57)

Mitchell and Snyder (2015) put forward a theory of curricular cripistemologies to illustrate that inclusionistic practices in higher education perpetuate professionalism as the supervision and management of the lives of people and normative as the functional mooring for assessment and diagnosis upon which deviance is created. The circularity exists as the academy produces professionals who are invested in creating others who do not meet the test of normalcy. Mitchell and Snyder suggest that we deviate from core curricular teachings to foreground disability based embodiment content, thereby revaluing the failures of crip embodiments to fit narrowly defined normative frameworks. The new pedagogy is not one of specialness, tolerance of incapacities, or overcoming toward humanness, but one of assessing how communities facilitate peoples' failure thereby creating spaces for understanding that nonnormative bodies harness the means by which to create and navigate alternate ways of living.

What constitutes essentialistic features of human embodiment is based upon culturally produced values (Vehmas & Mäkelä, 2009). For many, the normate body is not essentialistic to human embodiment. Disability is a form of embodied being, not a measurable, medical condition that is distinct from normate human embodiment (Mitchell & Snyder, 2015; Scully, 2009). Educating professionals toward the normalization of bodies raises strong ethical questions. In identifying and answering questions of ethical importance, alternate and more robust interdisciplinary knowledge may be fostered. Mitchell and Snyder (2015), for example, ask whether there is an educational avoidance at universities to opening discussions with disability studies' scholars around reimagined ways of "artfully living less productive, less consumptive, and less exploitative lives?" (p. 22). Nonnormative embodiment should be foundational to university professionalization, pedagogical responsibility, and instructional insight.

Disability is an ethical project that is always to some extent rooted in values, beliefs, and judgments of cultural origin, and as such, the subjective voices of disabled people need to be core to the disability discourse (Edwards, 2009). Further, people experiencing disability articulating their lives brings an ethical epistemological understanding that otherwise may go unrecognized, as space is created for discussions of valued alternate embodiments to those of tragedy and loss. In this way, "peripheral embodiments" can be revised, reinvented, and narrow views of disability through normative values can be transformed as many forms of embodiment are important to the understanding of humanity (Mitchell & Snyder, 2015, p. 14). Paterson and Hughes (1999) point to the impaired body as having a history that is marked by both biological and cultural experiences. Scully (2009) asserts that a phenomenological ontology or experiential knowing renders

> understanding the experience of disability from the inside, is an essential part of making ethical and ontological judgements about impairment. . . . [and] in some circumstances, disabled people have rather different takes on ethical questions relevant to disability than do nondisabled people. (Scully, 2009, p. 59)

In summary, the project of ethical professional practice involves reflection of taken-for-granted everyday practices aimed at normative functional change. Questioning professional circularity that perpetuates value systems that privilege ableistic knowledge over *other* embodied knowledge creates space for other ways of being in the world. By placing professional values and beliefs at the center of our reflections, wakefulness to other embodied (nonnormate) ways of being in the world may emerge.

Interpretations of Models of Disability

Interpretations of how disability is viewed have distinct implications for the way disabled people are viewed and treated (Smith, 2009). Disability can be mapped as the individual experience of lost function due to impairment or culturally imposed ambiguity and oppression (Titchkosky, 2003). Often referred to as the medical model of disability, disability is misrepresented as a fixed condition based in diagnosed medical conditions (Oliver, 1990, 2013; Shakespeare, 2006; Smith, 2009). Medically defined understandings of disability can be harmful in four ways. First, a medicalized embodiment can exclude people who deviate from ideas of the normal body from engagement in community physical activity opportunities (Goodwin, 2009). Second, disability identify is undermined (harmed) as the negative meanings of disability are internalized (Goodwin, 2008; Goodwin & Howe, 2016). Third, adherence to a medical or individual view of disability (personal troubles) can lead to paternalistic decision making by those who view their role to be that of the benevolent expert helpers with assumed authority of relevant knowledge for those suffering personal loss and tragedy (Smith, 2009; Vehmas et al., 2009). Finally, professional efforts may be extended to change the disabled person through structural disablism by decreasing the distance between the perceived deficient body or mind and standards or normality through expert interventions of professionals, such as medical, rehabilitation, and other allied health care providers (Reeve, 2009). Autonomy of disabled people is reduced as expert-based discourses of disability dominate. Rejecting the medical model does not necessitate the rejection of medical care or medicine (Withers 2012). It does, however, reject the tyranny of the normate, by replacing the medicalization of the body with disability models that come from the bottom up and focus on issues of social justice including othering, marginalization, and exclusion.

Proponents of the social model of disability state that disability is not a fixed medical state, but rather it is an experience dependent upon how society is politically and socially organized—a question of social justice (Smith, 2009). Exclusion, marginalization, access, oppression, and citizenship become central to the politics of disablement. Social models of disability emerge in resistance to the alleged disablement and moral authority of others' (e.g., medical practitioners) construction of disability identities (Oliver, 1990, 2013). Guided predominately by people experiencing disability, social models reframe the dominant understanding of disability as a tragic individualized deficit that is to be normalized to the fullest extent possible to that of social oppression (Oliver, 1990, 2013; Thomas, 2006; Wendell, 1996). Although a number of social models have emerged over the last 30 years (see Withers, 2012), each posits that sociocultural structures, be they attitudes, policies, or inaccessibly built environments, are oppressive and contribute to the disablement of people (Shakespeare, 2006).

Social model advocates of disability have attempted to sever the link between embodiment and disability by arguing that disability is about stigmatized and oppressed groups and not individually impaired bodies (Oliver, 1990). They have been criticized, however, for bracketing embodied experiences of impairments such as pain or fatigue thereby restricting subjective narratives of being a disabled person (Withers, 2012). Withers balances the argument in stating,

> Because many disabled people find pride in our disabled minds and bodies, this doesn't mean that we don't have difficulty with them. Sometimes, we do. But these difficulties are not because we are disabled; we experience them because we are human. (Withers, 2012, p. 115)

A justice commitment to equality based upon equalizing disadvantageous differences caused by social and economic environments refutes an individual demarcation of disability (Bickenbach 2009). The actions of social justice then become that of removing, modifying, or altering extrinsic sources of inequality that are imposed by social, cultural, and political institutions. People are different, and as such, equality does not mean that people be equalized (Bickenbach, 2009). In fact, using social, cultural, and political institutions to correct or ameliorate impairments and their impact on social function (decreasing inequality) through the distributive justice of medical, educational, rehabilitation, and assistive technological resources would be ethically questionable. However, failure to respond to needs created by individual difference also creates socially created inequities (Bickenbach, 2009).

The social model focus on barrier removal (e.g., physical access, educational access, and deinstitutionalization) has opened engagement with productive thinking about disabled embodiment beyond that of functional exclusion due to socially created barriers. Mitchell and Snyder (2015) in their book, *The Biopolitics of Disability* attempt to push through the medical and social models of disability, their iterations, and combinations toward new maps for living, embodied knowledge, and collective consciousness about alternate corporealities of disability. Similarly, Wendell (1996) referred to new maps for "the disciplines of normality" (p. 87) and McRuer (2006) for neoliberal "compulsory able-bodiedness" whereby there is no choice in how the body is experienced, as "compulsory able-bodiedness emanates from everywhere and nowhere" (p. 92) within a culture of consumer identities and market-driven systems.

Most lately, there is a call to bring together the embodied and social elements of the phenomenon of disability (e.g., Scully, 2009; Shakespeare,

2006; Smith, 2009; Vehmas & Mäkelä, 2009; Withers, 2012) thereby bringing a more nuanced and thorough understanding to normative judgments of human well-being. In bringing the biological (inner) and social (outer) influences together toward human freedom, Hull (2009) reminds us that only social or outer influences that disadvantage are to be equalized within a social justice framework. The pedagogical implications of bringing the embodied and social elements of disability together requires a blended understanding of the impact of the normative (biological) practices of modifying, accommodating, and adapting within physical activity contexts. Who desires it, for what reason it is being done, to what end, to whose benefit, and to what advantage or disadvantage? Alternately, what social influences are advanced through our pedagogy? What relationships are being developed, with whom, in what contexts, over what period of time, and how do they contribute to embodied knowing and flourishing? The marginalizing forces of pedagogy are often not known to us.

Whose Values Are of Most Importance?

When issues of social justice are applied to disabled people, the question of whose values are most important arises (Clayton & Williams, 2004; Edwards, 2009). Edwards (2009) supports the position that when it comes to questions of characteristics and responses to disability, disabled peoples' opinions have more weight than any other parties. Withers (2012, p. 11) further stated, that "social justice can never be achieved without working with disabled people and on disability issues." Withers cautions, however, that even though there has been an improvement in disabled people engaging with issues of social justice, it is difficult for disabled people to come forward, due to mistrust built on histories of stigmatization and exclusion. Moreover, disabled people are fighting for justice on multiple fronts: being women, queer, racialized, poor, or a combination thereof. Mitchell and Snyder (2015) also highlight how difficult it can be to elicit the values of people who experience disability due to the marginalization of embodied knowledge: "While disability identities can be recognized as 'clients,' 'patients,' and 'recipients' of services, they are walled off from the roles of knowledge-producers" (p. 64). They go on to provocatively suggest that this marginalization may be due to the destabilization that would be caused in the supervision and management of people they are there to help, because their credentials are a substitute for embodied experience of disability. A top-down expert generated approach to pedagogy, while important for the implementation of pedagogical technologies, does not create space for embodied knowledge to be viewed as a legitimately important knowledge form.

Ableism, Disablism, and Enlightened Ableism

Due to normalizing belief systems, three systems are at play that marginalize people: ableism, disablism, and enlightened ableism. Ableism is defined as "the compulsion to emulate ableist regulator norms resulting in a network of beliefs, processes, and practices" (Campbell, 2001, p. 44), which casts disability as a diminished state of being human. Inherent within ableism is the notion of normative (or the normate individual). Ableism constructs bodies as "impaired" and positions them as *other*, being different, lesser, undesirable, in need of repair or modification (Campbell, 2008). The project of ableism creates a different kind of people, the inferior other. Disablism is defined as "social oppression involving the social imposition of restrictions of activity on people with impairments and the socially engendered undermining of their psycho-emotional wellbeing" (Thomas, 2007, p. 73). The key element of ableism, then, is control through disablism of the inferior other.

An example of how ableism can influence professional practice (disablism) is evident in the work of Hodge and Runswick-Cole (2013) in their thinking about the leisure of disabled children. Leisure, defined as taking a break from activities or doing nothing at all, is useful as it promotes the value of space *to be* and the right to step out of *doing* for a while. Leisure can be about being rather than becoming. For many, however, leisure is framed as opportunities for doing, and in the case of disabled children, that doing is often akin to rehabilitation to meet developmental milestones–or the work of passing (Leary, 1999). In the former, there is no normative comparator to what leisure is beyond being. Bringing the notion of ableism back to the social model, and it becomes apparent, that those without impairments or the experiences of disability, through our professional practice and research may be party to disablism and the exclusion of people from full participation in society even if that participation is to do nothing at all (Shakespeare, 2006; Withers, 2012).

A social justice lens highlights the labor involved in passing as nondisabled to reap the benefits of those who meet normative expectations (Scully, 2010). Passing involves becoming, or the "body politics of normalcy" (Titchkosky, 2003, p. 76). It involves two forms of work: the first is the development of a map of ordinariness and living in a state of liminality in the "land of normalcy," and the second is what to do with this knowledge and judgment of difference (Titchkosky, 2003, p. 70). Passing involves the expectation of living as disabled and nondisabled simultaneously. McLaughlin, Goodley, Clavering, and Fisher (2008) point out that so powerful is the ableistic premise in leisure, physical activity, and fitness pursuits, that we have nurtured families to this way of thinking. Families work, through hidden labor, to create opportunities for their children to pass so their disabled children can spend their time enjoying the privileges afforded to the dominant group or what has also been referred to as chasing normal (McLaughlin, et al., 2008). Families labor to improve and modify themselves and their children in pursuit of acceptance and social inclusion in community physical activity settings (Hodge & Runswick-Cole, 2013; Scully, 2010).

Mapping disability against normalcy promotes injustice by not seeking to know the unobservable, but rather perpetuating, defining, documenting, and examining observed differences, inability, and lacking at the expense of relationship building (Bergum & Dossetor, 2005). Mitchell and Snyder (2015, p. 4) suggest that passing "allows for the embrace of some forms of difference through making them less apparent. The magical resolution of diversity-based integration practice is achieved by 'making bodies that look different' invisible, more normative." Rather than the individual creating and managing personal maps, mapping of the influence of cultural maps and cultural power on lives may bring a deeper understanding of the meaning and experience of disability. Without phenomenological understandings, epistemological transformation is very difficult. Without an understanding of meaning and experience of disability, professional practices such as helping, assessing, measuring, modifying, adapting, adjusting, correcting, and rehabilitating become comfortable and taken-for-granted as the difference gap is being addressed, but in doing so, may be causing significant harm (Goodwin & Rossow-Kimball, 2012). Although the social model of disability is purported to underpin our understanding of disability, enlightened ableism may be masking the potential impact of the social model as a mechanism for shedding light on the experiences of disabled people and how cultural value systems work to impede or advance one's ability to function in the world (Lyons, 2013). The term enlightened ableism has been used to describe teacher-speak surrounding inclusive practices in school contexts (Lyons, 2013, p. 237). Lyons argues that although teachers were supportive of inclusion and could articulate its benefits, but sadly it was not evident in practice. Enlightened ableism "presents a rational, modern, well-informed view of the world, yet allows the continuation of practices that marginalize people" (Lyons, 2013, p. 240). Slee (2008) suggests that the rhetoric of inclusion has been applied to such levels of saturation that it clouds the path needed to seek real change. Mitchell and Snyder (2015, p. 14) in a similar vein, coined the term inclusionism. "Inclusionism requires that disability be tolerated as long as it does not demand an excess degree of change from relatively inflexible institutions, environments, and norms of belonging" (Mitchell & Snyder, 2015, p. 14).

Goodley and Runswick-Cole (2013) challenge us to assume political and social justice readings of impaired bodies, seeing them as "possability" (p. 1) by adopting the stance that they are unique embodied entities. In doing so, we reject cultural norms of ability imposed on impaired bodies that positions disability as "private troubles" (Oliver, 1996, p. 48). Parents assume the responsibility and labor for finding, educating, and employing people to support their children in community physical activity programs (e.g., fitness buddies), rather than the responsibility resting with professionals and service providers (Goodwin & Ebert, In press). The hidden labor continues the institutional unconsciousness of taken-for-granted exclusion in inclusive physical activity settings, yet through a social justice lens, exposes the pervasive, systematic, and public nature of ableism (Hodge & Runswick-Cole, 2013). Either consciously or nonconsciously we perpetuate exclusion for families through our ableistic inclusion criteria of "be more like us" (Mitchell & Snyder, 2015, p. 60).

Where Does This Leave Us?

Understanding disability through a social justice lens will assist in knowing disability differently (Titchkosky, 2011). The way in which disability is created, explained and understood constitutes the basis for social justice actions that are aimed at removing hardships and distributing resources (Vehmas et al., 2009). Currently, however, much of the thinking about social policy, resource distribution, and access to opportunities is dichotomous: a person is impaired and/or disabled or not (Bickenbach, 2009).

Disability presents an opportunity to teach and learn about the organization of culture and what it means for some members of society, through ontological phenomenological understanding of the human condition (Titchkosky, 2003, 2006). With reflection and reflexion on our professional practice, research, and roles in preparing professionals, cultural discourses of labeling, treatment, rehabilitation, and training may be displaced by disability being as a way of being-in-the-world (Scully, 2009; Titchkosky, 2006).

Integration of disability studies scholarship into the preparation of adapted physical activity professionals and researchers will widen understanding of the disability experience. Alternative modes of nonnormative being in the world will arise to legitimize the lives of those experiencing peripheral embodiments (Mitchell & Snyder, 2015). McRue (2006) calls for "cripping" (p. 5) of heteronormative texts as a way in which to bring to light socially stigmatized and culturally [re]produced embodiments.

In conclusion, the positive gains made in the field of adapted physical activity over the past decades have been due to the placement of the individual in the middle of our understanding (e.g., individualization of our instruction). We have done this by modifying, adapting, and accommodating to "meet unique needs and achieve desired outcomes" (Sherrill, 2004, p. 7). The shortcoming that is becoming apparent with the theory of adaptation that promotes a top-down instructional model of intervention (Sherrill, 2004) or an individual in the middle approach is the focus on changing the individual, with little impetus to change the social and cultural influences that gave rise to the creation of the individual (e.g., assessment, prescription, intervention, evaluation, classification, labeling, and monitoring). By placing marginalizing forces in the middle (including professional beliefs, attitudes, and practices, the focus shifts to changing that which excludes, devalues, and others—rather than changing the individual, bringing a turn to adapted physical activity. To quote Sherrill (2004), "Education and service delivery are *adapted,* but behavior is *adaptive*" (p. 9). Adaptive professional practice, then, is what we do to ourselves that fosters flourishing in others (Seligman, 2012). The social justice work (project) of professionals and researchers in adapted physical activity is to reflect on our ableism, disablism, and perpetuation of the normate as the desired state of being, our need for ethical responsiveness, and the desire for relationship building.

NOTE

1. The term *disabled person* is used over *person with a disability,* to reflect the cultural and theoretical tradition of the social model of disability. Those who adhere to the social model posit that disability is not an inherent characteristic of the individual, but rather a set of socially and structurally produced relationships that isolate, confine, neglect, and devalue thereby actively disabling people (Peers, Spencer-Cavalier, & Eales, 2014).

REFERENCE

Asch, A. (2001). Disability, bioethics, and human rights. In G. Albrecht, K. K. D. Seelman, & M. Bury (Eds.), *Handbook of disability studies* (pp. 297–326). Thousand Oaks, CA: Sage.

Bergum, V., & Dossetor, J. (2005). *Relational ethics: The full meaning of respect.* Hagerstown, MD: University Publishing Group.

Bickenbach, J. E. (2009). Disability, non-talent and distributive justice. In K. Kristiansen, S. Vehmas, & T. Shakespeare (Eds.), *Arguing about disability: Philosophical perspectives* (pp. 105–123). New York, NY: NY: Routledge.

Campbell, F. (2001). Inciting legal fictions: Disability's date with ontology and the ablest body of the law. *Griffith Law Review, 10,* 42–62.

Campbell, F. (2008). Exploring internalized ableism using critical race theory. *Disability and Society, 23,* 151–162.

Clayton, M., & Williams, A. (2004). Introduction. In M. Clayton & A. Williams (Eds.), *Social justice* (pp. 1–18). Malden, MA: Blackwell.

Edwards, S. (2009). Definitions of disability: Ethical and other values. In K. Kristiansen, S. Vehmas, & T. Shakespeare (Eds.), *Arguing about disability: Philosophical perspectives* (pp. 30–41). New York, NY: NY: Routledge.

Goodley, D., & Runswick-Cole, K. (2011). The violence of disablism. *Sociology of Health and Illness, 44,* 602–617. doi: 10.1111/j.1467-9566.2010.01302.x

Goodley, D., & Runswick-Cole, K. (2013). The body as disability and possability: Theorizing the 'leaking, lacking and excessive' bodies of disabled children. *Scandinavian Journal of Disability Research, 15*(1), 1–19. doi: 10.1080/15017419.2011.640410

Goodwin, D. L. (2008). Self-regulated dependency: Ethical reflections on interdependence and help in adapted physical activity. *Sport Ethics and Philosophy, 2,* 172–184.

Goodwin, D. L. (2009). The voices of students with disabilities: Are they informing inclusive physical education? In H. Fitzgerald (Ed.), *Disability and Youth Sport* (pp. 53–75). London, England: Routledge.

Goodwin, D. L., & Ebert, A. (In press). *Physical activity for youth with impairments: Hidden parental labor.*

Goodwin, D. L., & Howe, P. D. (2016). Framing cross-cultural practice in adap[tive] physical activity. *Quest, 68,* 43–54. doi: 10.1080/ 00336297.2015.1117501

Goodwin, D. L., Johnston, K., & Causgrove Dunn, J. (2014). Thinking ethically about inclusive recreational sport: A narrative of lost dignity. *Sport, Ethics & Philosophy, 8,* 16–31. doi: 10.1080/17511321.2014.891644

Goodwin, D. L., & Rossow-Kimball, B. (2012). Thinking ethically about professional practice in adapted physical activity. *Adapted Physical Activity Quarterly, 29,* 295–309.

Hodge, N., & Runswick-Cole, K. (2013). 'They never pass me the ball': Exposing ableism through the leisure experiences of disabled children, young people and their families. *Children's Geographies, 11,* 311–325.

Hull, R. (2009). Disability and freedom. In K. Kristiansen, S. Vehmas, & T. Shakespeare (Eds.), *Arguing about disability: Philosophical perspectives* (pp. 93–104). New York, NY: NY: Routledge.

Ikäheimo, H. (2009). Personhood and the social inclusion of people with disabilities: A recognition-theoretical approach. In K. Kristiansen, S. Vehmas, & T. Shakespeare (Eds.), *Arguing about disability: Philosophical perspectives* (pp. 77–92). New York, NY: NY: Routledge.

International Federation for Adapted Physical Activity. (2016). *Definition.* Retrieved January, 19, 2016, from http://ifapa-international.net/definition/

Kuusela, O. (2011). *Key terms on ethics.* New York, NY: Continuum.

Leary, K. (1999). Passing, posing, and "keeping it real." *Constellations, 6,* 85–96.

Lyons, L. (2013). Transformed understanding or enlightened ableism? The gap between policy and practice for children with disabilities in Aotearoa, New Zealand. *International Journal of Early Childhood, 45,* 237–249.

McLaughlin, J., Goodley, D., Clavering, E., & Fisher, P. (2008). *Families raising disabled children: Enabling care and social justice.* New York, NY: Palgrave MacMillan.

McRuer, R. (2006). *Crip theory: Cultural signs of queerness and disability.* New York, NY: New York University Press.

Mitchell, D. T., & Snyder, S. L. (2015). *The biopolitics of disability: Neoliberalism, ablenationalism, & peripheral embodiment.* Ann Arbor, MI: University of Michigan Press.

Nordenfelt, L. (2000). *Action, ability, and health,* Dordrecht, the Netherlands: Kluwer.

Oliver, M. (1990). *The politics of disablement.* Houndsmills, England: McMillan Press.

Oliver, M. (1996). *Understanding disability: From theory to practice.* New York, NY: St. Martin's Press.

Oliver, M. (2013). The social model of disability: Thirty years on. *Disability and Society, 28,* 1024–1026.

Paterson, K., & Hughes, B. (1999). Disability studies and phenomenology: The carnal politics of everyday life. *Disability and Society, 14,* 597–610.

Peers, D., Spencer-Cavaliere, N., & Eales, L. (2014). Say what you mean: Rethinking disability language. *Adapted Physical Activity Quarterly, 31,* 265–282. Retrieved from http://dx.doi.org/10.1123/apaq.2013–0091

Rawls, J. (2001). *Justice as fairness: A restatement.* Cambridge, MA: Belknap.

Rawls, J. (2004). On justice as fairness. In M. Clayton & A. Williams (Eds.), *Social justice* (pp. 49–84). Malden, MA: Blackwell.

Reeve, D. (2009). Biopolitics and bare life: Does the impaired body provide contemporary examples of *homo sacer?* In K. Kristiansen, S. Vehmas, & T. Shakespeare (Eds.), *Arguing about disability: Philosophical perspectives* (pp. 203–217). New York, NY: Routledge.

Scully, J. L. (2009). Disability and the thinking body. In K. Kristiansen, S. Vehmas, & T. Shakespeare (Eds.), *Arguing about disability: Philosophical perspectives* (pp. 57–73). New York, NY: NY: Routledge.

Scully, J. L. (2010). Hidden labor: Disabled/nondisabled encounters, agency and autonomy. *Journal of Feminist Approaches to Bioethics, 3,* 25–42.

Seligman, M. (2012). *Flourish: A visionary new understanding of happiness and well-being.* New York, NY: Free Press.

Sen, A. (2009). *The idea of justice.* London, England: Allen Lane.

Shakespeare, T. (2006). *Disability rights and wrongs.* London, England: Routledge.

Sherrill, C. (2004). *Adapted physical activity, recreation and sport: Crossdisciplinary and lifespan* (6th ed.). Boston, MA: McGraw-Hill.

Sherrill, C., & DePauw, K. (1997). Adapted physical activity and education. In J. D. Massengale & R. A. Swanson (Eds.), *History of exercise and sport science* (pp. 39–108). Champaign, IL: Human Kinetics.

Slee, R. (2008). Beyond special and regular schooling? An inclusive education reform agenda. *International Studies in Sociology of Education, 18,* 99–166.

Smith, S. (2009). Social justice and disability: Competing interpretations of the medical and social models. In K. Kristiansen, S. Vehmas, & T. Shakespeare (Eds.), *Arguing about disability: Philosophical perspectives* (pp. 15–29). New York, NY: Routledge.

Standal, O, & Rugseth, R. (2016). Experience, intersubjectivity, and reflection: A human science perspective on preparation of future professionals in adaptive physical activity. *Quest, 68,* 29–42. doi: 10.1080/00336297.2015.1117000

Standal, O. F. (2008). Celebrating the insecure practitioner: A critique of evidence-based practice in adapted physical activity. *Sports, Ethics and Philosophy, 2,* 200–215. doi: 10.1080/17511320802223527

Tawney, R. H. (1931). *Equality.* London, England: Allen & Unwin.

Thomas, C. (2006). Disability and gender: Reflections on theory and research. *Scandinavian Journal of Disability Research, 8*(2/3), 177–185.

Thomas, C. (2007). *Sociologies of disability, 'impairment', and chronic illness: Ideas in disability studies and medical sociology.* London, England: Palgrave.

Titchkosky, T. (2003). *Disability, self, and society.* Toronto, Ontario, Canada: University of Toronto Press.

Titchkosky, T. (2011). *The question of access: Disability, space, meaning.* Toronto, Ontario, Canada: University of Toronto Press.

Updale, E. (2008). The ethics of the everyday: Problems the professors are too posh to ponder? *Clinical Ethics, 3,* 34–36.

Vehmas, S., & Mäkelä, P. (2009). The ontology of disability and impairment: A discussion of the natural and social features. In K. Kristiansen, S. Vehmas, & T. Shakespeare (Eds.), *Arguing about disability: Philosophical perspectives* (pp. 42–56). New York, NY: Routledge.

Vehmas, S., Kristiansen, K., & Shakespeare, T. (2009). Social just and disability: Competing interpretations of the medical and social models. In K. Kristiansen, S. Vehmas, & T. Shakespeare (Eds.), *Arguing about disability: Philosophical perspectives* (pp. 1–11). New York, NY: Routledge.

Wasserman, D. (1996). Some moral issues in the correction of impairments. *Journal of Social Philosophy, 27,* 128–145.

Wasserman, D. (1998). Distributive justice. In A. Silvers, D. Wasserman , & M. B. Mahowald (Eds.), *Disability, difference, discrimination: Perspectives on justice in bioethics and public policy* (pp. 147–207). Lanham, MD: Rowman & Littlefield.

Wendell, S. (1989). Toward a feminist theory of disability. *Hypatia, 4,* 104–124.

Wendell, S. (1996). *The rejected body: Feminist philosophical reflections on disability.* New York, NY: Routledge.

Withers, A. J. (2012). *Disability politics and theory.* Black Point, Nova Scotia: Fernwood Books

CHAPTER 14

STUDENTS WITH DISABILITIES IN BRAZIL, JAPAN, SOUTH KOREA, AND THE UNITED STATES

Implications for Inclusion and Social Justice in Physical Education

Justin A. Haegele
Old Dominion University

Jihyun Lee
San Francisco State University

Bethany L. Hersman
Wright State University

Amaury Samalot-Rivera
The College at Brockport

Samuel R. Hodge
The Ohio State University

Mayumi Saito
University of Tsukuba

Takahiro Sato
Kent State University

Anselmo de Athayde Costa e Silva
Federal University of Pará-UFPA

Inclusive Physical Activities, pages 287–308
Copyright © 2017 by Information Age Publishing

On the world stage, the United Nations Educational, Scientific, and Cultural Organization (UNESCO, 2005) articulates that disability of any kind cannot be a disqualifier from general education. Conceptually and practically, inclusion is a social justice fulcrum that "involves adopting a broad vision of education for all by addressing the spectrum of needs of all learners, including those who are vulnerable to marginalization and exclusion" (UNESCO, 2005, p. 11). Inclusive education means the inclusion of all, "regardless of race, ethnicity, disability, gender, sexual orientation, language, socioeconomic status, and any other aspect of an individual's identity that might be perceived as different" (Polat, 2010, p. 51). Globally, the inclusion of students with and without disabilities in integrated classes is an educational philosophy and practice that is gaining increased acceptance (Hodge et al., 2009). For example, in the United States inclusion is often defined as students with disabilities (e.g., autism spectrum disorder, visual impairments) educated together with their peers without disabilities in general education programs (Hodge, Sato, Mukoyama, & Kozub, 2013). In Brazil, the philosophy of inclusive education extends beyond students with disabilities to also include students from poor families and impoverished communities who may or may not have disabilities (Chakraborti-Ghosh, Orellana, & Jones, 2014).

Although the concept of inclusion has expanded internationally, countries around the globe are at different places practically with regard to implementing inclusive practices in physical education. For example, research in the United States suggests that most students with disabilities are educated in the same physical education context as their typically developing peers (Hodge, Lieberman, & Murata, 2012). However in Japan, for example, most students with disabilities are taught in separate physical education classes or special schools and have little opportunity to interact with typically developing peers (Sato, Hodge, Murata, & Maeda, 2007). The strategies necessary to improve physical education experiences and promote physical activity for students with disabilities internationally depend greatly on the educational context in which they receive physical education. In order to begin to understand physical education for those with disabilities internationally, a review of its current status across a number of countries is necessary. To that end, the purpose of this chapter is threefold. First, the authors will explore the current status of physical education services for students with disabilities regarding inclusionary practices across Brazil, Japan, South Korea, and the United States including Puerto Rico. Second, the current status of physical education for students with disabilities in each of the aforementioned countries will be comprehensively compared and contrasted. Lastly, strategies to effectively promote physical activity for students with disabilities will be articulated.

Throughout this chapter, the term individuals with disabilities is utilized to generalize individuals with various disabilities. As described, the term disability is socially constructed (Hodge, Lieberman, & Murata, 2012). This means various societies around the world construct their own meanings of disability types. As such, disability types can and often do mean something different in each country that is highlighted in this paper. For example, in the United States, federal legislation defines disability in 13 different categories, including those with (a) autism, (b) deaf-blindness, (c) deafness, (d) emotional disturbance, (e) hearing impairments, (f) intellectual disabilities, (g) multiple disabilities, (h) orthopedic impairments, (i) other health impairments, (j) specific learning disabilities, (k) speech or language impairments, (l) traumatic brain injuries, and (m) visual impairments including blindness. We recognize that factors that may influence the inclusion of individuals with different disabilities may not be the same, and when possible specific disabilities will be discussed. However, this information is not available in disability specific categories in all of the research pertaining to the inclusion of students with disabilities in physical education in each of the countries described in this chapter.

INCLUSION IN PHYSICAL EDUCATION: AN INTERNATIONAL ANALYSIS

In brief, the concept of inclusion generally means the instruction of students with and without disabilities together in integrated classes, including physical education (Hodge, Sato, Mukoyama, & Kozub, 2013). Inclusion has become a global phenomenon (Hodge et al., 2009; Son, Hodge, Chun, & Kozub, 2012) and has become prevalent in many countries over the past decade (Qi & Ha, 2012). However, the meaning of and practices in inclusion vary in countries around the world.

United States

Prior to 1975, school-aged individuals with disabilities in the United States were likely to experience educational services, including physical education, in a segregated environment separate from their typically developing peers (e.g., Haegele & Sutherland, 2015). At that time, many children with disabilities were isolated from peers and educated in residential or separate schools, such as schools for the blind (Hodge et al., 2012). The introduction of education legislation and advocacy from special education and adapted physical education professions has helped shift experiences

290 ■ J. A. HAEGELE et al.

in education, including physical education, from mostly segregated to predominately inclusive (Hodge et al., 2012).

Two federal laws enacted in the 1970s have had a profound impact on the education of individuals with disabilities in the United States. In 1973, Section 504 of the Rehabilitation Act, Public Law 93-112 was published into federal law with the intention of prohibiting discrimination on the basis of disability in programs that receive federal assistance. Now known as the Americans with Disabilities Act (ADA; reauthorized in 1990 and amended in 2008), this law requires that all entities that provide extracurricular services, including those in physical activity contexts, must afford those with disabilities opportunity to participate equitable to that of peers without disabilities. Furthermore, ADA requires barrier-free physical accessibility to programs and program areas (e.g., gymnasiums, fields) to allow for equitable access for those with disabilities.

Following the 1973 Rehabilitation Act, Public Law 94-142, the Education of All Handicapped Children Act provided protections specifically focusing on education for students with disabilities. Now known as the Individuals with Disabilities Education Improvement Act (IDEA; reauthorized in 1997, amended in 2004), this law provides federal funds to state and local education agencies to guarantee special education and related services for children with disabilities (Hodge et al., 2012). According to IDEA, special education is defined as specially designed instruction used to meet the unique needs of learners; and physical education as a direct service was included in the definition (Lieberman & Houston-Wilson, 2009).

A number of mandates that were introduced by IDEA have influenced inclusion in the United States, namely least restrictive environment (LRE) and the individualized education program (IEP). IDEA mandates that students with disabilities must receive physical education in the LRE, or with their peers without disabilities, to the maximum extent appropriate (Hodge et al., 2012). Under IDEA a number of placement options are available in the LRE; however, preference is made to education in inclusive settings as long as such placements provide educational benefits (Block, 1996). The implementation of LRE and IDEA changed the traditionally accepted practice of immediately excluding children with disabilities because they were different without first determining if the student could benefit from inclusive education. Now, educational placement is made on an individual case-by-case basis based on assessments and decision making by experts and family members, and is linked to an IEP (Block, 1996). An IEP is a written document about special education (including physical education) and related services for a student with a disability that is developed, reviewed, and revised annually (Hodge et al., 2012). This document represents an agreement that is signed by education officials and parents. If parents are dissatisfied with the educational services being offered to their child, including the placement of the child, they have the option not to sign the document and request different educational services or opportunities to be presented to their child.

IDEA also stipulates that physical education services must be provided by "highly qualified teachers." According to Kelly (2006), highly qualified APE teachers are those who can demonstrate competency in 10 comprehensive areas (e.g., report writing, special education law, assessments). Unfortunately, however, in the United States a shortage of highly qualified adapted physical education and special education teachers exists (DeMik, 2008), and many students with disabilities receive physical education services from individuals with little to no background in this area.

In addition to IDEA (PL 108-448), the enactment of Goals 2000 Educate America Act (PL 103-227) and Every Student Succeeds Act promote a comprehensive approach to educating all children in the United States (Alliance for Excellent Education, 2015; U.S. Congress, 1994). Goal 3 of the Educate America Act specifies that all students will have access to physical education and health education to ensure they are fit and healthy. As inclusion has become a more popular and global phenomenon in education, parents have increasingly requested that children to be educated in inclusive environments (An & Hodge, 2013).

Because of the implementation of federal laws, as well as efforts from special education and adapted physical education advocates, an increasing number of students with disabilities are receiving physical education services inclusively in the United States. Currently, approximately 6.4 million students in public schools are receiving special education services (U.S. Department of Education, 2014). This amounts to about 13% of the national school-aged population (U.S. Department of Education, 2014). As a result of the inclusion movement in the United States, more of these students are now being educated in physical education classes with their typically developing peers than ever. As such, recent estimates suggest that as many as 93-96% of children with disabilities are experiencing general physical education classes (Block & Obrusnikova, 2007; Hodge et al., 2012; Lieberman & Houston-Wilson, 2009). Furthermore, the percentage of students with disabilities spending 80% or more of their school day in inclusive classes doubled (30% to 60%) between 1990 and 2012 (U.S. Department of Education, 2014). This shift represents the culmination of an increase in the number of children being educated in inclusive physical education classes over the past several decades (Block & Obrusnikova, 2007).

Puerto Rico

Puerto Rico is an island located between the Caribbean Sea and the North Atlantic Ocean and is a commonwealth of the United States. In addition to federal laws of the United States (e.g., IDEA), individuals with disabilities in Puerto Rico are also protected by laws of the commonwealth. The first commonwealth law to provide educational services to individuals with disabilities in Puerto Rico was created in 1977 (Educacion Especial PR, 2015). This law was titled Public Law 21, better known As Special Education Program Law, and influenced the creation of the Special Education Program (part of the Education Department of Puerto Rico), which provides services to school-aged (under 21 years) individuals with disabilities. In 1996, this law was amended by Public Law 51, better known as Integral Educational Services for Individuals with Disabilities Law (Educacion Especial PR, 2015). This law guarantees integrated educational services for individuals with disabilities. Included in this is an initiative for different government agencies to work together for the well-being of individuals with disabilities (Santini-Rivera, 2004). Further, and similar to IDEA, it provides a free public and appropriate education, including physical education, in the least restrictive environment to those with disabilities (Samalot-Rivera & Hodge, 2008). This includes a more rigorous planning through a multidisciplinary approach to develop students' IEP, more efficient individualization and inclusion classroom, assessment to determine present level of performance and to write clear goals and objectives, and more organized school programing.

Another important commonwealth law of Puerto Rico is Public Law 238 (August 31, 2004), known as the People with Disabilities Rights Letter. This law ensures the rights of people with disabilities on the island of Puerto Rico have access and an equal right to public services, including health, education, and rehabilitation services. Still today, however, this is one of the areas that as a society Puerto Rico is struggling. Many youth with disabilities are still segregated from society due to a lack of opportunities (Samalot-Rivera, Aleman, & Volmar, 2015).

Prior to these commonwealth laws, many school-aged individuals with disabilities in Puerto Rico experienced segregation and discrimination (Santini-Rivera, 2004). This was also the case in schools. On many occasions, for example, children with severe learning disabilities were left out of educational services (Santini-Rivera, 2004) and were unlikely to receive physical education. Today, education, including physical education, in Puerto Rico is compulsory for all youth 6 to 17-years-old. There are a total of 1,457 schools on the island serving approximately 434,609 students (ED Data Express PR, 2015). From these student populations, 116,936 students with disabilities receive special education services (United States Department of Education, 2014). These data demonstrate that more than one-fourth (26.9%) of students with disabilities are receiving services in the public school system in Puerto Rico. It is important to continue promoting and advocating for strategies to improve educational services, including physical education contexts, for these student populations. Further, there is a critical need to improve and increase professional preparation opportunities for future and current physical education teachers serving this population in inclusive settings. The beliefs of physical education teachers on the island is that even if there is legislation and better services now compared to the past, lack of professional preparation and support from the government affects their ability to appropriately serve students with disabilities (Samalot-Rivera & Hodge, 2008).

Brazil

According to the Brazilian Institute of Geography and Statistics, Brazil is a country of continental proportions that has approximately 190 million inhabitants (Brazil Ministry of Planning, Budget, and Management [Brazil Ministry], 2010). Of those, approximately 23.9% present with some type of disability, amounting to nearly 45.6 million people (Brazil Ministry, 2010). The large proportion of this population group demands the existence of public policies to secure their basic rights, including the right to an inclusive education. In this sense, the phenomenon of inclusion is supported by the Brazilian Federal Constitution (Brazil, 1988). The federal constitution considers education to be a right for all citizens, and Article 208 of this document states that preference should be made that educational services be provided in the general education system for students with disabilities.

In addition to the federal constitution, other legal documents also impact inclusion for those with disabilities in Brazil. For example, Public Law 7853 (October 24, 1989) established a national policy for the integration of people with disabilities. This law, amended by the Presidential Decree 3298 of December 20, 1999 (Brazil, 1999), determines that public entities and agencies should secure the basic rights of those with disabilities, including the right to education. More recently, the Brazilian Law of Inclusion (Law 13146 of July 6, 2015) was enacted to secure and promote, on equal terms, the exercise of basic rights and freedoms by people with disabilities aiming at their social inclusion and citizenship. The Brazilian Law of Inclusion mandates consideration of the concept of universal design during the conception of programs and services, including school-based physical education to be used by everyone. Unfortunately, however, there are few current efforts to put this principle into practice. For example, many architectural barriers in buildings still exist because they were built before the law took place. Paragraph 15 of the first chapter of this law is of particular interest to physical education because it indicates that people with disabilities should have equitable access to games and recreational activities, sports, and leisure in the educational system.

Formerly, the education of people with disabilities in Brazil was held in a segregated manner in special education institutions. Proinclusion efforts have resulted in an increased number of students attending the general education network, with 79% and 77% of those with disabilities being enrolled in basic and early childhood general education schools, respectively (Brazil, 2014). The growing number of students with disabilities or special needs who are enrolled in general education schools is associated with a reduced number of enrollments in special education institutions. In 2003, 71% of students with disabilities were enrolled in special education institutions, and in 2004 this proportion was reduced to 21% (Brazil, 2014). For the students between the ages of 4 and 17, approximately 84% were educated in schools with typically developing peers (Brazil, 2014). However, although students with disabilities are more frequently educated in schools with their typically developing peers, they are commonly educated in special rooms in those schools (currently called multifunction resource rooms). This model remains partially in use to the present day; and while inclusion has been adopted in most Brazilian states, some still use the special rooms.

Even with the existence of legislation supporting the right to inclusive education and consequently inclusive physical education, and despite improvements in indicators of access of children and adolescents with disabilities to general education schools, there is little information about the quality of inclusion in physical education classes in Brazil. For example, Alves and Duarte (2012) conducted an observational study with children from the third grade and reported that a student with Down syndrome was unable to establish positive social relationships with schoolmates. Later in another observational study, Alves and Duarte (2014) reported that the feeling of exclusion for students with disabilities occurs as a result of the lack of adaptations of the classes, social isolation, and feelings of inferiority in relation to their classmates. Currently, the literature in Brazil still lacks consistent research demonstrating that inclusion is in fact occurring in physical education classes.

Japan

In Japan, two national laws influence physical education for individuals with disabilities; the School Education Law (2015) and the Basic Act for Persons with Disabilities. In 1947, Japan's Basic Act for Persons with Disabilities was enacted, which established school systems with a philosophy of equal opportunity for all (Franz, 2007). Within this law, there are three educational purposes that national and local governments are responsible to support in terms of academic opportunities for individuals with disabilities. These are that the national and local governments (a) shall take necessary measures to improve and enrich contents and method of education to enable persons with disabilities to receive adequate education in accordance with their age, capacity, and conditions of disability; (b) shall promote research and development and accommodations of school facilities for education of persons with disabilities; and (c) shall promote mutual understanding between students with and without disabilities through positively implementing exchange and cooperative study (Cabinet Office, 2015). Under this law, prefecture governments and local departments of education require that all individuals with disabilities are educated in inclusive settings, including physical education contexts, to the greatest degree possible and with the least amount of restriction. This law was created to avoid any discrimination against individuals with disabilities, to support individual and unique learning needs of individuals with disabilities, and to respect human rights (Ministry of Education, Culture, Sport, Science, and Technology [MEXT], 2015). This law has influenced Japan's educational system to promote interactive education *Koryu Kyoiku*, which emphasizes that students with and without disabilities are to be educated within similar academic learning environments, including physical education settings (Kusano & Chosokabe, 2001; Sato & Hodge, 2009).

In 2007, the School Education Law was partially amended to include the *Tokubetsu Shien Kyoiku* (Special Needs Education) policy (Goto, 2008). This policy defines special needs education as "education for students with disabilities, in consideration of their individual educational needs, which aims at full development of their capabilities and at their independence and social participation" (MEXT, 2015). The School Education Law mandates further the development of *KOBETSU-shido-keikaku* (individualized teaching plans [ITP]) for each student with a disability, which calls for individualized instruction and support to meet the needs of students (MEXT, 2002). This document includes annual goals, short-term goals and objectives, academic progress, assessment, evaluation, and support service requirements. Currently, ITPs are only mandated at special needs schools. This means that general public schools (elementary, middle, and high schools) that provide inclusive instruction are not mandated to develop ITPs. Because of this, only about 30% of public school teachers in Japan have experience reviewing, observing, or developing ITP forms for students with disabilities (Kanayama & Yamasaki, 2010).

Following recent national laws and mandates, revisions to the teaching license requirements mandate that teachers in Japan must be trained to teach inclusive classes because, predictably, students with and without disabilities will increasingly be educated together (Kusano & Chosokabe, 2001). Unfortunately, higher education program curricula, including physical education teacher education (PETE), does not lend credence or support to preparing teacher candidates to teach students with disabilities in inclusive settings (Sato & Hodge, 2009). Many PETE programs do not offer training that provides disability content, inclusive practices, or adapted physical education (APE) courses in general as a part of graduation or student teaching requirements. In fact, few Japanese colleges and universities offer one or more APE courses within secondary (45%) or elementary (13%) physical education programs (Kanayama & Yamasaki, 2010). Further many PETE teacher candidates only receive one credit hour (15 contact hours) and two days of APE practicum experiences as the graduation requirement of teacher education programs. However, progress is being made. In 2014, all members of the Division of Adapted Sport and Physical Education of the Japanese Society of Physical Education, Health, and Sport Science unanimously agreed and created a proposal that APE courses should be required as part of the PETE academic program of study for student teaching as well as graduation requirements. At the time of this publication, the proposal was under review and discussed at MEXT in Japan.

While advocacy for inclusion in Japanese education is current, many public schools are in transition from segregation to an inclusion philosophy. There are many issues and concerns to successfully promoting inclusion in Japanese schools, and the paradoxical nature of the educational context makes establishing a consistently positive learning environment difficult. Many students with disabilities are integrated physically ("dumping"), but not socially included in the classroom (Murayama, 2014). Such educational arrangements allow physical, social, and emotional separation of students with and without disabilities from each other, which may lead to social isolation or marginalization in the classroom (Sato & Hodge, 2009). One specific issue with inclusion in Japan is small class sizes. For example, Saito (2008) found that many physical education teachers had fewer than five students per class and struggled to teach ball games and group activities in inclusionary ways. Low class size is a country-wide trend that is a result of a rapid national population decline, which has also influenced the closing of many public schools per year (Menju, 2014).

Currently in Japan, approximately 41,000 students with disabilities between the ages of 6 and 18 years attend public schools. This amounts to about 3% of the national school-aged population. As a result of special education and the inclusion movement in Japan, MEXT (2015) reports that just 33% of students with disabilities attend special needs schools. Many of these students continue to attend special needs schools because family members believe that these schools can better educate students to develop skills while receiving extra support from teachers and staff. Conversely, though, 67% of students with disabilities currently attend inclusive (12%) or special education classes (45%) in public schools. It is unknown what percentage of these students participate in inclusive physical education classes. These figures do not include an estimated 6% of the national school-aged population not diagnosed with hidden disabilities (e.g., learning disability, attention deficit hyperactive disorder, or Asperger syndrome) who receive services in public schools (MEXT, 2015).

South Korea

Until the late 19th century, students with disabilities in South Korea were home schooled due to the lack of systematic special education programs (Kwon, 2005). In 1949, the Education Law was enacted and stated that all students had the right to an education and should receive an equitable opportunity to learn; however, education for students with disabilities was still greatly neglected (Park, 2005). In 1977, the Korean Special Education Promotion Act (SEPA) was enacted to ensure free mandatory education services for students with disabilities in public elementary and middle schools (Korea Education Newspaper Office, 1998). Since then, nine revisions have been made to SEPA, which mandates high quality special education programing including free education from kindergarten through high school, inclusive education, individualized education programs, therapeutic education, and vocational education (Yoo & Palley, 2014). SEPA has had a great impact on the education for students with disabilities. For instance, there was only one special school in 1935, but the number reached to 137 in 2003 (Ministry of Education and Human Resources [MEHR], 2014). However, concerns still existed regarding unspecified responsibilities of the federal and local governments in implementing special education programming and providing support for students who were at risk of having a disability (Yoo & Palley, 2014). In 2007, the Act on Special Education for Disabled Persons (ASED) was established to reflect international standards and rapidly changing educational needs of students with disabilities in South Korea (Yoo & Palley, 2014). Currently, disability categories in the revised ASED (Act No. 11384, 2012) are similar to the Individuals with Disabilities Education Act (IDEA, 2004) of the United States.

Three separate educational settings are available for students with disabilities in South Korea: special schools, special classes in general schools, and general classes (Kwon, 2005). Even after SEPA was enacted in 1977, most students with disabilities in South Korea were educated in special schools (Kim & Park, 2011). Similar to other countries, inclusion has been a powerful philosophical movement for the past few decades in South Korea. Unlike IDEA (2004), which uses the term least restrictive environment, SEPA introduced the term inclusive education in 1994. However, Korean special education related laws use the terms inclusion, mainstreaming, and integration interchangeably (Park, 2003). For example, in SEPA (1994), the term inclusion refers to educating students with disabilities in general classes or teaching students with disabilities in special schools using the general curriculum. The major justification of educating students with disabilities in general schools in South Korea has been increasing those students' social adaptability to interact with typically developing peers (e.g., Law 4716, Article 15, 1994). ASED (2007) defines the term inclusive/integrative education as educating students who are eligible for special education in general schools with typically developing peers to meet individual students' needs without discrimination based on the type and severity of their disabilities. However, both SEPA and ASED explain the term special classes as classes created to implement inclusive education for students who are eligible for special education in general schools. The definition of inclusion in legislation, existence of special classes in general schools, and legislative regulations for the ratio of the number of special classes and students with disabilities may encourage separation of students with disabilities in general schools. In 2014, among 82,535 school-aged students who received special education, 26%, 55%, and 19% were placed in special schools, special classes, and general classes, respectively (Korea National Institute for Special Education, 2014). Thus, still a large percentage of students with disabilities are being educated in special schools or classes.

Researchers in South Korea have addressed the needs for and benefits of inclusive physical education as well as its problems and challenges (Kang & Kim, 2012). In particular, lack of connections between special education laws and actual practices in schools have been addressed by: (a) training physical education teachers in general schools, (b) changing attitudes of typically developing peers and parents, and (c) adding more facilities and systematic support for students with disabilities (e.g., Lee, 2005). Despite the increasing number of students with disabilities in general schools, many of those in inclusive physical education often are observers instead of actual participants, are excluded, and do not receive sufficient instruction and monitoring from the teacher (Cho, 2003). Researchers have attributed these experiences to insufficient education for school staff, teachers, and typically developing peers, and lack of their understanding of individuals with disabilities (e.g., Kang & Kim, 2012; Lee, 2005, 2007). In particular, insufficient knowledge, skills, and understanding of how to teach inclusive physical education have been regarded as major problems for physical education teachers in South Korea (Lee, 2007).

Unfortunately, teachers often feel that they have not been adequately prepared for such a rapid influx of students with disabilities in general schools. In South Korea, inclusive physical education is often implemented without clear guidelines and the quality of education heavily relies on the individual teachers including students with disabilities (Lee, 2007; Kang & Kim, 2012). Research demonstrates that both pre- and in-service physical educators tend to have negative attitudes toward including students with particular disability types, such as emotional disturbance, autism, and moderate to severe intellectual disabilities (Cho, 2003; Kang & Kim, 2012; Lee, 2007). A number of steps must be taken to alleviate teacher concerns about inclusive physical education, such as offering: (a) carefully designed field experiences for adapted physical activity/education courses, (b) more training opportunities about teaching and assessing students with disabilities, and (c) instructional support for teachers in implementing instruction and managing classes. In fact, training needs for physical education teachers in general schools to assist them in implementing inclusive education are universal across all subject areas. According to the Special Education Annual Report to Congress in 2006, among 26,469 general education teachers who teach inclusive classes, only 20% completed more than 60 hours of training. In 2014, among 88,848 respondents, 47.6% completed more than 60 hours (MEHR, 2014). This indicates that while education in this arena is increasing, the majority of teachers in general schools do not have adequate knowledge and experiences in educating students with disabilities.

SUMMARY AND COMPARISON ACROSS COUNTRIES

Although inclusive practices are growing internationally, the meaning of and practices in inclusion in the physical education context may vary in countries around the world. The previous sections in this chapter describe factors that influence and the current status of inclusion in five distinct geographic regions. A number of similarities and differences between these areas are evident. Specifically, the early actions toward individuals with disabilities in educational settings, educational law, and the current education of those with disabilities is of particular interest.

Across geographic regions, services for individuals prior to legislative action and advocacy were poor at best. In several countries (e.g., Brazil, Japan, United States), school-aged individuals with disabilities were segregated from their typically developing peers and educated in separate institutions, such as special schools (e.g., residential schools for the blind in the United States). In other locations, students with disabilities were homeschooled (e.g., South Korea) or disassociated from education (e.g., Puerto Rico). Central to the evolution of inclusion to each of these locations, however, is the necessity for change in educational services for those with disabilities and the implementation of federal or state laws to enhance service delivery.

Across globally dispersed geographic locations, legislation was a major catalyst in promoting physical education for individuals with disabilities and inclusive practices. A number of influential laws across countries are summarized in Table 14.1. Early federal legislation, such as the Basic Act for Persons with Disabilities in Japan and the Education Law of 1949, set a

TABLE 14.1 Summary of Laws Impacting Inclusion Across Geographic Locations

Country	Law (Year)	Impact
United States	Public Law 93–112 (1973) Reauthorized (1990) Amended (2008)	Requires that all entities that provide extracurricular services must afford those with disabilities opportunity to participate. Barrier-free physical access.
	Public Law 94–142 (1975) Reauthorized (1997) Amended (2004)	Introduced LRE and IEPs. Included physical education within the definition of special education. Guaranteed a free and appropriate public education.
Puerto Rico	Public Law 21 (1977) Amended (1996)	Provided services to school-aged individuals with disabilities. Amended version guaranteed integrated education services. Guaranteed a free and appropriate public education. Introduced IEPs.
	Public Law 238 (2004)	Access and equal right to public services for people with disabilities.
Brazil	Public Law 7853 (1989) Amended (1999)	Established a national policy for integration and a universal right to education.
	Public Law 13146 (2015)	Mandates the consideration of universal design in program conceptualization. Promotes social inclusion and integration.
Japan	Basic Act for Persons with Disabilities (1947)	Promotes research, development, and accommodations of school facilities. Requires students with disabilities to be educated in inclusive settings to the greatest degree possible.
	School Education Law (2007)	Individualized instruction and support through ITPs.
South Korea	Education Law (1949)	All students had the right to an education and should receive an equal opportunity to learn.
	SEPA (1977) Revisions (9 times)	Free mandatory education services for students with disabilities in public schools
	ASED (2007) Revisions (2012)	Established disability categories similar to that of IDEA.

precedent for legislation in this area. Unfortunately, however, many of these early laws were neglected or not regularly enforced (Park, 2005). For instance, Ferreira (2003) asserts that despite the various laws and regulations enacted in Brazil regarding the rights of individuals with disabilities for equitable and inclusive education, "The legislation is still widely unknown, is not complied with, is neglected or, even worse, is consciously violated by decision makers who do not fear legal retribution" (p. 4). Watson (2013) also asserted laws and policies, such as the 1996 Guidelines and Basis of National Education, intended to assure the rights of students with disabilities are rarely enforced. In short, the rights of individuals with disabilities have been systematically violated over the years (Ferreira, 2003; Watson, 2013). In contrast, across South Korea, the United States, and Puerto Rico the emergence of special education/disability related laws and legislative policies in the 1970s may have driven an important watershed time period in this area. Across these culturally and geographically distinctive locations, laws were implemented that mandated a free and appropriate education for those with disabilities as well as equitable access to activities and services in society. Slowly, similar laws in other countries provided similar rights to those with disabilities internationally, including countries not included in this chapter, such as the Special Educational Needs and Disability Act (2001) of the United Kingdom.

In many of the locations discussed in this chapter, educational legislation impacted a shift from experiences in educational settings away from segregated or homeschooled settings. However, there is still a substantial degree of difference in the way students with disabilities are educated across geographic regions. For example in Brazil (84%), Japan (67%), South Korea (74%), and the United States (93–96%), most students with disabilities are now educated in the same school as their typically developing peers. Yet, the type of educational settings these students experience within these schools can be somewhat different so these figures can be misleading. For example in Japan, while 67% of students with disabilities are in schools with typically developing peers, just 12% of those, however, are in inclusive classes. This trend is similar to those being educated in South Korea, where 19% of students are educated inclusively. Other students are educated in self-contained, or "special" classes, where there is limited interaction with typically developing peers. Of the countries described here, the United States has the highest growth in this area where 60% of students with disabilities spend 80% or more of their day with their typically developing peers (U.S. Department of Education, 2014).

STRATEGIES TO INCLUSIVELY INSTRUCT PHYSICAL EDUCATION

The philosophy of inclusiveness demands that students with disabilities are included in physical education with their same-age peers to the maximum extent possible. Scholars insist that teachers who implement inclusive culturally responsive pedagogy and promote favorable interactions between and among children with and without disabilities build meaningful relationships (Hersman, 2007; Hodge et al., 2012). Further, physical education teachers should construct instructional goals and design task progressions that promote students' active participation in various physical activities including sports and recreational activities (Columna, Fernández-Vivó, Lieberman, & Arndt, 2015).

Across countries and cultures, physical education teachers should demonstrate cultural competence and responsiveness through their interactions and pedagogies (Hodge & James-Hassan, 2014). A teacher's use of culturally responsive pedagogy positions the languages, values, and cultures of all students within the educational process (Hodge et al., 2012). This means the "cultural knowledge, prior experiences, frames of references, and performance styles" of all students are given relevance within the learning environment "to make learning encounters more relevant to and effective" for all students (Gay, 2000, p. 29). Teachers who are culturally competent use student-centered strategies that empower students in their intellectual, social, emotional, and political maturation (Ladson-Billings, 1992). Student empowerment fosters competence, confidence, and a will to act (Gay, 2000). Table 14.2 presents guidelines to help teachers create high quality and socially just physical education programs (Hodge et al., 2012).

To ensure meaningful cultural bridges in today's richly diverse schools and communities, educators advocate a curriculum framework that emphasizes cultural competence and awareness, uses culturally responsive pedagogies, and encourages dialogue and reflective practice (Hodge et al., 2012). In such a curriculum framework, there are factors physical education teachers should consider in planning and implementing class activities where students with disabilities are included. These important considerations are: (a) know about each student's culture, (b) know about each student's type of disability and the student's behavioral tendencies, (c) know if the student has any other disabilities, (d) know what the student's prior experiences were, and (e) know if there are any contraindications (Hodge et al., 2012). For a further explanation of these considerations, readers are referred to the text *Essentials of Teaching Adapted Physical Education: Diversity, Culture, and Inclusion* by Hodge and colleagues (2012).

Generally, environmental adaptations and curricular modifications for a student with disabilities depends in large part on the interaction between the salience of the student's particular disability-related behavioral limitations, the demands (e.g., task structure and pacing) of the learning task(s), and the student's previous experiences in similar lesson activities. As educators have asserted, students with disabilities can be successfully included in physical education programs usually with few modifications (Block, 2016; Hodge et al., 2012). Generally speaking, highly organized and structured physical education settings are beneficial for all students with and without

TABLE 14.2 Guidelines for High-Quality and Socially Just Physical Education Programs
• Listen carefully to students with disabilities while seeking to gain an understanding of the meaning they ascribe individually to their physical activity experiences.
• Scrutinize your own pre-existing beliefs about students with various disabilities and determine in what ways such beliefs might affect your expectations and interactions with such students.
• Become culturally competent and responsive practitioners. For all students, seek an understanding and appreciation for the interaction style(s), cultural norms, customs, traditions, common foods, and dominate language(s) of family and peers used in the homes and communities.
• Establish positive home-school relationships with the parents, guardians, or caretakers of all students including those whose cultures differ from your own and of students with disabilities.
• Be consistent in relating to students from diverse backgrounds to build trust between you and your students.
• Learn and pronounce students' names accurately; reward and praise students' positive efforts and hold students to high, yet appropriate, expectations.
• Become culturally literate (e.g., learn cultural traditions) and regularly include various cultural practices in relevant activities.
• Follow a *no tolerance policy* concerning disability-related stereotypical phrases or demeaning remarks, such as "You are a retard."
• Follow a *no tolerance policy* for bullying, negative stereotypes, and racist, homophobic, or sexist comments. Use any instances of such behavior to reemphasize social responsibility and encourage cooperation among and between diverse groups.
• Be mindful that you communicate messages in verbal and nonverbal ways (e.g., facial expressions); thus, avoid instances of exhibiting negative body language toward any particular student, including those with disabilities.
• Seek equal close proximity, at random, yet distributed across both female and male students with and without disabilities during instruction, practices, and demonstrations.
• Listen attentively and respond respectfully to students with and without disabilities in positive and constructive ways.

Source: Adapted from Hodge et al. (2012).

disabilities. This can best be accomplished by (a) using on-going assessments; and (b) by using teaching tactics such as peer partnering, consistent daily routines and warm-ups, well-planned lessons, fun activities, and relaxing closure activities such as adapted rhythmic dance and movement exploration (Hodge et al., 2012). An easy way of supporting on-going or regular assessments is through peer assessment activities, which can be used to augment more teacher-directed assessments.

Peer assessment is a student-centered approach wherein students analyze the performance of their classmates. Usually students are assigned to small groups to work cooperatively as they follow a set of pre-established guidelines for expected performance in evaluating their classmates. This assessment strategy supports effective, inclusive, and culturally responsive pedagogy. A teacher's use of peer assessment can facilitate the process of determining whether students are making progress toward culturally relevant lesson objectives. This occurs through peer interactions, which help hold students accountable for inclusive learning and social maturing. What's more, this approach helps students become competent in evaluating their peers' skill performances, and by doing so imbues students with a greater sense of self and social responsibility in giving and receiving feedback. When used properly, peer assessment can help develop students' understanding of teamwork, promote a sense of shared responsibility for learning and performance of culturally relevant activities, promote respect among diverse groups of students with and without disabilities, improve communication among students, and build trusting relationships (Butler & Hodge, 2001).

Internationally, physical education generalists and specialists need to know that with appropriate instructional planning, best practice strategies, proactive behavior management, proper modifications, and culturally relevant pedagogical practices, teaching students with disabilities (mild to severe) typically result in meaningful and successful learning and interactive experiences for all (Hodge et al., 2012).

REFERENCES

Act on Special Education for Disabled Persons. (2007). *Act No. 11384*, Republic of Korea.

Alliance for Excellent Education. (2015). *The Every Student Succeeds Act: Replacing no child left behind.* Retrieved from http://all4ed.org/esea/

Alves, M. L. T., & Duarte, E. (2012). The participation of students with Down syndrome in physical education classes: A case study. *Movimento, 18*(1), 237–256.

Alves, M. L. T., & Duarte, E. (2014). The perception of students with disabilities on their inclusion in the classes of physical education: A case study. *Revista Brasileira de Educação Física, 28*(2), 329–337.

Americans with Disabilities Act. (1990). *Pub. L. No. 101-336.* Retrieved from http://www.ada.gov/pubs/ ada.htm.

An, J., & Hodge, S. R. (2013). Exploring the meaning of parental involvement in physical education for students with developmental disabilities. *Adapted Physical Activity Quarterly, 29*, 147–163.

Block, M. E. (1996). Implications of U.S. federal law and court cases on physical education placement of students with disabilities. *Adapted Physical Activity Quarterly, 13*, 127–152.

Block, M. E. (2016). *A teacher's guide to including students with disabilities in general physical education* (4th ed.). Baltimore, MD: Brookes.

Block, M. E., & Obrusnikova, I. (2007). Inclusion in physical education: A review of literature from 1995–2005. *Adapted Physical Activity Quarterly, 24*, 103–124.

Brazil Ministry of Planning, Budget and Management. (2010). *Brazilian institute of geography and statistics: Population census 2010.* Brasília, Brazil.

Brazil. (1988). *Constitution of the Federative Republic of Brazil.* Brasília. Brazil

Brazil. (1989, October 24). *Law No. 7853: Provides for support for people with disabilities, their social integration on the National Coordinating Office for Integration of Persons with Disabilities.* Brasília, Brazil.

Brazil. (1999). *Decree law 3298: National policy for the integration of persons with disabilities.* Brasília, Brazil.

Brazil. (2014). *Key education indicators literacy, diversity and inclusion of people with disabilities.* Brasília, Brazil.

Brazil. (2015, July 6). *Decree law 1314: Brazilian law inclusion of people with disabilities (status of persons with disabilities).* Brasília, Brazil.

Butler, S. A., & Hodge, S. R. (2001). Enhancing student trust through peer assessment in physical education. *Physical Educator, 58*(1), 30–41.

Cabinet Office. (2015). *Policy for persons with disabilities.* Retrieved October, 16t, 2015, from http://www8.cao.go.jp/shougai/english/index-e.html

Chakraborti-Ghosh, S., Orellana, K. M., & Jones, J. (2014). A cross-cultural comparison of teachers' perspectives on inclusive education through a study abroad program in Brazil and in the U.S. *International Journal of Special Education, 29*(1), 4–13.

Cho, J-H. (2003). The undergraduates' attitudes toward integrated physical education for individuals with disabilities. *Korean Journal of Adapted Physical Activity & Exercise, 11*(1), 191–202.

Columna, L., Fernández-Vivó, M., Lieberman, L., & Arndt, K. (2015). Recreational physical activity experiences among Guatemalan families with children with visual impairments. *Journal of Physical Activity and Health, 12,* 1119–1127. http://dx.doi.org/10.1123/jpah.2014-0257

DeMik, S. A. (2008). Experiencing attrition of special education teachers through narrative inquiry. *The High School Journal, 92*(1), 22–32.

ED Data Express: Puerto Rico. (2015). *Puerto Rico state snap shot.* Retrieved October 31, 2015, from: http://eddataexpress.ed.gov/state-report.cfm?state=PR

Educación Especial PR. (2015). *Leyes.* Retrieved from http://www.educacionespecialpr.info/leyes.html

Ferreira, W. B. (2003). *Public policies.* Retrieved from, www.cnotinfor.pt/inclusiva/report_politicas_publicas_en.html

Franz, D. (2007). The revised fundamental law of education and Japan's bid for educational reform. *Journal of Current Japanese Affairs, 15*(10), 52–64.

Gay, G. (2000). *Culturally responsive teaching: Theory, research & practice.* New York, NY: Teachers College Press.

Goto, Y. (2008). Cultural commentary: Critical understanding of the special support education in social contexts. *Disability Studies Quarterly, 28,* 15.

Haegele, J. A., & Sutherland, S. (2015). Perspectives of students with disabilities toward physical education: A qualitative inquiry review. *Quest, 67,* 255–273.

Hersman, B. L. (2007). *The effects of adventure education on the social interactions of students with disabilities in general physical education* (Doctoral dissertation). Retrieved from http://etd.ohiolink.edu/view.cgi?acc_num=osu1186493320

Hodge, S. R., & James-Hassan, M. (2014). African American males and physical education. In J. L. Moore III & C. W. Lewis (Eds.), *African American males in preK-12 schools: Informing research, practice, and policy* (Vol. 2; pp. 305–344). Bingley, England: Emerald Group.

Hodge, S. R., Lieberman, L. J., & Murata, N. M. (2012). *Essentials of teaching adapted physical education: Diversity, culture, and inclusion.* Scottsdale, AZ: Holcomb Hathaway.

Hodge, S. R., Sato, T., Mukoyama, T., & Kozub, F. M. (2013). Development of the physical educators' judgments about inclusion instrument for Japanese physical education majors and an analysis of their judgments. *International Journal of Disability, Development and Education, 60,* 332–346.

Hodge, S., Ammah, J. O. A., Casebolt, K. M., LaMaster, K., Hersman, B., Samalot-Rivera, A., & Sato, T. (2009). A diversity of voices: Physical education teachers' beliefs about inclusion and teaching students with disabilities. *International Journal of Disability, Development, and Education, 56,* 401–419.

Individuals with Disabilities Education Improvement Act. (2004). Pub. L. No. 108–446, Sec. 602, 118 Stat. 2657.

Kanayama, C., & Yamasaki, M. (2010). Physical education classes based on special needs education and teacher training therefore: Implementation of adapted sports education in training courses for elementary and junior high school physical education teachers. *Seiwa Ronshu, 37,* 9–18.

Kang, B., & Kim, N. (2012). Study on the actual conditions of the unified physical education class for disabled students in general secondary school. *The Journal of Special Education: Theory and Practice, 13,* 447–469.

Kelly, L. E. (Ed.). (2006). *Adapted physical education national standards* (2nd ed.), Champaign, IL: Human Kinetics.

Kim, C., & Park E. (2011). The effects of self-determined learning model of instruction on job performance behavior for students with mental retardation. *Korean Journal of Special Education, 46*(1), 125–148.

Korea Education Newspaper Office. (1998). *Korean education yearbook.* Seoul, Korea: National Textbook Co.

Korea National Institute for Special Education (2014). *A nation-wide survey on special education.* Seoul, Korea: Korea National Institute for Special Education.

Kusano, K., & Chosokabe, H. (2001). Teaching programs and teachers' attitudes toward inclusion of disabled children into regular physical education. *Japan Journal of Physical Education, Health, and Sports Science, 46,* 207–216.

Kwon, H. (2005). Inclusion in South Korea: The current situation and future directions. *International Journal of Disability, Development, & Education, 52*(1), 59–68.

Ladson-Billings, G. (1992). Reading between the lines and beyond the pages: A culturally relevant approach to literacy teaching. *Theory into Practice, 31,* 312–320.

Lee, H. S. (2005). A study on the reasons for negative attitude of middle schoolers without disabilities towards inclusive physical education. *Korean Journal of Adapted Physical Activity & Exercise, 13*(1), 17–28.

Lee, S. C. (2007). The perspectives of physical education teachers in general elementary school on inclusive physical education. *The Journal of Special Children Education, 9*(1), 1–18.

Lieberman, L. J., & Houston-Wilson, C. (2009). *Strategies for inclusion: A handbook for physical educators.* (2nd ed.). Champaign, IL: Human Kinetics.

Menju, T. (2014). Can Japan welcome immigrants? A shrinking population spurs a growing debate. *Civil Society Monitor: Japan Center for International Exchange.* Retrieved October 5, 2015, from www.jcie.or.jp

Ministry of Education and Human Resources. (2014). *Special education annual report to congress.* Seoul, Korea: Author.

Ministry of Education, Culture, Sports, Science, and Technology. (2002). *Special support education in Japan: Education for children with special needs.* Retrieved November 10, 2008, from www.mext.go.jp

Ministry of Education, Culture, Sports, Science, and Technology. (2015). *Tokubetsu Shien Kyoiku.* Retrieved October 4, 2015, from http://www.mext.go.jp/a_menu/shotou/tokubetu/main.htm

Murayama, M. (2014). *Teachers should acquire a viewpoint of adapted physical activity to achieve inclusive physical education.* (Unpublished Master's thesis). The University of Tsukuba: Tsukuba, Japan.

Park, H. C. (2005). Overview of Korean special education. In D. Y. Jung, H. C. Park, S. W. Ahn, H. G. Lee, S. C. Oh, J. H. Kim et al. (Eds.), *Special education* (pp. 2–18). Seoul, Korea: Kyoyoukgwahaksa.

Park, S. H. (2003). *Hankuk jangae haksaeng tonghap kyoyuk.* [Inclusion for students with disabilities in Korea]. Seoul, Korea: Gyoyuk Guahaksa.

Polat, F. (2010). Inclusion in education: A step towards social justice. *International Journal of Educational Development, 31*(2011), 50–58.

Qi, J., & Ha, A. S. (2012). Inclusion in physical education: A review of literature. *International Journal of Disability, Development and Education, 59*(3), 257–281.

Rehabilitation Act. (1973). PL 93-112, 29 U.S.C. §§ 701 et seq.

Saito, M. (2008). The status of adapted physical education in elementary school in "A" prefecture. *Sport Education Studies, 27*(2), 73–81.

Samalot- Rivera, A., Aleman, A., & Volmar, V. (2015). Increasing transition opportunities for youth with disabilities: Existing successful programs and steps to follow in program selection. *Journal of Physical Education Recreation and Dance, 86*(4), 57–61.

Samalot-Rivera, A., & Hodge, S. (2008). Secondary physical education teachers' beliefs on teaching students' with disabilities at schools in Puerto Rico. *Lecturas EFDeportes,* 123. Retrieved from http://www.efdeportes.com/efd123/secondary-physical-education-teachers-beliefs-on-teaching-students-with-disabilities.htm

Santini-Rivera, M. (2004). *Teoría y práctica de la educación física elemental y adaptada* [Theory and practice of elementary and adapted physical education]. Hato Rey, Puerto Rico: Publicaciones Puertorriqueñas.

Sato, T., & Hodge, S. R. (2009). Japanese physical educators' beliefs on teaching students with disabilities at urban high schools. *Asia Pacific Journal of Education, 29*(2), 159–177.

Sato, T., Hodge, S. R. Murata, N. M., & Maeda, J. K. (2007). Japanese physical education teachers' beliefs about teaching students with disabilities. *Sport Education and Society, 12*(2), 211–230.

School Education Law. (2015). *The enactment of school education law.* Retrieved from http://www.mext.go.jp/b_menu/hakusho/html/others/detail/1317423.htm

Son, Y., Hodge, S. R., Chun, H., & Kozub, F. M. (2012). South Korean undergraduate collegians' beliefs about inclusion and teaching students with disabilities. *International Journal of Human Movement Science, 6*(1), 153–174.

Special Education Needs and Disability Act. (2001). London, England: Her Majesty's Stationery Office.

United Nations Educational, Scientific and Cultural Organization (UNESCO). (2005). *Guidelines for inclusion: Ensuring access to education for all.* Paris, France: Author.

United States Congress. (1994). *Goals 2000 Educate America Act (PL 103–227).* Washington, DC: United States Congress.

United States Department of Education, Office of Special Education and Rehabilitative Services, Office of Special Education Programs. (2014). *36th annual report to Congress on the implementation of the Individuals with Disabilities Education Act.,* Washington, DC: Author.

Watson, S. M. (2013). Lessons from Brazil: Separate and unequal educational systems. *Preventing School Failure, 57*(3), 148–151.

Yoo, J. P., & Palley, E. (2014). The diffusion of disability rights policy: A focus on special education in South Korea. *International Journal of Disability, Development and Education, 61*(4), 362–376.

ABOUT THE CONTRIBUTORS

Tânia Bastos is a lecturer in adapted physical activity at the University of Porto and University Institute of Maia (Portugal). She has a joint doctoral degree in sports sciences and in biomedical sciences by the University of Porto and by the Catholic University of Leuven, respectively. She is member of the Centre of Research, Education, Innovation and Intervention in Sport (CIFI2D) and of the Research Center in Sports Sciences, Health Sciences and Human Development. Tânia Bastos supervised several master's and doctoral thesis in the field of adapted physical activity. She is a researcher whose interests are focused on inclusion in physical education and sports settings, psychological preparation of athletes with disabilities and Paralympic movement. (tbastos@fade.up.pt)

Ken Black has worked as a practitioner in the area of inclusive physical activity and disability sport for more than 35 years. This has included 10 years working in special education, 2 years for a disability sport organization (UK Sports Association for People with Learning Disability), 6 years as a disability sports development officer for Leeds City Council sports development team, 6 years as the inclusive sport officer with the Youth Sport Trust (the UK-based national youth sport agency), 3 years as sports consultant with the Australian Sports Commission, (working in the Disability Sport Unit), and 2 years running a research and development center on disability sport at Loughborough University. He has worked independently as an adviser and consultant since 2008. His latest role is as inclusion adviser and lecturer at the University of Worcester (since 2013). He serves on the board

Inclusive Physical Activities, pages 309–324
Copyright © 2017 by Information Age Publishing

of the English Federation of Disability Sport. He is a Scot, originally from Clydebank, near Glasgow. (ken@theinclusionclub.com)

Martin E. Block, PhD., C.A.P.E., is with the Department of Kinesiology at the University of Virginia, where he teaches courses in adapted physical education and motor development. He is the author of several peer-reviewed articles and chapters in books, and he has authored or co-authored seven books on adapted physical education and motor development including *A Teachers' Guide to Adapted Physical Education: An Inclusive Approach*, and *Developmental and Adapted Physical Activity Assessment.* Block also has been a consultant with Special Olympics, Inc. since 1988, where he was the primary author of the *Motor Activities Training Program* (MATP), a sports program for athletes with severe intellectual disabilities. Professor Block is the editor of the journal *Palaestra*, he is president of the International Federation of Adapted Physical Activity (IFAPA), and is past president of the National Consortium for Physical Education for Individuals with Disabilities (NC-PEID). (meb7u@virginia.edu)

Elinor L. Brown is an associate professor at the University of Kentucky, is internationally recognized in equity and social justice education for her series co-editorship of International Advances in Education, Equity, and Social Justice Research; publications in distinguished national/international referee journals; numerous national/international refereed presentations; invited international workshops; and hosting an international conference on cultural identity. Her commitment to teaching, research, and service is evidenced by student-nominations awards including Teacher Who Made a Difference; peer nominations for AERA Early Career Award; University of Kentucky's Teacher of the Year and President's Award for Diversity; and an administrative award received for Outstanding Service. (elbrown@uky.edu)

Brigid Byrd is a PhD candidate and graduate assistant in the Division of Kinesiology, Health, and Sport Studies with a concentration in sport and exercise psychology, at Wayne State University, College of Education. She completed her master's in kinesiology with a concentration in sport and exercise psychology at Wayne State University. Her research interests include psychosocial benefits of youth sport and physical activity, and psychosocial predictors of well-being in university athletes. (brigidbyrd@wayne.edu)

Anna Cadzow is a graduate of the University of Otago School of Physical Education. Her interest in teaching led her to participate in the movement development clinic in New Zealand as an undergraduate student. Since graduating with a bachelor's of physical education in 2012, Cadzow has completed a graduate diploma in teaching (early childhood) and now works as a teacher for 2 and 3-year-old children. In the early childhood sector, Anna has used her knowledge of physical education to work alongside physiotherapists in order to provide learning environments for children with a range of developmental delays. Anna is designing play spaces at her current early childhood center that are interesting, stimulating, and designed to promote the development of balance, strength, and coordination skills thus enabling all children to participate and learn through play. (anna.cadzow@hotmail.co.nz)

Attilio Carraro, PhD, is an associate professor of the methods and teaching of physical exercise in the Department of Biomedical Sciences at the University of Padua, where he is the cohead of the Health, Sports and Exercise Sciences Research laboratory. He is the director of the Psychomotor Rehabilitation Service at the Parco dei Tigli Psychiatric Hospital in Villa di Teolo, Padua, Italy. His current research focuses on health and exercise, and particularly on the relationships between exercise and mental health, and on sport pedagogy, mainly on values-based education and inclusion through physical education and sport. He has published extensively in peer-reviewed journals and is the author or co-author of several international and Italian books and books chapters. Carraro is currently a member of the board of directors of the AIESEP (International Association for Physical Education in Higher Education). (attilio.carraro@unipd.it)

Janine Coates is a lecturer in qualitative research methods in the School of Sport, Exercise and Health Sciences at Loughborough University. She has research interests in inclusive physical education, childhood disability, and behavioral interventions for children with behavioral and emotional difficulties. Coates has a particular interest in applied research, which aims to improve the well-being and experiences of marginalized children in education settings. She has contributed to a range of research projects including studies exploring the children's experiences of inclusion in physical education lessons; inclusion training for physical education teachers; perceptions of children with disabilities about the Paralympic Games and the effectiveness of parent training for children with attention deficit hyperactivity disorder (ADHD). Her research has been published in a number of high quality peer-reviewed research journals. (J.K.Coates@lboro.ac.uk)

Rui Corredeira is an assistant professor at the University of Porto, Faculty of Sport. He has a PhD in sport sciences, is the director of the master course on adapted physical activity, and coordinator of the Adapted Physical Activity Department at the Faculty of Sport at the University of Porto (Portugal). He is a member of the Research Centre in Physical Activity, Health and Leisure (CIAFEL). He supervised several doctoral and master's thesis candidates and his teaching and research special interests are related to the analysis of psychosocial variables in inclusive settings. More recently he is being developing a research line on mental health and its correlation and determinants with physical activity. (rcorredeira@fade.up.pt)

Mariana Amaral da Cunha is an assistant lecturer at the University of Porto (Portugal), Faculty of Sport. She cooperates with the Department of Sport Pedagogy as a teacher educator of a master's in physical education teacher education and with the Department of Adapted Physical Activity as a co-researcher. She also supervises master's students' thesis of both departments. She is member of the CIFI2D. Her research interests revolve around physical education teacher education, teacher professional identity, teaching, learning, and assessment issues within school physical education, inclusive physical education and qualitative methods. She has been involved in funded research projects in sports, educational, and psychology fields at University of Évora and University of Porto. (marianacunha@fade.up.pt)

Monica Cuskelly is professor of education and associate dean (research) at the University of Tasmania, Australia. Her research focuses on individuals with intellectual disabilities and their families; she has a particular interest in Down syndrome. A central aspect of her work is a longitudinal investigation of the development of individuals with Down syndrome across the lifespan. Recent publications have reported on cognitive and language development from 4 years until 30 years of age. Additional current projects include the examination of the aspirations of young adults with an intellectual disability and those of their families, the development of self-regulation in vulnerable populations, and the contribution of mastery motivation and self-regulation to adult outcomes. She has received a number of grants from the Australian Research Council, has published in the most influential journals related to disability, and has co-edited two books for clinicians on therapeutic practice with children and their families. (monica.cuskelly@utas.edu.au)

Ruth Cutfield completed a bachelor's of physiotherapy at the University of Otago in 1997. After working as a rotational physiotherapist at Dunedin Public Hospital from 1998 to 2000, she worked as a pediatric physiotherapist on a child development team in Wellington from 2000 to 2007. During this time, she gained considerable experience working with children with a wide range of disabilities, aged from 0–16 years. In 2005 she earned a postgraduate certificate and postgraduate diploma in physiotherapy, endorsed in neurorehabilitation from the University of Otago. In 2008 she returned to Dunedin and worked for the research project described in the book chapter, Family Focused Intervention for Children with Developmental Coordination Disorder. Ruth also completed in 2008 a Postgraduate Diploma in Physiotherapy, with distinction, endorsed in neurorehabilitation, University of Otago. Her studies focused on DCD and on the assessment of balance in children. Since then she has worked as a pediatric physiotherapist at Dunedin Public Hospital and taught pediatric physiotherapy in the School of Physiotherapy at the University of Otago. (Ruth.Cutfield@southerndhb.govt.nz)

Rhonda G. Craven is a professor and institute director at the Australian Catholic University's Institute for Positive Psychology and Education. She is a highly accomplished researcher having successfully secured more than $8.67 million in nationally and highly competitive funding for 51 large-scale research projects, including 30 Australian Research Council grants. This performance is arguably one of the strongest for an Australian educational researcher. She is the recipient of the Meritorious Service to Public Education Award, the Betty Watts Award (Australian Association for Research in Education), the Vice Chancellor's Award for Excellence in Postgraduate Research Supervision and Training, and the Vice Chancellor's Award for Excellence in Social Justice Research. Her research interests include: the structure, measurement, development, and enhancement of self-concept and key psycho-social drivers of well-being and performance; the effective teaching of Indigenous studies and Indigenous students; maximizing life potential and enabling people to not just succeed, but flourish in diverse settings; and interventions that make a tangible difference in educational and industry settings. (Rhonda.craven@acu.edu.au)

Yolanda Fernandez is an occupational therapist at Child and Youth Community Health Service, Children's Health Queensland, Australia. She is also a PhD candidate in the School of Health and Rehabilitation Sciences at The University of Queensland. She has held a variety of roles including clinical, teaching, and project positions with both a local and statewide remit. Her clinical expertise has centered upon the needs of children and youth who experience developmental difficulties and vulnerabilities that impact on their participation in everyday life activities and occupations. Family-centered practice, promotion of children's participation, and approaches that support self-determination, strengths and resilience, are particular areas of interest. The focus of her doctoral studies is on promoting children's participation in physical activity and leisure to optimize health and well-being. (yolanda.fernandez@uq.net.au)

Alex C. Garn is an associate professor in the School of Kinesiology at Louisiana State University. He currently serves as an associate editor for the *Journal of Teaching in Physical Education,* resides on numerous editorial boards, and has served in multiple positions in the American Education Research Association organization. His research interests focus on achievement motivation and emotion in academic and physical activity settings. He has published more than 50 peer-reviewed articles and secured more than $100,000 in external funding. (acgarn08@gmail.com)

Erica Gobbi, PhD, has a postdoctoral fellow position linked to a research project that focuses on values education through sport and physical education in the Department of Biomedical Sciences at the University of Padua. Her research interests include the development of inclusive practices in physical activity and physical education settings, and the promotion of active lifestyles among a general and clinical population. As an assistant professor, Gobbi is currently teaching physical education for elementary school children in the primary education course of the University of Padua. (erica.gobbi@unipd.it)

Donna Goodwin is a professor and associate dean of graduate programs in the Faculty of Physical Education and Recreation at the University of Alberta, Edmonton, Alberta, Canada. Her research focuses on issues pertaining to disability and physical well-being. Goodwin's research has given literal, metaphorical, and political voice to children, youth, and adults with disabilities. Her work has consistently brought the voices of those experiencing disability and their family members to discourses of inclusion. Her current research explores ethical professional practice in adapted physical activity. She also is interested in qualitative inquiry as a form of social justice. (dgoodwin@ualberta.ca)

Michelle Grenier, PhD, C.A.P.E., is an internationally recognized expert in the field of physical education for elementary school children. She has served as editor for a human kinetics publication entitled *Physical Education for Students with Autism Spectrum Disorders: A Comprehensive Approach.* She is coordinator of the Health and Physical Education Option in the Department of Kinesiology at the University of New Hampshire and oversees the adapted physical education concentration at the undergraduate and graduate levels. Dr. Grenier has presented her research on inclusion and best practices at the state, national, and international levels, and acts as a consultant to schools throughout the country. She is the adapted physical education representative for the New Hampshire Association of Health, Physical Education, Recreation and Dance, former chair of the national AAHPERD association, and serves on the Adapted Physical Activity Counsel for SHAPE America. (michelle.grenier@unh.edu)

Justin A. Haegele is an assistant professor in the Department of Human Movement Sciences at Old Dominion University. He is an accomplished young scholar in adapted physical education, and has published numerous articles in national/international physical education and disability-related academic journals, as well as a number of textbook chapters. Haegele has received the 2015 David P. Beaver Adapted Physical Activity Young Scholar Award (National Consortium for Physical Education for Individuals with Disabilities) as well as the New York State Adapted Physical Education Teacher of the Year award in 2012 (New York State Association for Health, Physical Education, Recreation, and Dance). His scholarly interests include physical activity participation, including in physical education, of individuals with visual impairments; physical education and physical activity experiences of individuals with autism spectrum disorder; and inclusion in physical education and physical activity settings. (jhaegele@odu.edu)

Bethany L. Hersman is an associate professor and assistant department chair in the Department of Kinesiology and Health at Wright State University, Dayton, Ohio. She is the creator and director of the Adapted Physical Education graduate level endorsement program at Wright State, which is a mostly online program. She is also a reviewer for several journals and is an associate editor for the *International Journal of Kinesiology in Higher Education*. Hersman has published and presented on various topics related to adapted physical education and physical education as well as educational technology. Her research interests mainly focus on social inclusion of students with disabilities in physical education settings and on using adventure education and cooperation games to better include students with disabilities into inclusive physical education classes. (Bethany.hersman@wright.edu)

Samuel R. Hodge is a professor in the Department of Human Sciences in the College of Education and Human Ecology at The Ohio State University. He is the recipient of the Adapted Physical Activity Council's Professional Recognition Award (American Alliance for Health, Physical Education, Recreation and Dance [AAHPERD]); E. B. Henderson Award and Charles D. Henry Award (AAHPERD); and Distinguished Scholar Award (National Association of Kinesiology in Higher Education). His scholarship focuses on diversity, disability, and social justice in education and sport. He has published extensively including the popular textbook, *Essentials of Teaching Adapted Physical Education: Diversity, Culture, and Inclusion* (Hodge, Lieberman, & Murata, 2012) and the case study book, *Case Studies in Adapted Physical Education: Empowering Critical Thinking* (Hodge, Murata, Block, & Lieberman, 2003). Furthermore, he is lead author on edited book chapters such as: "African American Males and Physical Education" (Hodge & James-Hassan, 2014), and "Health, Nutrition and Physical Activity" (Hodge & Vigo-Valentín, 2014). Hodge serves on the editorial boards of the following journals: *Adapted Physical Activity Quarterly, Quest, Multicultural Learning and Teaching,* and the *Research Quarterly in Exercise and Sport.* Lastly, Hodge has advised and mentored more than 50 master's and 13 doctoral students to degree completion. (hodge.14@osu.edu)

Yeshayahu (Shayke) Hutzler is the head of the graduate school at the Academic College at Wingate and former editor-in-chief of the *Adapted Physical Activity Quarterly*. In addition, he has been a visiting professor in various workshops and academic programs including the Lithuanian (Kaunas), Beijing, and Warsaw sport universities. Hutzler is also functioning as an adviser of the National Insurance Institute of Israel for exercise and sport in persons with disabilities. He has served as president of the International Federation of Adapted Physical Activity, wrote numerous articles and chapters concerning physical activity and disability, and contributed to the development of various sport programs for persons with disability. (shayke.hutzler@gmail.com)

Elizabeth Huynh received her MA at the University of Manitoba within the Faculty of Kinesiology and Recreation Management. Her thesis explored the meaning of social support among Manitoban youth living with type 2 diabetes using Grounded Theory. At the University of Manitoba and Red River College, she has supported research initiatives involving First Nations people, youth with type 2 diabetes, children and families with cystic fibrosis, university students with disabilities, and school-aged children. Previously, her research interests included the promotion of physical activity to improve psychosocial well-being, strategies to provide children and youth with meaningful opportunities to thrive, and working with children and youth to develop relevant interventions in community settings. She has now expanded her work to finding strategies to better serve populations affected by cancer. Currently, she is the Projects & Evaluation Coordinator at CancerCare Manitoba, with the Underserved Populations Program, where she is responsible for assessing the needs, and coordinating the planning, implementation and evaluation of health equity-focused initiatives. (ehuynh@cancercare.mb.ca)

Jihyun Lee is an assistant professor in the Department of Kinesiology at San Francisco State University. Her teaching and research focus is on two complementary areas: adapted physical activity/education and motor development. She has been involved in organizing community-based adapted physical activity programs as well as motor development programs. Her primary line of research investigates the effect of physical activities on behavioral changes in children with autism spectrum disorders and their families. This line of research aims to identify ways to promote health, quality of life, as well as movement proficiency in this population. Her second line of research focuses on issues associated with the promotion of motor skills and physical activities in pre-K children who are from low-income families or who are at risk of having a disability. Her research has been published in well-known journals and also presented at state, national, and international conferences. (jlee@shsu.edu)

Anthony Maher achieved a first-class degree in sports development with physical education from Liverpool John Moores University in 2007. He then studied for a master's in sociology of sport and exercise at the University of Chester, where his thesis was awarded the Norbert Elias Prize for its "originality and theoretical sophistication." He then moved to the University of Central Lancashire for his doctoral research, which is related to the sociology of special educational needs and physical education. Maher joined Leeds Beckett University in September 2014 as a senior lecturer in physical education and sport pedagogy. In January 2017 he then joined Edge Hill University as Senior Lecturer in physical education and youth sport. His research and teaching interests relate to diversity, equity and inclusion in education, special education, teacher education, and sociological theory. (mahera@edgehill.ac.uk)

Christophe Maïano is an associate professor in the Département de Psychoéducation et de Psychologie at the Université du Québec en Outaouais (Saint-Jérôme, Québec, Canada) and holds an adjunct appointment at the Institute for Positive Psychology and Education (IPPE) at the Australian Catholic University that is related to ongoing research collaborations with members of IPPE. His expertise broadly covers psychosocial interventions, adapted physical activity interventions, and health prevention and education interventions. Overall, his research activities aim at improving the physical and psychological well-being of individuals with an intellectual disability (ID), physical health problems, or mental health disorders. His current research projects are centered on the assessment of self-conceptions, mental health, and well-being in youth with or without an ID; the identification of social factors related to the development of self-conceptions in youth with or without an ID; the interrelations between social factors, self-conceptions, and the biopsychosocial adaptation of youth with or without an ID (obesity, eating disorders, well-being, etc.); and the effects of physical activity (behaviors or interventions) for furthering positive outcomes for youth with special needs (conduct disorders, intellectual disabilities, obesity, etc.). (christophe.maiano@uqo.ca)

Jeffrey Martin is a professor at Wayne State University in Detroit, Michigan, where he has been for the last 24 years. He has published more than 175 research articles and book chapters and has received more than $5 million in federal funding to support his research programs. His major research agenda is on the psychosocial aspects of disability sport and physical activity. Other research lines include a focus on understanding physical activity engagement with underserved children in urban settings and the psychology of distance running. He has published extensively in the *Adapted Physical Activity Quarterly*, the *Journal of Teaching in Physical Education* and the *Journal* *of Sport and Exercise Psychology.* Martin is the founding editor of *Sport, Exercise and Performance Psychology.* (aa3975@wayne.edu)

Nate McCaughtry is a professor and assistant dean in the Division of Kinesiology, Health and Sport Studies at Wayne State University, as well as director of the Center for School Health. He is the primary investigator of all three phases of the Detroit Healthy Youth Initiative and has secured more than $5 million in external funding. His research interests include: urban school reform, physical education teacher development, and sociocultural issues in physical activity and physical education. (aj4391@wayne.edu)

Motohide Miyahara has been interested in the body-mind relationships, and studied relevant academic disciplines, including psychology, health education, and the art and science of human movement in Japan and the United States. After completing his PhD in kinesiology at UCLA, he conducted his postdoctoral research at the University of London and the Free University of Berlin. Since taking up the academic staff position at the University of Otago in 1996, he has been teaching and researching in the areas of development and disability, while directing the Movement Development Clinic in New Zealand. He conducts disability research with a main focus on developmental disabilities, such as developmental coordination disorder, autism spectrum disorders, and attention deficit hyperactivity disorder. He takes advantage of a wide range of research methods to suit purposes. The examples of the methods that he has employed to date include case study research, qualitative interviews, psychological experiment, brain-imaging techniques, systematic review, and meta-analysis. He serves on the editorial board of *Research in Developmental Disabilities and Experimental Aging Research.* (motohide.miyahara@otago.ac.nz)

Fiona Moola, PhD, is an assistant professor at the University of Manitoba and a scientist at the Children's Hospital Research Institute of Manitoba. She completed her undergraduate, master's, and doctoral degrees at the University of Toronto and her postdoctoral fellowship at Concordia University in Montreal. Working out of the Toronto Hospital for Sick Children and the Winnipeg Children's Hospital, she has amassed a wealth of scholarship pertaining to the psychological and sociological effects of childhood illnesses on children and families and the role of physical activity in their lives. Moola has contributed more than 30 publications to this burgeoning international literature. She maintains a counseling-based research program at the Winnipeg Children's Hospital and is a strong, grassroots activist for the chronically ill and disabled community. She has a particular interest in the role of counseling as a therapeutic intervention for chronically ill children. (Fiona.moola@umanitoba.ca)

Alexandre J. S. Morin is a professor in the Department of Psychology of Concordia University (Montreal, Quebec, Canada). He is a highly productive researcher having produced more than 120 articles, many of which are in top-tier journals, as well as book chapters with reputable publishers. His research has also attracted multiple prestigious external grants in Canada (e.g., Social Sciences and Humanities Research Council of Canada) and Australia (e.g., Australian Research Council). He defines himself as a life span developmental psychologist, with broad research interests anchored in the exploration of the social determinants of psychological well-being and psychopathologies at various life stages and various settings, such as schools and organizations. Most of his research endeavors are anchored in a substantive-methodological synergy framework, and thus represent joint ventures in which new methodological developments are applied to substantively important issues. A significant part of his current research program aims to understand how to foster more positive futures for children with intellectual disabilities, through the identification of drivers of psychosocial and physical well-being. (alexandre.morin@concordia.ca)

Jack Neylon is a teacher at Coláiste Muire in Ennis, Ireland. He graduated from the University of Limerick in May 2015 with a bachelor's degree in physical education with an elective subject area emphasis in mathematics. In June 2015, Neylon returned to the University of Limerick to complete an eight-week research internship examining the use of adventure education on the social development of students with autism spectrum disorders. His research interests include the implementation of the adventure education curricular model within the secondary school setting, inclusive physical education in secondary schools, social skill development of students with autistic spectrum disorders, and the promotion of lifelong physical activities for students with autism spectrum disorders both within and beyond the physical education environment. (jack97neylon@gmail.com)

Kwok Ng completed his PhD from the Faculty of Sport and Health Sciences at the University of Jyväskylä, Finland. He specializes in adapted physical activity currently combining educational sciences with sport and exercise psychology as well as researching in health indicators of adolescents with disabilities. He also has an international coaching qualification for volleyball and authored the book, *When Sitting is Not Resting: Sitting Volleyball.* He is the European representative on the board of the International Federation of Adapted Physical Activity (IFAPA) between 2015 and 2017. Prior to that, he served on the managing council of the European Network of Young Specialists in Sport Psychology in the education department between 2011 and 2015. (kwok.w.ng@gmail.com)

Melissa Parker is a lecturer in the Physical Education and Sport Sciences Department at the University of Limerick, and professor emeritus in the School of Sport and Exercise Science at the University of Northern Colorado. She teaches undergraduate and postgraduate courses in physical education teaching and learning, and outdoor education. Her scholarly interest areas include accessing teacher and student voice and the professional learning of teachers and teacher educators. Parker is coauthor of two textbooks, *Children Moving* with Graham and Holt/Hale, and *Serving Underserved Youth through Physical Activity: Toward a Model of University-Community Collaboration* with Hellison, Cutforth, Kallusky, Martinek, and Stiehl as well as numerous articles and book chapters. She is a recipient of the Metzler-Freedman Exemplary Paper of the Year Award from the Journal of Teaching in Physical Education, a Research Fellow in the Society of Health and Physical Educators (SHAPE) America, and an International Fellow in National Academy of Kinesiology. (Missy.Parker@ul.ie)

Michel Probst is a professor in the Department of Rehabilitation Sciences and Physiotherapy of the Faculty of Kinesiology, Catholic University of Leuven (Belgium). He is head of the research unit Adapted Physical Activity and Psychomotor Rehabilitation and coordinator of the Rehabilitation Sciences in Mental Health Care studies. Probst is founder and president of the International Organization of Physical Therapy in Mental Health (WCPT-subgroup). His expertise and research interests and activities focus primarily on enhancing the body image and the physical activity of persons with common and severe mental health problems. (Michel.probst@kuleuven.be)

Matthew Rogers is the founder and leader of Volley*SLIDE*, the world education program for sitting volleyball. He previously led the creation and establishment of the English Sitting Volleyball club network and was the program manager of the British performance teams prior to the London 2012 Paralympic Games. He went on to hold a key games' delivery role with the organizing committee for both volleyball and sitting volleyball. Rogers now combines his voluntary involvement in sitting volleyball with his professional position at the Confédération Européenne de Volleyball (CEV) as the competitions coordinator. On the academic side, he recently completed a master's in physical education and sports pedagogy at Loughborough University and is a trained secondary school sports teacher. (volleyslide@gmail.com)

Mayumi Saito is an associate professor of health and sport sciences, adapted physical education and sport studies at the University of Tsukuba, Japan. Saito's scholarly interests focus on adapted sport coaching and sport coaching and performance for athletes with hearing impairments. In 2015, she became a principal investigator of national investigation of exploratory studies of pedagogical issues and concerns of adapted physical education in Japanese preschools through high schools requested by the Ministry of Education, Culture, Sport Science, and Technology in Japan. She serves on the board of directors for two academic organizations: Asian Society for Adapted Physical Education and Exercise, and Japanese Society for Adapted Physical Education and Exercise. She also serves as an evaluator of adapted physical education and adapted physical activity research citation and impact factors of academic research journals. (mayumi@mail.taiiku. tsukuba.ac.jp)

Amaury Samalot-Rivera is an assistant professor in the Kinesiology Department at the College at Brockport. He teaches in both general and adapted physical education programs, and works as a recruiter and mentor for an adapted physical education federal funded grant. His areas of scholarship are the development of the affective domain through the physical education class, transition from school to the community for youth with disabilities, and the impact of social skill interventions in urban education physical education programs for students for whom English is their second language. Samalot-Rivera also collaborates with university programs in the island of Puerto Rico, where he offers workshops and presentations in various topics in their yearly national convention. Recently, he published various papers and book chapters in the aforementioned areas. (asamalot@ brockport.edu)

Takahiro Sato is an associate professor in the School of Teaching, Learning and Curriculum Studies at Kent State University. Sato's scholarly interests focus on physical education teachers' beliefs on teaching students with disabilities, diversity and social justice of students and teachers of color in physical education, and international students' experiences in higher education. He has published articles in national/international physical education and educational journals. He has run several research grant projects to explore and analyze diverse students' experiences (e.g., African American students, Asian international students, English language learners, and students with disabilities) in schools and higher education. He is a nationally certified adapted physical educator and was a fellow of the Research Consortium of the American Alliance for Health Physical Education Recreation and Dance (SHAPE America) in 2014. Sato is currently offering Ohio Adapted Physical Education (APE) graduate endorsement approved by Ohio Department of Education starting from fall semester in 2014. (tsato@kent.edu)

Anselmo de Athayde Costa e Silva is a professor of faculty of physical education at the Federal University of Pará in Brazil. His area of expertise is adapted physical activity and he has conducted a number of studies regarding exercise for people with physical disabilities. His research interests include exercise for people with physical disabilities, and inflammation and body composition of those with spinal cord injuries. In Brazil, his research is in APE and APA, two areas that are not mutually exclusive. He is currently teaching courses in adapted physical education, and acting in collaborations regarding the inclusion of people with disabilities in the Amazon region. (anselmocs@ufpa.br)

Deborah Tannehill is an emeritus faculty member recently retired from her position as senior lecturer, course director of the professional diploma in education: physical education, and co-director of the Physical Education, Physical Activity and Youth Sport (PE PAYS Ireland) Research Center at the University of Limerick. Tannehill's teaching, research, and professional service is focused on teaching and teacher education in physical education and sport, as well as continuing professional development, communities of practice, and curricular initiatives, assessment, and instructional strategies. She continues her involvement in numerous professional development opportunities for teachers and research projects related to teaching and teacher education. Tannehill has authored six published textbooks, 24 book chapters, more than 60 refereed research/teaching journal articles with four in review, 23 newsletter/brochure publications, 41 keynote/invited addresses, and more than 100 conference workshops/sessions, in addition to being a reviewer of several scholarly journals and past coeditor of the *Journal of Teaching in Physical Education*. (Deborah.Tannehill@ul.ie)

Joana Teixeira is the team manager of the adapted sport department at FC Porto, which includes sports such as boccia, swimming, football, basketball, and table tennis. She is also an adapted physical activity teacher in a primary school and regularly collaborates in the organization of activities promoting the dissemination of the adapted sport. Previously to this work, Teixeira worked in hydrotherapy and implemented her own senior boccia project. She has a master's degree in adapted physical activity and the subject of her thesis was the implementation of a Paralympic educational program. Teixeira's research interest revolves around improving the attitudes of children without SEN toward disability. (joana.teixeira@fcporto.pt)

Daniel Tindall is a lecturer in the Physical Education and Sport Sciences Department at the University of Limerick. He is the course director of the physical education programme at UL and teaches courses in physical education teaching and learning, and adapted physical education (APE). His scholarly interest areas include the attitudes and perceptions of preservice physical education teachers and the facilitation of inclusion within the Irish educational system. His current research projects focus on the physical activity levels of children with disabilities, the individual education plan (IEP) process as it relates to physical education in Ireland, as well as the perceptions of stakeholders (principals, teachers, special needs assistants, and parents) toward the IEP process. Tindall has published book chapters and refereed research-based/practitioner-based journal articles as well as presented numerous conference presentations in the areas of physical education teacher education and APE. Currently, he is the codirector of the Inclusive Play & Leisure Activities for Youth (i-PLAY) program for children and young people with special educational needs. (Daniel.Tindall@ul.ie)

Danielle Tracey is a senior lecturer in educational psychology in the School of Education at Western Sydney University. She is a senior researcher within the Centre for Educational Research, and the academic course adviser for postgraduate inclusive education courses. As an accomplished mixed-method researcher, she has been awarded multiple prestigious external national and international research grants to the value of $2 million. The impact of her work is achieved through both publication in scholarly outlets, and recommendations to industry via the adoption of a community-based participatory research framework. Her research interests focus primarily on enhancing the psychosocial well-being of children and young people with disabilities through the application of mixed-method longitudinal and evaluative research designs. Tracey's research expertise and activities have been informed by her extensive experience working as an educational and developmental psychologist within the community sector supporting children and young people with intellectual disabilities and learning difficulties. (d.tracey@westernsydney.edu.au)

Philip Vickerman is a professor of inclusive education and learning at Liverpool John Moores University. He received a national teaching fellow awarded by the Higher Education Academy (U.K.) and has published widely on practical and theoretical approaches to including children with special educational needs (SEN) in physical education (PE). Vickerman is currently Pro Vice Chancellor for Strategic Initiatives at LJMU and leads on a number of university wide projects. Vickerman has advised United Kingdom and international governments on inclusive education. He has a keen interest in research on children's perspectives of inclusive PE and in recent years this has been a core focus for his research activities. (P.Vickerman@ljmu.ac.uk)

Jenny Ziviani is the inaugural professor of children's allied health research with Queensland Children's Health Service and the University of Queensland, Australia. Her 30-year background as an occupational therapy clinician, academic, and researcher has focused on the well-being of children at risk of a range of physical, developmental and psychosocial conditions, their families, and the communities in which they live. As an active researcher, she has successfully managed large national and international competitive grants, published more than 200 internationally peer viewed articles, 32 book chapters, and four books, as well as presented more than 210 conference papers. She has been awarded the Open Award for Research Excellence and the Sylvia Docker Award for her contributions to the profession by occupational therapy in Australia. In 2016, she became a member of prestigious American Occupational Therapy Foundation, Academy of Research. (j.ziviani@uq.edu.au)

CPSIA information can be obtained
at www.ICGtesting.com
Printed in the USA
FFOW01n2221110717
37695FF

9 781681 238524